THIRD EDITION

Adolescent Portraits

Identity, Relationships, and Challenges

Andrew Garrod

Dartmouth College

Lisa Smulyan

Swarthmore College

Sally I. Powers

University of Massachusetts, Amherst

Robert Kilkenny

Harvard University

Allyn and Bacon

Boston • London • Toronto • Sydney • Tokyo • Singapore

Senior Editor: *Carolyn O. Merrill*
Editorial Assistant: *Amy Goldmacher*
Director of Field Marketing: *Joyce Nilsen*
Editorial-Production Administrator: *Annette Joseph*
Editorial-Production Coordinator: *Susan Freese*
Editorial-Production Service/Electronic Composition: *Omegatype Typography, Inc.*
Composition Buyer: *Linda Cox*
Manufacturing Buyer: *Megan Cochran*
Cover Administrator: *Jenny Hart*
Cover Designer: *Susan Paradise*

Library of Congress Cataloging-in-Publication Data

Adolescent portraits : identity, relationships, and challenges /
[edited by] Andrew Garrod ... [et al.]. — 3rd ed.
     p.   cm.
   Includes bibliographical references (p.   ) and index.
   ISBN 0-205-27779-9
   1. Adolescence—Case studies.   2. Adolescent psychology—United
States—Case studies.   I. Garrod, Andrew.
HQ796.A3343   1999
305.235—dc21   98-6091
                                                                                  CIP

Text Credits: Excerpt on page 33 and poem on page 36 reprinted by permission of the publishers and the Trustees of Amherst College from *The Poems of Emily Dickinson*, Thomas H. Johnson, ed., Cambridge, Mass.: The Belknap Press of Harvard University Press, Copyright © 1951, 1955, 1979, 1983 by the President and Fellows of Harvard College.

Printed in the United States of America

10   9   8   7   6   5   4   3   2   1   03   02   01   00   99   98

CONTENTS

Cases Categorized by Theme

continued

Cases Categorized by Theme (continued)

PREFACE

This third edition of *Adolescent Portraits* includes three new cases, an expert anlysis of one of these cases, and two Reflections by earlier contributors looking back on their lives. In choosing new cases and removing others, we have considered feedback from faculty and students using the book and our own understanding of the important issues facing adolescents in the 1990s. We welcome further comments on the usefulness of particular cases and the varied ways in which you may use them in your courses. We particularly value suggestions about critical adolescent themes that are not yet addressed in our text.

This third edition is accompanied by an Instructor's Manual, which includes further suggestions for teaching strategies and assignments for using the cases. The manual also contains an expanded review of films, along with three cases from the second edition—"To Be the Best," "Forever an Awkward Adolescent," and "Turning Against Myself"—and two cases from the first edition—"Distilling My Korean American Identity" and "Guilt Was Everywhere Around Me."

ACKNOWLEDGMENTS

The following students provided editorial and research assistance on the book: Megan Cummins, Jay Davis, Patrick Lynch, Theresa Shay, Hae-Seon Song, James Stascavage, Lisa Wilson, Samantha Zee, and Keith Zorn. We thank them for their skill and energy throughout the project. In the preparation of the third edition, we are deeply grateful for the editorial suggestions of Karen Maloney and for the administrative skills of Hae-Seon Song, a senior at Dartmouth College, who skillfully prepared the manuscript for publication. We also appreciate the faculty research grant awarded by Swarthmore College in support of the project and the comments on many cases provided by Stephanie Beukema, Assistant Dean at Radcliffe College.

The cases in this book are the words of college students who have taken our courses, individuals who were willing to share their life experiences with many outsiders. Although we cannot thank them by name, we wish to acknowledge their personal strength as well as the time and energy they invested in this project. In addition, we want to recognize the many students who worked with us on cases that have not been included in the book; they, too, gave tremendous amounts of themselves as we worked to shape the final manuscript.

We would like to thank the following reviewers for their comments and suggestions for this edition: Roger A. Johnson, Old Dominion University; Suzanne M. Morin, Shippensburg University; and William George Scarlett, Tufts University.

OVERVIEW

The Study of Adolescence

The way in which we view adolescence depends, to a large extent, on our perceptions of human nature and the relationship of the individual to society. Those who study adolescence today draw on past perceptions but also bring a new set of lenses to the field. Many have begun to realize the diversity that characterizes their individual subjects and the difficulty in generating theory that captures their experiences. Using the lenses of class, ethnicity, race, and gender, they work to describe and explain the complexity seen in adolescent thought, behavior, and relationships.

Twentieth-century understanding of adolescent development has some of its roots in earlier studies of human development (see Elder, 1980; Muuss, 1988; Sisson, Hersen, & Van Hasselt, 1987). The first consideration of adolescence as a separate stage of life is often attributed to Plato (1921) and Aristotle (1941), both of whom described the adolescent as unstable and impressionable. They suggested schooling for girls and boys that would shield them from society and help them develop the self-control and reason that characterize a mature individual. In the Middle Ages, the prevalence of Christian views of human depravity and of knowledge as external to the individual led to a less developmental perspective. Children and adolescents were seen as miniature adults who had to be socialized into acceptance of adult roles, values, and beliefs (Muuss, 1988).

John Locke and Jean-Jacques Rousseau helped to restore society's belief in the qualitative difference between children and adults. Rousseau, in particular, emphasized a process of development during which innate knowledge and character unfold throughout childhood and youth. In *Émile*, Rousseau presented his view of this process and the role of society in nurturing and schooling young people as they develop into responsible citizens. Rousseau attributed different natural characteristics and social roles to males and females and suggested that, while the process of development is similar for both, schooling toward the end product differs as a result of their divergent natures and responsibilities.

In the nineteenth century, several social and intellectual movements influenced perceptions of human nature and adolescence. Charles Darwin's *The Origin of Species* included humans as a part of the natural world, providing a more biological and evolutionary view of human development and growth. The Industrial Revolution led to a gradual deemphasis of the family's role in socialization for work and relationships and a discontinuity in an individual's experience of home and work. Accompanying movements such as child labor laws and compulsory schooling contributed to society's perception of a phase of development between childhood and the assumption of an adult role in society, a phase that G. Stanley Hall named "adolescence" in 1904 (Bakan, 1972).

Hall (1904) described adolescence as a key stage of life in the evolution of the mature individual. Drawing on Darwin's work, he postulated a scientific theory of recapitulation in which the individual develops through stages that parallel those of human civilization. Like Rousseau, he saw development as a natural, largely innate process that could be guided and supported by society. Hall characterized preadolescence as the "savage" stage in the life of the individual. Adolescence followed, a transitional period to adulthood filled with contradictory emotions and behaviors: selfishness and altruism, sensitivity and cruelty, radicalism and conservatism. Through the struggle of adolescence, the individual is reborn; a new self is created, ready to assume a role in modern society.

Hall's work has influenced the study of adolescence throughout the twentieth century, but it has also been modified and challenged over the years. While Freud and those whose ideas developed from his work (e.g., Blos, 1962; Erikson, 1968; A. Freud, 1946) continued to focus on biological imperatives and their influence on the individual's psyche in the process of development, others began to take a more sociological perspective on adolescence. The work of Margaret Mead (1958) and Ruth Benedict (1950) suggested that society determines the behaviors, roles, and values of its adolescents. Others focused on the effects of social disorganization, social class, and social institutions on the life of the adolescent, documenting the role of environment in the shaping of experience (e.g., Havighurst, Bosman, Liddle, Mathews, & Pierce, 1962; Hollingshead, 1949). In the 1950s, studies of adolescence tended to emphasize the role of the peer group and the uniqueness of the adolescent experience; adolescence was seen as discontinuous with both childhood and adulthood. Adolescents had their own culture, comprised of a unique language, patterns of interaction, and beliefs.

While events of the 1960s contributed to this perception of an adolescent subculture, they also led those who study adolescence to focus on the intersection between the life course of the individual, the age cohort, and the historical context within which the individuals act (Elder, 1980). Some researchers and theorists, following Mead's emphasis on cultural influences on adolescence, focused on the social–historical context of adolescent development. They challenged Hall's view of adolescence as necessarily stressful by examining continuity and change in adolescent behavior over time. Others began to reexamine the period of adolescence within the context of an individual's lifespan. Research in child and adult development and in ego, cognitive, and moral development led to an understanding of adolescence as one of a sequence of life stages during which the individual addresses key issues such as identity, autonomy, attachment, and separation. The emphasis in this work has been on phases or stages of development that cut across social, historical, and cultural boundaries (e.g., Erikson, 1968; Kohlberg & Gilligan, 1972; Piaget, 1972).

Some of the most recent work in the study of adolescence has challenged approaches that emphasize either sociocultural determinism or universal developmental theory, suggesting that understanding adolescence involves a consideration of how social categories such as race, class, and gender interact with processes of individual development (e.g., Berry & Asamen, 1989; Gilligan, 1982; Josselson, 1987; McAdoo & McAdoo, 1985). The historical and cultural context is important in understanding adolescent experience, but it may not be sufficient to explain an individual's behaviors, beliefs, and sense of self. Stage and phase theories of development tend to overgeneralize from small, nonrepresentative samples and often ignore key variables such as race and gender that have a profound impact on an individual's experience and identity. The study of adolescence, then, has become more inclusive in terms of who is studied, what questions are asked, and how experience is analyzed. It has also become more complex, as we take a range of variables and contexts into consideration when examining individual development.

Even as researchers and teachers try to understand the multiple aspects of each individual's identity, the context within which American adolescents develop continues to change, further complicating the picture. Adolescents in the 1990s grow up in a society that takes technology and global communication as givens. On a large scale, this adolescent cohort's historical and cultural context is one in which international shifts toward democratic governments and market economies mean changing relationships between the United States and former Cold War antagonists. Increased international communication will lead to greater knowledge and understanding of other people around the world and, perhaps, to greater interdependence. Closer to home, these adolescents experience a society that is working toward greater acceptance of diversity—one, for example, in which women and minorities strive to define and work toward their goals while simultaneously trying to change society. Although they are growing up in decades of change and progress, today's adolescents also face persistent social problems: educational systems struggling with declining enrollments and shrinking resources, urban (and some suburban and rural) communities focusing on teenage drug use and the spread of AIDS, and a resurgence of racial and ethnic questioning and occasional violence. The social questions and issues that surround them demonstrate to today's adolescents that society does not have all of the answers and that it often seems to lack the direction and commitment needed to find them.

Research in the past twenty-five years has also refuted the "storm and stress" model of adolescent development that grew out of Hall's work. This approach sees adolescence as a time of severe turbulence, during which relationships disintegrate as the individual rebels against internal and external value systems (e.g., Blos, 1962; A. Freud, 1946, 1958). In contrast, more current work in the field emphasizes continuity and renegotiation as processes that characterize adolescence. "Normal" adolescent development encompasses a wide range of experiences, including a variety of family structures, sexual experimentation and orientation, and ethnic and racial exploration. Although some adolescents may experience more environmental stressors than others during these years, they occur within a meaningful personal and social context for that individual. Researchers have come to accept many variations within their definitions of normality in adolescence.

The Case Study Approach

Those of us who teach courses in adolescent development continue to search for materials that address our students' lives and illuminate emerging approaches in the study of adolescence. Such materials help students learn what past and present theorists and current research have to say about the adolescent experience and engage students in asking questions about those theories and approaches as well as their own lives. We want our students to be thoughtful and critical participants in the study of adolescence, contributors to our growing understanding of how this phase of life relates to the larger life cycle.

The authors of this book found this kind of material in a book called *Experiencing Youth,* first published in 1970 by George W. Goethals and Dennis S. Klos. We used this book in our own study of adolescence and have since incorporated it into the courses we teach. *Experiencing Youth* is a set of first-person accounts written by undergraduate and graduate students (the latter appear primarily in the second edition) that highlight key issues in adolescent development: autonomy, identity, and intimacy. These cases demonstrate how powerful narrative can be as a way of examining individual lives within a framework of theory and research on adolescence.

By listening to the voices of individual adolescents, students and teachers of adolescent development can gain a greater understanding of the issues facing some of today's adolescents. Case studies illustrate the complexity of the individual experience and the interactions among an individual's needs, ideas, relationships, and context. Each case, taken alone, helps us begin to know one more adolescent and his or her experience; taken together, the cases provide a rich overview of the field of adolescence. Through them, students come to a greater understanding of key theorists and current research findings as they examine patterns in their lives and the lives of others. We are indebted to Goethals and Klos for helping us and our students learn the value of the case study.

Despite the strengths of *Experiencing Youth,* we felt a need for cases that reflected the experiences of today's adolescents—their social and historical context, their diversity, their concerns—and for theoretical frames that reflected more recent work in adolescent research. In this book, we build on the model provided by Goethals and Klos, bringing together the voices of students in our own classes and some key theories and approaches used in the study of adolescence. Each case in this volume was written and revised by an undergraduate or very recent graduate, most of whom have taken a course in adolescent development.

Although it is never possible to be completely representative, we chose students and cases with the goal of achieving a cross section of ethnicities, class backgrounds, and experiences. The book includes cases written by first-year college students who reflect primarily on their early adolescent experience and by students who have recently graduated from college and look back on those years as well. Case 1 was written by a first-year student; Case 15 by a sophomore; Cases 2, 3, 9, 11, 13, 14, and 16 by juniors; and Cases 4, 5, 6, 7, 8, 10, and 12 by seniors. Of the sixteen case writers, ten are white, two are African American, one is Native American, two are Asian American, and one is half-East Indian, half-white. Ten are women and six are men. Case writers come from the West, Midwest, South and East; from urban, suburban, and rural environments; from more and less privileged backgrounds; from single- and two-parent homes; from situations that have stimulated reflection and those that have allowed the writers to develop without thinking deeply about the implications and meanings of their actions and ideas. Although we have included each case under a major topic (as listed in the Contents), each case addresses a number of issues. The charts at the front of the book provide a guide to the themes present in each case, as do the abstracts at the beginning of each case. See the Instructor's Manual for further suggestions for using the cases in this book in a variety of classroom settings.

PART ONE

Identity

Theoretical Overview

The seven cases in the Identity section of this book show a pattern of a struggle for meaning and a quest for wholeness. Within the categories of gender, work, values and ideology, ethnicity, and sexuality, the adolescent writers wrestle with important choices—who they want to be, how to relate to others, what values should guide them, and what their place is in various spheres of their lives. Though the content of the autobiographies may differ from case to case, the reader will see that they share common explorations and preoccupations with the self, the self in relation to the self, the self in relation to the other, and to the broader society. We offer here a framework for approaching the cases in this section.

Erik Erikson (1968), who has helped shape our understanding of identity, proposed a detailed and widely applied psychosocial theory of identity development. Convinced that the study of identity is as crucial to our time as the study of childhood sexuality was to Freud's, Erikson forged a radical rethinking among psychoanalytic theorists about ego structure and the role of culture and environment in personality development. As is inevitable, his writings have, over the last decades, been expanded (e.g., Marcia, 1967) and debated (e.g., Gilligan, 1982) by a succession of theorists, some of whom have significantly broadened his theory's applicability. Its general acceptance, however, remains widespread, and his ideas form the foundation of the psychological approach we take to the cases in this section.

When asked to describe his adolescence, one of our students recently wrote: "I don't know where it started and have no more idea if it's ended. Something inside of me tells me I'm in transition between something and something else, but I don't know what." In transition between two "somethings," this young man is not at all sure where he has come from and even less sure of his destination; he is Kurt Lewin's (1939) "marginal man," uncertain of his position and group belongingness. As an adolescent, he is in a stage of his life in which pressures, both internal and external, to define himself become simultaneously impossible to ignore and impossible to satisfy. He is working to establish a self-concept while at the same time realizing that this concept is changing as rapidly as he can pinpoint it. Like Lewis Carroll's Alice, he may well reply to the question, "Who are you?" posed by the Caterpillar, by saying, "I, I hardly know Sir, just at present—at least I know who I was when I got up this morning, but I must have changed several times since then." In Erikson's terms, the adolescent has entered a psychological moratorium—a hiatus between childhood security and adult independence.

Adolescence is a critical stage in the individual's development. Adolescents are intensely aware of how they are seen by others—aware, as V. S. Pritchett (1971) observes, that "other egos with their own court of adherents invade one's privacy with theirs." It is a time in which the values and perspectives of others become clearer to the developing mind. The adolescent must first attempt to evaluate his or her different options—different ethical positions or religious beliefs, acceptance or rejection of societal norms, attitudes toward sexuality, ideological stance in relation to family and friends—before he or she can choose among them. In this sense, the search for identity is not only the process of molding an image of oneself, it is also the attempt to understand the fundamental components of the clay that will be used.

The ego of childhood, strengthened by identifications with significant others and by growing mastery of the tasks of school and family life, will no longer hold; the challenge now for the adolescent is a creative synthesis of past identifications, current skills and abilities, and future hopes—all within the context of the opportunities the society offers. This challenge is made immeasurably harder because of the technological society we live in, in which multiple roles and careers tantalize us with choice. Mead (1930) suggests it might be easier to live in a society in which roles are inherited through birth or decided by gender! Yet the autonomous creation of identity, the redefinition of one's relationships, the crystallization in various domains of a sense of who one is, what one stands for, and how one relates to the world, is the critical task of the developing adolescent.

Erikson's theory of ego identity formation focuses on the concepts of ego identity, the identity stage, and the identity crisis. He defines identity as "the capacity to see oneself as having continuity and sameness and to act accordingly. It is the consistent organization of experience." As Côté and Levine (1987, p. 275) point out, there are two dominant characteristics defining the concept of ego identity: (1) the sense of temporal–spatial continuity of the ego, a requisite indicator of ego identity (Erikson, 1964, pp. 95–96), and (2) the self-concepts (the configuration of negative identity elements) that unify individuals' experiences of themselves during interaction with the social world. "The development and maintenance of the sense of ego identity is dependent upon the quality of recognition and support the ego receives from its social environment" (Côté & Levine, 1987, p. 275). In contrast, those who have challenged psychosocial notions of identity have suggested that we should think of defining identity in terms of the individual's connections/relationships in the world and see the individual as embedded in the social context rather than outside of it.

The concept of the identity stage introduces us to the notion of ego identity formation and the process by which identity is transformed throughout the life cycle. Erikson held to the epigenetic principle of development in which "anything that grows has a ground plan, and that out of this ground plan the parts arise, each part having its time of special ascendancy, until all parts have risen to form a functional whole" (Erikson, 1968, p. 92). The stages are not merely passed through but instead add cumulatively to the whole personality; Erikson saw the quest for identity and the crises that it often produces as the defining characteristics of adolescence. His psychosocial stage theory is founded on the belief that life is composed of a series of conflicts that must be partially resolved before the developing individual can move to the next one. He proposes eight general stages of conflict: trust versus mistrust, autonomy versus shame, initiative versus guilt, industry versus inferiority, identity versus identity confusion, intimacy versus isolation, generativity versus stagnation, and integrity versus despair (Erikson, 1968). Following psychoanalytic theory, these stages appear in sequential order but are never completely resolved. The formation of ego identity does not then take place only in the identity stage; the degree to which one satisfactorily resolves the identity crisis is heavily dependent on the resolutions to the challenges of the first four stages in Erikson's eight-stage life cycle theory. Each item exists "in some form," Erikson tells us, before its decisive and critical time normally arrives (Erikson, 1968, pp. 93, 95). That is, there are identity elements in all preceding stages just as there are in the succeeding stages, and if the conflicts in these earlier stages are concluded satisfactorily, the healthy development of the ego is more probable; if the conflicts are resolved unsatisfactorily, negative qualities are crystallized in the personality structure and may impede further development.

The psychosocial moratorium—a time of deferred choice—is the period in an adolescent or young adult's life for resolving the identity crisis. It is a time when role experimentation is encouraged and where there is little expectation that the individual will commit to permanent responsibilities or roles. The identity crisis "is precipitated both by the individual's readiness and by society's pressure" (Erikson, 1980, p. 130). The age at which the identity crisis occurs may vary "according to such social structure factors as class, subculture, ethnic background, and gender" (Côté & Levine, 1987) or socialization factors such as child-rearing practices and identification with parents (Jordan, 1971). The moratorium must end, with the experience of role experimentation complete and the achievement of a resynthesis of positive identifications that enables the individual to find "a niche in some section of society, a niche which is firmly defined yet seems to be uniquely made for him" (Erikson, 1968, p. 156). This niche is dependent on the adolescent's feeling that commitment in the areas of values, vocation, religious beliefs, political ideology, sex, gender role, and family lifestyle are accepted, settled, and expressions of personal choice. Other more critical theorists, Jackson, McCullough, and Gurin (1981) for example, have suggested that the option of having a moratorium and being in a position to choose in the area of commitment are limited by social, political, and economic structures and dominant ideologies.

Allied with Erikson's faith in ego identity is his understanding of the difficulty with which adolescents must create and maintain this identity. Identity confusion, and the resulting identity crisis, result from the individual's inability to understand the "mutual fit of himself and the environment—that is, of his capacity to relate to an ever-expanding life space of people and institutions on the one hand, and, on the other, the readiness of these people and institutions to make him a part of an ongoing cultural concern" (Erikson, 1975, p. 102). Feeling pressured by society and his or her own maturation to choose between possible roles even as personal perspectives are rapidly changing, the identity-confused adolescent experiences a confusion that challenges his or her ability to form a stable identity.

Erikson believes that the success with which the adolescent resolves these crises is extremely important for the eventual achievement of intimacy with others. It is only through the commitment to sexual direction, vocational direction, and a system of values that "intimacy of sexual and affectionate love, deep friendship and personal abandon without fear of loss of ego identity can take place" (Muuss, 1988, p. 63). Identity achievement, as opposed to identity confusion, allows the individual to move smoothly from preoccupation with the inner core of identity to exploration of the potential roles this self will play in intimate relations with others.

Erikson's construct of identity versus identity confusion has been expanded by James Marcia (1966, 1980). Marcia, whose work on ego and identity development began with his dissertation "Determination and Construct Validity of Ego Identity Status" (1966), establishes two concepts already mentioned by Erikson—crisis and commitment—as the determining variables in identity achievement. "Crisis refers to times during adolescence when the individual seems to be actively involved in choosing among alternative occupations and beliefs. Commitment refers to the degree of personal investment the individual expresses in an occupation or belief" (Marcia, 1967, p. 119). Using these variables as the determining standards, Marcia breaks Erikson's fifth stage down into four substages: identity diffusion, identity foreclosure, moratorium, and identity achievement.

The identity-diffused individual is characterized by having neither an active involvement in the search for identity roles nor a commitment to any of these roles. He or she is not questioning alternatives. At this point, the adolescent is like James Joyce's Stephen Daedalus, "drifting amid life like the barren shell of the moon." Identity foreclosure is characterized by commitment without crisis; that is, the individual has chosen a set of values or an ideological stance, most often that of his or her parents or valued others, without examining these values or searching out alternatives. In moratorium, on the other hand, the individual is in the midst of the crisis, actively questioning and searching among alternatives without any commitment to one option. He or she is exploring possible alternatives but temporarily unable to commit to one or the other. In achievement, the individual has experienced the crises of moratorium and has successfully made a commitment. Identity achievement is most often attained in the college years, with moratorium and diffusion characteristic of earlier adolescence (Santrock, 1990). It should be pointed out that differences exist between societies and between groups and individuals within societies in the length of the sanctioned intermediary period, the psychosocial moratorium (Manaster, 1989). Also, those not afforded the time or opportunity to engage in identity seeking may well not undergo an identity crisis in adolescence or young adulthood.

Adolescent identity formation also varies, as has been suggested by Signithia Fordham (1988) and Janie Ward (1989), in accordance with the ethnic background of the individual. In her examination of black identity formation, Fordham considers the phenomenon of "racelessness." She explores the relationship between group (black) identity and academic success, and concludes that black adolescents follow one of two paths. Some respect an "individualistic ethos," disregarding their mandatory membership in the black group—a path that may lead to academic success. Others consider this to be "selling out" and espouse the "collectivistic ethos" of their minority group in order to avoid becoming "nonblack," although they may sacrifice academic success in the process. Ward (1989) examines identity formation in academically successful black female adolescents and discovers that racial identity formation is compatible with academic accomplishment. Considering not only the factors of beliefs, values, attitudes, and patterns of family socialization but also "the girls' own subjective understanding of the role that race plays in their lives" (p. 217), she concludes that racial identity must be considered in order to gain a complete understanding of identity formation.

Other theorists, among them Miller (1976) and Surrey (1984), have suggested that theories of identity development have been theories of separation and autonomy rather than connection and relationship. They believe that whereas adolescent boys seem concerned with separation and individuation, adolescent girls create identity more in connection to peers and members of their families. Carol Gilligan (1982) writes of her reservations about Erikson's theory in *In a Different Voice*. Gilligan points out that Erikson recognized sex differences in identity development and discussed how for men identity precedes intimacy and generativity in the optimal cycle of human separation and attachment, but for women these tasks seem to be fused (the woman comes to know herself through relationships with others). Erikson nevertheless retained the sequence of identity preceding intimacy. The sequencing of Erikson's second, third, fourth, and fifth stages, Gilligan suggests, little prepares the individual for the intimacy of the first adult stage. "Development itself comes to be identified with separation, and attachments appear to be developmental impediments, as is repeatedly the case in the assessment of women" (Gilligan, 1982, pp. 12–13).

An alternative perspective on the process of identity development in adolescence, then, focuses on the examination of the individual in context. Development is thus seen as a process of renegotiating relationships, redefining oneself in relation to individuals and social groups (family, ethnic group, class, gender) of which one is a part. Along these lines, the reader may follow Carol Gilligan's approach to examining Courting Danger (Case 1) and focus on how the writer represents his or her *self* in the larger narrative, how the *self* is seen in relationships, and what words, themes, and images are repeated. Such an approach acknowledges that the narrator is speaking, constructing a meaningful account of his or her life.

In the eight cases that make up the Identity section of this book, we include, in addition to the sexual and gender aspects of identity development, cases that address three other aspects of identity development—work, values and ideology, and ethnicity. Any one writer may well focus on a particular area of identity formation. We encourage the reader to examine these autobiographies through a consideration of the following questions. What roles do issues of trust, autonomy, initiative, competence, and identity play in each person's case? Within what contexts does the author define himself or herself? What relationships and connections contribute to his or her sense of self, and how are they changing? Advisable, too, is an exploration of identity status—the evidence of crisis and/or commitment—in relation to each case, an approach similar to that followed by Ruthellen Josselson (1987) in *Finding Herself: Pathways to Identity Development in Women.*

Whatever theoretical perspective one adopts, and we suggest an eclectic approach, the essential components are a simultaneous discovery and creation of self leading to a deepening self-understanding. We believe the cases in this section capture that process in both tone and substance. In each case there is a greater sense of understanding and acceptance of oneself at the end than at the beginning. Each author makes clear that the process continues, but they seem here to have reached at last a plateau from which they can look back and survey their progress. Readers may do well to suspend somewhat their theoretical assumptions while reading a case, lest they miss the sheer spectacle of lives unfolding. Though different identity theorists provide a useful framework for interpretation of these cases, the best of them are but a scaffolding for understanding. We should try to listen first to each author in his or her own terms, to see the authors' evolution through their own eyes. In the unique and intimate details of their individual lives we can discern the outline of a universal struggle to identify our true selves. Your readings here should influence your understanding of theory at least as much as theory influences your reading.

1

Courting Danger

A 19-year-old English woman describes her coming of age in the context of a private British girls' school. Melanie enters puberty as a vulnerable and uncertain young woman, torn between compliance with her family's standards of propriety and her own need to crash through what she perceives as the stagnation and regimentation of her life. She finds a haven in an art class where her teacher demands that students break the rules and go beyond conventionality into creativity. This adult validation of her unspoken belief that she is emotionally suffocating gives Melanie the courage to trust her own intellectual, emotional, and physical instincts. She begins to see her needs as having at least as much validity as her parents' expectations of her. The world of intense peer friendships begins to open to her and with it comes a sense that she is attractive and capable in her own right and can make her way in the world on her own terms.

I still have not fully resolved why, at the age of 13, I stood in the corner of a chilly classroom and calmly took off all my clothes in front of twenty or so of my peers. It was a cold, crisp day and I remember watching goose pimples form on my very ordinary legs. There was absolute silence in the room as I carefully undid the buttons and stepped free from our horrible green uniform. The school sweater and skirt lay crumpled round me and my little white panties circled my feet. I felt a strange lack of emotion or horror at what I had done: My eyes stared blankly back at the girls' uncomprehending eyes, and I stood straight and certain. I was very white, very cold, very vulnerable, but very unemotional. Puberty had barely hit me: My breasts were still small and unformed and any waist, as yet, unidentifiable. There was nothing special about my body—I certainly had nothing either to show off or to hide.

I was not aware of doing this for anyone in particular: The girls present in the room were acquaintances rather than friends or enemies, and none knew me that well. The seconds passed slowly; I wanted to ensure that everyone had the opportunity to recognize what I had done. Was it merely the first raw shock of adolescence causing me to act in such an "odd" way? Was this simply a new awareness of the body and an expression of awakening sexuality? What was I trying to say and why did I have to resort to such lengths to make my point? I heard the delayed reactions—"Melanie, *what* are you *doing*?" and "Hey, Emma, come and see this, will you?"—and felt as if I wasn't there at all. I was completely isolated from my body—my pale limbs really had nothing whatsoever to do with me. I have no recollection of dressing again: All I have is that frozen moment when I see myself from an outsider's point of view. I see the goose pimples on my legs as if I were another person looking at this "freak" from a substantial distance. In the weeks to come, my mind would be filled again and again with images of that small figure standing alone in the shadowy corner.

As I started writing this paper, I had no real idea of where it would lead or what, if anything, would be the cohesive factor pulling my adolescence together. Of course the stripping incident had an impact on me—for one, I had never before done anything "unacceptable" in the eyes of society. However, how would all the other ensuing things that mattered to me fit in with that one isolated happening? Many hours of contemplation have led me to believe that stripping was perhaps a first cry to establish who I was—to find some kind of wholeness in my muddled mind. It was a bold statement in order to dare myself, and others, to think about me in a new, and in many aspects, scary way. Although I never did anything quite as "dramatic" again, I see many of the other things that I subsequently describe as further attempts to clarify who I truly was. Things have been painful and often incomprehensible; I have faced an eternal struggle between solidifying my own individuality and maintaining connections with others important to me. As I stood shivering and exposed in that classroom, I still remember realizing that this was the first time that I had been truly "alone"—there was something intangible separating me from "the rest."

A few other crazy things also happened that year. Surrounded by several friends, I stripped down to the waist on the exposed playing fields (faint half-broken voices echoed in the background from the neighboring boys' school) and returned to math without my underwear on. I did cartwheels between the desks in history lessons when the teacher's head was turned, almost longing for her to catch me and punish me. I threw my shoes out of third floor windows in the midst of physics lessons and watched them tumble into the out-of-bounds quad where no girl was allowed to trespass. I leaned over the banisters on the top floor of the school until I was nearly vertical with my head below my feet pointing skyward. That entailed going right to the brink of my physical capabilities and I trembled at the fact that one slight loss of concentration would result in paralysis or death. I was courting danger, but there was something else going on, too—falling from those banisters was the only way I could imagine of doing something truly irreversible, permanent, strangely beautiful, and perfect. No one would be able to brush that off lightly or complain that I could have done it better. It was an absurd thought, but it appealed to the part of me that was wanting some kind of permanence and perfection. There was little, if any, *acceptable* logic behind these acts: I never thought of the reaction my peers would give and never planned my actions in advance. I just knew that I was never caught or upbraided, and that each time I tried a new escapade, I was in part attempting to have my sense of justice restored: Why was I never punished when others so frequently were?

My friendships were, at least superficially, unaltered by my "demonstrations," and there was no noticeable stultification or intensification in my relationships with the rest of my peer group. They certainly regarded me as "weird" and unusual, but, fortunately, I had just enough "normal" endearing qualities to allow me to stay within the realms of their conforming cliques.

Thus began my adolescence in a flurry of self-exposure. I have always been a very shy and vulnerable person, and it has therefore taken me some time to understand why I did things so blatantly *obvious*. I pondered earlier that stripping was maybe the first glimmer of a search for identity. But why did I have such a need to make myself noticed and distinctive when, at the same time, I shied away from drawing any degree of attention towards myself? To begin to answer this question, I shall have to explore my intense feelings of self-doubt and low self-esteem.

Ever since I can remember, I have felt a fraud. I usually surpassed my schools' and my parents' expectations and failed to achieve my own. Often things have been easy academically, but from age 7 onwards teachers have said, "You must be prepared—in your *next* school, things won't be like this. You'll suddenly find yourself a small fish in a very big pond." The problem is that whenever I moved into another academic environment, I was *still* considered a success—still a "big fish." I always fear that the next time will be the one—the next time I move on I'll be exposed for who I really am. Suddenly all these grand perceptions of me will be crushed. When in a new setting, I am often convinced that everyone else is more socially and intellectually capable than I. The more "successful" I become, the more inadequate I feel: *Why* can people not see my limitations when I find it so easy to fault myself and not live up to my own expectations? Although my drive for perfection means I often fail in my own eyes, to others, I have *never, ever* failed. That is absolutely terrifying; I feel I have come so far now that if I do stumble in front of others, it won't merely be a fall, it will be tumbling right over a precipice. Paradoxically, although I don't really value external praise for my success, I still yearn to be reassured and affirmed; I need to be told I am achieving even though I can never fully hear it. And paradoxically also, my perfectionism is complemented by an awful self-sabotaging urge: One part of me seems determined to teach me how to fail in front of others. How can I relate my arrogant perfectionism—which is unable to accept my mediocrity—to my severe lack of self-confidence and feelings of inadequacy?

Sadly, the conscious and logical mind often cannot explain my thoughts. Much of my fear of being a fraud is, I know, irrational, yet I still find it painfully difficult to acknowledge that *really* I am okay. Underneath all this self-doubt, there is something worth valuing. The world of green uniforms was a private girls' school where my scholastic achievements were particularly highlighted (we were valued for what we could *do* rather than who we could *be*). I was the model "do-er," and how I hated it. Thus all my shoe throwing, clothes stripping, cartwheel turning were, in part, attempts at throwing off the role that had been cast in marble for me—that of the good, obedient, successful student. For far from giving me a feeling of pride, achievement, and worth, my role as a "good girl" was making me feel more and more isolated, empty, and disoriented. They were measuring my worth totally on a scale of tangible success. This had two major implications in my eyes: (1) any part of me that couldn't be measured on that scale—that is, who I was as a *person*—was inconsequential and worthless, and (2) since I had no true belief in my own intellectual and creative talents, I was certain that I was the largest con artist ever. I became increasingly shocked that I did well in exams; I rationalized it by saying that exams were simply a "knack" that I was fortunate enough to possess.

My ability to analyze myself and spot my fallibilities fits in very well with the general ambience of my family and house where intellect and reasoning are very much admired and where action fades into the background. My family has always been stable and permanent in my life. My relationship with my sister Sarah (two years younger) is particularly untroubled. I have always been very fond of, and protective toward, her; she is a very imaginative and almost unworldly girl who seems to exist for much of the day on another planet. Her naïveté and innocence occasionally irritate me, but usually I am amazed and impressed that she has reached midadolescence so pure, old-fashioned, and untainted by the grubbiness of the world. She very much looks up to me and is ever so proud of me. She is incredibly shy in front of other people; I worry about her low self-esteem (it runs in the family, I think to myself, wryly) and the fact that it is very difficult for her to live up to what she perceives as my enormous successes. Her own very special talents and strengths are unfortunately not as obvious as my damned ability to pass exams with flying colors. It makes me furious to think that my success damages not only me (in a topsy-turvy way) but poor Sarah as well.

Both my parents completed higher education and it was a matter of course that I would do the same. My father is very proud of my academic successes and both my parents nourish and encourage "intelligence." Thus our house is very nurturing to all cerebral functioning. However, because all four of us are shy—we all find listening so much easier than asserting ourselves—I have always believed my affective and social development to be rather stymied at home.

My father especially has a fear of emotions and instability, and he copes by being the most centered and unflappable person I know. Life for him is divided into organized, categorized sections. People, time schedules, objects, relationships, and events all have a defined place in his hierarchical scheme. His constant companion is a big scribbling diary incorporating every aspect of his life. Birthdays, for example, are slotted in with an "A" alongside—"A" stands for annual event; "wash sox" has a "3W" (for three times a week); and emptying the vacuum cleaner has an "M" for monthly. Everything is crossed off once it has been recognized (Christmas Day is lined through early on in the morning—thank goodness that doesn't need to be thought of for the rest of the day). He was "green" decades before the concept of "greenness" had even filtrated our society; wrapping paper has always been ironed and the scotch-tape removed by steam so that it can be used again; baths are always two inches deep to conserve water. I see him now, bending over the pine kitchen table and wielding a paper knife and the tissue paper in which wine is wrapped. He folds the paper and carefully cuts it up into six-inch squares that can then be used for toilet paper. My mother always has to rush around the house before our (infrequent) visitors arrive to remove telltale signs of "eccentricity." Our attic is filled with eighty or so identical, numbered boxes which contain all that we don't need on a day-to-day basis. When we need to put up the Christmas decorations, I simply look on his handmade index under C for Christmas, notice subsection 1 (decorations as distinct from wrapping paper), and know that all I require is in box 53.

For years it was wonderful for me to be able to believe that life was simply a question of putting numbers on boxes and letters in diaries: It was very reassuring to see a means of control. Although I have never been physically tidy, perhaps some of my mental perfectionism was derived from observing my father's amazing exactitude. He has managed, somehow, to exist throughout his life in this manner, but I gradually became aware of many uncategorizable things. I couldn't just compartmentalize people or feelings—that would be denying their very interconnectedness with other people/feelings—and thus I had to reject my father's philosophy. Nevertheless, I still had to live in a house where emotions were kept very much under control and social interaction was treated as nonessential. I believe my father could exist perfectly well by communicating with no one but the rest of his family. People really are a terrible burden to him, probably because they are unpredictable and tend to resist simplistic categorizing. He gets on very well with strangers when he has to, but can go months without getting in touch with any of the few friends he wishes to keep. He is a very private, mysterious man, and I wish I understood better his way of thinking. He adores my mother and is very fond of both my sister and me but could not recognize that I needed to be meeting new people, talking with my peers about new things, going to parties, and doing all the other "foolish" things that adolescents so desire to do. I think that because I was so successful in the things that were of paramount importance to him (academic work, musical achievement, being a "nice and polite" daughter), he assumed that my social skills were just as advanced.

He regarded nights out with my friends as a waste of time and would usually say no in answer to my supplications. I think his objections to my socializing also implied a real concern with protecting me from the irrational, dangerous world. I found it poignant when he gave as a reason for his negative reaction, "Your mother would be worried out of her mind if you just waltzed off into the night"; of course my mother would be anxious, but the truth was it would be *he* who would be more frantic. As I grew older, I often did not even bother to disturb the family's harmony and ask to go out when I knew they would not approve of the occasion; I thereby forfeited many evenings with my friends to which I felt entitled. I think this issue became somewhat enlarged in my mind: I was convinced both that my father wanted to keep me under lock and key, and that he would never listen to me. In reality, I often didn't even voice my needs to give him a chance to hear me.

In connection with this, I was becoming more and more concerned about my ability to relate and communicate with others—particularly those of the opposite sex. I have always been scared of "maleness." I choose that word carefully; I am not afraid of men as individuals, but I am certainly uneasy about the whole concept of masculinity. I find it difficult to pin down this fear, but I suppose it must be at least tenuously connected to many things: my fear of my father's categorizing, the fact that I never had brothers and their friends round the house, my eleven years in an all-girls' school, my father's lack of social interaction with anyone but his family, and my belief, between the ages of 14 and 17, that I was profoundly repellent and that no man would ever look twice at me as a possible friend, or—God forbid—girlfriend. It was a short step from my shameless undressing in the classroom to a state of shameful embarrassment about my physical presence.

Trapped in a world of schoolgirls where physical beauty was the prime standard by which to judge and compare peers and where the most complimentary adjectives were *fashionable, trendy,* and *slim,* I longed to exist in some dark cupboard where my vulnerability would be invisible. The ultimate aim was to be "trappable"—worth trapping by a member of the boys' school over the wall. (It has always amused me that the school proudly regards itself as very feminist when we as pupils held such conventional and degrading notions of the function of females as simply an object of desire and adjunct to males.) I suffered acutely because I knew that I didn't quite live up to the cliques' standards of fashionable, trendy, and slim. I have vivid recollections of nearly our entire class of thirty-two sitting in lines during lunch breaks comparing the various merits of our shapely and shapeless legs. There were two marks out of ten: one for length and another for "general impression/shape." I, too weak to protest at such behavior, was an unwilling participant. I remember being relieved, and also disappointed, that I was classed as a "double five"; thank goodness I was within the realms of leg normality, but, yet again, I wasn't going to make it into trappable class.

I wasn't really that concerned with my legs: There were, for me, far more worrisome things to think about. I hated my hair, detested my glasses, and was ashamed of the braces on my teeth. For several months, much of my energy was devoted to feelings of physical inadequacy. I defined myself by how others would regard me—and since I was sure that to others I was ugly, awkward, and gawky, I didn't end up with a very strong self-image. Those were days of torment and despair, of hours in front of the mirror trying on every conceivable combination of clothes to make me look the least objectionable. I would curse the inane values against which I was powerless to resist: I knew most of the standards set amongst my peers were insubstantial and trivial, but I was caught up in them all the same—I wanted, and needed, to belong. My early flouting of their rules of normality by undressing in front of them had given way to a desire simply to fit in.

I was desperately trying to define my own identity but was failing so miserably that I turned to others to help me unify my sense of self. My time of conformity was dark indeed, since I had no real core to my being and all was fragmented and amorphous. In addition, I was suffering from bouts of incapacitating depression—day after day of black woodenness and despair. I was sure that if someone were to open me up they would find absolutely nothing there—if such things as souls existed, I wouldn't have one. I would wake in the morning with nothing but a dull headache filling my entire being, and often I would cross off the hours left before I could get into bed again and escape into the oblivion of unconsciousness. I would long with all my feeble heart to sleep for six months so that I wouldn't have to face any of the awful and draining responsibilities that I saw my life entailed. Depressions were deepened by awful feelings of guilt and remorse: What right had I to be feeling this way? I was physically healthy, had a loving family, did very well at school, was treated by all as someone with abundant reasons for having high self-esteem and self-worth. It was plain contrary of me to feel I had a right to suffer. The very fact that I didn't think I had a right to my depressions made them seem all the more immovable and permanent. I remember gazing from a top story window at school (only yards away from those treasured banisters where I had hung so precariously two or three years earlier) and imagining what would happen if I threw myself from it. I saw my body banging heavily through the air and landing on the lawn below. What glorious peace and permanence that would bring—no more mundanities of everyday existence and no more people making me feel so scattered and disjointed.

I would cry monotonously and regularly, both at home and school. My sobs would be silent to the world but huge and deafening to myself. All I could see were the long days stretching effortlessly and emptily to the end of time. How could I possibly fill them, and what good could I do anyway? My family of course sensed that I was not at my happiest, and made a special effort to be understanding, warm, and trusting. However, I was so good at constructing a façade—a semblance—of okayness for the outside world that soon they too began to believe that everything was just fine and treated me accordingly. As I became increasingly competent at maintaining this veneer of togetherness my internal screams shrieked louder and louder, and I felt I must surely be smothered by this dual existence.

But it would be wrong and misleading to pretend that my adolescence was simply month after month of despair, separateness, confusion, and fragmentation. Now I regard all that blackness as a positive force in my development—I *was* thinking, questioning, and acknowledging that everything wasn't all just "fine, fine, fine." I was being torn and stretched, twisted and distorted—but this was a molding into something new and fresh. Indeed I experienced moments of great lucidity and joy between those weeks of deadness. For a few fleeting seconds, existence would seem purposeful and comprehensible. Often it would be merely the tilting of a head, a certain shadow on the sidewalk, a few piano notes caught in the stillness—suddenly I would sense an acute beauty in life that would be almost too expansive to hold inside me. I would struggle to hold onto that sensation for I knew that I was filled with something precious and valuable; my sense of self then was strong and constant.

The depressions began to wane with my first glimmerings of meanings in the world; this coincided both with my achievement of a satisfactory physical identity and with my escape from the acceptance of others' definitions of me. Actually, my transition from—what I considered—a dowdy, gauche 16-year-old to a presentable, even perhaps attractive woman, was the one fairy tale-like thing that has happened in my life. In the space of one short evening I threw off the shackles of physical insecurity that I had been carrying with me for so long.

Everyone had been talking about the school ball weeks in advance, a joint occasion with the boys' school. All of a sudden I was filled with a crazy and wild desire to make an impact at this silly occasion. I was sick to the back teeth of losing at games where others had made the rules; if I couldn't make my own rules, then at least I'd beat them at their own game. If the aim was still to be eminently trappable, then I would do all I could to be as ravishing as possible. I think my intense desire to succeed made things fall into place—how otherwise could it have chanced that I was to have my braces taken off, contact lenses fitted, and my hair cut all the weekend before that damned dance?! I riffled gleefully through all the dresses hanging in the shops the Saturday before and chose the brightest I could find. The "in" color that winter was black, and so I chose crimson. I still remember the sensation when I pulled the red satin over my head and felt its smooth coldness over my flushed skin.

That night my faith in the world and myself was unshakable. I stood before the mirror with my glasses gone, my hair sleek and sophisticated, teeth proud and white, and that wonderful dress hugging me close in all its glory. Somehow, without my acknowledging it, I had become someone reasonably all right to look at after all. I stood there for several minutes: Gradually it dawned upon me that that strange figure in the shadows was a woman, and that woman was me. There was no longer any need to separate my psychological and physical selves: I hugged myself, reveling in that wholeness. That was the real moment of Epiphany: The rest of the evening was perfect but predictable. Everyone was amazed at the "transformation"; by the end of the evening I was satiated with declarations of approval. I danced and danced and smiled and wept. At long last I had no cause or need to feel inferior: Conversely I had no desire to live up to some ideal of perfection. I was *there*: concretely and earthily there. I actually *felt* my feet aching and I laughed in the knowledge that for once I wasn't "floating all over the ceiling" (as I so often tend to do when I feel ungrounded and unsure) and that I had overcome the enormous hurdle of denying my own physicality in a matter of hours.

To this day I have not had a close or intimate relationship—platonic or sexual—with a man. Despite my acceptance of the interdependence of my physical, emotional, and intellectual self and my newly found physical self-confidence, I still feel unprepared and nervous about tackling a close relationship with a male. Remnants of my own fear as a sexual being remain, and as time goes on, I feel relatively less and less experienced in comparison with others. That is not to say that I do not have strong sexual drives or fantasies; even now I occasionally wonder (1) does everyone else think about sex as much as I do? and (2) are other women just as obsessed with the muscles in a man's legs and bum when he walks? Even after one brief introductory meeting I have a distinct and vivid memory of the exact shape of a man's lower body. Faces may fade; legs do not.

Anyway, I have not yet found anyone with whom I feel I can develop a strong feeling of trust. My vulnerability still makes me terribly wary of revealing parts of my psychological or physical self. I kiss and pet as required, but I am never fully at ease—I can never lose myself in the experience alone and never shrug off the question, "Is this right; am I doing okay; is this what's supposed to happen; is this what

I'm required to do?" I feel the hands on my back and glimpse my slip rising up my thighs and think "Is this actually me here—are these my hands, my lips, *myself?*" I search for some ideal notion of that overused word "fulfillment" and all that seems to happen is a taste of soggy mouths and sweaty skin.

Occasionally I wish for a constant boyfriend. People cannot understand why I don't "go out" with someone; many of my friends go from one long-term relationship to the next almost without pause. But I still have to find someone with whom I want to make some kind of commitment. I cannot see the point of dating just for the sake of it; I cannot afford to expend a lot of energy on a relationship I don't care about. I have no wish to give a lot of myself to someone I don't truly respect. Thus most of the time I am happy with my decision not to fall into a relationship to be like my peers; I like being free and I am thankful not to be called so-and-so's "bit." I used to believe that vulnerability was the only thing holding me back. "If only I weren't so shy," "If only I didn't worry so much about being wounded." Now, however, I have come to cherish it as one of my inherent strengths. I believe vulnerability has made me all the more sensitive to the vagaries of both myself and others, and I feel that it has helped me to be more self-questioning and willing to take risks. Life for me has never been solid or secure, and so I am all the more aware of what a "risk" is, and how exposed I am to change and new circumstances.

When, at the age of 14, I suddenly found myself immersed in art, its teacher, and the fellow students, I found it incredibly exciting to explore a new part of myself. Art wasn't something I could automatically do and it was wonderfully refreshing to grapple with something that couldn't be classed as "right" or "wrong." In addition, no one had preconceptions of my ability, and I had no one to live up to but myself. However, at the beginning it was not art *per se* that thrilled me; it was the art teacher, Ms. Madeleine Tremayne, in all her strange, beautiful mystery.

To me Madeleine is quite unforgettable. I don't quite know where to start—she is still such an important element of my life that I find it difficult to see her objectively, and I feel a strong obligation to portray her as well as she deserves to be presented. Every moment she is *alive*—questioning us, herself, events, imaginings—and I think it is this constant searching for some kind of ultimate truth of faith that makes her so exciting. It is almost possible to feel the zone of her impact and influence; to my unformed mind this "magnetic field" was fascinating and mesmerizing. She drew people towards her—they would come with love and hate but never with indifference.

I would be painting and slowly my paintbrush would droop and my wrists go limp. I would turn and look—trying to identify what on earth made this woman special. Her uniqueness definitely had something to do with her physical presence and aura—there was a steeliness *and* a softness about her—but I think ultimately her great strength was both her integrity and her sense of risk-taking inherent in her teaching style. Every day she would come in with some new theory about "life's rules"—mingling Buddhist meditation with astrology, reincarnation with existentialism. She did not talk for her own benefit—I am sure she was trying to get us to think about life and art in different and often unconventional ways. Her own life was hardly rosy even now (I remember her saying, "Life's no less shitty to you even when you have got bits of it worked out"). She would ask for our advice and cherish our support when life was being a "real bugger." We would sit enraptured by this woman who actually considered us worthy enough both to share her life experiences and to nurture her in crisis. She would also listen limitlessly to our own tales of conflict and confusion and seemed to possess infinite quantities of compassion, empathy, and suggestions. She forced us to look at what we were creating for ourselves, and pushed us into a new state of awareness and responsibility for our actions.

"It's no good thinking that it's always the other person's fault when things go wrong for you, Melanie," she would say, skewering me onto the wall with the intensity of her gaze (escape or evasion was never possible). "You're always going to be part of the equation when other people are involved, and so you have to work out what you're doing to cause this response." I would look at her feeling peeled and exposed. How did she always know exactly what was happening for us?

"You're still being a victim of your fate instead of an instigator. You *do* have the means to control rather than to be manipulated. In the meantime, instead of faffing around and 'floating around on the ceiling,' put some of this anguish into your picture and give yourself twenty minutes to get emotion into those contorted figures. You see, that's what art is—a means of showing *yourself*, a vessel in which to pour your soul. If you have nothing to show, then all we get is a cluster of meaningless, empty lines. And if I were you, I would go home tonight and meditate for half an hour—you clearly haven't been doing that, have you? Your aura's all over the place." (I would admit that I hadn't been meditating: It was impossible to lie to her.) "And ask yourself why your parents aren't hearing you. The blame's not necessarily entirely theirs. Are you really speaking to them, or are you simply talking in a half-hearted way? By the way, I've just noticed: That tiny bit of blue in the center is really singing; you're beginning to understand the pictorial tension. Maybe something is moving inside you after all."

Madeleine was the one member of staff who acknowledged passion, insecurity, and sexuality—both in herself and in her pupils. She recognized our adolescent turmoils as healthy, joined in with our wildness, rejoiced at our unpredictable inflammability, and treated us as sexual beings. Other teachers denied us the right to be disruptive, sexual, and confused; she loved us for what and who we were and knew that all our "madness" could be harnessed to improve our art. She would stride into the room saying, "Come on. Figure drawing—we're really going to get the hang of internal form today. I want you to see the model as monumental." We looked at the 11-year-old posing in front of us in her green school uniform, her legs skinny and her breasts flat. Monumental was not the word that would have automatically jumped to mind.

"Her legs must be solid—they've got to be big enough to support her. Imagine her as a baronial hall: overwhelming the paper, spilling over. You must be like a little ant crawling around her. If you get this going, you're going to be creating masterpieces—I'm telling you, the experience of drawing magnificently is way, way better than sex. I'm completely serious—so let that be an incentive to you!"

My instinct believed that in the chaotic art room my battered soul could be rebuilt, and that here what I had to give would be valued. For those brief months during my last two years, Ms. Tremayne and the other three members of the art class provided in abundance all the love, frustration, inspiration, and despair that I needed. For good or bad, everyone else—parents, other friends—faded into the background. Although I had always managed to be fairly popular with my peers (even without reaching the upper echelons of "cliquedom"), I had never before felt a real sense of belonging or connecting. It was with joy that I heard Madeleine talking of:

"Our raft. Our raft's sinking. We've got to support each other. We're all in the middle of this bloody great ocean and the only way we can keep above water is to paddle like mad *together*. It's no good you all standing in your separate corners beavering away at the old still life." All four of us turned, looked at each other guiltily, and dragged the easels closer together.

"The great thing about learning art together is that you pull everyone else along. We create a pool of energy and everyone draws from it. No more of this trying desperately to be better than everyone else. If you're doing awfully, just be grateful that Sophie over here is making up for you."

Art became the focus and the purpose of our passions—a means of catharsis and purging and an outlet for all my emotional and sexual frustration. At home suppers were still pedagogical affairs, but at least now filled with a sense of excitement; my family could recognize that something was happening to me even if they did not fully approve. They realized that I was living in another world, but still struggled to make me hold onto the image of a loving, considerate daughter. After one particularly lengthy argument between my father and me, he said quietly, "Oh, don't be silly, Melanie—just try and be more demure. That's what you should be aiming for—everyone values demureness and femininity." At that moment I was at last able to conceptualize and clarify one of the primary struggles in my development: I was becoming a woman but was fighting tooth and claw against that image of "womanly goodness and obedience." I wasn't only trying to throw off my role as "good student": I was aiming to get to the much bigger issue of what it is to be feminine. I hated the vice-like grip of the word *demure*. Why had I stripped naked, why had I hated those "marks out of ten for leg shape" discussions so much, why was I unhappy with the power wrapped in the words *fashionable* and *trappable*? My fight was *against* the whole belief of girls being quiet, predictable, and dainty. Even when I had joined in that game by going to the ball, it was in a red, angry dress which defied conventional notions of prettiness. I was just learning how to express my darkness and energy through some creative channel, and the last thing I needed to hear was that I should be aiming towards some traditional notion of femininity.

At last I was destroying the semblance of "good girl/good student" and starting to unleash my hidden and suppressed anger. I felt as though I were bringing into the light a half of me which had been hidden and etiolated for years. Occasionally I would stand back, look at my picture, and be amazed that it was the product of my own hand: Did I really have that much blackness and badness in me? It was both liberating and terrifying to be able to see art revealing some of my murky depths. Even so, still I felt choked: If the right point were tapped I would be faced not with a slow welling up of emotion but a full-scale avalanche of desires, bitterness, half-formed needs, unresolved fears. . . . It's a good job that we learned how to do "anger release."

It was a muggy summer's day—the sort of day when one's pores feel saturated with humidity and nothing much seems to be happening. Madeleine was getting fed up with our slowness to get down on paper "what was really happening for us":

"Is this what you really want to say about yourselves through art? All I can see at the moment is a namby-pamby schoolgirl picture—you're painting the wallpaper and thinking about the next tea break at the same time. Do you really want your pictures to look so flabby? I want to see something 'yummy': I want it to look so good that I could eat it. Find the 'wow' effect—do anything but make bloody sure that it's strong enough to knock off anything beside it on the wall. Where's the internal form? The heart? The passion? I want to be *convinced*."

For once, none of us could respond to her exhortations, and so she led us—Jessica, Joanna, Sophie and me—downstairs to the deserted gym. The school was almost empty since it was after four o'clock, but there was a badminton practice going on in the next-door hall. Madeleine was completely fair: Each one of us was free to leave at any point and we certainly felt no obligation to do what she was suggesting. As I sit here typing, I can still recall the touch of those faded mats as we unpacked them and piled them a foot high; I still see the dust motes hanging in the gym; I still sense that tension of nervousness and expectancy as we stood round those mats waiting to begin. Madeleine began talking in a slow, calm voice:

"Okay, now, I am trained to do this, so you don't need to feel in any way that I am merely experimenting or messing around. I want you all to watch closely and give me energy as I go first. I'm not going to do it fully since none of you would know how to replenish my energy if I let myself go completely."

As usual, my brain understood some of her meanings but not all. What was all this talk of energy and replenishing? What was she actually going to do? I could feel myself beginning to "float on the ceiling"—as I am still wont to do when apprehensive—and I struggled to get both my feet back on the ground. I watched her take off her cardigan and expose her lithe, strong arms and artist's hands. She knelt in front of the heavy pile of mats and locked her arms together by grasping her hands firmly.

"In order to keep me going, I want you all to say insistently something that really pisses me off. I always hate it when people tell me to calm down and so I want you to say just that. 'Calm down!'—again and again. I'm going to shout back 'Shut up.' Okay?"

She gave one of her enormous, reassuring smiles to each one of us in turn. Everything sounded perfectly run-of-the-mill and ordinary. I wondered how she was possibly going to get angry in the middle of a school gym at 4:30 on a Monday afternoon with no real provocation. As I pondered, her face changed: There was absolute focus and concentration, and she started to radiate an almost tangible sense of drive and life force. We felt the tension enveloping us, saw the old, overused mats and heard childish voices from the badminton room. Suddenly there was a whisper of the unknown and the irrational. Madeleine raised her arms high in the air and—Jessica walked out. Her face was filled with an awful fear— perhaps a fear of seeing anger, exposing a weakness, overturning some stable notion of the world? We turned and watched her slam the door, and then drew closer together.

Madeleine didn't break concentration even for Jessica. As if wielding an axe, she raised her arms in a great arc and hurled her full body weight onto the mat. In the same motion she let out a huge and gut-felt cry, "Shut up." The two words lost all meaning as they penetrated the lofty hall. Again and again she drew herself up and thundered back down as we began the slow provocations of "Calm down. Calm down." Her body and voice worked rhythmically; she was both brutal and graceful as the energy surged through her and exploded on the mats. For the first few seconds I was paralyzed by shock and fear. I watched the muscles trembling in her strong arms, the hair in her armpits glistening with sweat, the skin stretching over her temples and the blood flowing to her lips. Gone were all vestiges of what society so admires and needs: control, etiquette, niceness, and obedience. The figure before me had stripped all our superficial coverings away and taken us back to our brutal and real nakedness. So this is humanity: This is what we all so desperately try to cover with manners and social graces. This untamed beast in all of us. My fear subsided and I looked with admiration at the power curving through my teacher and snarling in her throat. What on earth would a "full" anger release have done to me?

It was hard not to feel overwhelmed and self-conscious as I knelt down and gazed at the mats before me. Why did I have to be the first one after Madeleine? I tried to empty my mind but I could not shut out the sound of girls screaming in the next hall. What if they look through and see us here? How could this be explained to 12-year-olds? I focused on my charcoal-covered jeans and swept the hair out of my eyes. Delaying tactics. I felt an absurd desire to rush out of the room into the sunlight.

"Come on, Melanie," I whispered to myself. "Don't let yourself down; if you get this, think of how much you'll move. Even if you can't do it for any other reason, do it for your picture. Your picture needs it; you need it. Don't think about inhibitions, don't think about what society wants. Come *on*, Melanie." Part of me reeled with the thought of exposing the power within me—acknowledging in public the strength of my dark side. I struggled, finally overcame that fear, lifted my arms, and began. As though from a great distance I heard them shouting—shouting the very phrase my father uses which drives me to distraction. "Don't be silly, don't be silly, don't be silly." I registered Madeleine's voice strong against the rest and shouted back with all the power I could muster, "No!" It wasn't very much of a word, but it was all I could manage. I felt vibrations in my throat and gradually everything— the badminton game, the dusty hall, my friends—became lost, and I was overtaken by wild instinct. I was sucked up into a glorious unity and was expressing that deep and unheard wholeness. As I struck the mats, I had no awareness of my hands growing numb with pain and my voice growing hoarse and incoherent.

There was only a sensation of deep and exhilarating release—something was at last pouring from me and I was cleansed and revitalized. I have no idea how long I managed to carry on, slowly the presence of my friends reasserted itself and I collapsed onto the mats, drained and limp. My hands were burning and my throat parched.

I lay there feeling like a newborn babe and recalling the temper tantrums of my childhood years. When had I last been able to express emotions physically? Had I really been keeping so much inside for so long? Madeleine's olive arms extended towards my white ones and swaddled me in a blanket. I curled over onto my side; Madeleine's breath was hot on my back as she drew me near and held me close, one arm pressed onto my lower spine. My ability to hear seemed to have vanished temporarily and her voice sounded thick as she spoke: "That was good, did you feel good? It was wonderful seeing what no one has seen of you for such a long time. Just lie still—stay still. I'm holding you like this to create a big circle of energy so that my energy can flow back into you. I'm going to refill you. This is, in many ways, the most important part: It's essential that you have someone to give back what you just gave out. I'm trying to make myself as open as possible."

I murmured in reply and felt her body strong and warm beside me as I began to expand and re-inflate. I lay quiet and clean amongst the marks made by years of scuffling feet and sweaty toes. The minutes passed and I began to experience a magnificent sense of power and liberation: All the matted junk had been cleared away from my inside and I felt ready to begin again. I saw my big picture—the culmination of our five years of learning with Madeleine—waiting for me. Its primary function was to express, in any way I wished, what really concerned me at that moment in time. Easily six feet long and filled with agonized, contorted horses and humans, it had become nightmarish and abstracted. I was trying to express the enormous conflicts raging inside me, but still couldn't quite get the dynamics working. I had been feeling for the past two weeks as though I were hitting my head over and over against the ceiling.

Ten minutes later (the mats put away and my friends gone home—they were going to do their anger release next week) I swept along the corridor feeling as though I were running on air. I saw exactly what I had to do to make that picture work. It was growing dusky outside and the janitors were beginning to thump around with mops and buckets in the next room. I picked up my pastels and felt entirely alone. The anger release had filled me with such energy that I was sure I could carry on all night if I had to. Taking courage in both hands, I obliterated all the flashy, superfluous marks, rubbed over all the superficial highlighting, erased all parts which were just trying to make me look like an "expert" artist. What would be left? My throat was dry and scratchy and my fingernails filled with the grease of oil pastels. After two hours I stood back, terrified that I had destroyed it all: Had I simply gone overboard with this "anger" and killed everything? My eyes skimmed the image; to an outsider the board looked a mass of messy and unintelligible marks. I exhaled noisily: To me the picture, although now stark and unpolished, had jumped forward more in this one night than it had for the past two weeks. A force was moving within it—oh the joy that that brought. So this is

CASE 1 / Courting Danger

what commitment feels like. I rested on my haunches and thought: This is the first time I have really exposed my anger; this is the first time that I have really experienced commitment to anything. As I sat in that gloomy room, art and that picture were the most important things in my life. Take that away and my life would be meaningless.

By deliberately evading mundanities and trivia by condemning them as the antithesis of art, we had entered a dreamworld where creativity, irrationality, and insubstantiality flourished. It was by no means a stable and realistic existence, but it came at a vital time in my life—all at once no one was forbidding me my rights to feelings of insecurity and inadequacy. I was actually being allowed to ask "What really matters to me?" instead of having to maintain a pretense of okayness. Wow—my art actually improved each time I realized and accepted some previously hidden weakness. The world for me extended not much further than the ends of my finger tips; anything beyond my reach seemed distant and relatively unimportant. I was concerned with how I fitted into life's workings, not how the great impersonal world functioned by itself. I was completely wrapped up in the personal, and set great store on the value and effect of emotion. I began to shun all people—including my father—who appeared to exist without them. Emotion gave my life at that time color and excitement. Experiences were heightened simply because I felt them so keenly; my newly formed relationships were stronger because they were born through feeling. All seemed intense and vital because my spirit was at last being succored whilst my cerebrality and cold intellect were being starved. At last I was a "do-er" no more.

Unleashed from the restrictions and pressures of cliques, I formed my first real friendship with one member of the art group in particular. Jessica is an extremely powerful, exciting, obsessive, and invigorating woman. She was all that I had been aspiring to be: strong in her convictions, sensitive in her vulnerability, creative in her unpredictability, and powerful in her femininity. She was also incredibly unstable, and there would be days when she was beyond us all—uncontrollable, mad, and irrational. Although she was sensitive and vulnerable, she couldn't really get in touch with her feelings so that she could express this insecure and compassionate side: witness her inability to participate in the anger release. I saw these hidden emotions lurking within her and I longed to tap those resources.

I loved her as I wanted to love myself. My deep compassion for her was intense and exclusive; I didn't have much left to give to other people. Jessie, because of her own need for companionship and security, transferred much of her love onto me. We succored and nourished each other with our crazy devotion. I experienced moments of liberation and commitment that I have never since transcended: Both of us were managing to get over our great fear about exposing and trusting, and we knew that there was much invested in our "other half." But this progress was made painfully; our friendship developed most rapidly at times of suffering.

One rainy afternoon I picked up the phone and I heard her voice devoid of any panic but with a hardness and a tension which meant she was in one of her mad days. Never, till now, had she been able to come to me during one of her deepest crises (she would simply retreat into herself), and I was therefore exhilarated and terrified.

"Mel, Mel . . . um . . . is there any way you can come over?"

"Right now?" (Thoughts fluttered through my mind; two papers to be in the next day, a major piano concert that coming week, my father's refusal to let me out since I was under "such pressure." I had to go; I just had to.)

"Yes. It's that . . . well . . . it's just me. I don't know . . . what's happened."

I placed the phone on the receiver, having assured Jess that I would be over as soon as I could. I faltered on the threshold of the kitchen where my parents were sitting. What do I say—that my friend needs me, that my papers don't matter? I had to find some strength to center my energy so that I could not fail.

"Um, Mom and Dad . . . well, actually, Jessie's just rung. She's desperate and she's come to me for help. I have to be with her. I know you'll understand—and understand how much Jessie means to me." I looked at them, amazed that I was for once being open. As I looked, I suddenly saw their love for me in their eyes. I did know at the moment that they would understand: Why had I always been so afraid of enunciating my needs to them before?

An hour later, I was sitting with Jessica in her room. Of course my parents hadn't thought my papers more important than the bonds of a friendship. On the train I had experienced a new self-confidence: I had come to understand my parents better, and we had opened a new line of communication. Even so, as I stepped into the room my confidence evaporated. Jessica was there but not there: She seemed abstracted from life itself. How the hell could I reach out to her? She was sitting on her bed, her face white and unmade-up and her expression fixed. She looked as though she were made of clay; nothing was going to give. Around her, on the paint-stained rugs, lay half-finished self-portraits, sinister abstracts, angry figure drawings. Her full-length mirror had been propped up against a cupboard. Suddenly there were dead and heavy words amidst this chaotic silence.

"Thanks Mel. Thank you." I looked at her, trying to convey by my eyes what my mouth couldn't express. No, that's inaccurate: I didn't even know exactly *what* I was trying to convey. All I wanted was to make some kind of connection with her.

"I was sitting . . . I was sitting in front of my mirror for ages. I wanted to try and get my self-portrait more intense and mysterious."

Was this some kind of explanation? Terrified, I picked my way across the floor and sat down at the end of the bed. There was something almost inhuman about Jess's lack of emotion and the hardness in her voice. Where had she retreated this time? Do I talk, or sit silently and use my body energy to empathize with her? I had never before been in a position when such responsibility was falling on my shoulders—Jessie had come to *me*.

Again she spoke—continuing the monologue, "And I looked, and after a while, after I had sat there for ages, there was nothing there. I looked in the mirror and—I had disappeared—there was just a crazy head there. Desperate—I couldn't find myself anywhere—I had vanished."

I glanced at her self-portraits—wild eyes, pained cheeks—and back to her own impassive, motionless face. "Maybe we should go for a walk," I suggested pathetically. At least then we could get out of this claustrophobic room and maybe the fresh air would help me clarify what I could do to help her. I led her out into the drizzle and felt as though there were a ghost walking beside me. Impulsively I turned towards her and hugged her stiff and cold body close and hard. I felt the energy in my gut and stomach, and tried with all my force to transfer some of it to her. I could feel myself wanting to cry—wanting to show some emotion myself if she couldn't. My knuckles turned white, and Jess's head drooped onto my shoulder. Suddenly she was limp all over, but still no outburst of feeling came.

We carried on walking, and slowly her voice rose in a whisper, a monotone. It came in fragments: her intense fears about not growing up to be a great artist, the terrifying agony when she feels she "must have vanished." Her days of utter irrationality when she cannot even remember the words with which to have a conversation, the spiderlike fatality of her attraction which draws people towards her only for her to suck them dry, her uncontrollable tantrums. I heard her words and wept inside; my best friend had at last removed her "I'm okay" façade and I loved her all the more for entrusting me with the blackest parts of her character.

What did I say in those next two or three hours before I led her home? I know that I was trying desperately to allow her to let something break inside her. This deathlike passivity seemed so unnatural and unhealthy. I myself felt very strange: I had never—even momentarily, as now—been in a "dominant role" in any relationship, and I struggled to relax. Gradually I managed to forget myself and focus entirely on Jessica. As we tramped homeward through the dismal rain, I began to feel the first flames of energy licking through Jessie's body. She had lost that hardness, but I had to acknowledge that Jessie could not, and would not, recognize her emotions that night.

It was with trepidation that I glimpsed her dark head bent over a book in class the next morning. She looked up, gazed at me, and looked down again; I glimpsed serenity in her eyes. Was this a good sign? Do I stay here or do I leave her to her own intimate thoughts? She lifted her head again and tears were trickling down her face. She did not even attempt to brush them away. I watched the pure clean sorrow in her face and felt real warmth in her pale hands as I grabbed them. I had never seen even a hint of a tear in the past and now she was crying openly and beautifully before me. I could feel in those tears the outpouring of all the tension and deadness of last night, and I rejoiced that Jessica had at last let down her final and most firmly established mask—her mask which stated proudly, "Nothing can get to me: My emotions are totally under control." In the following weeks, our friendship blossomed even further since the remaining few barriers against intimacy had been destroyed. Well, temporarily at least.

You see, this sharing of our lives couldn't last for ever. We began to come into school wearing the same clothes without even realizing it, and started using each other's mannerisms and vocabulary. We began to function interdependently—almost as one person. In effect, we were each other's life-support machines. The nature of our union became symbiotic: Our combined power was so strong that it was uplifting to exist as one, rather than to return to our separate loneliness and lack of security. Writing this now, our relationship seems unhealthy in the extreme;

the emotions and intensity invested in the relationship were comparable to those in a love affair. But at that time, it was wonderful to know, for the first time, that what I had to give was valuable. The sense of standing alone and being somehow separated was temporarily extinguished.

But the very closeness that was our strength also engendered in me seeds of envy and mistrust. Art, the common ground on which we both stood so firmly, provided the means for comparison. Which of us had more talent? Which of us had greater depths of character to nourish our creativity? The competition inspired our art and put an invisible, paper-thin divide between us. Also, I began to fear that she didn't need me as much as I thought she did. She seemed scared of our closeness, and I sensed that maybe she was starting to reject me. Her periods of withdrawal returned, and in the holidays she would go weeks without contacting me. I would often call her but she was nearly always out with her boyfriend Andrew (was she substituting our interdependence for a new interdependence with Andrew?) and rarely got back to me. Was it possible that she had sucked me dry and was now discarding the empty shell? I hated myself for thinking that, and so whenever she did either write or phone I would forget all my doubts and everything would be wonderful once more. Even so, it was becoming increasingly complicated: Jessie was now deeply attached to Andrew, and therefore there was a third variable to be considered.

I struggled constantly to give the two of them enough room to grow. Whenever the three of us were out with other people, I knew that it was Andrew's, and not my right to be with Jessie. But still Andrew felt in competition with me for her trust and companionship. Jessica is a very striking woman, and I knew he was very proud of her and felt I had no right to claim her. The strange thing is that she defies all standard definitions of femininity—there is something distinctly masculine (if we can call characteristics "masculine" and "feminine") about her "grit" and stubbornness. I would stand there and think: My "best" friend is at the same time the male ideal image of sexual beauty. How does that affect me; *where* does that leave me?

Although one of Madeleine's axioms rang constantly in our ears—"When you feel you can't exist without someone/something, then that is the time to give him/her/it up"—neither Jess nor I had the strength to make a *real* split. Our partial separation had to be forced by the physical dividers of leaving high school and beginning our separate lives. I wonder now: Was it right of me to expect such loyalty from her? Was it right of me to sacrifice so much of myself for her (even now I forgive her every time she "forgets" about me or treats me in an offhand way)? I remember Madeleine's words clearly, "It's no good thinking that it's always the other person's fault when things go wrong for you, Melanie. You have to work out what you're doing to cause this response." Much of my ongoing doubt therefore stems from myself: Is my concept of friendship too intense and distorted? What was I doing to make Jess shy away? Even now I am reluctant to admit the close of that chapter in my life of which I was so desperately fond. In my turbulent and joyful "art phase" it was so clear that I was developing and learning. The storms of midadolescence—with all their agonies and their ecstasies—are over and I now face a period of consolidation rather than complete reformation. It's harder now: I have to look very carefully indeed to identify the few millimeters' progress that I aim to advance each day.

But there have been gains; partially freed from ties with Jessica and the art group, I have been able to reincorporate and reaccept my family. Although I had managed to break down the fear of communicating openly with them during my time of intense friendship with Jessica, I still wasn't treating them as an integral part of my life. My *real* life was my hours spent in the art room; coming home was like having to return to a hotel to sleep and recuperate for the next day. Now, my eyes are free to observe my parents and accept them both as parents and as people in their own right.

The turning point arrived in the form of my first major piano recital. The two weeks preceding this event I had stayed home with my mother and I had felt a real strengthening of bonds between us as we entrusted each other with our intimate selves. On the day of the concert itself, she couldn't eat one thing; it was almost as though she was going to be playing and not me. My father had been like a shadow during this time; he was often there but I never really acknowledged his solidity.

The hundreds of hours of practice for my recital condensed into one short evening. Those rare moments of happiness when I'm playing well—when I feel that I *have* achieved my full potential, and near perfection doesn't seem *quite* so impossible—were quickly over and I was standing bowing. At first I could focus on no one, but then I spotted my father's snowy hair near the back (at the back so as not to distract me). In between bows I strained to see them all clearly. I blinked rapidly and caught my mother's beautiful joyful face and the tears in Sarah's eyes. Thank God I had played my best. I felt on top of the world. Then I saw my father's strong hands clapping and—my father was crying. My father was *crying* because of me. He was being more damned emotional than anyone else in the entire room. I snatched back a sob in my own throat and clutched the bouquet closer to my chest.

I had been so critical of my father's categorizing, and yet I had neatly classified him as "not able to have emotions." I remembered Jessica's tears and now I experienced the same joy as I had then. What tears could do to me! As I lay in bed that night, I knew my eyes were opening to the world; with a sharpness in my chest I realized that my father, and indeed all other people to whom I am closely attached, are infinitely more varied and magical than I had previously been willing to admit. As I lay there in the darkness, I again felt that degree of separateness that I had experienced in that drafty classroom several years ago. But this time I wasn't scared; although there was a thin line separating me from "the rest," there was also a thin line separating each individual from "the rest." (What is "the rest" anyway? Surely it is merely a collection of struggling, lonely souls.) It was incredibly comforting to know that I would never be able to understand fully the workings of someone else—people could never be truly figured out. They would always be able to shock me by their inconsistencies of behavior. One person would cry or one person would strip naked and someone else's notion of the world would be overturned. Yes, it was wonderful to be able to perceive at last each person's own, precious uniqueness and complexity.

Yesterday I was strolling along the sidewalk. It was quite a nice day and my glance fell on my elongated shadow gliding along beside me. I paused: That was *my* shadow. I could never get rid of it, add to it, swap it with someone else, or change its fundamental characteristics. It would always be mine. Just as my "Melanieness" will always be mine. I had never formulated that thought quite so clearly—no matter whom I get involved with, what I do with the rest of my life, there is absolutely no way that I can ever change or add to my shadow. There will always be just one. The only companion it will have is me. I carried on walking and heard a voice inside me: "We must die alone: We *shall* die alone. *We* are our own constant companion. Surely therefore we must learn to live and stand alone." Just as I was about to go inside into the gloom I heard my voice again, "Here I am, whole, eager, vulnerable, and alone. I'm walking alone. I'm existing alone. And I'm *living* . . . not merely surviving."

Response to Melanie

Reflections on Case 1

CAROL GILLIGAN

Ourself behind ourself, concealed—
Should startle most—
—Emily Dickinson

I felt as though I were bringing into the light a half of me which had been
hidden and etiolated for years.
—Melanie

I am listening to Melanie, tuning my ear to her voice, letting it enter my psyche, picking up its resonances, its familiar themes and cadences, and also its distinctiveness, its Melanieness. Because Melanie's voice is my guide, taking me into the realm of her psyche and leading me across the terrain of her adolescence. Preparing to speak in response to this voice, I take my bearings by asking four questions about myself and also about Melanie: Who is speaking? in what body? telling what story about relationships—from whose point of view or from what vantage point? in what societal and cultural framework? And I realize that I am familiar with the fugal structure of Melanie's composition—the two-part invention or the counterpoint of Melanie's narration where one voice begins with a startling story about self-exposure and disconnection (from her body, from herself, from her feelings, from others, and from the society in which she is living) and then, midway through, a second voice enters—picking up the themes of self-exposure, relationship, and challenge and telling a vibrant story of living in intense connection with herself and others.

This doubling of voice and vision—this simultaneous telling of two stories that are fundamentally at odds with the portrayal of self, relationship, and reality—is a familiar landmark of girls' adolescence because it is a creative solution to what Melanie describes as a "painful and often incomprehensible" problem: the seemingly "eternal struggle between solidifying my own individuality and maintaining my connections with others who are important to me." This split between "self" and "relationship" is psychologically painful and also incomprehensible because it marks the taking of self out of relationship, paradoxically for the sake of maintaining relationships as well as for the sake of solidifying one's self. With this withdrawal of self from relationship, the moving life of relationship stops. The voice of the opening section of Melanie's self-portrait—in portraying a self feeling all alone and disconnected and relationships that feel inauthentic or fraudulent—bespeaks this stillness and this disjunction.

For the opening voice is a voice that is in some odd relation to Melanie—an observing "I" who speaks about herself from somewhere outside of her body, who is preoccupied with questions of judgment (is she ordinary or special, a con artist or an artist, a fraud or a person of worth and value), who stands alone—apart from "the rest," and who speaks in partial quotation, as if taking on some foreign language ("odd," "freak," "unacceptable," "alone," "weird," "normal," "big fish," "successful," "do-er," "knack," "intelligence," "maleness," "categorizing," "trappable," "fashionable, trendy, and slim," "togetherness," "separateness," "fine, fine, fine").

This is the no-voice voice in which psychology is commonly spoken—a voice that speaks as if it is disconnected from a person and a body, that tells a story about relationship that is at its center a story about separation, within a setting that is supposedly culture-free or universal. And in this voice Melanie tells what is, to psychologists, a familiar story of female adolescence: about self-sabotaging urges, feelings of worthlessness, a drive for perfection, intense self-doubt, a wooden depression, suicidal impulses and gestures, poor body image—all in a girl who is physically healthy, doing very well in school, who has a loving family, who is treated by all as someone with abundant reasons for feeling good about herself, who is the daughter of highly educated parents—a girl who is musically gifted and living in the midst of educational, economic, and racial privilege.

Melanie, however, portrays herself as a weary survivor of a relational struggle—wanting to expose herself but also wanting to stay in connection with others who are important to her. This crisis of connection is accompanied by a feeling of seemingly hopeless relational impasse: To be with others, she has to cover herself with "our horrible green uniform" and to free herself means to be at odds with other people—angry, passionate, and presumably too sexual, dressed in red at a dance where everyone wears black. In her most direct answer to her opening question as to why she took off her clothes in the chilly classroom, Melanie says, "It was a bold statement in order to dare myself, and others, to think about me in a new, and in many ways scary, way." This healthy, if dramatic, act of resistance to her pervasive experience of disconnection is, as she says, the beginning of her move to join her "psychological and physical selves" and to connect her thoughts with her feelings. Melanie seeks to bring herself into her relationships—at first by expressing her point of view on what is happening and thus revealing her experience of the world in which she is living.

Because, like a member of the underground, Melanie has become facile "at constructing a façade—a semblance—of 'okayness' for the outside world," so convincing that "they too began to believe that everything was 'just fine' and treated me accordingly." But the psychological darkness that encroaches on Melanie—the incapacitating bouts of depression and the feelings of emptiness—comes from her sadness about living in such isolation and her uncertainty in this radical aloneness as to who she is and what is reality. Her "veneer of togetherness" covers over and muffles "internal screams which shrieked louder and louder," leaving Melanie feeling that she "must surely be smothered"—kept from breathing, kept from speaking, physically and psychologically dying. The more she sees herself fitting into the roles that have been cast in marble for her—"good girl/good student" and also "loving/considerate daughter"—the more she feels "isolated, empty and disoriented": disconnected from others, drained of feelings, without a soul, and out of touch with reality.

But this is only half of the story. Midway through her chronicle of despairing choices (between being true to herself and appearing perfect in the eyes of others), Melanie suddenly backtracks and retells her story, beginning now at the age of 14 rather than 13 and changing the location from the chilly classroom where she stood all alone in a shadowy corner to the art room where she "suddenly found [herself] immersed in art, its teacher, and the fellow students." The catalyst for this transformation is Ms. Madeleine Tremayne, and the medium is genuine connection, or real relationship.

The shift in Melanie's voice is striking as the remote "I" (or eye) of the first section who *looked at* and *spoke about* her in ways that ultimately were terrifying, holding up an image of perfection that, like virginity, could be lost irretrievably with one false step or careless moment, gives way to an "I" immersed in feelings, in art, in herself, in her teacher, and finding it "incredibly exciting," "a deep and exhilarating release" of creative energies that had been bottled by concerns about perfection and overbearing judgments. Rejoicing at being able "to grapple with something that couldn't be classed as 'right' or 'wrong'," Melanie now is able to take risks that are developmentally essential, because imperfection no longer means "failing in front of others," or "tumbling right over a precipice," or losing everything.

The quotations drop off as Melanie no longer struggles against the voice of constraint but instead is drawn by her teacher into an experience of alive and moving relationship. Lapsing briefly into the voice of the first section, she attempts to be dispassionate and to judge Ms. Tremayne "objectively," feeling at the same time "a strong obligation to portray her as well as she deserves to be presented." But this voice now sounds stilted and artificial, remote and judgmental, and Melanie quickly shifts into a language that is for the most part free of quotation, grounded in her own strong feelings and thoughts rather than "floating on the ceiling," and a voice that bespeaks living in a world of emotional generosity, joy, pain, and abundance rather than a world that is sparse, spare, and judgmental.

Again Melanie feels peeled, exposed now by the eyes of her teacher who wants to see her, who wants to be with her, who calls on her to speak the full range of her feelings with unmodulated intensity: to show her passion, her insecurity, her sexuality, her confusion, her anger, her desire for closeness, her wildness, her power, her weakness, her love of her artwork, her inflammability, her wish to be alone with her painting, her relief at being comforted—in short, her humanness. The "madness" that previously had seemed so dangerous and disruptive now could be "harnessed to improve our art." Art was "a means of showing *yourself*, a vessel in which to pour your soul."

It is essential to stress the relational context in which this self-exposure takes place and to note that what Melanie refers to as her teacher's "uniqueness" and "her great strength"—"her integrity and her sense of risk-taking inherent in her teaching style"—was her readiness to bring herself into relationship with her students. The risk Madeleine took was the risk of relationship, exposing herself, peeling herself, revealing her vulnerability—her ability to be wounded or her humanness, her imperfection, her need for closeness, for comfort, for nurture, and also her irritation, her impatience, her steeliness, her anger. Her listening, compassion, empathy, and suggestions seemed infinite—abundant and limitless—because they were given so openly, so freely. Here Melanie could expose herself and release her feelings without feeling herself "silly" or finding herself all alone and abandoned. And this release is carried in Melanie's language as she actually feels feelings ("I felt choked") rather than thinking about what she must surely be feeling ("I must surely be smothered by this dual existence").

In the world of the art room where Madeleine and the other students "provided in abundance all the love, frustration, inspiration, and despair that I needed," Melanie felt for the first time "a real sense of belonging and connecting." On this raft where they were "paddl[ing] like mad together," she was "at last able to conceptualize and clarify one of the primary struggles in [her] development: [She] was becoming a woman but was fighting tooth and claw against that image of 'womanly goodness and obedience.' "

In "the chaotic art room" where Melanie's "battered soul" could be rebuilt—where what she had to give "could be valued," where she "felt a real sense of belonging or connecting," and where she experienced "the joy" of "learning together . . . [and] creat[ing] a pool of energy"—Melanie speaks about becoming a woman, having to fight against being trapped in the conventions of "femininity" and having to speak back in anger to the voices that say everything is fine, nothing is wrong, calm down, don't be silly.

> Much Madness is divinest Sense—
> To a discerning Eye—
> Much Sense—the starkest Madness—
> 'Tis the Majority
> In this, as All, prevail—
> Assent—and you are sane
> Demur—you're straightway dangerous—
> And handled with a Chain—
>
> —Emily Dickinson

When I become confused in listening to Melanie is when she refers to the vibrantly colored interior of her self-portrait as "a dreamworld," "insubstantial," "unrealistic," "unhealthy," while calling the shadowy outer story of aloneness and separation reality—the way "we must live," and the way, she implies, she shall live in order to ensure her survival. Because in doing this, Melanie covers over problems of relationship that she has revealed and gives up both a healthy resistance to disconnections that are psychologically wounding and also a political resistance to an order of living that denies the "interconnectedness [of people and feelings] with other people/feelings." Thus Melanie moves from the healthy resistance that opens her narration into the political resistance that characterizes her "turbulent and joyful art phase"—the resistance that, with Madeleine's encouragement, leads her to speak openly of her desires to her parents, and then, finally, to what is clinically known as a psychological resistance: a reluctance to know what she knows, about belonging and connection, about passion, commitment, closeness, love, pain, and struggle.

This pattern, whereby a healthy resistance to disconnection turns into a political resistance or open struggle for honest relationship, which then is under pressure to turn into psychological resistance—a reluctance to know what one knows—reflects girls' sense at adolescence of coming up to a chasm: the place where their experiences in living divide from what is generally taken to be or socially constructed as reality. Melanie, for example, "gradually became aware of many uncategorizable things. I just couldn't compartmentalize people or feelings— that would be denying their very interconnectedness with other people/ feelings—and thus I had to reject my father's philosophy." And yet, "I still had to live in a house where emotions were kept very much under control and social interaction was treated as nonessential"—the house she grew up in.

Which brings me to the silence—the fact that her mother says nothing, has no voice. Madeleine speaks, Jessica speaks, Melanie speaks, her father speaks, the girls in the opening classroom scene speak, but not her mother. Like Jessica who looked and looked and "couldn't find myself anywhere—I had vanished," Melanie's mother has disappeared or appears only as a pale shadow of Melanie ("it was almost as though she was going to be playing [the piano] and not me"). And their relationship, said to be intimate and trustworthy, is overshadowed by Melanie's father who, in the end, cries at her near-perfect performance.

Whether this assent on Melanie's part to the ideal of perfection and the conventions of femininity that she had resisted is sanity or madness remains in question. Her mother silently models capitulation as Madeleine had exemplified resistance, and perhaps Melanie's relationship with Jessica serves as the passage leading away from intense and powerful relationships with women that now seem to her "unhealthy in the extreme" and toward the overriding claims of the patriarchy—"I knew that it was Andrew's, and not my right to be with Jessica. I had no right to claim her." Melanie's questions, "How does that affect me? *where* does that leave me?" orchestrate the ending.

Moral language returns to cover the loss of relationship and to justify giving up a way of living that was "joyful and turbulent," that "chapter in my life of which I was so desperately fond . . . [when] it was so clear that I was developing and learning." With her "eyes opening to the world," Melanie comforts herself with the realization that she is safe from detection ("there was a thin line separating each individual"; "people could never be truly figured out") and also with the recognition that notions of the world can be suddenly overturned by crying or sudden nakedness. As her sentences shorten and relationships dwindle to a shadow, the words "never," "ever," and "always" convey her sense that what was moving within her has come to a stop ("there is absolutely no way that I can ever change or add to my shadow, there will always be just one"). Living away from her art world and also from her family and her country, she is now her only companion. In the end, the voice that spoke earlier in partial quotation now speaks in full regalia: "We must die alone: We *shall* die alone. *We* are our own companion. Surely therefore we must learn to live and stand alone." And yet, going into the gloom, Melanie hears "my voice again"—speaking as if from some underground cavern: "Here I am, whole, eager, vulnerable and alone. And I'm *living:* not merely surviving." Like many adolescent girls, she is surviving in the underground, has gone into hiding.

My sensitivity to the disjuncture in Melanie's narration between the first person "I" and the cultural "we"—this chasm between experience and "reality"—comes from the fact that although I am much older and grew up in a different country and in a different family and culture, I too am a woman, was also a girl, and like Melanie, I know standards of physical beauty, the voice of the father, the lure of perfection, the realization that this is deadly, the feeling of being a fraud, the persona of "good girl/good student," the feeling of "being smothered by this dual existence," the split between self and relationship and the urgency to heal that division. And, like Melanie, I too have experienced passion, insecurity, sexuality, wildness, confusion, abundance, "a real sense of belonging [and] connecting," joy in being in it and "paddling like mad together," the power of "unleash[ing] hidden and suppressed anger," the feeling of being choked by the fear that "if the right place were tapped I would be faced not with a slow welling up of emotion but a full-scale avalanche of desires/bitternesses/half-formed needs/unresolved fears," a tendency to "float on the ceiling" when apprehensive and a struggle "to get both my feet back on the ground," the feeling of vibrations in my throat, of "deep and unheard wholeness," the comfort of being drawn near and held close, of taking in the energy of others, the exhilaration of discovering "what really matters to me," of realizing and accepting weakness, of knowing love and closeness instead of having to stand alone and maintain a façade of "okayness."

Melanie, with the discerning eye of an artist, the ear of a musician, and the candor of one who is willing to undress in public, has drawn an exquisite and powerful portrait of adolescence—psychologically compelling, beautifully rendered, and in the end deeply unsettling, because she covers over what she has revealed. Like a painter working in oils, she layers her canvas by telling two overlapping stories about her adolescence. And the resonance of her voice comes in part from the dissonances between these stories and the way in which she is thus able to convey what otherwise, perhaps, cannot be heard or spoken: that her adolescence at once fits into the models of adolescent development that she has studied and also deeply calls into question the models. Her readiness at the end to fit herself into a simple story of developmental progress and in doing so perhaps to perform for her father or reassure him that she is all right, that what has been lost is inessential, is what I find distressing. As I listen to the silent aligning of her first person "I" with an unspecified "we" intoning aloneness, I find myself wondering what Melanie might say if we were able to talk with one another directly.

2 Working Through My Adolescence

In this case, the 20-year-old author describes his experience working at a local art film theater in early adolescence. As the only child of parents who married and had him before entering college, Bill was expected early on to "pull his own weight" and learned the independence that would carry over into his work experience. By far the youngest employee at the theater, he finds that he can play "little brother" while being exposed to a range of people and experiences he would not otherwise have encountered. The movie theater serves as an arena outside of the home in which Bill gains self-confidence and develops a sense of responsibility and where he begins to experiment with drugs and sexuality. At the same time, he is a "model" student and family member. His feelings of self-confidence and self-knowledge are challenged by his realization that his overdependence on drugs affects his relationships with women and other aspects of his early college experience. This case study explores Bill's sense of leading two lives and of his more recent attempts to reconcile them.

To set the scene: It is 12:30 on a Saturday night. I am working at the Palace Theatre while *The Rocky Horror Picture Show* plays in the background. It is my first job, and I am excited to be there. After all, I am 14 years old, handling lots of money, candy, and late-night zaniness every weekend. I am the youngest worker there, but because I work hard my age isn't often remarked upon. Furthermore, I don't look 14, with my wide shoulders and 5'10" frame, my well-spoken manner and air of confidence. And I don't worry too much about being younger—I simply do what I have been raised to do: be responsible and work hard.

I was raised to work hard, since hard work is what has kept my family together from the start. I am an only child, the son of parents married at age 18. My mother and father had been dating a few months when my mother became pregnant with me. My parents were high school seniors at the time, and I can imagine the leaden feeling in their stomachs as they faced the reality of this unplanned pregnancy. The circumstances have been described to me in snatches, small bits so as not to flood the memory with pain. My mother told me that I wasn't the reason for their marriage—a catalyst, but not *the* reason. Neither of them would have been comfortable with a forced marriage. Their options were limited: They could get married, and face the tremendous pressures of a young marriage, or my mother could go away and have the baby with relatives, away from the eyes of friends and neighbors. Abortion was not an option due to the limited resources available in my state. So they thought and cried about it and decided to get married and try to make it work.

Both sets of parents were extremely disappointed and angry. The extended family's anger did not help the situation any; now my parents were scared *and* alone. My father's parents were especially hard-hit, since they, too, had faced a similar problem at age 20. They had gotten married, but theirs was not a happy union: There was a lot of bitterness and anger between them, which my father had seen all of his life. To see their son repeating their mistake was hard for them to handle. Their disappointment was multiplied by my father's academic success up to that point. A good future was in store for him if he played his cards right. He was president of the Honor Society, a scholarship recipient, and the vessel of his parents' dreams. They were angry about his predicament, furious with my father's failure, and they gave him only minimal help. There was no emotional support from my father's side of the family.

My mother's situation was different, but no less difficult. While not the academic superstar that my father was, she worked hard and took college prep classes. She has told me that every year she had to go and argue with her guidance counselors to be allowed to take those college prep classes. In a way, her pregnancy confirmed the low expectations that her guidance counselors had for her. As for her family, it appears that they kicked her out. Through their accounts I have vicariously experienced the coldness and anger that they faced from both sides.

My parents' marriage required a complete renegotiation of expectations, dreams, and lifestyles. I feel that my father had to change his expectations the most, having been a high school superstar looking eagerly towards college. My mother had less to prove, but less to fall back on. She was the only one convinced of her own abilities. Together these young people entered college as married freshmen, with a child on the way. I arrived in February and was an ever-present reminder of the reality of the situation. Despite living in college housing, my parents had to work all of the time. Whoever was not in class or at work was taking care of me. There was never enough money, time, or energy for my parents to relax while our family was young. Never enough of the things which make college fun.

So long as I can remember, my parents have always placed a lot of confidence in me. Their confidence came with the responsibilities which they gave me. As soon as I was able, I was asked to do my share in our household. Anything that I could contribute lessened the overwhelming amount of work my parents faced. My first responsibility was to take care of myself. I was a latchkey kid during grade school, taking care of myself after school. This self-monitoring allowed my mother to finish her classes and student teach without worrying about being home in time to meet me. Being a latchkey kid was the first responsibility I remember having, and while I was helping my parents out, the confidence they had in me was clear in their choice to leave me alone during the afternoons.

The effect of placing their confidence in me at a young age can be seen to this day. In my household I am accustomed to being held accountable for my actions, as well as being responsible for my share of the housework. When I first spent the night at a friend's house, I noticed that his mother never asked him to clean up after himself, or share the cookies with all of the family. By seventh grade I had realized that I did much more housework than any of my male friends and most of my female friends. Yet I am glad that I learned how to be responsible as a young boy, for I also learned about the corollary of responsibility—the promise of freedom.

For me, our household philosophy meant several things. First of all, I was expected to think as a member of the household, and not as a boarder. If there was work to be done, I should do it, without complaint, as a natural reaction to my commitment. Some of my friends' families were set up with the mother doing the housework, the father making the money, and the kids just being kids. With my chores and self-regulation, and two working parents, the same rules did not apply in my household. But if the rules weren't the same, neither was the way in which I was treated. My responsible nature won my parents' respect and earned me more understanding for my occasional youthful indiscretions, without which this narrative would be entirely unbelievable. Moments of poor judgment, like the time that I did a forward somersault in the family room, kicked the TV with an awkward foot, knocked over the flower vase on top of the TV, and blew up said television. Rather than telling me how awful and immature I was, my parents told me to go outside and play. In retrospect I think their understanding was due in part to their respect for me, which gave them the understanding that this was an isolated incident and not a typical stunt. Hearing how some of my friends were put down by their parents for being lazy or immature, I was glad for the way my household was set up. To this day, however, one will never find flower vases on our television.

By the time I was 12 or 13 years old, my responsible nature had won me a bigger share of independence than that which my friends enjoyed. My parents did not question every decision I made; instead they trusted that I had thought out my choice and would accept the consequences. I was not forced to take music lessons against my will, although my father had been; my stabs at adolescent romance were not overly lampooned as immature; and my school life was my domain. I enjoyed this relationship with my parents, and the faith they had in me gave me a lot of self-confidence. Their faith also allowed me a lot of room for self-expression. I could stop playing the saxophone if it sounded like a moose's mating call to me, since my feelings were considered valid. I could be very silly without worrying what my parents would think, since they knew the depth of my responsible nature. Their faith, however, was tested when I was 13, and a friend of the family offered me a job working at his movie theater.

I was in the seventh grade and in braces when he asked my parents, with my eager approval, if I would help him deliver schedules for upcoming movies and events. They consented to the proposal after some thought. If there was to be a good entry into teenager work, this was it: working for a friend of the family in a simple job. I felt as if I had been offered the chance of a lifetime. I rode around in the back of a gutted-out Volkswagon van, not noticing the severity of the accommodations—due to my euphoria I never felt a bump. When it came to working, I was enthusiasm incarnate, a teenage whirlwind running, literally running, from door to door. I acted as if I had received a great honor to be able to deliver movie schedules. It seemed a task of almost heroic proportions—defying large dogs, paranoid residents, and the imminent clumsiness of a 13-year-old frame were just some of the dangers I faced. I jumped whole flights of stairs, and mastered a certain way of throwing the schedules so that they landed face-up. My first day at work was tiring, not for me, but for those who watched me be so energetic.

That day of delivering schedules began my involvement in one of the most important experiences of my life, for having impressed the owner with my speed and eagerness, I was adopted into the Palace Theatre organization. My parents' decision had opened the door to a whole new set of experiences, and the lessons I had learned in our household had primed me for success.

The Palace Theatre was an old-fashioned movie house which sported a brass rail balcony and showed movies in a double feature format. It is best characterized as a repertory/art film theater, showing Hollywood favorites, foreign films, and midnight cult classics. My parents and I were regulars there, and our affiliation with the theater certainly influenced their decision. My parents' knowledge of and affection for the theater was important, since the place had a bad reputation. It had previously been owned by hippies and was associated with drugs and loose morals. My friends' parents thought that by allowing me to work there, my folks were throwing me into a den of corruption. In casual grocery store conversation, they often commented so. My mother had to deal with my peers' parents, all of them at least eight or ten years older than she, and their condemnation of the decision to let me work. Both of my parents stood firmly behind their decision and never showed any sign of wavering.

So I worked. After my debut as a schedule deliverer, I was asked to help clean up the theater on weekends. During seventh and eighth grades, besides my standard school subjects, I learned all of the intimate details of broom. I graduated from my household responsibilities to a larger scale of work. Instead of cleaning my bedroom, I was cleaning up a 400-seat theater. Hard work took on a new meaning as I worked against the mess and chaos created by *The Rocky Horror Picture Show*.

I could only imagine what happened during the film, since I had never seen it, but being confronted on a Sunday morning by a floor covered with rice, playing cards, toasted bread, and toilet paper gave my imagination room to roam. When I finally saw *Rocky Horror* a few weeks after I began cleaning, the reality of it was stranger than any scenario I could have dreamed up. All sorts of people, hundreds of them, came dressed up like it was Mardi Gras. They carried bags of rice, squirt guns, toast, and bags of assorted projectile goodies. As I watched the movie I was engulfed in an audience participation event of cultish proportions. At different points and lines in the movie, members of the audience shout responses and humorous profanities in response to the characters' lines and queries. At other intervals they cover their heads with newspaper as a massive water gun fight erupts, mimicking the storm in the movie. Still other moments call for flying toast and toilet paper to soar through the air. I was enthralled by the film and its consuming atmosphere, but not pleased with the aftermath and the way it shaped my Sundays.

But I wouldn't have traded places with any of my friends who played outside on Sunday afternoon. I was having a lot of fun, working with other teenagers in a whole different world. As a matter of fact, many of my friends wanted to join me at work; there was definitely a Tom Sawyer phenomenon, a romantic notion about working in a theater. I myself won't deny the real romance of the Palace. The balcony, the loud stereo sound system, free candy, soda, change for video games, movies—for a young adolescent the Palace had it all.

The most important thing that the Palace offered me, however, was an extended family which I didn't have at home. Most of my co-workers were four years older than me, 18 when I was 14. The Palace was the center of their social lives, since they were all close friends and the Palace was an exciting place. The theater had a homey feel to it, since there was almost always friends hanging out while others worked. And if we were a family, I was certainly the little brother. They even called me Little B, a way of commenting on my position in the "household" (and differentiating between the four or five Bs who worked there).

I was forever being wrestled, chased, and wrangled into doing extra work—the life of a little brother. One of the favorite pastimes of the theater family was getting into each other's business. I could never have a date without it being commented on and joked about. I often took my dates to the Palace, with all of its secret spaces and the dark and romantic balcony. My love life was a favorite topic at the Palace, with its share of embarrassing moments for myself. Moments like being caught half naked in the backstage dressing rooms, caught in the heat of my eighth grade mating dance.

But if the Palace gang observed my romantic development, they also helped prompt it. My co-workers were my role models, both good and bad. By interacting with 18-year-olds on a regular basis, it was inevitable that I would use them as a standard, and reach for their level of maturity. After all, at work I had been admitted into a circle of older people, and in a way this signaled my acceptance as a 14-year-old who was mature enough to enter the 18-year-old strata. For anyone who is growing up, maturity is the goal, a prize to be attained. It was my goal, too.

From early adolescence on, I was thought of as a mature young man. I did all my chores, got good grades in school, and never got into any big trouble. Being a good kid and not causing trouble are the two most important measurements of maturity. I lived up to everyone's expectations, and then some. But I think it was my intelligence and the lessons of my upbringing which led to my fulfillment of adult expectations. I was used to working hard and doing a good job. And I had learned that if I did a good job I would be trusted with a greater share of freedom. That was the way I considered maturity when I was younger, as a social contract. If you do this, you get that.

In my free time, away from adults, I played and acted like a child. I was a silly boy. The Palace was the perfect place for me to express both my more adult and more childlike sides. Our cleaning work was often interrupted with play. We played tag with rolls of toilet paper, long white ribbons trailing behind. Once or twice we turned off all of the lights and threw a glow-in-the-dark frisbee around. The more usual form of recreation was our spontaneous concerts on stage. The theater had an excellent sound system, and we fueled our cleaning efforts with really loud music. Sometimes the pull of the stage would overcome us, and we would perform. Brooms became guitars, and "Rocky Horror" costumes were pulled out of the dressing rooms. In a few seconds we were all transformed into superstars, as we air-jammed our favorite songs. Our all-time classics were "Won't Get Fooled Again" by the Who, "ABC" by the Jackson Five, and the tasteless "Big Bottoms" by Spinal Tap. We played our hearts out on the stage. I share these antics with you in order to dispel any notion that I actually was mature. I knew *how and when to act maturely,* but I still had a lot to learn. Since my sense of maturity was very circumstantial, that is, about when I needed to be mature or not, I learned about maturity as I faced new situations at the Palace. One particular incident stands out in my mind, when I was taken to task for not living up to the expectations which accompanied being a mature worker.

The scene: 2 A.M., the abandoned lobby of the Palace, during *Rocky Horror.* I sat in the warm ticket booth, watching the lobby while the movie played. Or rather I alternately watched the lobby and the insides of my eyelids. I was very sleepy. My boss suddenly appeared before my groggy eyes, quite irate with my sleepiness. He proceeded to berate me for not looking cheerful and businesslike at two in the morning. From his point of view, boss to worker, I was not living up to his expectations. In my mind, I was thinking, "Give me a break! I'm 14 years old! I'm in eighth grade! What did you expect?!?" He told me what he expected. When dealing with customers you have to be at your best. You're not at home. You're getting paid for this. At the time, his speech was very upsetting, almost unfair. Who was he to expect so much of me?

After my anger and upset due to this conflict had passed away, I thought more about what he had said. I thought about his image of a good worker, and his image of me. I wondered if he had forgotten how young I was, and if he had overstepped his bounds by having such high expectations of me. In reviewing the incident, it became clear that my boss *had* forgotten how young I was. He certainly wasn't treating me like a 14-year-old whom he expected to be less mature. No, he had the same expectations of me which he had of all the others. The same adult expectations of worker cordiality that he demanded of the other older workers were demanded of me.

Suddenly I realized that this interaction was not an indictment of my immaturity, but rather a pronouncement of my mature image. He *did not* think of me as a 14-year-old! This was made clear by his expectations. And it made sense, since I did the same work as the others, with an equally high level of efficiency and energy. The realization that my boss did not consider me as a 14-year-old had amazing consequences. It was like getting your eighth grade CAT tests back and scoring "college level" in reading. The incident with my boss and my subsequent realizations made me conscious of the fact that people considered me to be as old and mature as my 18-year-old coworkers.

My image as an older teenager, maybe 16 or 18, was helped by a host of personal traits. I was an intelligent young man who spoke easily to adults, without the paralyzing self-consciousness which impairs many adolescents. I was physically larger than many of my same-age peers, with wide shoulders and a deep voice. I also had a knack for thinking practically and handling problems easily. The last, and perhaps most important factor contributing to my older image, was that I was very responsible, and carried out my duties competently. After the confrontation with my boss, it was apparent that all of these qualities spoke louder than my biological age, and it was clear that I was being judged by my appearance and performance, and not some age measurement. The realization that I had successfully, unconsciously projected the image of an 18-year-old gave me a lot of confidence.

But what did all of this mean in my life? In simplest language, it encouraged me to grow up a little faster and involve myself in some of the activities that my 18-year-old friends were engaged in. They were my role models, and their actions functioned as a subtle encouragement to do the same. They were my standard. Most of my male friends from the Palace were college freshmen, eager to meet women and explore the realm of sexual activity. Don was particularly libidinous, taking great pride in the length of his penis. There is a Palace legend of a great showdown between him and Adam, but the result is fogged in a haze of drunken, inaccurate measurement. The openness of sexuality, this phallic exuberance if you will, was a central component in the male experience at the Palace, a topic of continual joking and question. Once I began seeing girls, I was often quizzed on my sexual progress by the men at the Palace.

Another aspect of their involvement with women was commitment, and longer term relationships. Having had more experience with dating, they had longer relationships than most of my same-age peers were having. My contact with the examples at the Palace helped shape my notions about relationships and sexuality. I had never had a BIG TALK with my dad, but my Palace peers educated me by example. In retrospect I am surprised that my parents and I didn't talk about sexuality more, but they did give me a book. Maybe they didn't want to talk about it, since it was an especially sore subject with them. Anyway, the characteristics of my Palace peers' relationships with women influenced my eighth-grade interaction with girls, by informing my ideas about sexuality and commitment as I became involved in my first relationships.

The place to meet girls in eighth grade was school. At the beginning of eighth grade, having come from a smaller public school, a feeder school, into a huge sea of adolescent hormones and strange faces, I would characterize my social situation as "King of the Geeks." I was the coolest of the geeks, geeks being smart, weird, nonathletic types who had not entered into the ranks of the popular. I sat at the far end of the geek table in the cafeteria, closest to the "cool" tables, in a very hierarchical setup. With the confidence gained at the Palace, however, I was primed to make the jump from "geek" to "cool." With a self-awareness about the effect of appearances gained at the Palace, I made the connection between fashion and social strata. Just as by acting mature I was considered mature at the Palace, so perhaps by dressing cool I would be considered cool. I put my theory into practice by adopting the oxford shirt and upturned collar look of the cool kids.

Amazingly enough, my theory worked. It seemed as if the lesson I had learned at the Palace could be widely applied: Appearances were very important in creating an image. After a month or so of dressing cool, I found myself being eyed by a girl from the cool group. She was very nice, an intelligent, talkative girl who also gave me the chance to enter the popular crowd. With the confidence I had gained at the Palace, and the lessons I had learned from my male co-workers in mind, I entered into an eighth-grade romance. I was to go out with this girl for nine months, practically an eternity by eighth-grade standards, and it was in this relationship that I first had sex.

Our relationship was even more passionate than that of the average horny eighth grader. This was the result of the precocious maturity which both of us brought to the match. She came from a very social neighborhood where kids start dating early, in fifth or sixth grade. I came from the Palace, my special realm of social interaction, and brought to the relationship my vision of a long-range commitment. There was the sense that both my girlfriend and I were growing up faster than most of our friends, and we formed a relationship which was very mature for 14-year-olds. I forgave her the time that she messed around behind my back, and she was happily surprised by my faith in her. She brought a willingness to explore our sexuality together. She encouraged me to explore her body and the pleasures associated with it, while I encouraged her to think of our relationship as a long-term thing. Together we said "I love you" for the first time, and together we made love for the first time.

I was pretty nervous when we first had sex. I had good reason to be nervous, too, considering the way my parents had been put in a difficult situation by their lovemaking. There were signs of a family curse in the air, what with both my father and grandfather impregnating their girlfriends premaritally. Despite the lack of a BIG TALK, my household had an implicit message for me: Be careful. And I was; I always used a condom. But I still had to get over my nervousness, and I can see how three subtle pressures helped me make the choice to have sex. First of all, all of my male role models at the Palace were openly sexual, and I did want to be like them. Secondly, my girlfriend's willingness and desire to make love were very influential. I remember almost backing out when we were about to have sex, and she told me straight out that she wanted me to make love to her. That was a pretty powerful pressure. The third influence was more general—the adolescent desire to explore the mysteries of being adult, and the actions and privileges associated with maturity. When all these factors came into play within the course of our six-month-old relationship, the result was the mutual loss of our virginity.

Having sex for the first time didn't change much. I guess I was still a little nervous, because we did not proceed to have sex all of the time; in the course of the next three months we only made love twice more. What was more important was my discovery of the powerful sexuality within me. In the course of our relationship, I got in touch with my sexual feelings, and was able to express them. In this way, my early sexual experiences helped to shape my future sexuality, which continued to be a powerful force. It takes a powerful force to make me ride my bike six miles uphill to see a girl, as I did in eighth grade.

Throughout the course of my first serious relationship, I continued to work at the Palace. Between these two simultaneous events, I increased my self-confidence weekly. In my relationship I was loving and being loved for the first time, and just having a relationship gives you confidence that you aren't an ugly pimply nosed geek. Being in a relationship is a sign of success, just like a promotion, an acknowledgement of your worth. At work, I was also being acknowledged, as I moved up from cleaner to usher and finally to assistant manager by the summer before ninth grade. I was regularly responsible for lots of money, crowd control, and the nightly running of the theater. As my job experience expanded, I got more practice in public speaking, problem solving, and organizational tasks. All of these tasks require a high level of self-confidence: One cannot move a grouchy, chaotic crowd into the rain without a confident presence. In order to get anyone to do anything, you need to seem like you know what you are doing. To my mind, the measure of this ability is confidence. And I had it.

Others seem to think I had it too. It is interesting how this period of precocious autonomy affected my relationship with my parents. As I worked at the Palace, confident in my own abilities, my parents became less and less mothering. (By mothering I mean a certain mode of close-watched connection between parent and child.) The early decision to trust me as a latchkey kid had evidenced the fact that there was not enough time or energy for a full-time mother. Once I began taking care of myself after school, my mother finished school and started her job as a teacher, solidifying a two-job household. As I learned to take care of more and more of my needs, the duties of my parents became less and less, and they took on the role of providers and advisors, rather than keepers. As advisors, my parents usually waited for me to bring things up for discussion. So if there was no glaring need, and no manifestation of a desire to talk about it, a subject would not be freely discussed in my household. Sometimes the distance between mother/father and advisor can be great.

In retrospect, I can remember several situations in which my parents probably should have said more than they did. Like the time that my dad found a condom in my jeans pocket as he did the wash. Rather than taking the opportunity to talk about early sexuality, he just "hoped I was being careful." Other times when I was caught drunk, my parents didn't talk to me about it, but let me get out of it without discussing it. Without reprimanding my parents for bad parenting, I am suggesting that I would have benefited from more parental involvement. I can easily understand why they trusted me so, but when the trust became an unquestioning confidence, some of my faults grew into problems.

Without the direct supervision/intervention of adults either at home or at work, I found myself becoming involved with both drugs and sexuality. I became exposed to marijuana at both school and the Palace during my freshman year. At work many of the workers and regular patrons smoked dope, and the Palace was a safe, dark, and hassle-free environment to try marijuana. I could hide my pipe and stash at the Palace, and spend my stoned hours safely inside the movie theater.

At school, I was also setting up a safe environment by gaining the confidence of the adults. As a freshman I ran for class president, and won. I continued my involvement in student government throughout high school, eventually becoming the president of the student body in twelfth grade. My work in student government had much the same result of my chores at home, earning me a greater share of trust with my handling of responsibility. By the time I met some "stoner" friends at school, I had established myself as a mature young man in the eyes of the teachers. This image was to ensure that no adult ever thought I was stoned. Within this safe reputation, I began to explore marijuana use when I was 15.

Smoking pot was an activity which linked my Palace existence and my social life at school. I would go out and smoke pot with my school friends on Friday night, and then smoke more at work on Saturday night. My school friends often met me at the Palace, with its free candy and soda, and its safety. I used the theater as my home away from home, where my friends and I could party without the fear of getting caught. With all of the worries gone, smoking dope was a fun thing to do, with its wild times and altered state of mind. I loved climbing out on the roof of the theater, forty feet up, and relaxing in the sun with a beer and some pot. The abundance of intoxicants was certainly the result of my collegiate co-workers, for whom beer and dope were readily available. Again, by working and growing up at the Palace, I was steeped in the attitudes and actions of my co-workers. When I found a group of friends at school who were also into partying, I connected to my same-age peers.

I continued to smoke pot throughout high school. I also continued to be an honors-student-class-president type who was the opposite extreme from a stoner. For me, there was no opposition. I saw the two sides of myself, the honors student and the stoner, as the two sides of the freedom and responsibility of maturity. Since I was successfully negotiating my duties as student and class president, I had earned a certain amount of freedom. My student government advisor gave me a permanent hall pass, allowing me to walk freely around the school. I used the pass to do my government work, organizing dances and Homecoming and whatnot, as well as to leave campus for McDonald's or to go get stoned. My permanent hall pass was formal acknowledgement of the freedom that comes with responsibility.

My parents never caught on to my regular pot smoking. Even when another parent called my house to tell my mother that he had heard his son saying how he could buy pot from me, my mother dismissed his claim. "Oh, no," my mother said, "you must be mistaken. Bill gets associated with that stuff because of where he works. The theater has a bad reputation, you see, and . . ." I was out back, shitting bricks. When my mother came outside and saw me upset, she commented on how frustrating it must be to be falsely accused of pot use. "Yeah, it sucks," I said, shocked by her nearsightedness. Yet I did not leave much for her to see. I was careful to use breath mints and to wash my hands after I got stoned, and I usually came home from partying after they had gone to bed.

Since no one caught on, I became more and more involved in marijuana use. During the summer after freshman year in high school, I was almost always stoned. Stoned and free and doing my own thing. I used to get stoned before I did almost anything. Get stoned and play basketball. Get stoned and go to classes. Get stoned and lie in the sun. Get stoned for no reason at all. Just like some friends always go to Friendly's for ice cream, me and my friends always got stoned. By the time I entered college, I was getting stoned way too much. I began to see it as a problem.

Looking back, I do recall three of my closest friends talking to me about marijuana. These friends were the three women with whom I had gotten very close in high school. I went out with all three of them at different times throughout high school, and they knew me better than anyone else. From these three women came the first criticism of my pot use. Their experiences with me both physically and mentally, in school and at parties, left them with a total picture of me which showed some inconsistencies between my responsible image and my irresponsible behavior, between my natural silliness and my desire to get stoned. They would talk to me about their feelings, but I didn't consider what they described to be inconsistencies, simply different sides of myself. I was very confident, perhaps too confident, that I knew what was going on. In the course of my relationships with women, however, I discovered I was not as mature as I thought I was.

My eighth-grade experiences had allowed me to discover my own sexuality, and I was very comfortable with it. For me, sexuality was a natural means of expression, and with my charm and intensity I often found myself becoming very passionate with young women in high school. I would get myself, and my partner, into intensely physical situations early on in our relationships. In retrospect, I know that I was unaware of what sexuality meant to the women I was fooling around with. In my mind, it was simply fooling around. I wanted to express myself physically with these women, but I was unaware of their needs, or unwilling to admit them to myself. In other words, I was a prick. I would mess around with someone, naked by candlelight one night, and then act as if it was nothing special. I wasn't acknowledging the emotional needs behind their physical expression. They would feel used and angry, and I would be angry at their anger, thinking it was the woman who was being immature. Nice male bullshit, huh?

By the time I graduated from high school, none of those three women were talking to me anymore. One of them was so angry that she took a cassette tape I had given her, threw it into the road, ran over it ten times, back and forth, and shoved the broken mess of tape into a manila envelope and left it on my doorstep one Tuesday morning before school. I did not expect such anger, and I did not understand it. I didn't see the cassette tape incident as an indictment of my immaturity but rather as a sign of hers. After all, lots of adults were telling me how mature I was, at work and in school. It is memories like that of the broken tape which make me realize that I was not as mature as I thought I was.

As I entered college, my most intimate feedback from my most intimate friends told me that I needed to do some thinking. By this point the Palace had been closed for a year and a half. No longer did I have that safety net, that other arena to act in. Now I was alone, going off to college, and leaving behind broken relationships and anger. But I didn't leave it all behind. I carried a lot of guilt and self-critical anger inside of me, astonished at how immature I had been.

I had always been very introspective and self-critical of my actions, but until this moment I had continued to be confident in my introspection and feel good about myself. Now I felt that I had failed my own test, miserably. This feeling of failure, and my guilt about hurting my past girlfriends, fueled my harshest self-criticism yet. In response to my strong feelings of guilt, I decided to refrain from any sexuality during my freshman year, in order to clear my head and think. My first priority, then, was to reconsider my sexuality, and the way in which I expressed it. After a long time thinking, I decided that the safest thing to do would be to let my partner, whoever it would be in the future, initiate any sexual activity. I decided that my sexuality had to be contained, and it was a year or so before I felt ready to date women again.

As sophomore year in college began, I got involved in my first relationship after that long hurt. It was also during sophomore year that I began to see my pot smoking as a problem which needed to be dealt with. It was always in a relationship in which the pot smoking became a problem, because if you are stoned and your date isn't, the conversation, and the whole relationship, tends not to go well. Pot creates a distance, since the other person doesn't know when you are stoned, or if she does know, she may be resentful of the difference, resentful about the choice you have made to be different than her. Now I was finally beginning to understand.

My understanding about how pot can be a problem came at the time when I began to make all of my own decisions. I was deciding what courses to take, which interests to pursue, and what activities to engage in. Pot smoking became an activity like any other, with a cost and a benefit. For the first time, I began to realize how high the costs of smoking pot were. Now I don't mean that I was worried about cancer or mutated babies—it was simpler than that. Pot smoking as a habit can take up a lot of time. Being stoned began to feel like a waste of time, now that I was making all of my own choices. So during my sophomore year, I made a new choice—to cut back on my pot smoking.

This choice was harder than it sounds, since I had set up a friend network in which pot smoking was a regular activity. With my decision to smoke much less marijuana, I was afraid that it meant seeing less of my friends. I felt a lot of pressure to remain where I was, a pressure emanating from a fear of change. From a fear of losing friends. Slowly I thought the whole thing out, and realized after a few despondent days that I needed some help. I couldn't talk to my parents about it. They knew nothing about it, and when I would begin a conversation intending to tell them about it, I would invariably chicken out, and cast my troubles upon girls or something else. They were not the resources to tap for this problem. At first this angered me, but since then I have talked to them about it. In our talks I have realized that they are not the people to talk to about this part of my life. They have no experience with marijuana, and no desire to banter with me about it. To them, it's just bad.

So I decided to go and see counseling on campus. It was helpful just to go and admit that I had a problem. By admitting it, I was telling myself that I had something to work on, in much the same way that I worked on containing my sexuality. Counseling confirmed this feeling, telling me to treat each incident individually, without a past and without a history, and make my decision based on what I want there and now. Since what I want is to be free to engage in a variety of activities, without the eight-hour time loss of marijuana, pot smoking has fallen from among my favorite activities.

By that time, the end of my sophomore year, I knew that I couldn't just wish marijuana away. It was something I would have to work on, like an alcoholic, for the rest of my life. I came to understand that problems have to be worked out slowly, without the haste of extreme decisions. I had also come to realize that I had been too extreme in "containing" my sexuality. I had learned the dangerous outcome of my decision to banish my sexuality during the summer after sophomore year, when I felt attracted to a woman, and she to me, but I could not find my passion anymore. I did not trust myself to even kiss her. This was a very empty feeling. It seemed as if I had taken a step backwards rather than a positive movement towards growth. As I spent some time getting in touch with my strong feelings again, I came to see that just hiding my feelings and depending on the other person was an extreme, and immature, strategy. There was no way for me to keep learning how to express myself in relation to others so long as I didn't allow myself any chance at expression. Guilt and confusion were the result of my disowning my own strong feelings.

So I decided to repossess my sexual feelings. I needed to be honest, to myself and to my future lovers, and talk out my feelings with them. Being honest about my feelings unlocked my sexuality again. I acknowledged my strong feelings, and began to reintegrate them into my current, junior-year relationship. My partner and I have talked out our feelings about sharing the responsibility for our sexuality and our self-concepts concerning sexuality. This open communication has been very successful; we both know where we stand and how our partner feels about the relationship and our mutual sexuality. Being honest to myself and to my partner turned out to be a very positive way to clear up that confusion and work it out together.

This more realistic approach to my problems was helpful in dealing with my sexuality and my pot smoking. These were both things to be worked on, without going to extremes as I usually did. I now feel that the extremes I would go to were a sign of my immaturity. Now I am much gentler with myself, talking things out with my girlfriend, and not whipping myself into submission with guilt or ideals. No, maturity seems to be a process of realizing what you need to work on, and working gradually towards change. An acknowledgement that I was not perfect, not totally mature, was a first step towards maturity.

I still look back to my days and nights at the Palace as the place where it all began. This case study has helped me to integrate other factors, such as my home and my social life, into that picture. I participated in several arenas simultaneously, as we all do, day to day. Maybe it was the novelty, the difference, the movies, and the good times which lead my mind back to the Palace. Perhaps it was a den of corruption in some people's eyes, but for me it was a safe place, a loving place, with a group of friends whom I shall never forget. I have attempted to share some of my feelings and experiences, without moralizing, although some of my decisions seem to veer towards conformity. No, all of my decisions were my decisions, made from my beliefs and my feelings. If this case study prompts reaction, so be it. But I'll have no moralizing!

3 Running Hurdles

This autobiography focuses on the author's determination to overcome obstacles in the way of becoming a doctor. Stacey describes a regimen of self-improvement begun in junior high school and carried on through college. Though she has many successes along the way, her status as a premed student in a highly competitive college brings her up against the fact that she cannot maintain the high grades she had been used to in high school. She also reconsiders her single-minded striving for academic achievement as she becomes active in demonstrating against racism on her campus. Though shaken in her belief in herself, Stacey invokes religious faith as the means for survival. Her experiences at college emerge as a means for her to take a larger perspective on the philosophical notion of the good life and the meaning of personal success. Though her ambition remains, she moves toward a deeper understanding of her own fallibility and a spiritual acceptance of life outcomes beyond the grip of self-determination.

I don't feel no ways tired,
I've come too far from where I started from.
Nobody told me that the road would be easy,
but I don't believe He brought me this far to leave me.

As I think about the words in this gospel song, I can only look upon my past with relief and anticipate the future with hope. I ask myself what it is that has guided me to this, my junior year in college and my twentieth year in the world. The answer is, in short: motivation, hard work, determination, love, and, of course, God. There have been frequent ups and downs—times when I did much soul-searching. During these periods I learned to dig deep. I tried to understand why what was happening at that particular time was so important to me and then plan my future course of action accordingly. I was not always sure that the steps that I was about to take were the right ones. However, I did know that no matter what the outcome, there was a lesson I could learn. Often there were tears that could flow river-deep. Nevertheless, I knew that I would never give up on a dream, for my faith and hope reached far into the sky. Barriers became temporary hindrances which, once over-come, would make me a true victor—fit and able to handle future problems.

My mother often explained to me that I must never let others set limitations for me. She said that if I believed with all my heart that I could do something, I shouldn't let anyone tell me that I can't—at least not without giving it a try first. She added that only God knew what was to become of my future, not men. My mother believed in me and, more important, I believed in myself. I started to read books on how to succeed in high school and, using a self-teaching guide I got at the thrift store, I worked hard on doing algebra problems. Despite the teacher believing I was not yet ready for the challenge of the algebra course, I took the class in the summer and got an "A"! This experience helped me to learn a lesson of self-confidence and determination that I have never forgotten.

In high school I encountered new battles. Even though I had an "A" average and was taking a couple of honors classes, I realized that my English class was far from honors level. I remember talking to a teacher who said that the level I was on was *average*. That was difficult for me to accept. My eighth-grade teacher once said, "You should always strive to be above average and should never let anyone consider you as average." Oh, no, I was not going to let someone look down his nose at me; I was just as capable of excelling as anyone else!

I used another self-teaching guide to aid me in preparation to take a place-ment exam to move to a higher level class. My book bag went with me everywhere: on long trips to grandma's, to my parents' meetings, to church, and even on the way to shopping centers. During this time people thought of me as a "little brain." I didn't pay much attention to this, because the only thing that concerned me was getting ahead. I was not going to let those who teased me distract me from the tasks which would one day help me to become a great doctor. I knew that once I had accomplished my current academic goals, I would have time to move on to other things. Sure enough, I was put in a higher level English class after passing a placement test.

Having realized that I was academically sound, I then went out for track where I made only a small contribution, but I still remained dedicated. I enjoyed getting to know upperclassmen on the team, and I began to look forward to going to practice. I felt that by talking to older students I was taking a sneak preview of possibilities for my own future. More and more I wanted to complement my acad-emic success with other types of accomplishment; therefore, I added reducing my hurdle times to my list of goals. The feeling of being down in the starting block, waiting for the gun to sound, gave me a sense of perfect concentration. I was filled with excitement as I cleared the hurdles and passed the finish line. I was inspired by the senior awards ceremony where I saw students acknowledged for their out-standing achievements in academics and athletics. I wondered if the same types of honors were to be a part of my future.

In my sophomore year I challenged myself by taking mostly gifted and tal-ented courses. My enrollment in these classes was a result of careful planning. Freshman year I had looked through the course guide and noted all the honors courses that I wanted to take before I graduated. I talked to teachers about the courses well ahead of time to see how I could best prepare. If I was to be a doctor, I knew that I would have to start working at it then. While I still continued to play sports, I managed to keep my priorities straight and maintain an A average. However, that year I failed the state writing test. I cried, and I never told my friends because I knew that I was the only one who could correct the problem. Because passing the exam was a graduation requirement, I had to figure out my next plan of attack. Recalling that some members of my family couldn't read or write very well, I knew it was important for me to work hard to overcome these deficits in my basic skills. With all this in mind, I worked diligently and passed the test the next time.

I didn't have a sibling at home to whom I could express my frustrations. Because my brother was ten years older, I didn't get to know him well until he was in high school. The next thing I knew, he left home, got married, and had kids. The good things in life always seemed to be at the *next* stage of life or educational level. My boyfriend was the only person other than my family members with whom I felt comfortable sharing my goals, dreams, and frustrations. I never thought that my friends at school could understand my tendency to think so far into the future. They knew that I did well in my classes, but they really didn't know how hard I worked and why. Jason, however, was aware that I wanted to be a doctor and that it was my first priority. I had fun like everyone else, but whenever I had the chance, I read books on study skills or about being successful. Jason and I became very close, probably because he was a little older and was thinking about life plans as well. I learned to trust him in a way that I had not known before. I learned to love and to be loved, and thus felt good about myself. Jason was there for me throughout many ups and downs until my senior year.

Stories about how difficult it had been years ago for blacks to obtain education of any sort made me strive even harder towards my goals. I knew that my grandmother, as brilliant as she was, didn't have much education. Even though she was the most insightful and loving person that I had ever known, it hurt me to know that she did not have the same opportunities that I had. It was almost as if she, along with many others, had been cheated out of something that they rightfully deserved. Although no one in my family ever pressured me to set high standards for myself, I knew that they hoped that I would succeed. Through much support and encouragement, they made me believe in myself to such a degree that I felt nothing was impossible for me to obtain. I never wanted to let opportunities pass me by; so many people had sacrificed so much so I could have them. Deep down inside, I knew I was able to overcome academic obstacles just as my family members had endured hard times in their lives. My family has always stressed that God made it possible for them to overcome prejudices and other barriers they encountered. I knew that if I continued to encounter academic stumbling blocks, I needed God to guide me through any problems that I might encounter.

During my senior year in high school, I spent most of my free time in the lab at the state university. Having participated in a fellowship program the previous summer, I developed a project that I could work on independently for a science research class. I had a key to the lab and was allowed to work there whenever I could. During the times that I processed rat nerve tissue until midnight, Mom or Jason stayed in the lab with me. Having such strong support from the people I cared about was crucial; I was able to develop the self-confidence and skills which made my interest in science increase. Filled with energy and enthusiasm, I felt a sense of satisfaction in knowing that my classwork had some practical applications in the real world. As senior year came to a close, I had succeeded in meeting most of my academic goals. I presented my project at a science fair and gained assurance that my skills in science were apparent in the work that I produced. I received many awards and scholarships at the senior awards ceremony, which made both my parents and me proud. However, in spite of all this success, I had failed to strengthen my relationship with God. I realized this to be true when I became haunted with both Jason's words, "You need to have God in your life," and a recurring nightmare. The nightmare horrifies me today as much as it did years ago. I dread the thought that my fate in the nightmare could ever take place. If by chance it did happen, I would know that I was in Hell or some other inferno.

In my nightmare, I find myself on a ship looking out at a dirty brown-grey body of water divided by a large brick wall. Boundless, the wall stretches as far as I can see up into the sky and out in every other direction. As I look into the water, I notice an object floating in its center. A strong and powerful force then pushes me forward, making my body press close to the ship. As the pressure intensifies along my upper spine, I begin to feel weak against the force, but somehow dominant over the unknown floating object. As the force increases, I am able to dive in the water and swim toward the object. Swimming fast causes my back to ache and arms to tire. Each stroke, though painful, seems to take me closer to the object. However, this feeling changes after about a minute. Suddenly it seems as though the object is moving away from me and towards the brick wall, which now seems more vast and blocks all light. I try to swim faster, but it does not seem to make much difference in the distance that I am from the object. Tired and puzzled, I stop swimming and reach out towards the object expecting to grasp nothing. Immediately I feel myself sinking. There is nothing that I can do to save myself; therefore, I take one last look at the object and the brick wall. I have arrived at the end of my journey.

As I now look back upon the dream, I can understand why I consider it infernal. In my interpretation of the dream the ship that I am standing on is my home. The force coming from my home represents my parents and other role models. They are trying to lead me toward the distant object symbolizing my goals. Those who support me are trying to make me see that my goals are real and obtainable. Their belief in me gives me confidence to dive into the world, symbolized here by the water. Unfortunately, once I am on my own, I begin to take on too many tasks without really knowing what I am getting myself into in the long run. As I begin to think that I am reaching my goals, I find out that times have changed. My goals are leaving me and are about to crash into a brick wall. I begin to believe that my goals are now unobtainable, but I reach out in vain, feeling that I still might have some dominance over them. After doing this, I begin to sink into the lower parts of the world. By losing hope of obtaining goals, I become a victim of my own efforts. Because of this, I enter the bottomless lower world which is indeed Hell.

My worst fear has always been to have goals and not be able to obtain them. At the time when I had the nightmare, I never considered the possibility that it could come true, nor that God was a possible savior. I had not yet found the connection between my goals and Him. It was only while in college that I began to understand what a relationship with God could mean. Before then, I remained confused about how he would affect my personal development.

I am the daughter of a preacher. Though my father works many long hours in the church each week, he also has another occupation to help support us. As a preacher's kid (P.K.s, we call ourselves) I came face to face very early with many special expectations and problems. Most of the time I was puzzled by church members' inconsistencies and seeming hypocrisy. The biggest problem was watching people criticize one another. Being present at most of the church events, I became increasingly aware of jealousy. I have seen people upset with others for holding a particular office in the church, for singing too many solos, for dressing differently, and even for trying to become "buddy-buddy" with the pastor and/or his wife. This has always bothered me because, in seeking to learn more about God, I became more and more confused by the actions of those who claimed to be Christians. Inconsistencies became increasingly apparent as I became aware of these people's testimonials about how much the Lord had done for them. How could it be that these people could be so unkind to one another? Weren't these people supposed to be kinder than those who were in the "world"?

I became even more confused when it came down to matters concerning my father. I felt severe pain whenever I heard someone say something bad about my father. I became very bitter towards these people, mainly because I would hear these comments behind my father's back, yet see them smile to his face. I wondered how these Christians could be so cruel. Wasn't my father a servant of God? Did he, as their leader, deserve this treatment? I remember overhearing one particular woman challenge my father's judgment. I was hurt, for I truly believed that my father would not intentionally do anything that was wrong; however, I realized that my father was still human. I knew that he was not God and was only a messenger. Let me say that I never have been close to my father, probably because deep down I wish that he was perfect and all that the church members think he ought to be. For most of my life I have seen Dad in two lights, the one who I knew through his thoughts in his sermons, and then as the man I could never open up to about my feelings. I love my father, but I have always wished that we had been able to communicate more as I was growing up and to know each other more personally. Instead, I became quite close with my mother, since she had stayed home to raise me.

There came a time when I could not merely rely on my family's opinions or views of God. I began a search to find out who God was for myself. My freshman winter in college was the first time that I learned to depend truly on God. This was because I found myself walking around in disbelief at actions going on about me. There was an incident in which a black professor was harassed, insulted, and tape-recorded without consent. I remember seeing a terrifying picture of the professor on the front page of an ultra right-wing newspaper on campus. The photo, taken in the heat of fury and chaos, angered me just to look at it. I thought the newspaper staff had gone too far this time. It was not the first time that this professor had been harassed. Because of the newspaper's history of articles negatively portraying blacks and other minority groups, I suspected that racism was involved. However, it was not purely a white-versus-black issue; it was also about threatening one's dignity and reputation as a type of sophomoric blood sport. I was sick and tired of seeing articles in that newspaper that tried to make blacks seem inferior. I was tired of these pompous guys acting as if only they knew how things should be. With some self-proclaimed authority they figured that they could say or do anything they wanted and get away with it, hiding their racism behind the smoke screen of freedom of the press. What was so scary and almost intimidating was the paper's persuasive style; many people could read it and say "Yeah, that's a good point." A little serious thought and consideration of undertones would reveal that something was wrong. Unfortunately, the newspaper's writing style swayed quite a few people into believing that its presentations were accurate and true.

This and much similar outrageous racism on the part of the newspaper turned my resentment into a force which propelled me to protest. I began to participate in rallies, to picket stores advertising in the paper, and to express views and concerns in ways that were unthinkable for me before coming to college. The people to whom I felt closest during that time were those engaged in these activities with me. I felt a common bond with them because we were working for the same cause. While walking on campus, I was always on guard, just waiting to hear someone talking about the incident with that professor, or to see someone stare at me or the ribbon symbolizing black liberation pinned to my jacket. The air was filled with bad vibes.

Living next door to one of the newspaper's editors made those days much more trying. One day as I was studying at my desk, I heard a loud conversation going on just outside my door about the "reactionary blacks blowing things out of proportion." This comment presumably was made in response to student protests and TV and newspaper reporters flooding the campus. I was struck motionless at my desk. I felt trapped within the confines of my room. I was tense and angry and full of pain and frustration. I badly wanted to go out there and give an argument that would put all those men into a state of awe and speechlessness. It angered me even more when they spoke of the Afro-American Society and its predominantly black dorm. They put everything down, yet admitted that they had never stepped foot inside the building. I doubt if any of them even had a black friend. I wondered how such otherwise intelligent people could be so closed-minded and ignorant about others. Every time I heard the pipsqueaky voice of one young man who was talking in the hallway when the comments were made, I became extremely annoyed and angry. I was frustrated because, although I was angry at the students for being so uninformed and insensitive, I also was disappointed with myself for being so bothered by their actions. I longed to be stronger.

Dorm events didn't end there. Every day as I passed my editor-neighbor's door there were mean and degrading statements written about minority groups and feminists on his memo board. It would include things like: "No radicals, feminist witches, black racists, or gays wanted." With each glance, I wanted to rip the board down, or just scribble on it. I wanted to kick that stupid door—do something that showed that someone was not afraid of him or his malicious words. Something, however, always restrained me. No matter how great my resentment, I told myself I could not stoop to the level of that hateful young man who lived in the room next door. I prayed that I might maintain my dignity and self-control. Each day my roommate (who was black) and I talked late into the night about everything that was happening and our growing concerns. I always felt like a captive in the dorm, for even these private conversations were whispered so that none of our white neighbors would hear what we said. We were not really afraid of what might happen if others heard us, but we didn't want to run the risk of having our comments misinterpreted or purposely distorted.

It was during the days of protest that I began to understand the pressures upon people in the civil rights struggles of the sixties. More than twenty years later, efforts to correct situations of injustice continued. My uncle told me before I went to college, "Always remember where you've come from, where you're going, and who and what has helped you to get where you are and hope to be." There is no way that I can ever forget or ignore my past or the problems that still exist today.

During those days, I spent my mornings in class and my afternoons and nights protesting. I studied during any free moment I had. It was hard to do, but I had put protesting high up on my list of priorities. This was in spite of the fact that I knew other freshmen who had been asked to take a one-year leave to reevaluate their goals after a poor performance first term. I had to do what seemed right at the time. I worked hard to do the best I could in my classes—I had tutors and went to see my professors regularly. I was glad they all were understanding and knew the position I felt obligated to take. My Chinese language professor asked me to see him after class one day. He said he knew that I was involved in the protests and wanted to know how I was doing. We talked for quite a while and both of us had teary eyes. I could tell that he cared and that what was happening was affecting him too. He was willing to work with me to make my classwork more manageable during this period. I knew that he and other professors understood the situation, and many were actively involved in the protests. For example, I met an English professor while we were both out picketing. He chatted with me then and whenever I saw him throughout the rest of the term.

I really valued the friendships that developed during the days of protesting. It seemed rare to find people who would *really listen* to what you had to say: not just hear your words but not your meaning. This was because we discussed, in addition to the incident with the black professor, many issues about student life which came to the surface. For example, many whites wondered why blacks seemed to separate themselves at dinner. Blacks wanted to know why we so often had to take time away from studying to protest things which shouldn't be happening in the first place.

In the midst of all the confusion, I learned to pray continuously. My time in prayer seemed to be the only time when I was at peace and the only thing that gave me strength to make it through the day. At the end of the term, in a class where I was the only black, we had a discussion about all the things that had happened. After hearing the comments about the "typical black" (which I didn't know existed) as well as some other radical and conservative views from my classmates, I felt obligated to say something. Before I did, however, I prayed briefly that I would be understood and not just heard. After stating my opinion and feelings, I thanked God for making me stronger that term than I ever had been in my life. From that day onward, I valued my college more than before because it had, however unintentionally, taught me to communicate with people from a wide variety of backgrounds and outlooks. It is only too bad that it took a crisis for people to start expressing their true feelings and concerns.

As I started to develop new friendships in college, I tended to share only parts of me, almost like a puzzle. Each piece would fit well with certain individuals, and not so well with others. I learned how best to mix and match those pieces so as to get along with different types of people. No matter how great the differences are between people, there has to be a common ground somewhere. It is unfortunate that a person's skin color, religious beliefs, nationality, or difference of views can sometimes distract us from other traits he or she might possess which could bring us closer. My friends who are Jewish, gay, foreign, and Caucasian have helped me to recognize the basic good in everyone.

Though I value the relationships I have with others outside my race, just as I do those within it, my four closest friends are black. They have seen me both at times when I was bubbling with energy and stressing out over something. There are few other people I feel are trustworthy enough for me to open up to. I can't imagine what my life at college would be like without them, because they have not only been friends since I arrived on campus, but have also been family. Combined, I can say they know almost as much about me as I do. It was really strange when I went abroad one term and did not have them to lean on. However, I did get to know God as a friend who would be wherever I went.

In the summer after freshman year, I was able to go abroad for the first time in my life. Looking back, it seems evident that in Taiwan I learned more about myself than I ever thought possible. This knowledge helped me to gain increased confidence and direction. Most importantly, I became close to God in a way that I had never known. By taking classes and having Chinese roommates, I was able to learn a great deal about the language, lifestyles, and traditions of the people. I felt so at peace at this Christian university because religion seemed to be a part of many people's lives. I was able to respect those who were of different faiths because they were not ashamed to express their beliefs in any setting. All these things made me eager to develop my own spiritual life.

On my nineteenth birthday I was awakened by an alarming announcement recounted here from my journal:

> I heard something or a voice say "You are going to die young." What a scary thought to wake up to on your birthday. I don't know if it was my conscious self, the end of a dream, or God. All I know is that I won't forget these words ever. I must take each second seriously, and value it, because the next moment is not promised.

New doors will open up to me, and I must be sure to live as a Christian and take advantage of those gifts. I don't want to separate myself, I just want to be me—a goal-oriented, religious, and successful person. It's not ambition, for sometimes that's bad. It is determination to do the very best I can. As long as I follow God's word, there is nothing that I can't do. No matter how short a life I live, I must be first and foremost thankful to God who gave it to me. I hope that I make the right decisions and can in some way be a positive influence on someone else. I love the Lord and pray that he will always be with my family and me. . . .

Praying continuously, I came to know God as my personal savior. I did whatever the holy spirit led me to do, and reaped many blessings because of it. I was unafraid to go into any church on the island and sit down. I jumped on buses, and trusted that whoever I met would help me reach my destination. Listening to the English translations of the sermons at the chapel made me believe in the power of God that was touching my life halfway around the world. I never felt alone or afraid because I knew the Lord was watching over me. I continuously thanked God for the blessings that he had bestowed on me each day.

As my faith grew, I also looked to God for direction with my future. By taking the time to be still and listen for an answer, it was revealed to me that I would spend my life going to different countries and helping people with their health problems. Afterward, I would spread the word about the goodness of God and His ability to make all things possible. Having been given this awareness of my destiny I felt fulfilled and content. I knew where I was headed and felt happy about the enormous possibilities for growth in my work in serving the Lord. Soon, I began to meet missionaries who were doctors and other health care workers. After talking with them, I couldn't wait to get home and share the news with others about my future career.

When I returned to college in my sophomore year, I was on a spiritual high. I worked with the chaplain and for the first time realized what a wonderful calling my father had. I couldn't think of anything more satisfying than dedicating one's life to God. As I continued to think about my future in health care, I became obsessed with the idea of doing everything I could to make God proud of me. Gradually I spent more time thinking about the future and less time in my daily devotions without fully realizing that I was doing so.

As the year progressed, I started to feel empty and unsatisfied with my academics. I initially thought it was because of the difficulty of college; it never occurred to me that God was trying to tell me something. I was reminded of the picture that my high school guidance counselor tried to paint for me of what life at a highly competitive college would be like. She told me to imagine the smartest person in my most difficult class who seemed to get As without really working hard for them. I should then think of a school where almost everyone was that type of student. She said that she knew that I got where I was (at the top of my class) by working extremely hard and by putting in extra time, and that was an accomplishment in itself. She warned me, however, that it might become unfulfilling or burdensome later. I found it difficult to accept that what I had always taken pride in (working hard) was now something that might not lead to success in the future. Once again in my life, someone was trying to discourage me from getting ahead. By reading extra books, doing additional problems, and asking about the practical applications of the course in class, I felt I was preparing for my future as a physician. That was my motivation, so although I was competing with people who caught onto some principles quicker than me, my concern was not with them, but with my goals.

As a college student I am beginning to see that perhaps Mrs. Riley was right in warning me about what I was going to be up against. I know that I have potential to succeed, so I have worked extremely hard in my classes and met with professors, obtained advice from grad students, had a tutor every term, and frequently met with my premed advisor and the academic skills director. Regardless of my efforts, my academic standing is not high. I have become disgusted with the grading system at my college. First of all, the science courses are graded on a curve. I hate to always have to compare myself to the mean, or actually all the other students in the class. I despise that, since learning is something that I feel is very personal. If my grade falls below the mean, my attitude toward the class changes. No longer is my emphasis on doing the best I can on an exam, but instead it is on getting at least the mean. I realize now that I was lowering my standards and settling for doing about the same as everyone else.

For the first time in my life, I have become accustomed to Cs and being a satisfactory student. I have had professors say to me "Cs are not bad. You'll still get into med school." By being on a campus where my right (or any other minority's) to be there is continuously being questioned, I have come to realize that it is necessary to excel and get As and Bs. Otherwise, people will doubt my credibility, and even worse, my ability.

It has been difficult for me to accept doors being closed due to the GPA. I remember that when invitations were sent out to students in my class to discuss the honors program as well as internship opportunities, I wasn't invited. Many people asked me why I wasn't there. Since I always walked about with a positive attitude, was involved in a professional society, and knew many important people on campus, they assumed I was somewhere near the top of my class. I couldn't really answer them because the pain I felt was unimaginable; I knew that I should have been there and I felt left out. As a result, I had to make a special appointment to discuss these programs. It hurt to realize that I had learned about them not because the college thought that I should know about them, but because of my own efforts. My mom always told me that sometimes you have to make things happen for yourself. I had to work very hard to get into higher levels of English and math years ago, so I naturally continue to seek out people and opportunities now that I am in college. I try to overcome any obstacles in my path, for my success has always come about because I have refused to settle for anything—regardless of the situation.

It was at a national youth leadership meeting in high school that I realized the true leader in me. Since that time I have been coming up with ideas of things I'd like to do. A while ago I developed a project that would try to encourage middle school students to become interested in science through role models. This project meant a lot to me, for I knew from personal experience that when you talk to people who are where you want to be, you begin to believe that you really can get there, too. During breaks, I had always called physicians, med students, or anyone else in health care who could tell me about the field and steps to get into it. In turn, I often spoke to students at different churches to try to get them interested in continuing their education. I believed these things could keep dreams alive for someone.

After spending a couple of months meeting with different people who could give me ideas about how to get my project started, I was just about ready to get it off the ground. I had a meeting with my former professor and friend, whom I always go to when there's something on my mind or a new thing I'm interested in doing. After he agreed to help me carry out the project, I said to him, "I know that there still might be some trouble getting funding to do this, since my grades could be stronger." When I told him my standing, the expression on his face was that of shock and disappointment. He suggested that perhaps I should try to constrain my ideas until I was in a position in my life to make the greatest contribution. He went on to say that he knew that I was going to make great changes one day, but all good leaders need a solid background. It was his wish to see me concentrate my energies on improving my grades, so I could get into the best medical school in the country. Though I did not doubt his sincerity, I felt all alone and stripped of the very thing that had made me feel so fulfilled for so long—a project that would spark energy and enthusiasm in kids who, like me, may have to overcome many academic obstacles. What would I do now? I left that office and tried to come to grips with the fact that things don't always work out as planned.

In the next term, I tried to concentrate more on my studies. After laying my project aside for a while, I became confused about where my life was headed. Some mornings I would lie in bed wondering why I should get up. Why should I put myself through so much pain for so little gratification? Why couldn't I stop school, get a job, and do whatever I wanted? Even though these thoughts kept running through my mind, I knew that they wouldn't make me happy. I always felt a great sense of accomplishment and joy when I worked in the lab all night, completed a paper or problem set, or developed ideas for the future. These things made me see that academics were a necessary part of my life.

At the term's closing, I felt drained of all energy. I had hit a burnout point. It was during these days of physical and emotional strain that I realized I had been leading a life that was not dependent on God. For many months I had been taking my life into my own hands. Because I wanted to take advantage of anything associated with being a doctor, I rushed through the first half of college. There were many warning signs and people telling me to slow down, but I overlooked them or simply regarded them as more barriers that I had to overcome. It never occurred to me during that stressful time that perhaps God was trying to tell me that great things can be accomplished only through His will. Attainment of my goals will not come through my efforts alone; only He possesses the master plan for my life. I had to take some time off from school in order to understand at last that if I was to *succeed*, I needed to turn over my life to God and let Him choose my path.

Presently, my attention is focused on increasing my happiness, flexibility, and spirituality. I no longer take for granted the relationships I've had or lessons learned. After breaking up with my college boyfriend, I realized that too often I have let my goals draw me away from those whom I love the most. I can become so involved with what I am doing that I don't give others the time to show me how they feel about my actions. I need to take time out to listen to others. I realize that my friends have always been there for me when I needed them. Therefore, I have no real reason to believe that they will disappear if I allow them to see my inner-most fears of not being able to obtain the very high goals I set for myself. Often they have been the ones who have given me happiness and support that I couldn't find elsewhere.

It has been this type of support that has helped me to see my potential and to go after my goals with an almost uncontrollable desire. It is only after reading the biographies of those who have inspired me in the past that I now realize they achieved success by hard work *and* strong spiritual beliefs. They were all happy people, who had endured pressures, by trusting that God would lead them through those times. Even though I have overcome barriers in the past, I have always carried a bit of resentment towards those things or persons who I felt caused them. I should have actually been thankful for them, since God had control over my future and knew what was best.

My first response to any advice conflicting with my goals has been to first regard it as a barrier, and then try to see what *I* can do to prevent it from having a negative effect. I need to spend more time praying to God to see how *He* wants me to deal with the situation. I know He is able to do this because while I was abroad it was from His word that I received direction in all parts of my life. I long to have this type of relationship with God again.

While growing up I used to wonder how God would influence my life. I have heard some older folks say that He is a "heart fixer, a way maker, and a mind reg-ulator." God is able to be all these things for me. My life is in God's hands, and it is through His guidance that tomorrow's joy, treasures, and perhaps even a medical degree, shall be mine. I am so glad God forgives those who, like me, make the mis-take of vainly trying to completely control their own lives. I truly believe the mes-sage in the words of the gospel song I have paraphrased in the first person to fit my own story:

> I know somehow, and I know some way,
> I'm gonna make it!
> No matter what the test, whatever comes my way,
> I'm gonna make it!
> With Jesus on my side, things will work out fine!

4 Someday My Elders Will Be Proud

This Native American woman recounts her experience of living in two worlds. Jean describes how her mother raised her and her three brothers after her father abandoned the family when she was quite young. These circumstances, along with abuse at the hands of her uncle, leave lasting emotional wounds she will not address until much later. While firmly rooted in and proud of her Native American culture, Jean becomes a scholarship student at an elite secondary school. Her family's relative poverty and the condescending attitudes of her classmates further feelings of self-doubt, low self-esteem, and ethnic inferiority. Her transition to college does not succeed; she turns to heavy drinking, fails academically, and returns home. She gets a job working with troubled Native American adolescents, and through helping the self she sees in them, she finds a purpose in returning to college.

I grew up in Bismarck, North Dakota. My parents met through a relocation program. Relocation attempted to assimilate Native Americans into urban life from their reservation or tribal communities. The goal of the program was for an individual to gain economic self-sufficiency by means of a vocation or technical school education. My parents were in just such a program in Denver, Colorado, where they met and married. That is where my three brothers and I were born. My mother, a Cheyenne, was 22, and my father, a Blackfoot, was 21 when they had me. I am the oldest.

My father ran back to his reservation in Montana before my youngest brother was born. I must have been almost 4 years old. I have no concrete memories of him. My mom says that he taught her how to take care of me, because she didn't know that much about babies. He began drinking when I was born, and he was a womanizer. Soon his drinking got out of control. Despite her problems with our dad, Mom would always tell us how he loved my brothers and me and that he was a good father to us. Whenever he came home we would run and crawl all over him. We never saw him again after he left Mom and us behind. Dad died on the reservation when I was 7 years old, from alcoholism. He was only 28. I don't remember exactly when Mom told us, but it held no meaning. It seemed that he had already died when he left.

By the time I was 6, my mother had moved to Bismarck, where many of her relatives and immediate family lived. We did this because family was important to her tribe, and they would help us as much as they could. Initially we lived off welfare and the help that our relatives could give us. My mother decided she didn't want us to live like that forever. She wanted to be a good example for the four of us, so she worked during the day and went to school at night to get her bachelor's degree in social work at the state university. We grew up in a single-parent family with the benefits of an extended family.

Mom worked through temporary services at factories, and we got some monetary help from our father's Social Security benefits after he died, food stamps, and AFDC. We were very poor. We went to garage sales, Salvation Armies, and Goodwills for most of our clothes, furniture, and toys.

During those years when my mother pushed herself, my brothers and I were watched by one of my mom's younger brothers. She had no choice; he needed a place to live, and we needed a babysitter. I think he was in his twenties. He stayed with us from the time I was in first grade until I was in the sixth grade. He was always there after school when we came home. He taught us good things, like to stick up for each other when we used to get chased home from school by the white kids, and not to be afraid of fighting for ourselves.

However, our uncle was alcoholic and had a violent streak in him. We became convenient scapegoats for him when he was sober or drunk. Even though my mom forbade him to drink in her home, he still did. There are lots of stories about how we couldn't wear shorts because the belt or switch marks were too vivid. He never hit us when Mom was home. When he did whip us, he'd say to us after he was finished, "You'd better keep your mouths shut and not tell your mother." And we stayed silent.

It was for stupid reasons that we got whipped. Who moved his magazine, who messed up the kitchen, who lost his sock and where was it? Who did it? Guilt, innocence, truth, right, wrong, what did any of that matter? It meant nothing. We could have been perfect children but that wouldn't have changed anything. We learned to clean the house as soon as we got home, and maybe it was good enough, maybe it wasn't. We learned to hide in our rooms until Mom got home. We used to be mean to our dogs, and sometimes to each other. He made everything seem our fault.

Why didn't we say anything? I don't know. I remember one time how our uncle picked up my brother Lance by the hair, and Lance was screaming. I never felt so helpless. I was mad, but I was afraid too. I knew it was all wrong, but I was glad in a way too, because it wasn't me. Mom kicked him out finally when I was in the sixth grade. All that mattered to us then was that he was gone. I still remember the relief I felt.

Why so long to get him out? Mom had to know. All I can think of is how her tribe is strongly patriarchal; men rule the home, and women must listen to and abide by what their brothers say. You never tell them that they're wrong; it would be disrespectful. In the traditional way, uncles are a second father to their nieces and nephews. Alcoholism ran through her side of the family and our dad's. I know that our two uncles had a violent father and uncle too. Those behaviors were probably passed on, and were allowed to continue because men have so much power to do what they want. Mom hadn't quite broken out of that mindset when our uncle was living with us, and she tried so hard to make our lives better at a cost to hers. I couldn't really be angry at her, because I remember how she tried to make us happy.

When I first started actively remembering everything that our uncle did to us, I hated him. I was glad that he couldn't hold a job, that he had a rotten marriage, that his own kids were uncontrollable and spoiled, that his drinking gave him critical liver and heart problems. But I tell you, it's strange. He loves us. I'm not going to live fueled by hate, and so I tried to understand what there was in him and his life that let him beat four little kids. He never had it easy himself, and he is the one who has to live with what he's done. He doesn't need another person who hates him, or another part of his life to make him more bitter.

Many of our relatives on my mother's side lived in Omaha. Lots of these relatives were members of the newer religion, Native American Church. NAC integrates Christianity, adapting to urban life by getting an education or keeping a job, and being aware of what's good and beautiful in life, in other people, and in yourself. At least that's what it means to me.

An NAC meeting lasts throughout a night; you pray for whoever the meeting is for, including your family. You get no sleep, people sing "hymns" that are in the native language, and you eat a bitter-tasting cactus called peyote. The old school relates the Bible to life, and others talk about what their elders told them about being good people. People talk about how to cope with problems, talk about why things are the way they are, how you can look at your misfortunes, and how we must appreciate and recognize the good that we have. They talk about humbleness and realizing that so much of what we deal with will pass in time. It was there that I felt awe for wisdom and reasoning.

We drove back to Nebraska frequently for NAC meetings and for traditional religious ceremonies, where we prayed and made offerings to the gods and spirits, holding feasts and dances to honor what was being done for the people. We used to travel around the surrounding states for powwows—intertribal gatherings where dancers and singers from different tribes got together to dance and visit with one another. We also stayed with close relatives with whom my mother's generation had grown up. They told us stories from long ago, and they fed us and took us along with them in their areas. The four of us liked going out of town; our world was not defined by the city.

When I finished sixth grade at the public school, Mom had me tested for a private school that an uncle's wife highly recommended. They wanted me to go to a school better than the public junior high. I was accepted and given a scholarship, and when seventh grade came around I went there. At the time, I didn't want to go. I wanted to go on with my friends to the public junior high.

I remember feeling that I didn't fit in, and being apprehensive. It was an affluent Episcopalian college preparatory school, grades K–12. It wasn't race that made me an outsider, though there were undercurrents of it. If anything, it seemed to be worse in grade school, where my brothers and I had come home crying, until they told us to fight and stick up for each other. I'd say that poverty made me an outsider.

The first day an English teacher had us write essays on the furthest place in the world we had been. After we finished, we placed them up on the bulletin board. I wrote about Nebraska, and when I looked at the other essays, I saw people saying, "I've been around the world on a cruise ship." A larger majority than I could have imagined said countries in Europe, California, all over. Showing off seemed to occupy a great deal of time at school.

Kids were mean there, not physically, but with their words. "*Who* does your shopping for you? You've *never* been to the Calhoun Club? *Where* do you get your clothes from? You mean you *haven't* been out of the U.S.? You *rent* your home? You mean you don't get an *allowance?*" I couldn't have what they had or really understand the importance of it all, and I felt it acutely. There were the times when I would be talking with someone, and instead of listening to whatever it was I was saying, they'd be staring at my clothes.

It wasn't anything that my family or relatives understood. We all knew that it was a good thing for me to go to school there; they wanted us younger kids to be able to work at jobs we wanted and not struggle like they had. Being poor was awful, the bills were too many and too much. I knew all of that in a vague sense way down, and I suppose that's why I stuck it out. But still, it didn't help me in dealing with the daily questionings or scornful looks from my peers. When they did that, I just looked away or down, shoulders slumped, because I felt self-conscious.

Learning the stuff from the books wasn't ever really hard; it was just memorizing most of the time. So I'd memorize and forget everything later. Mom made sure that I did homework when I was home. She always used to say to us how important school was, because if we had it, life wouldn't be as hard for us as it was for her generation. If anything, the material was boring. I noticed that the kids were highly conscientious about doing their work. Grades mattered to them in a way I never really understood. Mom never said to me, "Jean, I want you to get As," and she never acted disappointed when I didn't get an A. All Mom ever said was, "Did you try?" and that was enough. The other kids did their work because they wanted a good grade. For me, it was a way out.

The only way I could figure out to make things better was to bug Mom incessantly about clothes. She tried her best, but it wasn't good enough in my eyes to catch up to the other kids. So I started stealing from stores and from unlocked lockers at school. And then it happened; I got caught. I felt hunted, and I knew the other kids would really talk. "Can you believe what she did?" Most of all, I knew that I would hurt Mom. That's what mattered the most to me. I got suspended for a couple of days. When my mom and I came in to talk to the middle school director, and I was asked "how come?" I ended up crying, and talking about how people called me names, looked at me funny, and that I couldn't take feeling bad about myself anymore. I hadn't realized that those things preyed on my mind, that they hurt, and that's why I was stealing.

So Mom and I went home and she talked with me. She said that it was wrong to steal, and that it reflected on myself and the kind of upbringing I had. She said how it was easy to steal, it was cheating, and that it was hard to tell the truth and live by it. She said that we all make mistakes and that it was all right. "Just learn something good from this." And then she talked to me about the things that I had been called. "They're wrong and cruel and do not know you or your strengths. They're just a bunch of kids." I knew what I had done and felt ashamed about myself, but she made me believe in her love and in myself. From Mom, I learned to be compassionate.

I think I learned that I couldn't be myself at that school. I had to be like the other students to be happy there; I had to be rich and snobby. Because of my family's poverty and our tribal gatherings, I couldn't be like them. Not really anyway. Most of the time I was bored, or distracted by home. So what if the football team lost? So what if you're pissed off because you can't talk on the phone past 8:00? What kind of problems are those?

I felt that I had to put on airs, or have a dramatic life that people would be interested in, otherwise I was a lonely person. I needed to find a niche somehow, somewhere. So for about two years, somewhere between eighth and ninth grade, I became a liar. I made up the death of a relative, talked about things like drinking, or weed. I told people that I was part Greek. I quit when someone asked about my Greek grandmother. I knew what a lie it was, and I thought to myself, what about your real grandmother? Why can't you be proud of her and everything back home? It was like I had erased her life, said it was nothing by making up another woman who never even existed. I knew something was really wrong with me then. I cringe at the pitiful person I was. I see why I did what I did, but still . . . I decided that never again would I lie like that, because it takes away from the truth of my life. It's "cheating." Parts of my life were ugly, and not understood, but it was mine. My life was no less important than my schoolmates'. Life can't be for everyone what it is to the affluent or sheltered, and none of that makes them better than those less fortunate or different.

By this time I realized how hard it was for my mom to support the four of us on her own. I know the bills and our teenage wants that got more and more expensive were getting to her. She would lash out at us about "never being satisfied" or about not helping enough around the house. She used to point out our faults to us, not in a nice way, during those times. For myself, I cowered during those times when she lost her temper. I couldn't help it. But it wasn't anything like those times with our uncle when we were kids—I understood why she was frustrated and yelling. Even so, Mom always came through for the four of us. She would tell us how smart we were, and how strong we could be. If we did something wrong, she would understand what drove us but always tell us to learn from it all.

There were other times when we went to an NAC meeting, powwow, lodge feast, or a meal with the relatives. I loved all those things. I didn't think about why I felt that way, all I did was feel good. I remember being back at school in the ninth grade after one weekend when we'd been to a powwow. I was in math class, looking around and listening, but my attention kept fading. I kept staring out the window, remembering. We had been to Canada, and the powwow was by a huge network of lakes. During one of the breaks, my brother and I had gone out onto the lake on a motorboat. He killed the engine in the middle of the lake and we were drifting; we could see the powwow ground, all the campers, smell the fires, hear the singing, see dancers walking around in bright colors, shawls and bustles, people laughing.

We tried to start the engine, but it wouldn't, and we had forgotten to bring oars along. We were drifting farther and farther away to the opposite shore, and right before we got tangled in the reeds by the shore, we tried one last time to start the engine. It started, and we were laughing, and the wind whipped our hair back as he gunned the engine. We sped around for awhile like that, and when we got back, we had a good story to tell.

People were always teasing each other about something. That's what I liked, laughter. At night you could see all the stars; coffee tasted the best when it got chilly after the sun went down. The smell of a wood fire was always around too, and you were up late and probably tired, but you were having a good time, so it didn't matter. Out of the four of us, I liked to dance the most. When I was small, I used to dance until I had blisters and they would make me rest for a while.

No one at school though would know what in the world I felt good about, or why. I felt caged. What did I care about a logarithm? I was disgusted when I kept hearing three girls across the aisle talking about the teacher, how nerdy she looked, and wasn't John hot, he just broke up with his girlfriend.

Reconciling school, our trips, and home life was hard. Keeping up with us and the bills was hard on Mom, and she was alone. Even though she finished up at college and got her degree, $18,000 a year didn't go far enough for the five of us. Mom was always stressed, and then there were the four of us being adolescents going through all of our stages. Sometimes I wasn't the nicest person, and got mad or upset when I couldn't do something because we didn't have the money. I would act like it was all Mom's fault. My brothers Rick and Lance were starting to hang out with the crowd at school that smoked weed, skipped school, and acted tough. Lance tried to run away one time when our uncle who used to live with us threatened to beat him up if he kept on smoking cigarettes.

My youngest brother Bill went to school with me. My other two brothers went to the public high school. They also tested for our school when they finished sixth grade, but there weren't any scholarships for them. By the time they were offered one, Mom couldn't swing it. As it was, the school was always hounding her to pay up. If she had paid on time, we would have gone without food, and probably heat and electricity too. Most of me wishes that my other two brothers could have gone to school with us, but part of me feels so glad they didn't. Basically, I didn't want them to feel bad about themselves. I know life would have been "easier" for them, but do years of ridicule have to go along with it?

By the middle of the ninth grade I developed some friendships. I found it easier to talk to other new students. For the first time in two years, I had friends. Most of the time our talks revolved around classes, boys, how hard track practice was. I liked it.

I think that high school for Bill and me was a time where we numbed ourselves to being poor and to forgetting the Cheyenne and Blackfoot ways. It was easier that way. It seemed that we had to learn to be one way at school, and another at home; but it was hard, how are kids supposed to do that? I went unwillingly to family functions. My family didn't see that much of me the last two years of high school. I was involved in sports, stayed over at friends, or talked with them on the phone incessantly. I didn't want to hear about how far we were behind in bills anymore. School was easier because it was shallow. I could handle talking about classes, etc., but I couldn't do anything to help Mom or not make us poor.

By the time I was a junior, my brother Bill was in the upper school, too. Only thing is, I didn't like him that much, because I saw things about myself from his behavior. He looked down on our family for being poor; he was ashamed. School and the people in it were the most important to him. I saw it in him when he brushed my mom aside. She was trying to tell him something, and he answered in a condescending voice to her. I was angry at him for not respecting everything she had done for us. He paid more attention to his friends than family. He said derogatory things to my other two brothers like, "Oh, what do you know?" and after a while they'd say things about our "rich private school." He looked down on them, and I thought, my God, it was only luck that got Bill and me in; it wasn't Lance's or Rick's fault they had to go to public school.

By the time it came around to applying for schools I had a sneaking suspicion that I had neglected something really essential by ignoring as best I could home and the tribes for so long. I applied to colleges because it was what everyone else did. I did fairly well on the entrance tests, had a good grade average, and got recommendations from teachers who liked me. When I applied to school, I applied to out-of-state schools because I wanted to see what it was like elsewhere. The whole process was funny, because I had all these ivy league schools interested in me. I didn't really care about going to a top school, but most of the other kids did, and a lot of them did double takes when one of my friends teased me loudly about Harvard calling for me. I liked the school I'm at now the most because it had a Native American Society. I knew that I would need some connection to my background to help me out in school without my family or relatives.

Again, my relatives and mother were encouraging. I'll amend that. Everyone but the traditionals were glad for me. As a young woman, I should have been starting a family, not running across the country for four years. They never actually said anything, but when Grandma told them, they'd look away, or talk about something else. In my eyes, going to college wasn't going to make me less Indian, or forget where I came from. If anything it would enhance it.

It used to bug me sometimes when Grandma would say where I was going, because the way she said it would make other people jealous of me. Lots of people she told this to had kids in state schools or community colleges, and I felt bad because they were just as good as me. I didn't want people to be envious, or think that I was snotty. There were a lot of relatives like that, who were proud of me, but I hated it when they would announce where I was going; they didn't always mention that Sue was doing something really good for herself by going into the

Marines, or that Bob was a supervisor in a plastics factory. They weren't any less than I was; in fact, the things they did demanded so much more.

Graduation was boring, and I wasn't crying like most of the other students were. I just remember being glad that school was finally all over with. I wouldn't yearn for my years in high school, and I wouldn't miss most of the people there.

My family brought me to the airport. Mom, Grandma, Grandpa, two uncles, two cousins, and my brothers were there. They took all kinds of pictures of me and my brothers, me and my cousins, me and Mom. I said goodbye to my brothers, and Mom was crying. She tried not to, but I knew she would miss me. And all of a sudden, I knew that I would miss her, too. It startled me. I had tears in my eyes and was biting my lips, and Grandma said, "You're going away to do a good thing. Nothing bad has happened. We don't have to cry." They called my name as I boarded, and I turned as they snapped a picture. I sat in my seat and looked out the window, crying. This man tried to make small talk with me, until he saw me crying, then he let me alone. The plane started to go towards the runway, and I looked at the terminal, and there they all were, standing and waving. I could still see Mom crying. Love. I was leaving love.

I was excited about going to school, partly to be on my own, but I thought because it was college, people would be wise and mature, that there wouldn't be the cliques like in high school. I was wrong. It was freshman week, and most of the people were *just like* my high school peers. I was horrified. I couldn't get into the class spirit, I didn't like my roommate, I didn't like most of the bubbleheads I met. I didn't really feel my purpose in being there—except possibly to meet all the self-important people and party as much as I could. It was a time when I had to stand on my own and rely on my strengths. The only thing was, I didn't know what my strengths were. It didn't feel like I had any.

I was sitting alone one night that first week looking at the stars, like I used to at powwows or in Nebraska. All of a sudden I had a tight feeling in my chest, and I said aloud "Why am I here?" I felt like walking into the woods and crying, because I didn't want to go through a repeat of being new, like when I started private school.

This is what I did my first term at school: I went to math class for the first week, I went to English for the first half of the term, and to my third class maybe once a week. I drank whenever I could. I remember being three or four papers behind in my English class. I read the books I had to; I just couldn't sit down and say something about the topic questions. I sat in front of a computer, and for the life of me, couldn't think of a damned thing to say about Conrad's imagery in the *Heart of Darkness* and its effect on the reader. I went to math for the first three classes, and it was all review, from like the eighth grade. The thing is, I always hated math. It was my earliest class, and I didn't feel a compelling need to wake up and go to it.

When I drank too much, I would end up crying and babbling. One time I was at a fraternity, looking at the mob of people dancing, watching people weave in and out through the tightly packed basement to get a beer, and I saw people jumping up and down and crowing with triumph about a beer pong game when a cup got knocked over. I was supposed to be having a good time. I ran out and stood under a pine tree, fists bunched up, crying for my relatives. I was always embarrassed about crying or babbling like that, and would act like I had never done it the next day. I was homesick, more than I had thought possible, but I didn't know it. I felt empty and knew something was wrong with me because I should have been having the time of my life. After all, I was young and at college.

People tried to help me. Friends would ask if I'd gone to class, if I'd caught up in math and English. I'd say no, and they'd say, "Jean, you've got to or you're going to be in trouble." I'd laugh, or say nothing. I got called in by my freshmen dean, and he asked how come I was having trouble. I said I didn't know. I was nervous and afraid of what he'd say to me. He said, "You went to a private school, you did well there, you are more than capable of doing well here. You're messing up. Why aren't you doing well?" I didn't say anything. He asked if I was homesick, and almost sobbing, I said yes. He told me that I had to go to classes, and that I could do it. I walked out of there, and composed myself. Crying, what good did it do anyway?

I used to talk with my mom about once every week. She always asked about the people who I was meeting. So I'd tell her about the people I hung out with, what we did or talked about—except the drinking parts. Mom hated to see any of us ending up alcoholic. She asked about classes, and I'd say that they weren't going so well. She'd ask about how I was doing, and I'd say, "I don't know, Mom, not so good." She always said "You can come home if you want to, Jean. You know that. We want you to be happy."

Somehow I imagined that if I had a boyfriend, everything would be okay. I had met this Native American guy my freshman week. I went looking outside of myself for what I lacked. I liked it that he still had close ties to his tribe, that that was where he drew his strength from. I had spent the night with him a couple of times after parties during the weekend. Platonically, I mean. We spent most of our days together. People were always wondering if we were ever going to get together. I wondered too.

John came up and said he wanted to talk. I had had a knot of anxiety and yearning in me, and it loosened up. He said something about wanting to wake me up with a kiss when I had slept in his room, taking it slow, how he had fun when we were together, and that he respected me. But it was almost like he was dictating a letter to me or something. Maybe I should have gotten up and gone to him when he finished talking. Instead, I said that I needed to go to the bathroom, because I really did.

When I came out, he had gone downstairs, and I felt disappointed. He ended up drinking until he passed out, and then I knew that we didn't have anything. I felt immensely alone, and sad. The next day we studied together, and that was it. He wasn't very talkative. We went back to his room, and he said I would probably hate him, because he had decided to get back together with an old girlfriend, and that he didn't want to date someone who wasn't Navajo. I told him I hoped it worked out for him, and felt surprised that I meant it. But that was the last straw for me, and I set myself on the path of self-destruction. I just drank whenever I could, tortured myself with dreams of getting him back, and forgot completely about classes.

The end of the first term came, and finals. I wouldn't get up to go to my math final. Why go? I was going to fail anyway. I still needed to finish three or four papers, and I hadn't done my term paper for my third class.

I got a call over break, and my dean said that I had been suspended. So when I went back to school it was to pack. Dimly, I regretted it. I had been on my own out there, and I was just beginning to see that there was a lot I could have done, such as pulling my act together, being independent, and maybe learning to loosen up with people my age and have fun.

Mom was supportive of me, as were most of my relatives when I got home. I didn't really know what to do with myself in terms of getting a job, or going to the state university. I didn't really feel like doing anything. For about three months I stayed home a lot, cleaned, cooked, hung out with Mom and my brothers. I tried to escape from thinking about myself and what I would do. The only things I made an effort for were to go to Nebraska with my grandmother and to go to as many NAC meetings and powwows as I could.

I started to drink on the sly. I'd drink when there wasn't anything for me to do, or just to liven things up. One time, I had been slipping into the bathroom to take a shot of vodka every now and then, and I got carried away. My brother Rick told Mom that I was acting weird, and I remember sobbing as she rubbed my back. The next morning I woke up, and I thought, "Oh my God, what have you done?" I felt apprehensive, I couldn't remember anything, and I couldn't really believe that I had gotten stinking drunk like that.

Mom came home, and this is what she said: "Jean, you can't do this to me. This happened to your dad. If something happens to you because of drinking, I'm going to feel really bad. What's the matter? Why are you doing this?" And I didn't know what to say. But I realized that the parents are supposed to die first, not the kids. I saw in her face that Mom knew that she couldn't help me. I had to help myself, and drinking like there was no tomorrow wasn't going to do it. I saw how my not thinking had led me to so many things, and that somehow I needed to make sense of what was bothering me. I said how sorry I was, and for the first time in my life, I meant it.

So I enrolled in a religion and psychology class during the evenings and I got a job tutoring math and English at an inner-city alternative high school for Indians. Most of these students were from the reservation and had come from North and South Dakota, Nebraska, and Montana. Indians flock to Bismarck for jobs or for excitement. Most of us are poor, lots are alcoholic, and many come from dysfunctional families. What smacked me in the face was seeing that abuse was a way of life, the only way of life they knew and accepted. Their education: poverty; alcohol; drugs; emotional, physical, and sexual abuse.

There was a girl named Sharon who did her work and was quiet. When people picked on her she would cower. When she was called on in class her voice shook and she wouldn't look up. If I told her she was smart or looked pretty that day, she'd say, "No I'm not." If she had to ask me for some help with some problem she'd say, "I'm so stupid, I can't do this." I heard Sharon's boyfriend sneering, "Why am I even with you, I could have any woman I want." Sharon said, "I'm sorry, please don't be mad. I'll be how you want me to be." When I heard that I winced and ran into the bathroom. I tried to block out the echoes of her beseeching him. Those were my words whenever anyone was mad or displeased with me. I knew how that felt in your gut.

They had nothing. So those that still had any fight left in them latched on to being tough, independent, and reckless, all for pride. Everyone needs something. I don't know why the kids talked to me and told me about their lives so much. I don't know why they picked on almost all the other teachers and aides (to their faces most of the time) and left me out of their ridicule. Maybe it was because at 19 I wasn't that much older than them. Or because I was Indian. I liked to laugh with them or tease them when I could. And when they talked to me, I listened, because what they were telling me about was their lives.

All I could say to them was, "It doesn't have to be that way, you know." Those kids are the trapped, the bereft, the haunted. They are the reason I came back to college. I have to find a way to open up a life and world outside of their childhood so that they can at least get through high school and get an adequate education, one that prepares them for college. I have to find a way that doesn't make them feel ashamed about their pasts. I want to change the schools somehow. Schools and your success in them determine what kind of life and career you're going to have. I see so many kids weeded out, and it has nothing to do with their intelligence. Why is the path through high school to college so narrow?

Working helped me decide what to do with myself in terms of college. Since my return, I have done fairly well in classes. I still have problems in making myself go to classes on a regular basis and doing all the reading that I'm assigned. I'm more caught up in my family life and what goes on there than in my studies or the issues at school.

I don't aim for straight As, but for learning what I can that will be useful to me when I go into education, or what will help me understand people in general. I also try to learn as much as I can about the culture here, what kinds of ideals and standards motivate the students and professors. It's still a pain a lot of the time, because for all the advantages that most students have here while growing up, and for all their intelligence, there's an incredible lack of compassion or understanding that there are people who live hard, hard lives. Their worlds and lives are closed, too, and it disheartens me lots of times. Sometimes I think that academic knowledge is how they gauge the wisdom and respect of one another. It's something I don't understand, because what does academic knowledge have to do with what we are as people? As far as I can see, wisdom has nothing to do with books and theories.

For a while when I first came back, I joined a coed house, but I found that I still drank a lot to pass the time. I was hung over at least three times a week. I drank so much that I ruined something in my body. Now, when I have more than three beers or mixed drinks, I'm hung over really badly the next day. Luckily, I only get carried away once or twice a year like that. Now, I'll have a beer with dinner once or twice a month, and that's about it. I don't really miss it because I finally figured out that drinking solves none of my problems. It only wastes my time.

Since I have been back I have been an active member of the Native American Society and have lived at the Society's house whenever possible. It feels like a home. Most of my friends are Native American, not because I'm prejudiced, but because I'm much more at ease with them. I am still really quiet and shy when I first meet people, and I avoid at almost any cost participating in class. Just this past year I decided that I couldn't always be like that, and for now that's enough. I also fell in love for the first time. We were together for two years but broke up three months ago. It was so hard—it still is.

Peter accepted me for who I was, faults and all. He used to say that he wanted the two of us to be able to do what we both wanted, and then be able to tell each other about it all. But I didn't know how to accept myself, and I demanded so much from him. It was as if I expected him to make up for things lacking within myself, within my life. Now I know that there's no one in the world that can do that for me but myself. Until I met Peter I was always lonely. With him I learned how to actually reach out to another person instead of being someone who just dreamed about love. He reached out to me and I learned to trust.

One time I went out with a high school friend, and she was talking about how her father went to meetings for abused children and children of alcoholics. She named off all the symptoms that these children have. And you know, as she listed off the characteristics, she described me. I sat there with my mouth open, and it felt like I had been punched in the stomach.

I saw a lot of the abused child behaviors in myself throughout the whole time Peter and I were together. It's like there was a lightness in me after I realized it. Even when I was with Peter I often felt hopeless and depressed. I was always afraid he would leave me. I never understood what he saw in me, so I would try to be what he wanted. I couldn't stand getting into fights with him, and if I was ever mad at him, I'd sulk around and keep it in because I was afraid to express it. I was so insecure with myself. Things would build up, and when we finally got it out in the open, I wouldn't even know myself what I was mad about. Somehow I felt inarticulate and that I didn't even have the right to be mad. I still have some of these tendencies.

I see how I turned him into a kind of addiction and couldn't give him what he gave me, love and acceptance. When I told Peter about the fact that my brothers and I had been abused, and that I wanted to do something about it, he held me. My voice was shaking, and I could barely get across what I had found out. Peter asked if I felt like crying, and when I said yes, he said, "come here" and hugged me. But I couldn't cry. And when he asked how I felt, I said I felt ashamed. He said, "Oh babe, you don't have anything to be ashamed about. It wasn't your fault." And then I cried.

As time went on, when we were apart I became more and more insecure. I demanded that he put me at ease and hounded him to keep me a part of his life. I smothered him. Slowly, I lost confidence in myself and in him. Then I knew that I had a long, slow battle to feel good about myself and to not revert to my victim reaction. Oh God, I just wish we had met years from now when I was normal. I wish I had not been abused. But that is not going to change the past. I need to deal with how things are now, and slowly get rid of the things from my childhood. At least now I am aware, unlike many people who never have an inkling about what beneath it all is really bothering them.

Graduation is finally in sight. I plan to go on to graduate school for Indian education. I want to work in curriculum and administration, but I will probably teach first so that I can get some practical experience. I find that because of my experiences away from home I've gotten a lot of perspective that has, in the end, allowed me to appreciate my heritage. I will always do my utmost to keep family ties, NAC, traditionals, and powwows in my life. I want all that, or something like it, for my children.

I've learned to think about myself as important and to know that I have strengths. I'm finally starting to be at ease with myself and with other people, and I look forward to the person that I'm becoming. It's been a long, slow haul. When I walk down that aisle for graduation I want my relatives to be there with me, and I'll walk proudly. I would do everything over again. I wrote this poem which speaks for me and for others:

> I wear a coat. I wear tennis shoes.
> I play a game and I am winning.
> I go to school. I feel the worth
> in the knowledge of my relatives.
> I play the game, I do not live it.
> Knowledge from all areas . . .
> My thought, my hope:
> someday that all my elders will be proud
> respectful of the little ones who follow them.
> I dream . . . to make a way for the small ones not yet here.
> The younger ones to play the game in a skillful manner.
> In a way that I never could.
> It is our wish, it is our wish.

5 I Reconcile the Irreconcilable

This 20-year-old African American describes his determination to be a leader of men. The death of Rob's father when he was 8 led his mother to relocate the family to the South, where she had grown up and would now pursue a medical residency. Concerned about the lack of male influence in her son's life, she introduces Rob to a number of institutions that are predominantly white and predominantly—or entirely—male: a military academy's summer camp; the Boy Scouts; a prep school. The author follows the pattern, joining a fraternity when he enters college. Active and successful in student government at college, Rob now has his eye on the presidency of the student body as he seeks to reconcile within himself those "seemingly contradictory experiences and paradoxes of race and privilege, disadvantage and advantage."

One of my first memories is my father teaching me how to spell my last name; "D-A-N-F-O-R-T-H," he would say over and over again, and I would repeat the letters until I had memorized them. My last name held a fascination for me. It is sufficiently rare so that I have never met a Danforth who was not in my family. I also was struck by the way that my family used our name; when they spoke it they always changed their tone, as if it was the most special word in the English language. Members of my family have always carried themselves with a certain sense of arrogance, and I do not mean this in a bad light. I have found that America's most successful blacks are rarely modest. Arrogance or cockiness is used as a sort of a drug to combat the sense of inherent inferiority that America places upon blacks. In my experience as a black person who deals in the white world, all of my peers who have demonstrated the so-called virtues of modesty and humility have, in almost every case, failed to achieve their desired goals.

From what my relatives tell me, my grandfather was an arrogant man. He was born in North Carolina into a family of landownership that could also read and write. His father had attended college, graduating sometime before 1920. He went on to get a degree in dentistry and, like so many black men of his era, moved to the North. In the thirties, after a first marriage that failed, he moved to New York where he met and married my grandmother. He set up his dental practice and they had four sons; my father was the third of these. My grandfather would always make a distinction between other blacks and himself. As far as he was concerned, his education and profession put him in a separate class. He passed this attitude on to his sons to a certain extent. Although I never heard my father articulate this sentiment, I could tell the difference in the way that most other blacks carried themselves and the way that my father and his friends carried themselves. My parents' friends were all college-educated blacks who seemed to be still celebrating the gains of the 1960s, which is appropriate since they were the ones who had benefited the most. I was expected, as these people had done, to take advantage of the new-found educational and social freedoms to the fullest. This meant college definitely, and graduate school most likely.

When I was 6 my mother entered medical school. A few months later my father was hospitalized for cancer of the colon. My mother hired a live-in housekeeper to take care of my sister and me; we would have such help around the house for the rest of my childhood. When I was 8 my father died at age 41. My memories of this are images of lots of people being around the house for several weeks. I understood what had happened, but my father had been gone for so long in the hospital that the situation seemed somewhat removed from me. I do remember my mother's grief, but I was so young that my emotions were not developed enough to understand anything more than the concrete changes in everyday routine. My mother graduated from medical school and decided to pursue her residency in North Carolina where her mother and younger brother lived, and where she had grown up. I felt indifferent to the move except for the fact that I had just recently learned that North Carolina was a slave state, and I was wary that there would be racists down there. I was 9 years old.

My mother's family in North Carolina was quite different from my father's. My grandmother worked as a waitress in a downtown department store, my maternal grandfather was a mailman who died soon after I was born. My mother had grown up relatively poor, though not impoverished. I did not see much of my mother since she was completing her residency as a pediatrician. We lived in a suburban home in a predominantly white neighborhood that had a few blacks. The house was larger than our first home and better appointed. I attended the public schools but didn't like them at all. They were large and impersonal, and it seemed the teachers really didn't care about the development of students. One positive aspect was my inclusion in the district's Talented and Gifted Student Program. I also served as the treasurer of the elementary school's student council. In middle school I became involved in the public speaking program in which we would choose poems or speeches and practice for the countrywide competition at the end of the year. I won two years in a row, once in poetry and once in prose. During my time in public school in North Carolina, I felt awkward and out of place. There were no other kids in the school who had a similar background. My earlier exposure to white kids in Connecticut contrasted with the starkly segregated world of my North Carolina town. The other black students teased me for not speaking in the Black English dialect. The middle-class white students did not really associate that much with the blacks. Maybe once a year I would hear an insult of "black boy" or an occasional "nigger." By the end of seventh grade my marks in school were dropping and I felt as if I was learning nothing. When my mother offered me the chance to go to private school, I jumped at it.

My mother was always afraid that my development would be adversely affected by having lost my father at such a young age, so she was determined to provide other strong male influences in my life. Partially as a result, I have always been exposed to institutions that were predominantly or entirely male. These include my attendance at a military academy's summer camp, the Boy Scouts, prep school, and my college fraternity.

My mother got the idea to send me to a summer military academy from my father's older brother, my Uncle Bill, whose son had also gone to this camp. I spent the four summers following my father's death at this military academy turned summer camp where all the traditional American values were stressed. We were awakened every morning by bugle and had to assemble in military formation. The days were filled with athletic events such as horseback riding, riflery, and archery. In the evenings we saw movies like *True Grit* and *Patton*. During these four summers I became accustomed to spending long periods of time in an entirely male environment. I also learned at an early age what it meant to be independent from one's parents. However, there were some corresponding disadvantages to the experience at the camp. It encouraged the boys not to be dependent upon parents or other adult figures, and to look with disdain at such needs for nurturance or guidance. Leadership and responsibility were emphasized at the camp. As each camper would return for another year he was moved up a notch in military rank. After four years I was made a second lieutenant. My duties included assembling my group of 100 campers, who would report to me and salute in military fashion. By the end of my last year I had become so enamored with the place that I wanted to return there and go to the military academy. My mother was not about to let me go that far.

When the decision came to send me to prep school, the fact that it was an all-male school did not matter. The school was undoubtedly the best college preparatory school in central North Carolina. The surroundings at St. Andrews School were so much nicer than public school that I was too dazzled to worry about the lack of women. Also, the work was so much harder that I spent much more of my time studying than socializing. The structure and atmosphere of the St. Andrews program appealed particularly to the male psyche. Almost all of the teachers and administrators at the school were male, athletics were mandatory, and success in sports was heavily stressed. Time and again it was emphasized that we were the future leaders of our community. Since there was not a woman among us, this message also carried other connotations. As we entered the ninth and tenth grades, girls from our sister school, St. Anne's, began to attend classes with us. They came to St. Andrews to take math, science, and English, although we were not allowed to take such courses at St. Anne's, since it was generally thought that the girls' curriculum was watered down. There were only two or three black girls at St. Anne's, and my contact with any of them was rare. After five years of this situation, I became used to functioning in an all-male academic environment. It seemed perfectly normal to me to attend meetings or plan activities that were entirely devoid of any female participation.

My first day at St. Andrews was rather strange. I noticed first the difference in the way students dressed; they were all wearing pastel-colored "dress shirts." There were no blue jeans allowed, but the students did not seem to care. In class, I was struck by how much control teachers had over their students, who simply didn't act up as much. Out of my eighth-grade class of sixty-five, four of us were black. Three of us were new students and the other one, Jonathan, had been at the school since fourth grade. I ended up in the same class with him. Though he seemed pleased that there finally was another black person in his class, his attitude toward me was somewhat patronizing. He would constantly stress to me the difference between St. Andrews and my previous educational experience.

One day not long after I had first started at St. Andrews, the teacher arranged the seating. I ended up sitting next to a boy named Scott, a typical West End white kid. I noticed that he stared at me constantly. I got the feeling he was staring because he didn't think I belonged there; he did not stare at the new white student in the class who also sat near us. Another incident also clued me in to the way that things worked at that school. Members of the class had to give an oral presentation. One student named Ben gave his talk and he stuttered very badly. No one laughed or even flinched, and at the end he was congratulated as if he had given a flawless presentation. Next, a student named Louis went up to give his speech and he also stuttered badly. This time the members of the class chuckled and made faces. After the class most of the boys, including Ben, made fun of Louis. I questioned Jonathan about the double standard, and he explained to me that it was "not cool" to make fun of Ben because he came from a very wealthy and prestigious family, and his father was a respected alumnus. Louis, on the other hand, was Jewish, and his family owned a discount furniture store. Also, Louis had only been at the school for three years, whereas Ben had been at the school since kindergarten.

I soon came to understand that the boys of St. Andrews were taught that there was an ideal best exemplified by members of the community's elite society. These men were always white, always wealthy, and always Protestant. There was only one black teacher at the entire school, and he was too immersed in his religion to worry about social concerns. The only other blacks at the school were the kitchen and janitorial staff; not just particular members of the support staff were black, but the *entire* crew. The only white who worked for the school in this capacity was the supervisor. The students would always call these maintenance employees by their first names, no matter how old they were. The janitors would simply nod their heads in response. To call any other member of the staff by their first name would be grounds for severe punishment.

At first the students in my class did not know exactly what to make of the black students, but by the end of our first year opinions about us had begun to gel. Al was the most popular black member of our class. He was a gifted athlete and this immediately gained him considerable respect from our classmates. He was middle class and did not live in a very fancy neighborhood but every weekend a different white guy would invite him to spend the night. I was treated quite differently. In English and history classes I was beginning to show a remarkable amount of verbal ability. This shocked the other students in class; they had expected me to be slightly below par, at best. Another thing that shocked them was my accent. Within a year I had so immersed myself into the life of St. Andrews that I had donned a near flawless southern gentleman's accent. On the other hand, my athletic skills left something to be desired. The other boys dealt with this by coating me in humor. I began to notice that many of my habits were being ridiculed. This would continue in earnest until the tenth grade. I was constantly questioned as to why I did not possess greater athletic skill. When I showed skill in the classroom they said the only reason I did well was that I had somehow been able to shirk the curse of ignorance placed upon my race.

Early in ninth grade I was confronted with overt racism for the first time at St. Andrews. A student named Tim came up to me and for no reason said, "Nigger, nigger, why so tall? Nigger, where's your basketball?" He then proceeded to laugh and walk away. When I told another classmate about this incident he dismissed it as not being so much a racial attack as a personal one. He pointed to the fact that Al was one of Tim's best friends. I was later to find out that Tim said that he just wanted to see what my reaction was, and that he would never have done such a thing to a "normal" black person. When I went to my faculty advisor to explain my problem to him, he asked that I not tell anyone else and said that he would handle the problem himself. I never got any sort of an apology from Tim. During my freshman and sophomore years I was a target for racial harassment. Guys would say things to me just to get a reaction, and often I supplied them with it. During this period my grades, particularly in math and science, began to fall. I failed two terms of chemistry and one term of trigonometry.

During the last month of my sophomore year we held elections for junior class leadership positions. When the nominations came up for student council, a kid named Tom decided it would be funny to nominate me. There was no way that I could win since such positions were reserved for students who could act as role models. When the time came to give the speeches, I argued that the people who had held the positions of leadership so far had rested on their laurels and had looked upon their positions as honors rather than jobs. People were surprised by this tactic; it had previously been unspeakable to condemn our class leaders. When election day came I actually had much support. I won my position handily, to the surprise of the students, faculty, and administration of the school. I therefore found myself in a very different position to deal with my junior year, and my self-esteem rose considerably.

During the following summer I spent most of my time working out in the school weight room and became close friends with Jonathan, the black student who had first greeted me in eighth grade. Now he had a new sense of respect for me due to my election as a class leader. Jonathan was the eldest son of wealthy physicians. His wealth did not in any way prevent him from acknowledging his black identity, and "blackness" was often a topic of conversation between us. By the time junior year began we were definitely the best of friends. Both of us had the desire to complete St. Andrews as successfully as possible, and we were willing to do anything to make this wish a reality.

As junior year began, I was hungry for opportunities to get involved. I entered the tryouts for the school's team for "Battle of the Brains," a TV quiz show in which area high schools competed in tournament-style competition. I did not make the competition team, but I did make first alternate, and I practiced with the team and went to all of the matches. The coach, Mrs. Morgan, took a personal interest in me and valued my capacity to learn and understand facts, especially in the area of history. By the next year I was to join the television team and I soon became a major force. Many people were surprised to see a black guy on the team from St. Andrews. We did very well, making it all the way into the semifinals. I even sent my tapes to the admissions committees at the colleges I applied to.

I didn't really search for all of the activities that I became involved in. When sign-ups were announced for the Drama Club's play, Tom, the same guy who had jokingly nominated me for a position on the student council, took the liberty of signing me up. To the surprise of many, I actually went ahead with tryouts for the play. I became involved in several productions during the course of my junior and senior year, which brought me into contact with the women from St. Anne's for extended periods of time. Jonathan and I began to go to the parties of our wealthy white friends. These parties were comprised of the "popular crowd" of the St. Andrews and St. Anne's students. These people began to take a new attitude toward me; I was no longer simply someone to make fun of. I had finally begun to turn my experience at St. Andrews into a positive one.

In the spring of junior year I found out that I was accepted by the AFS intercultural program and went to Israel to stay with a family for the summer. The group with which I traveled was a diverse mix of people from around the United States. About half of the students in the group were Jewish, and I was the only black. This was the first time I had come into close contact with people from all over the country, and I felt as if I had been living in a closet; the closed-mindedness of North Carolina had left its mark. We arrived in Israel and were taken to a youth hostel in Tel Aviv where we underwent further orientation. As we traveled around Tel Aviv, I remember feeling self-conscious because I was black, though this feeling left when I saw that there were actually a fair number of black Israelis. After I had been in the country for several days, my host brother, David, came to pick me up with a female friend of his. As I talked with them, I began to notice the differences between them and my peers at home; these people seemed to be a lot more mature and less materialistic. I also felt that they did not notice that I was black, or that if they did notice, it made no difference.

In all of my travels around Israel, I never felt that my race was an issue or a problem. I was referred to simply as an American. I remember only one conversation that concerned race. My host father had heard that things were pretty bad for black people in the United States and he asked me what my experiences had been. I told him that in my hometown there were still many problems that revolved around race. However, I explained that things were much improved since the days when my parents were my age. He replied that to his people, race itself meant nothing. He noted that when distinctions were made, they had more to do with religion than race. But what he told me and what I observed were two different things. The family that I stayed with were of European descent, and every once in a while they would make derogatory comments about Jews of Middle Eastern descent. I also saw the way Arabs were treated within Israel. Their neighborhoods were some of the most impoverished places that I had ever seen. And the Israelis to whom I spoke believed that if the Arabs wanted to live better they should go to another country. My eyes were opened to the fact that people could oppress others for reasons unrelated to race. I had heard that this happened around the world, but I had not seen it up close. I left Israel feeling that I understood much more that people had different perspectives on life, and that no one perspective was necessarily better than any other.

When the time rolled around to start thinking about college, my initial reaction was to apply for early admission to the University of North Carolina. However, this attitude changed when I noticed that Jonathan was looking at an entirely different set of institutions. His football prowess, along with good grades, had assured him of acceptance to most of the Ivy League schools. This sparked my interest in these schools, and when it came time, I applied to them. Most of the guys in my class thought that I was taking a shot in the dark; there was no way that I would ever get in. In the end, however, I was successful and was accepted into every school to which I applied.

The reaction by some to my acceptance into a top college was that I would soon fail or disappear into the woodwork. This seemed to be the attitude of the St. Anne's girl who was also accepted to the same college as I was. She had been part of the crowd that had given me such a hard time during high school. Whenever she and I would talk about heading off to college, she behaved as if the two of us were going to entirely different schools. I got the feeling that she could not imagine that our college experiences would be at all similar, primarily because I was a black student and could be expected to separate myself from the college mainstream. My stock did go up among the faculty of the school. I was encouraged warmly by faculty who had been cool toward me in previous years. The teachers even went so far as to award me an honor prize for outstanding citizenship at graduation, the culmination of two years of surprising people by succeeding where I was not expected to.

The fact that my Uncle Joe attended this same college has much to do with the attitude that I have developed toward it. Samuel Joseph Danforth, my Uncle Joe, was the oldest brother of my late father. He enrolled in my college as a member of the class of 1954. This was years before this college had any thought of diversity; there were only three blacks in his entire class. He even joined a fraternity. After graduating, he went on to medical school where he did well enough to earn a fellowship in research.

When first coming to college I sensed that, as a black student, I was expected to look upon the past of this institution as something that should be alien to me. I was supposed to reject its traditions and reactionary fraternity system. However, my family's connection did not allow me to take this stance to the extent that some of my fellow black students did. I was aware that in the past my college had many problems and prejudices; my uncle had been excluded from a fraternity that had an open policy of excluding blacks. However, I did not treat the past of this institution with the loathing which I sensed from other black students, and which I felt some administrators expected me to espouse. For some reason, I felt connected to that part of my college's past that my uncle represented. Part of this was a sense of pride in being a black second-generation Ivy Leaguer, and a fourth-generation college undergraduate. For this peculiar reason, I wished to experience that side of college life that most black students feared or even hated.

I lived my freshman year with two roommates from very different backgrounds. Phil was from the Midwest; he came from a wealthy background and had attended an exclusive day school, as I had. Jim was more middle class, his father was a football coach, and he had come to college primarily as an athlete. Interestingly, I was the intermediary between these two. Phil and I shared the same tastes in clothes and had shared a similar educational experience in high school. Jim and I could talk about football, had similar attitudes toward women, and enjoyed rap music. Phil and I developed the closer relationship. Jim did not drink, and alcohol would soon become a large part of my life at college. I also found it difficult to discuss my career goals and plans with Jim; he knew little, if anything, about corporate law or investment banking. On the other hand, Phil's experiences and aspirations were more congruent with my own.

During my first term at college, alcohol became the means to purchase my popularity. This popularity would make possible attainment of most of my student leadership positions ranging from class council representative, to student assembly representative, to class president. The college had a policy that excluded freshmen from the fraternities during their first term. As a result, wherever alcohol showed up, large groups of freshmen were sure to follow. One Friday a couple of my hallmates and I decided to buy a few cases and invite some people over. We set the beer out in a trash can with some ice and soon a crowd of about fifty to seventy had gathered in our hallway. Phil suggested that I go around and collect "chips" (small donations of one or two dollars to help defray the cost of the beer) and, as a result, I met more people in one hour than I had met during my entire first two weeks. Later, as people were beginning to file out, I heard people saying, "you guys are really ballsy" and "when's the next rager." We had these parties for the next six successive weekends. We started to buy our beer in kegs and people began to depend upon us for their weekly entertainment. Within three weeks our parties were 150 strong, and even upperclassmen were beginning to show up. I began to achieve widespread recognition, at first as the "big black guy who collected the chips." Eventually people whom I did not ever recall seeing before began to call my name around campus. I began to realize that if I had anything going for me, it was the fact that I had an image that stuck in people's minds.

Elections for class council were announced about the fifth week of the term. I decided to run and produced only one simple campaign poster. It used photographs from our several parties and the caption read, "Let's keep the tradition going." Therefore, in my first student government election I ran on a platform of "free beer" and parties. It worked, and I went to my first class council meeting the next week.

By the second term of my freshman year the fraternity system had become a major mental preoccupation of many of my fellow classmates, as well as myself. We had abandoned our weekly parties on the hall and had begun to consume beer at the expense of fraternity brothers. The Zeta Upsilon house had a reputation for being a haven for the wealthy and powerful. This reputation was taken seriously by the campus, and an article on this particular house had appeared in *Playboy* magazine just a year before. This did not intimidate me or my roommate, Phil. One Wednesday night early in winter term we went into the basement of Zeta. It was filled with about thirty guys wearing Brooks Brothers shirts with ratty jeans and dingy baseball caps. The Grateful Dead played in the background. I went over to a guy who appeared to be wearing a sweatshirt from one of St. Andrews rival schools. It turned out he had actually gone to Exeter, but he got excited when he found out that I had gone to a private school and he invited me to come back the next week.

Phil and I began to go to Zeta U on a regular basis. We became good friends with most of the brothers and we began to spend time outside the house with those guys whom we expected to become members of our pledge class. At the beginning of spring term, rush came around. Both Phil and I were let into the house and I began to spend all of my leisure time there. I would get up and go to class, eat, and then go straight to the house. For a relatively small fee each term, I would have all of the beer that I could drink, not only at my own house, but also at most of the other houses in the system. I began to partake of the system on a regular basis, but I did not feel that I would be any more productive if I was not in a fraternity.

The women who hung out at our fraternity were basically the female counterparts of my brothers. They were all white and wealthy and knew it. They were much more civil toward me than were the St. Anne's girls, but they were extremely image conscious. One thing that really struck me was the fact that I received odd looks from these people when they discovered that I was in Zeta U. I was the only black person in the house, and at many of the "social set" parties that I would go to, I would almost always be the only black person in the room. The one thing about the fraternity that would often cause me stress was the every-term chore of finding a formal date. Usually the only women who were interested in going were white sorority girls. I often shied away from asking black girls because I was afraid that they would not feel comfortable. I often had to reconcile within myself the fact that as a black person I belonged to this organization that made no effort to include blacks.

During the entirety of my sophomore year, I was the only black member of the house. When rush for the next class came along, I felt obligated to ensure that another black member got admitted. One black guy, whom I did not really know, rushed. When the time came for deliberations, I made a passionate plea for this person's acceptance as a member of the house. Several of the other brothers felt that I used "racial guilt" to force this member into the house. Therefore, they put pressure on me to ensure that person would become a good member. I felt that such an attitude was inherently wrong, but it is representative of what I have often had to deal with as a member of this fraternity. Even though I have been exposed to several incidents of racial insensitivity, to question these events usually brings about vehement denial of any racist motives. Often these incidents are passed off as jokes, or simply a matter of objective, intellectual fact. The style of racism may be different from the more blatant form I had to deal with at St. Andrews. However, the end result is the same; I am made painfully aware that I am different from those around me. One fear that I had when I joined a white fraternity was that I would be shunned by other blacks on campus, but this has not come about because I always made a point to speak to black students whom I know, especially when I am in the presence of my white friends.

The experience of being in a fraternity has opened my eyes to the true nature of this college. Though the administration preaches a "principle of community" that promotes the toleration and celebration of diversity, the student body is allowed to maintain an elitist structure. Most of the people in my fraternity are white and wealthy. The people that they eat with, socialize with, and compete with in athletics are also white and wealthy. I am the only black friend that most of these guys have, yet I do not bring them face to face with the poverty and injustice that most blacks must labor under. This causes me to wonder whether I am giving these people a false sense of security about their dealings with black people, and whether I should be more persistent in voicing black concerns in my dealings with my fraternity brothers. However, I believe that I should not seek to place a special burden upon myself to "educate" my white friends. To do so would reduce my ability to function and, hence, succeed.

Rushing my fraternity was rather easy; ten years in predominantly male environments allowed me to take to Greek life like a fish to water. By the beginning of sophomore year, as my skills as a student politician increased, I began to realize that it would be to my advantage to reassess my views toward women. I began to use the word "girls" less and use "women" more. My politician friend, Randy, persuaded me that my attitude was going to eventually get me into trouble. However, inherent in his criticism was a basic misunderstanding of why such attitudes had developed, his having always been in a coed environment where parity between the sexes was stressed. Even now, however, the part of student social life to which I belong is rather divided along gender lines. All of the major positions in student government, with one exception, are occupied by men. So my involvement in a male-dominated environment still continues, though my awareness and perception of this situation has changed.

My career in student government has, in several ways, been tied to my fraternity experience. First, I realized that if I was to assert myself as a leader at the college, it would be necessary for me to join a fraternity, which had to be well respected and traditional. Second, my closest partner in student government was also a fraternity brother of mine. Third, my fraternity experience has constantly brought me into contact with more and more people. Being in a fraternity such as Zeta U also has an effect upon my campus image. Just as black print is most distinctive against a white background, I, too, stick out in my college environment. This makes me more recognizable and, hence, more viable as a campus politician. There are also some drawbacks to my unique position. There are many on this campus who thrive upon their differences with other people, whether they be racial, socioeconomic, or religious. Many of these people have used their situation to gain prominence and power within the community. To many of these people, I represent a dangerous element because I reconcile the irreconcilable. By virtue of who and what I am, a Zeta U, a class president, and a black person, I mix experiences and attitudes that many in this community contend cannot coexist. It is these attitudes that can eventually hinder my progress in this community, if anything can.

My associations with whites are a result of the institutions and experiences that I have been exposed to. I never set out with the purpose of associating myself with the wealthiest, "whitest" people that I could find. I do, however, show great discretion in choosing the educational and social institutions in which I become involved. Blacks have traditionally been excluded from such organizations, but in the late 1960s a conscious decision was made to allow blacks access to these places. This is the situation into which I was born. The earliest decisions about whom I would associate with were made by my parents. They decided to settle in a predominantly white neighborhood because of certain perceived advantages. These reasons further led them to place me in a white nursery school. As a result, I learned from earliest childhood to be most comfortable in a predominantly white environment. My parents saw no harm in this, since they understood that the recognition of racial differences would come with age.

The motivation for associating with whites was not a desire to stay away from blacks. The minute number of blacks at traditionally prestigious schools and organizations forced me to modify my patterns of association and socialization. I had to associate with whites in order to have any social life at all. There are very few blacks who have shared my set of experiences, and to find someone similar to me who is black is rare. I guess that these shared contradictions and experiences form the basis of my friendship with Jonathan. Most of the time we spend together is consumed with the discussion of race and class . . . and women.

My relationships with women, or the lack thereof, are a result of my unique situation. Just as I am hampered by the lack of other black males who have shared my experiences, there are even fewer black females that I have come into contact with. This is not to say that I haven't met a few, but the field is very small. It is unrealistic to believe that I will be compatible with every upper-middle-class black female that I meet. To limit my relationships with women to one race is therefore foolish for me. In dealing with white women, another set of factors comes into play. Even in the 1990s it is not fully acceptable to have interracial relationships, especially for those women who are conscious of their class and position. They care about what their peers will think, as well as their parents. This is especially true in a conservative town like the one I grew up in, or the small, sheltered community of my college. When I have tried to initiate such relationships, I have encountered the barriers that society has erected.

As I look beyond my upcoming final year at college (with an eye on the presidency of the student body) I feel I have a good idea of what it is that I have to overcome. I must be sure that I have reconciled within myself these seemingly contradictory experiences and paradoxes of race and privilege, disadvantage and advantage. I am a young black man, socialized by elite white institutions, very aware of the racism that surrounds me; yet my perspective on life is one of empowerment and unfettered opportunity. If I do not reconcile these contradictions, then those goals that I have set for myself shall be much harder, if not impossible, to reach.

6 Falling for Someone

In this case, Graham traces his personal journey from withdrawn and awkward young boy—interested in girls but not knowing the "rules"—to self-possessed young man who values honesty and communication in his relationships with women. In a middle and high school culture where sex is viewed as a goal-oriented activity, Graham insists that for him emotional connection is an essential part of physical intimacy. He describes the significant romantic relationships he has had in high school and college, assessing why the year-long relationship with Sarah ultimately failed and why the burgeoning relationship with Nora holds more promise.

I wrote a poem about the first night we went to get coffee together. A couple of weeks later, on Valentine's Day, I printed the final copy and spent an hour making it into a card. We were in a play together at the time, so that night at rehearsal I set it slyly amidst the things on her dressing-room table after everyone had gone to warm up. When I saw her again, she was waiting out in the hall, smiling. "Thank you, Graham," she said breathlessly, eyes gleaming. "I'm almost in tears. I couldn't let everyone in there see me lose it."

"So you like it?"

"I love it." She threw her arms around my neck and gave me a fierce hug, and then she squeezed my hand again, smiling, before reluctantly slipping back down the hallway to finish costuming. We didn't know what to say to each other the rest of that evening, so backstage, we just smiled at each other and blushed.

A week later at senior cocktails, she pulled me aside. "I started writing this the same night you did," she said, placing an envelope into my hands, "but it's taken me longer to finish." She sat and watched me as I read it, the noisy crowd just around the corner. Both of our poems described the same feelings, the same lovely moments. She wrote more than I had dared to include in mine; it made me dizzy, reading and re-reading the lines, the subtext too strong to ignore but too good to be true. All I could do was blush and smile and giggle like a schoolboy; she started, too, and there we were—two college seniors on a couch around the corner from a large cocktail party, rocking and giggling like children.

Her name's Nora. She's pretty, she's funny, she's talented, and she's smart. We've got common interests, common viewpoints, common tastes in music and food, and the same sense of humor. We're attracted to each other, and you can tell by the shine we both get when we're around each other, the lovely little flirting that goes on. The kicker is that she has a boyfriend.

I'd come a long way from the shy boy I used to be. Throughout my childhood I was shy, quiet, and withdrawn. Most people find it significant that I'm an only child and that I am adopted. "Oh, really?" they murmur, with a click of their tongue. "That must be rough." Well, no, actually—it hasn't been rough. I can't remember a time not knowing I was adopted, and I can't remember a time when the concept has ever caused me any grief. My parents are my parents, and if you get to know them it becomes immediately apparent how like them I am. My parents treat me as an equal, and for that I respect them.

I've always felt as though I had a high degree of responsibility and freedom in my family. They never gave me the sex talk, though: I learned all I knew about sex from the kids at school between third and fifth grade. I was not one of those sexually precocious kids who leapt right into the act and got it out of the way. I saved myself for as long as I felt I could and still gave away my virginity at seventeen. That was pretty old by the standards in my town—there just wasn't much else to do. I hit an early growth spurt and was five-foot ten going into junior high. I towered over everyone and was husky in build—not exactly fat, but pushing the limit. I was clumsy with my size. I slumped. The subtle ways of fashion were mysterious to me— what to wear, what to say, how to posture myself—and my attempts at conforming to them seemed immediately transparent to the popular kids, who ridiculed me.

I've liked girls for as far back as I can remember, but I missed learning the rules somehow. I remember one time, when I was in seventh grade, at someone's birthday party. The room was darkened, and everyone was being social. I was standing with my back against the wall, watching it all, when I caught my own gaze in a big portrait-sized mirror hanging on the opposite side of the room.

I vividly remember feeling as though I was seeing myself for the first time: I stood head and shoulders above the reflected people, my lank and longish hair parted sloppily down the middle, with my bangs tickling my eyebrows. My almost-too-small shirt was open at the collar, and I wore a thin gold chain around my throat. My expression was blank, noncommittal; the corner of my mouth kinked up slightly in an expression of universal dismissal, but I held my own gaze for a long time. Dismissal was a safe expression to assume. People who seemed not to care about anything were the least fun to ridicule.

It was still common at that time to talk about sexual intimacy in terms of baseball: Making out was "first base," intercourse a "home run." Everyone was eager to know how far someone had gotten the weekend before. The analogy of a game was perfect, because it neatly removed emotion from physical intimacy; it reflected a perfectly goal-oriented mentality. This was a game I wasn't playing, partly because I didn't know the rules and partly because all that my parents had told me about physical intimacy as far back as I could remember was that it was something that you only did with a person that you loved.

Enter Melissa Reynolds, someone I had placed on a pedestal all through seventh and eighth grade. It didn't dawn on me until after the fact that we had been considered "an item" for about two months, which was pretty cool to me in retrospect, considering she was a year older and a grade above me; older loosely equaled cooler. Nothing ever came of it physically: Had someone suggested that I kiss her, I would have laughed in that person's face.

I saw Mel as untouchable, all encompassing. I was physically attracted to her, yes, but at that point in my life physical affection was a symbol of love, and I was so certain that I was unworthy of her love that any desire to hold her or to kiss her was buried by self-doubt. It *never occurred* to me at that stage of my life that I could be desirable physically to a girl who was physically desirable to me.

This leads me to think that physical and emotional development are related but ultimately different processes. In many of my friends, the desire for sexual release seemed to develop before the desire for any interactive emotional context, but I recall my desire to feel loved as dominant over the urges of my flesh. What did I want from girls? I certainly experienced simple physical lust, but in another sense I longed for emotional support, personal validation. These physical and emotional desires felt somewhat disconnected in me. Physical affection from my early girlfriends became a reflection of my self-worth, showing that I was attractive enough or witty enough to merit their attention.

Anyway, Mel must have eventually gotten tired of me because the next thing I knew we weren't speaking—it was as if we'd never met. This didn't surprise me greatly, and since I had never felt as though we were bound together by anything mutual, all I felt was disappointment. The advantage of a pessimistic attitude toward something is that when it goes wrong, you've been anticipating it. I suppose I thought pretty little of myself; I had no confidence with my peers because I felt as though I didn't understand them, didn't belong. I spent a lot of time talking about these issues with my best friend, Jeff.

Jeff is an only child, as I am, and we've ended up being like brothers. I guess I call him my best friend because I feel as though he is the one person who understands me the most completely. There was very little that I didn't share with him emotionally throughout high school, and he never judged me. He just accepted me for who I was. I could be completely honest with him and not fear his scorn or reproval.

Until high school, the female mind remained largely mysterious to both of us, a combination lock to which the cool guys seemed to share a secret code. They treated girls like trash, but the girls seemed to eat it up. All I knew was how to be polite, honest, and friendly. Self-deprecatory. I was the "nicest" guy everybody knew. It was in this mind-frame that I met Missy, My First Girlfriend. I asked her out on Valentine's Day of my sophomore year; she was a junior, and it was with her that I abandoned virginity.

My introduction to intercourse was somewhat anticlimactic, so to speak. In the back of my car, almost nine months after we had been going steady, we decided to "just see what it's like." The October leaves swirled in the dark parking lot behind the public library. We had parked beneath the farthest lamppost, which some kid had shot out with a pellet gun some months before, and the light across her anxious brow was silvery and dim. She nervously brushed a strand of her long blonde hair out of her mouth. Her blue eyes were wide and fixed on me. I was fumbling with my belt. She was as tall as I was, and the tiny backseat was cramped and uncomfortable. We were already more frightened than curious, and the sensation of momentary insertion was so unbearably sweet that it pushed us immediately over the edge into panic.

We leapt apart, buckling and zipping furiously until we were safely tucked back into our pants, and then we held each other tightly for a few moments, panting, before jumping into the frontseat and zooming out of the parking lot and onto the well-lit streets of town, windows down, the night breeze cooling our damp faces. The next day we were terrified that she was pregnant, even though our contact hadn't been but three or four seconds. The biological facts of the matter didn't seem relevant to us; no matter how brief, the mere pleasure of the touch seemed enough to doom us.

As our fear faded, however, our desire deepened, and within a week we couldn't get enough of each other and began having intercourse in earnest. At the time, I truly believed this was Love: "the real thing." I spent all of my free time with her, to the point where my parents began to suggest that maybe we were seeing too much of each other. This enraged me—I felt that they didn't understand our feelings for one another, didn't realize the depth of our connection. I began to feel as if I didn't need anyone else's affection or approval—I had all I needed emotionally in Missy.

Over the summer, I kissed another girl. I was disgusted with myself morally because my physical desire had gotten the better of my desire to remain faithful to my girlfriend. At the same time, though, I was overcome by the physical thrill of my bravado. Things between Missy and me deteriorated, and we broke up after she went off to college that fall.

I had a silly little relationship with a sophomore my senior year, but I was more concerned with college applications and with getting out of Dayton than I was with her. My first sexual encounter here at college, though, is worth mentioning: I was a bright-eyed, first-term freshman in this brave new world, and hence easy prey. A junior named Alice asked me to her sorority formal, and I accepted. We drank quite a bit and danced suggestively enough to earn cat calls from her sorority sisters. She came on to me very aggressively and brazenly, which I don't recall as particularly *arousing;* I was dizzy, and I remember a vague excitement of being in uncharted waters, the thrill of having someone come on to me like that. I didn't encourage her advances, but then I didn't discourage them, either.

When we got back to campus, Alice asked if I wanted to stay in her room that night rather than walk home. I was tired and drunk, so I went up with her into her room and collapsed on the bed. I lay there watching the ceiling slowly spin, and she suggested that I'd be more comfortable without all of my clothes on. This was undoubtedly true. She helped me undress and heap my clothes on a chair in the corner, and then we both crawled into the bed and pulled up the covers. Soon we were kissing and rolling around, and although we didn't have intercourse, things got awfully passionate. I remember vaguely the point at which it seemed to be over and I could drop off into an exhausted sleep.

I awoke the next morning around seven with mixed emotions. Alice was the first sexual predator I had ever dated, and I was realizing that it wasn't such a great experience. The complete lack of emotional substance to the whole affair depressed me, and I was angry at myself for having done such a thing. I got dressed and Alice walked downstairs in her nightshirt to the door with me. As I remember it, I never said a word the whole time; I just sort of looked at the floor and got out of there as quickly as I could. She made light comments, trying to start a conversation, I suppose, but all I really remember her saying was "give me a call" at the door as I stumbled out.

The irony of this, to me, is the gender reversal in this scenario. Isn't it supposed to be the older frat boy who asks the shy young freshman girl to the formal, gets her liquored up, and then convinces her to spend the night in his room? One difference is that I don't feel like I was taken advantage of; I never felt like any of the responsibility for my actions lay with anybody but myself. I didn't *have* to drink or stay in her room, I decided to. One thing I'll say to Alice's credit: She was clear about what she wanted, and maybe that kind of communication is better than none at all.

Communication is imperative. I think a major reason that my relationships at college have seemed different from the ones I had in high school is that people communicate more. For example, my buddies here are all important to me, yet there is no significant sense of hierarchy; no single one of them fulfills my every interpersonal need. That being said, my happiness still seems to some degree dependent upon my relationships with others. I get depressed when I feel unloved or unnoticed, which leads me to think that I *need* other people, I *need* friends around me. Is it possible to be completely self-sufficient? Is it desirable?

As a kid, I spent a good deal of time by myself. I guess I was lonely but then I never really remember being unhappy, as such. I often enjoy being alone; I *need* to be alone sometimes. Ideally, I have a balance of quality time with my friends, quality time by myself, and activities that combine social interaction with independent work.

For example, I like to act. I like to get up on stage and impress people. I like the attention and the freedom of my body on the stage—the freedom to expand my personal space until it encompasses an entire room. I unleash my voice and express my energy. I love the applause, washing over me in its thunderous *yes*. On stage, I can be graceful and funny and tragic; I control the dynamic. I can feel alone in a room full of people, letting them in and out of my life as I wish, and then enjoy their approval.

I am most exultant when I am living a scene moment by moment, never anticipating the next, not inhibited by the sequence of emotions I'm scripted to experience, but rather living a fictional story line as spontaneous, as now, as if I were the character. Acting is a strange mixture of awareness and spontaneity; I have the chance to figure out how my character will behave before the action takes place. When I walk onto the stage and into the world of the play, I'm living spontaneously in a self-controlled moment; there is nothing to be unsure of, so I can experience a range of passionate emotions without doubt, without unpredictable repercussions—everything's safely scripted beforehand.

I met Sarah the spring of our sophomore year. She was beautiful; she had dark, thick hair that fell to her jawline and big, brown doe eyes. When I looked at her, she'd smile and sometimes glance away and blush.

We began spending more and more time alone together. We'd go for a jog, grab a bite to eat, take in a movie, or just walk around and talk. At some point I realized we were sitting on her bed in her room one night, and the conversation had fallen into one of those comfortable silences. It occurred to me to kiss her, but then I thought I'd better ask, just to make sure. When I did, she smiled and blushed and said yes, and we kissed and it was bliss. It felt like chemistry; it felt right. "Why did this take us so long?" she smiled, as if she'd been thinking about it for a while. It occurred to me then that maybe I had, too. I suppose things happen at the pace they happen, and that's part of the beauty of courtship.

We saw more and more of each other. By the end of the term, we were going steady. I don't recall ever being that happy in my life, in the sense that *nothing* mattered. It was a mindless kind of happiness: The world could have ended and I would have been content to go down with it knowing that there was Sarah and me.

The romantic clichés are clichés for a reason—because they are indeed Fantastic, they are Magnificent, they are 100 percent true. It's bliss, it's beautiful—it's walking on air; it's as light as a feather. She was radiant, and when I looked at her I couldn't *stop* looking at her. I wanted to touch her and hold her and hug her close and melt right into her body, fuse like that, curl up like a kitten inside her and wrap around her and weave through her hair and fall into her eyes. I don't know if that's the healthiest phase of falling for someone, but it is certainly an exhilarating lack of perspective.

Every time I looked at her, I was struck anew. With other girlfriends, that sense of astonishment diminished over time. I'd "get used" to them, so to speak, in the sense that my aesthetic attraction to them became internalized, accepted, understood, not thought about consciously. But with Sarah, it was like seeing her for the first time every time I looked at her. She was also the most intelligent girl I'd ever dated; she thought in a wonderfully straightforward, logical way. We could discuss issues and never lose each other; our processes of deduction seemed to mirror each other's and work in exactly the same patterns. This is not to say that we never disagreed; rather, I mean it always seemed that we understood one another.

In her eyes I was funny, talented, intelligent, and diverse—"Is there anything that you *don't* do?" she asked early on—so different from the other boys she had dated before. She described me as passionate, inexplicable, dynamic, rational, emotional, ridiculous, sophisticated, sophomoric, artistic, communicative—unlike anyone she'd ever met. And my willingness to go head-over-heels, hopeless-romantic crazy for her was probably exactly what she was looking for at the time when a fling with another frat-boy, Econ-major, cookie-cutter, blue-blazer, third-generation-legacy stereotype had fallen through in her life. I fit. She fit. We were perfect for one another for impermanent reasons. We spent that summer together at school, and the whole term went by in a happy blur.

In the fall I went to study in London for two terms. Sarah took the winter off to go ski and work in Colorado. There was a general feeling of unease in me; I feared that she might get into an exciting new environment and fall for someone else. I also feared meeting some nice British girl and breaking my word to Sarah; I'd not yet been successful in a long-distance relationship. I came home to the U.S. over break and flew up to see her after Christmas; she was going to meet me in the airport. I wasn't sure what to expect—would she feel the same?

I was one of the last people out of the plane, and as I walked across the tarmac in the bitter night's wind, I felt a strange calm come over me. I was excited to see her, but perhaps I was steeling myself for a letdown. I walked through the door into the bright terminal.

She was sitting in a chair against the wall, leaning forward with her elbows on her knees when the crowd parted and we saw each other. Her hair was longer and I was again struck by how lovely she was. She rose and we embraced—it was wonderful; that sense of gently trying to pull the other person completely into oneself. For me, it was an ecstatically silent affirmation.

We drove home to her house in Albany, New York and tried to catch up on what had happened in the time since our last letters, the last phone call, the whole term in general. There was so much I wanted to say, but somehow we just sort of sat smiling in silence as we drove through the dark. I could smell her favorite perfume, the scent of her hair, the fabric softener she used on her clothes. The sound of her voice was so much different in person than it had been on the telephone.

We ended up spending almost the whole time with her parents. They were all better skiers than me, and they all looked like one big, happy family. Her parents always seemed a *shade* distant toward me. I wasn't sure if it was just that I was their daughter's first "serious" boyfriend, the fact that I was a creative writing major, something specific about my personality, or a combination of these things that inspired this coolness. She was Daddy's Little Girl, and I suspect that part of the odd feeling originated in the psychiatrist's evaluative eye he always seemed to be examining me with.

I think from those four days, I wanted definite confirmation of her feelings for me. Sarah wasn't the best at articulating her emotions. "The more we try to pack everything into four days," she said, "the harder it will be to go without it again." I wasn't sure what that statement implied.

Sarah was uncomfortable with the idea of her parents seeing us in any physically intimate way. We were very comfortable with one another when nobody else was around, but with her parents it was an almost visible fear, a tension that lasted the whole four days. When the day came to have her take me back to the airport, I was still confused.

I went back to London; she went to Colorado. I enjoyed hearing how animated her voice became over the phone when she told me about the crazy high jinks she had gotten into while working on the mountain that week. I was having a better time myself, meeting people and traveling around Britain. All seemed well until that fateful day when I talked to her, perhaps two weeks before the end of the quarter. We talked for an hour, but I never felt like she was actually in the conversation.

"You know, Sarah," I suggested, "I've been wondering if maybe this relationship is going to be the same when we both get back to campus in the spring."

"You know, I have, too," she replied with audible relief. "I mean, it's been so long and we've both been through *so much*. It's strange, isn't it? I'm not really sure how to feel about you any more." All of this in a light, *thank goodness we agree!* sort of tone. Well, I had to sit down.

"... Are you *serious?*" I asked, after a moment. "What exactly does that mean?"

Silence on the line.

"I thought you wanted us to be honest with each other," she said.

"Well, yes—I do. I do. But Jesus, maybe not *this* honest." I was floored. It felt as though a deep hole had opened up somewhere inside my gut, and everything was getting sucked down into it. My center of gravity had suddenly become a black hole. I couldn't let myself believe what seemed to be happening, not after all this time, not this way.

"Well, we can talk about it when I meet you in France, right?" She seemed to want to wrap up this discussion.

"You still want to do that, then?" This gave me some kind of hope.

"Of course I do! I wouldn't miss that for the world." Sarah's family and another family had a tradition of going to Europe biannually to ski. Sarah and I had made plans to go to Paris before their trip was scheduled to begin.

I mumbled a few shaky good-byes, and the conversation was over. I went into my room and lay down on my bed and stared at my ceiling for about two hours. I couldn't get over that hollow emptiness inside myself. A strange detachment came over me, and I was sort of marveling at how interesting a sensation it was. *I haven't just been dumped, that's for sure. She never said we aren't going out anymore—after all, she's still going to meet me in Paris over break, like we planned. That must mean something. We'll talk about it. She'll see that she still cares about me when we meet again face to face. This is not a disaster.*

Cut to a wide-angle shot of me two weeks later, sitting alone in Gatwick, waiting for her to deplane. I'm having a coffee and reading *Bleak House*. The crowd parts and there she is, walking toward me, smiling. She is deeply tanned from the slopes of Colorado, and her teeth are brilliantly white. She carries a large duffel sack over her shoulder, which she swings to the floor as I stand up to greet her.

A grandmotherly embrace. A dry peck on the cheek. There could be no doubt anymore, but somehow I managed to convince myself otherwise. It's amazing what things we won't let ourselves believe when we don't want to believe them. The taxi ride back to my room was mostly silent, uneasy.

We spent a day and a night in London. It was immediately apparent that things were different between us, but I denied the signs of this. There was no physical affection beyond the casual or the accidental—the few times she made contact with me were sisterly, almost reluctant. When we got to Paris, it was worse: She didn't want to talk about it; she didn't want to acknowledge that there was anything to discuss. "Less not spoil our time here," she said a couple of times. It was terrible.

The city of romance was gray and wet. A cold wind blew through the streets. We slept in the same bed, but she would not be touched—if I brushed against her, she rolled away. This was not done in a cruel way, which somehow made it worse. Her absence of emotion was harder to handle than love, hate, or anger: Anything would have been better than her wistful distance. It was as if I was fading out like an old photograph, slowly losing cohesion until light itself began to bleed through me; I could almost feel myself becoming more and more translucent and ghostlike.

Even when I would grab her and pull her close to me, hug her fiercely as if to say "See me! See me!" she would look into my eyes and smile vaguely, sadly, until I thought my heart would literally crack. She never wanted to face it, to discuss it, to admit that this was happening. I felt like she was lost, but she was always there—I'd look up from the bed while she was gazing out the window and it was *her,* in the *flesh,* and that kept alive in me a strange kind of hope.

Her family and their friends arrived in the city; we all spent the day together, and they all looked knowingly at me. That evening I left alone for London, as planned.

I spent the spring term at school, where it finally ended, almost a year after we met. Ultimately, I had to do it myself. We both arrived back on campus and got in touch; a week or two went by during which we ate lunch, met for coffee, and did the usual sort of things together, but as in Paris there was no spark at all.

Finally, I went to her room one afternoon. She was lying on her bed reading. I sat down in a chair next to her and said, "I think it's really time we talked about this." She stared at her book. Her tension was palpable; I wanted to make it as painless as possible.

"What do you want to talk about?" she said.

"I get the feeling that you don't care about me anymore," I replied.

Pause.

"That's not true. . . ." She was struggling with the words. "I just don't think I care about you in the same way that I used to. I think things have changed." I explained to her why it was important for me to *hear* this from her, to actually have it *said* and *deal* with it once and for all. I told her that not knowing for sure was the worst thing and that it was wonderful at last to be communicating sincerely again.

Her relief was visible and immediate. From then on, I asked if she was still interested in being friends and she gushed that of course she was. I hoped we could still spend some time together, and she assured me that she wouldn't want it any other way. I was so happy that she seemed at last to be looking *at* me rather than *through* me, that I seemed to finally *exist* again in her eyes, that I forgot about what was really being *said* here: We were breaking up.

It was maybe a day and a half before it began to sink in that things weren't going to be like they had been before. When I'd suggest activities, she always had other plans. She told me that she was sorry, that if she could make herself feel the same way that she had before then she would. I asked her if she had fallen for one of the guys she was living with in Colorado, and she flew off the handle. *That's not important. That's none of your business. I can't believe you'd ask me that.* Panic. A week later she's dating Kevin, a guy from school she'd met while out West. She began avoiding me.

I began to see Sarah in new ways, began to hear the things my friends were saying (that perhaps they had been hinting at all along) about our incompatibility. Had our relationship been doomed from the get-go? I wondered just how much of my affection for her had been based upon my emotional needs at the time. It seemed in my life that I just bumped into these girls I was serious about and that fate dictated my relationships. Not my own emotional state, but the chance meeting of one special girl. For a while after Sarah, I looked at it as almost entirely dictated by my own emotional state: I thought that if I was emotionally ready to have another big relationship, I'd find the girl to have it with and convince myself that it was destiny. As I see it now, big relationships in my life have probably been just as dependent upon my emotional needs at the time as they have been upon who it was I happened to meet during that period—a combination of chance and internal readiness.

I loved to hold Sarah, I loved to be close to Sarah, but did I love *Sarah?* What exactly was I waiting six months for? Why did the lack of physical intimacy over both of our vacations strike so fundamental a chord in me? Was she purely a beautiful object with whom I sexually validated myself?

No. The lack of physical intimacy at vacation time was a problem because it was the way in which we communicated. Since she didn't discuss her feelings very much, I read them in her body language. An affectionate hug around the waist was one sign that she cared for me. Being apart had a preservative effect on our relationship, then: Without communication there could be no unified evolution, and a relationship in stasis eventually goes stale. I got used to not seeing Sarah for so long, but without the physical we didn't communicate. We spoke on the phone but very seldom about how we felt, about "us" or what was going on emotionally. When I saw her in person, then, I needed that physical communication. Not because I couldn't stand going without the sex—I had done fine without it for three months—but sex would have given me a document to analyze, a script from which to interpret her feelings. I could have found affirmation in her physical interaction with me, but our halfway vacation was stifled by her parents' constant presence.

We never said that we loved each other. It didn't make sense to; I had told other girls before that I loved them and then proven myself false by breaking up with them. Telling someone that you love them is all very well and good, but where do you go from there? It's a rut. Once you say it, it immediately begins to lose its meaning. It fades. There is no greater emotional profession, but there are many types of love. I told Missy that I loved her, and I still believe that I did—I was madly, hopelessly, Romeo-and-Juliet in love with her. I wanted to surrender myself completely to our love. It was ridiculous. Wonderful, but ridiculous in the way only first love can be, with its talk of forever and eternity, of magnitudes beyond the mortal.

Sarah never got that into it. I don't know how Sarah saw love, but my guess is that she was saving it for later. This was fine by me, since I'd said it too often to other girls and soured it in my mouth. Clichés don't mean much, so we used little body language haiku. It felt like love, but perhaps both of us knew deep down that there was something missing (an element of clear and fundamental communication?), that there was some kind of unwritten expiration date between us that made it "not love." Further, although I feared it might expire within me, I now believe that from the beginning it was doomed to expire within her. That didn't stop us, though, from falling happily into whatever it was for the time being.

Looking back, I don't regret a minute of it. The experience changed my perspective on relationships. For a while I dated around, hooking up with friends and acquaintances, fulfilling the desire that flesh is heir to, but emphasizing the transience, the lack of emotional substance to such behavior. My partners and I would talk beforehand, making sure that what was about to happen "didn't mean anything." It was fulfilling physically and convenient emotionally—a handy kind of disposable love, you might say—or like instant coffee, one cup at a time. But after a year of that lifestyle, I began to feel a little hollow and hunger for something more emotionally substantial.

I often need someone to remind me that there is a broader perspective from which to look at my life: a girlfriend, a buddy, a parent. Usually, there is an element of understanding that exists between myself and my male friends that I don't think exists between myself and my female friends or my parents. I feel as comfortable with a girlfriend as I do with a best friend—I freely share my inmost thoughts and feelings—but sometimes there is some doubt in my mind as to whether or not they truly understand where I'm coming from in the same way that, say, Jeff would.

With Nora and me, it seems like an entirely new experience. Three weeks have elapsed. She broke up with her boyfriend a few days ago, and we've been seeing even more of each other since then. Both of us are happily in that phase of exultant exploration with which relationships characteristically begin, but I'm approaching this with a mixture of skepticism and hope. Will it be possible to develop our ongoing physical attraction as well as our actively evolving emotional and intellectual relationship? She tells me I'm unlike anyone she's ever dated before, but I've heard those words before. Still, she can explain her thoughts and feelings in detail, and I do feel as though we connect in a unique way. I don't want to kid myself any more—I don't want my actions to be dictated by my emotional needs.

I'd like to behave in complete accordance with my moral and rational convictions. I often catch myself doing otherwise, but I continue to make the effort. For example, there was a period of two days when the chemistry between Nora and me had become undeniable, but she had not yet formally ended her relationship with her boyfriend—"overlap," she calls it. I urged her to deal with that situation, even though I knew how difficult it must have been for her, remembering the pain and sadness I felt when Sarah was not straightforward with me. She discussed everything with him; she explained her feelings and why she felt the way she did. It wasn't easy for her to do, but he's an extremely mature and friendly guy, and she tells me that although he was hurt, he appreciated her honesty.

I hope that I'm better equipped to deal with this relationship because of what I've been through with Sarah. I'm very happy getting to know Nora, although I am wary of being hurt again. Communication is important to her, too, which is refreshing, and overall I feel good about the direction we've been taking. People may never meet Mr. or Ms. Right in their lives; the very concept of the perfect partner may be unrealistic in and of itself. If we all communicate, if we are willing to work at it, I do believe that any relationship can be an ultimately productive and therefore positive experience in our lives—and besides, isn't it almost more fun not knowing?

7 A Step in the Only Direction

This writer's central theme is coming to terms with being gay. The 20-year-old autobiographer recounts the emergence of homosexual longings in junior high school amid all the peer pressure toward heterosexual involvement. Ben has his first gay experience as a first-year college student, and he realizes that these feelings represent where he wants to go with his sexual life and that he must somehow come to terms with being gay in a straight world. He describes an excruciating coming-out scene with his parents that begins a period of coming-out to friends, though he avoids being openly identified as gay at his college because he perceives an antigay environment. Ben blames his parents for his reluctance to be more active in his advocacy of gay issues at his college. This resentment of his parents for their lack of true acceptance of his sexual orientation remains a powerful source of anger and insecurity for him, and it reflects his struggle to maintain both a sense of belonging and self-respect in a homophobic society.

"How can I study with *that* over there?" I asked myself over an open philosophy textbook. "Finals are coming so you'd better pay attention to your books and not to anything or *anybody* else," I warned myself. Still, I found myself rubbernecking awkwardly every time I heard one of the two doors at the west end of the study hall open. After reading the same paragraph about fifteen times due to my perpetual rubbernecking, *he* walked into the study room. Of course, I again awkwardly contorted myself in my chair in order to catch a glimpse of whoever may have entered the scene, and when I did this time, I found myself in a locked stare with a very attractive man. The stare, which seemed to last for minutes, could not have been more than a second and a half glance, but that was enough to make me forget about Mssrs. Kant, Hume, and Hegel.

Tim, as I later learned was his name, placed his things on the long wooden table right next to the door he had just passed through and sat down facing my back. I had to know if his glance was just casual or if it was more. I turned toward the clock and stole another glance at Tim. However, again, my attempt did not go unnoticed. Tim was waiting to meet my glance with his. My heart was racing! I was sure that everybody in the silent study hall could hear it pounding loudly in my throat. I could not keep myself from looking again, and I was greeted by an "inviting" glance. One time I was met by a rather forward raising of the eyebrows.

"Your attention, please. The library will be closing in thirty minutes. If you wish to check out books . . ." What was I going to do?! The library was closing, so I headed for the door—the door farther from me and closer to Tim. He had begun to pack up when I did, and he *just happened* to be at the same door at the same time that I was. He held the door open for me (literally and figuratively, as I'll explain later), and I passed within inches of him and choked, "Thanks."

"What's up?" he asked in a friendly voice as we headed for the stairs.

"Not a lot," I stuttered. "And you?"

"Where are you headed?" he answered with a smile.

My God. It was really happening. This beautiful man was making a pass at me. By the time we reached this point in our "conversation" we had reached the first floor of the library on our way toward the doors that lead to the west end of campus.

"Where are *you* headed?" I answered meekly.

"Would you like to go somewhere and talk?" he asked.

"Sure," I answered, choking on my heart.

Since that evening, I have had no doubt whatsoever about my sexuality. I am gay. I have always been gay. I will most likely always be gay. I am happy being gay. It is true that the fact I am gay creates some barriers in life for me, particularly in the political world and other professions. Also, the possibility of having a family is considerably decreased by the biological incompatibility with homosexuality. Finally, being gay has caused me to distance myself from people, like my family, to whom I would like to be closer. However, these are things that mean very little in comparison to the life I imagine if I tried to live a straight life as a homosexual. I couldn't live a charade like that. My happiness stems from my being me, and my being the only one who knows what is best for me. Homosexuality is not the cause of my happiness. My acceptance of it is.

But what about the first eighteen years of my life? Was I happy then? I will answer yes and no to this question. I answer yes because I was truly happy before my mind understood what it was to be sexual at all. When I did not understand sexuality (heterosexuality or homosexuality), I was ignorantly blissful. My troubles began when my body began changing and when my intellect began understanding those changes and the feelings they caused. Before I get into the inner conflict of my adolescence, let me say something about my early childhood.

I was the most self-confident child I knew. I wasn't afraid to say or do anything to anybody. In elementary school and in middle school I was always the "teacher's pet." Why shouldn't I have been? I was the model student: well-behaved, respectful, entertaining, and intelligent. It all came very easily and naturally. To behave in any other way would be to behave as I was not. As I look back on those years before high school, I see many things which I am now better able to understand.

In middle school I was very involved with the drama club. My singing voice is comparable to a cross between Elvis and Roger Rabbit, but I was always on stage in the school musicals. I was an attention "addict." My habit was more than adequately supported by the many attention "pushers" around me who were more than willing to give me a fix. I never had trouble dealing with people in the structured and regulated environment of school. However, out of the classroom I was out of my element and, therefore, a very different person. Still, I was very charismatic and self-confident until the subject of sex was brought up. I just couldn't participate in the "oogling" that my friends engaged in. I didn't find Danissa and her chest as inviting as everybody else did. John's conquest of Cindy wasn't the least bit interesting to me, particularly because I didn't yet have the sexual drive to engage in these behaviors myself. When I did develop this drive, I guess in eighth grade, I found myself equally disinterested in Danissa and her chest. Instead, I found myself very interested in Tony and his sharp features and muscular build.

Parties! I loved them then. I love them now. Soda and chips have been replaced by beer and more beer, but the idea of getting together with a group of friends (an audience) and sharing some stories and laughs is my favorite way to spend time. Well, maybe my second favorite way. Parties were great in middle school until I became sexual. An innocent game of spin-the-bottle among friends was a lot of fun. Actually, it seemed pretty inane to me. Why would anybody want to voluntarily enter a situation in which he or she would be forced to kiss somebody else? What was the big deal about kissing anyway? I must have played fifty games of spin-the-bottle, and not once did I get any pleasure from kissing. Kissing wasn't repulsive to me, but it wasn't attractive either, until I began to have sexual desires for men. I felt forced to play spin-the-bottle. If I didn't, I feared being labeled as gay. And I *wasn't* gay. That's what I told myself so often, in fact, that I actually believed it for a while.

Things got tougher, however, whenever one of my oversexed and underexperienced adolescent friends would suggest that we play a game of "French" spin-the-bottle. It sent a shiver up my spine and caused my stomach to contract to the size of a pea. They wanted me to put my very personal tongue into somebody else's equally personal mouth. No way! I wasn't even interested in putting my tongue in Tony's mouth. I don't know what I wanted to do with Tony. I think I just wanted to be with him, to admire him, to touch him. I put my foot down when it came to institutionalized French kissing, and this seemed odd to everybody else. "Why not?" my friends would ask. My answer was usually something like "I'll only do that with somebody special" and not "It's gross and I'm afraid to try it," which was the true answer. I laugh when I think of Susan (who later earned herself the reputation of being the class slut) trying to teach me how to kiss: "It's just like giving somebody a raspberry only into their mouth." Ick!!! More than four years would pass before I had my "first kiss." Needless to say, my attitude toward kissing is very different now.

Now, before I jump from middle school into high school, is the best time to say more about the relationship between my twin brother and me. First, I should note that I haven't told my brother Keith that I am gay. I do not feel that close to him, nor do I feel that he would react in a positive way to learning that his own twin brother, albeit fraternal twin brother, prefers intimacy with men over sex with women. Also, I have respected my parents' wish that I not tell my siblings about my homosexuality. Anyway, Keith and I always got along, and we always fought. We were best friends and worst enemies. In middle school we had different friends. He hung out with the tough Neanderthal jock crowd. I moved in more civil circles. My friends were students, actors, and other human beings.

Academically, I've always been a better student than Keith. I was enrolled in my school's Gifted and Talented Students program. Keith, on the other hand, excelled on the playing field, particularly the gridiron. I participated in athletics, as well, although I disliked most team sports and was equally as terrible at most of them. I even played full-contact football until the end of middle school when everybody got big and I didn't. I know that I only played in order to be "one of the guys." The pressure in my community to be this way was tremendous. I needed to be accepted by my peers, and the only way to do that was to appear to be like every other normal heterosexual young man. This pressure existed even before I became aware of my sexuality and was only exacerbated by my feelings of "abnormality," which I suffered when I began to have sexual feelings for men.

When we entered high school, the tables had turned. Keith was more relaxed and at ease than I was. I had a serious lack of self-confidence, especially in the social sense. I wasn't comfortable. I just couldn't bring myself to talk about girls and all of the other stuff that high school guys talked about. My friends loved to talk about all of the girls they wanted to sleep with, and I found it very difficult to feign interest all of the time. I did, however, more often than not, awkwardly participate in the talks about girls and sex. However, in the back of my mind was the ever-present feeling that I wasn't normal, and that I must change. This problem was exacerbated merely by being placed in the new physical surroundings of high school. Perhaps it is more accurate to call them "physique-ful" surroundings. My new, more physically developed age-mates of high school provided many more stimuli to remind me constantly of my feelings about men.

In high school our groups of friends changed. Keith and I started to hang out with the same people, most of whom were male and from the other middle school in town that we did not attend. Some played with me on the soccer team. Others swam with me during my one-season career on the swim team. I attribute my brief swimming career to the many distractions that the swim team offered. The only thing more brief than my career with the swim team was the "brevity" of the team's uniform. I barely made it all season without any very embarrassing moments.

My female friends were generally the same as those from middle school. In general, I never had any problems getting along with girls in school. I just never "got anywhere" with them sexually. Today, I am almost never intimidated by any woman, but I am often intimidated by handsome men. I don't know why this is, but I would venture to guess that it has something to do with my desire to be liked by men and my disinterest sexually in women. I am not sexist. This is not a sexist phenomenon; it is deeper and far more fundamental to my personality than any "ism" could be.

Keith and I are opposite in every way. He, as I've said, is a great athlete and a good student; I am a great student and a fair athlete. He loves the Grateful Dead; I love Beethoven. He is an engineering student; I am a liberal arts student. He is a registered Republican; I am a Democrat. He is a conservative thinker (an oxymoron if ever there was one); I am a liberal. He is heterosexual; I am gay. How do we get along? Honestly, I'd have to say that we don't get along. We were never very close except in proximity to each other. We don't agree on anything except that we never agree on anything.

I don't want to be like him in any way. Deep in my heart I feel that Keith is a fundamentally bad person, one who doesn't care about hurting others. I pride myself on my integrity, honesty, and open-mindedness. Keith, in my experience of nearly twenty-one years, lacks these elements of goodness. (He is very similar to my father, whom I will discuss later.) I must make it sound like Keith and I were and are constantly at each other's throats. That is not the case. It is true that we argue occasionally, but more frequently, I choose to avoid any argument by changing the subject at hand, particularly if it is one of the standard liberal versus conservative questions. I don't like to appear like a "flaming liberal," which in my home is equated with "flaming homosexual." As far as Keith is concerned, our relationship is a farce, a play in which one actor believes he is living his part and the other is simply humoring him. My sexuality, combined with my paranoia about discovery and then rejection, has caused me to isolate myself from my family and anybody else with whom I feel unable to be completely open. Nowhere were the fundamental differences between others and me greater than at home.

Keith and I are the youngest of six children. All together we are three men and three women. A regular Brady Bunch without the maid. There is a seven-year gap between my youngest sister and Keith and me. (Keith and I were not a product of Planned Parenthood. Instead, I believe that we were the product of the Catholic Church, or worse yet, my parents' ignorance about and inability to discuss sexual issues such as birth control.) Because of this dramatic age difference (thirteen years in the case of my oldest sister) I was never very close with my older siblings. The most time we spent together was when one of them (always one of my sisters) was forced to stay home and baby-sit. When I entered junior high school, my youngest sister was the last to leave home and go to college. Although I was never very close to any of my siblings, whenever we are together we always seem to have fun. Of course, all conversation revolves around very impersonal subjects, except for the standard "Do-you-have-a-girlfriend?" question which I have learned to dodge with great creativity and eloquence. I lie.

I lie because my family is very different than I am. I don't know how to explain this difference, but it has always existed, and I think it always will. It has to do with our fundamental natures, and mine was and never will be like theirs. They are racist. I am not. They care only about themselves and their families. I tend to look at life on a broader scale. This "bigger picture" has caused me to isolate myself from my siblings because I feel that they are unworthy of my attention. I am not going to agree with their racial slurs and homophobic remarks, and until I feel that I can tell them about my sexuality, I am unable to defend myself in the face of such remarks. My brothers and sisters are fun people to whom I would like to be closer, but until I can be honest with them, I will continue to alienate myself from them.

My relationship with my parents is very similar to my relationship with my twin brother. I love my parents very much and I appreciate all that they have done for me. At the same time, I detest their very existence. They stand for everything that I oppose. My relationship with my parents can be divided into two periods: our relationship before I told them that I was gay, and my relationship with them since.

Before I went to college, things between my parents and me were stable and simple. I succeeded. They praised. I did not spend a lot of time with them. Sure, they were proud of me, but, upon reflection, I don't believe that they really know what I accomplished. They were always more concerned about whether or not I needed a car than what pieces the Wind Band, of which I was the president, was playing for the seasonal concert, which they only went to out of a sense of obligation. We never discussed my interest in girls. Granted, it would have been a very short discussion, but they never even showed any interest. My father never had "the talk" about sex with me. I doubt that he has even said the word "sex."

I am grateful that my parents have been such good providers. However, I resent them for filling me with prejudices and hate which I still have to work to combat even today. Blacks are no good. Jews are no good. Puerto Ricans are no good. The English are no good because of what's happening in Northern Ireland. (My mother is a full-blooded Irishwoman who blindly believes that only the English are to blame for all of the violence in Ireland. I've since learned that this is not necessarily true and that my mother knows very little about her "homeland.") Finally, homosexuals are no good. This is what they have taught me through their actions and words. They have taught me to hate myself. I have learned to love myself since I have left home for college.

My relationship with my parents has been more of a farce since I told them that I am gay. Imagine that: raised in a household where the word "sex" was not even uttered, and I've told them that I am gay. I admit that telling my parents when I did was a mistake *for me*, but it has also reinforced my belief that they are fundamentally ignorant people. (I have a perhaps unfair tendency to freely interchange the terms "ignorant" and "conservative.") That was a lonely summer. I had lost Tim in the spring. He was nearly the only person who knew about me. (He had introduced me to a few other gay men, and I had met a few others after we broke up.) Working, eating, and reading. That's how I spent my summer of 1988. I worked all day long at two jobs. I'd come home and make my dinner. I'd then retire to my room where I read books with homosexual themes, like Mary Renault's *The Persian Boy*, Christopher Bram's *Surprising Myself*, and AIDS nonfiction like *And the Band Played On*. I used to leave these books around the house, and although I doubt my parents knew the content of them, I guess I left them out subconsciously hoping that they would get the message I wanted to convey. At the time, I consciously thought nothing of leaving the books out; I didn't want to appear to be hiding anything.

Periodically, my parents would confront me about my self-isolation during that summer. My response was always, "Everything's fine. I'm just tired." Then it happened. I came home from work one night and I was confronted immediately by my father. He said, "We know something's bothering you, and we don't want you to tell us that there isn't. We can't help you unless you tell us what it is that's on your mind. We are your parents and you can tell us anything. What's the problem?"

"I don't have a problem," I answered in a very insincere tone, but I was feeling rather pressured. My dad was getting equally upset. It was more than obvious that I was keeping something from them and that I wanted to let them know, but from where would I muster the courage to do so? I could barely speak. My breathing seemed to stop. I had to consciously remind myself to inhale or else I would find myself passed out on the kitchen floor.

"I do want to talk to you and Mom, but I would like to talk to you tomorrow." I needed time to plan what I was going to say, although I had done just that hundreds of times in my head already.

"No. I want you to talk to us now. We are your parents and we don't like seeing you like this."

I was nearly in tears. This was the big one, and I knew it. I had let the cat out of the bag (my parents hate cats), and it was only a matter of time before I would have to let them know. I suggested that we all sit down in the den. My dad turned off the television right away and sat down on the couch. My mom lit a cigarette and settled down in her recliner. I sat uneasily on a futon opposite my mom and next to my father. (I can't believe how all of the uneasiness is coming back to me as I sit here and recall what happened that evening in August. My hands are shaking as I type.) There was an incredible tension in the air, one which created the loudest silence I have ever had to break.

"I don't have a problem really. I just want to talk to you about me. First, I want to say that I love you very much and that what I'm going to tell you will not change that at all. I want things to be the same after as they were before."

"Of course. We love you and always will. You can tell us anything."

"It's hard for me to do this because I know you so well and because I treasure your love so much. I think that you both would agree that I am a good person who has never done anything to embarrass or shame you."

"No, you haven't. What are you trying to say, Ben?"

"This isn't easy for me. I want you to understand that I need you and that I don't want this to change your love for me. I haven't always been completely honest with you. There's something about me which I have to deal with, and I want you to know about it too."

By this time tears were streaming down my face. My mother was sniffling as she puffed feverishly on her cigarette. My dad was noticeably shaken and struggling to maintain himself.

"I'm not everything that I appear to be. Er, rather, there's more to me than is apparent. I'm not . . . I'm not exactly what you think, and it bothers me that I haven't been completely honest with you. I'm the same person, but there's something you don't know about me. I'm . . . I'm not . . . I'm not exactly . . . This is very difficult for me to do because I don't want to hurt you, but I also don't want to be dishonest. I'm not . . . I'm not exactly straight."

My God, I said it. It took me a while, but I came out to my parents. The silence was even more deafening than before. This time my father broke it by questioning me.

"What do you mean you're not exactly straight?"

I couldn't believe it. There weren't going to make this easy at all.

"I mean I'm gay." I barely choked that out through my throat, which had contracted to inoperable dimensions, and the tears flooded my face.

"How long have you known this for?"

"For a long time. Since the beginning of high school."

"Why didn't you tell us before?"

"Because I was afraid of being rejected. I don't want to hurt you, but I don't want to lie."

"Why are you telling us now?"

They were making this tough! "I want you to know about me. I don't want to be dishonest with you. I want some support in dealing with this. I don't want it to be something I have to hide or that we can't talk about."

"You say you are homosexual," (Did I actually hear my father say the "H-word"?) "but what do you mean by that?"

"I find other men attractive."

"Sexually?" (Wow! He just said the "S-word," too!)

"Yes, sexually."

"Why didn't you tell us before? We could have helped you."

"I wasn't sure before. Now I am, and I want your support."

Then it happened. For the first time in my life, I saw my father cry. He couldn't keep it inside any longer. He broke down in tears, jumped to his feet and hurried to the bathroom right next to the den. My mother and I sat and listened to him for a few minutes before I said, "This is what I didn't want to do. I didn't want to hurt you."

She choked through her own tears. Shaking, she said, "We're glad that you told us. We only wish you had told us sooner."

My dad returned after blowing his nose. He had pulled himself back together, but was still quite shaken. The inquisition recommenced.

"Have you told your brothers and sisters about this?"

"No, I haven't."

"Do you plan on telling them?"

"Yes, sometime."

"We don't think that's a good idea."

"Why not? I don't want to lie to them either."

"We don't think they will be very accepting of it."

"I'm not going to tell them right away."

"We hope that you don't ever tell them, but if you ever do, we'd like you to tell us that you are going to before you do."

"Okay." I wasn't about to make things worse by starting an argument. I haven't even considered telling my siblings after this fiasco, so this promise has been very easy to keep. After I graduate, I wonder if it will be as simple. We talked for a long time about me and how I feel and what they can do. My dad felt guilty and wanted to know if he did anything to cause this. I told him of course not, and that is not why anybody is gay. He needed to know why, but I couldn't answer that question myself. After about an hour spent discussing everything from AIDS to the destruction of the American family, my dad was again in tears. My mom had really never stopped. Instead of rushing from the room, this time he stood up and pulled me up to him and hugged me tightly.

"You're my son. We're always going to love you. We could never reject you. We only want you to be happy." This was the first time my father had hugged me in many years. He has only done so on one other occasion since, that being upon my return from my term abroad. My mother stood and joined our hug. All of us were crying. My father ended it and said, "I'm going to bed now." I don't think that anybody slept for about a week after that night.

Things were more than a little bit tense around the house for the next few weeks before I returned to school. We talked about my sexuality once more before I went back to school. They suggested that I not return to school for the fall term, and that I see someone professional in order to try to change my sexual preference. What preference? I told them that psychiatrists can't change people that way, and that I was going to go back to school. I was seeing a counselor there, and I would tell her all about what they wanted.

The theme of this second conversation was, "We're only happy if you are happy." I told them that I was happy and that I didn't know if I was going to ever change. They asked me to look into it by reading books and talking to a counselor. I said that I would, but I never did. I wouldn't know how to be anything else except gay. They told me that I had devastated them, but that they would never reject me as their son. They told me that they probably would never accept me as being gay, and that homosexual acts greatly repulsed them. I hate them for saying those things. The last thing I needed from them was guilt. I have to believe that they are not sincere in their claim of happiness in my own happiness, because they were making me very unhappy.

We have only discussed my sexuality on one other occasion during the next two years. It was in the car on the way up to school after my leave term abroad. They basically wanted a progress report on how my conversion to heterosexuality was going. I told them that there had been no progress, but that I had tried (another lie). They were terrified that their son was everything that the stereotypical "faggot" was. I did everything in my power to dispel these unfair and ignorant conceptions. I also told them that it wasn't something that anybody could change. That was the last time we have discussed my homosexuality.

If I had the opportunity again, I would never have told my parents about me. They have not been supportive at all of me and my inner conflict with my sexuality. In fact, it is an implicit understanding that unless I change, my sexuality will not be an acceptable topic of discussion. I am never to bring anybody home with me, as my brother would bring home a girlfriend. They have made it clear as well that unless I change, I will be unhappy and, therefore, they will be unhappy. What they don't understand is that when they ask me to be something which I cannot be, i.e., heterosexual, they cause me to be unhappy. I am happy being gay, and I could not be happy pretending to be straight. I refuse to live a life of self-sacrifice for the sake of my pseudo-happiness and their peace of mind.

My relationship with my parents since I came out to them has been a comedy at which I am not permitted to laugh. They worry about ostracizing me, and for this I am grateful. They do sincerely love me. What I don't like is the extreme overcompensation which occurs when I am around. When we dine out, they never bring up a controversial topic of discussion in fear that their flaming liberal, i.e., homosexual, son will embarrass them by dropping to his knees and performing fellatio on the cute waiter. Our conversations are very superficial, and tend to revolve around what I want to do after I graduate. I have cleverly come up with the interesting topic of law school in order to put their minds at ease. Basically, I am never told "no" anymore, which is nice, but not at all like the parents I had for the first eighteen years of my life.

One good thing has come from telling my parents about me, and from suffering the ensuing inquisition. It has forced me to examine myself and my sexual development in order to better understand why I am what I am today. I now understand why, when my father would take Keith and me to the racquetball club on Monday nights, I would be more interested in showering in the locker room and soaking in the whirlpool than I was in playing racquetball on the vacant courts. I also now understand why I could not help but have an erection when such showering and whirlpooling was accompanied, and please pardon the pun, by other club members. I understand now why I preferred to watch the men's gymnastics and swimming events in the Olympics instead of the women's basketball games.

The impetus for my first taste of sex was the men's gymnastics floor routine competition in the Olympics. (My first taste of sex was solo, so I should clarify myself by using the term "masturbation.") My parents, Keith, and I were watching the Olympics, which were on quite late as they were broadcasting live from Los Angeles. All three had fallen asleep, and I woke them to send them to bed. I, on the other hand, was not sleepy at all. I was glued to the set. In fact, I was mentally conjuring up some very interesting routines for two people. I decided to give one a try. I stripped down to my jockey shorts and watched the screen. Without making a lot of noise or breaking anything, I tried to imitate the more basic rolls and bends that were being performed three thousand miles away. I found myself with an erection. My tumbling was very pleasurable. Soon I discovered that my erection was leaking. As I had never masturbated before, and because of the intense pleasure caused by my movements, I mistook this pre-ejaculatory fluid for an orgasm. I hurriedly cleaned up, got dressed, and went to bed feeling less than completely satisfied.

It would be less than a week later, after several other similarly produced pseudo-orgasms, that I would experience my first true orgasm. It happened while I was asleep, but I still remember everything about my first and last wet dream. I was fantasizing about being at a swim team practice where none of the swimmers were wearing bathing suits. I remember the image of my being carried on the shoulders of one particular swimmer when I orgasmed.

The first sexual experience that I shared with somebody else occurred my freshman fall at college. It happened the night I described at the beginning when I met Tim for the first time in the library. I will never forget that night for as long as I live. I have to believe had Tim not had the courage to approach me that night that I might not be able to write this paper today. In fact, I might still be denying my homosexuality. I'd hate to know the miserable me if I weren't consciously gay.

As I have already said, Tim and I met at the library. We then went to talk in a classroom in the math building. We chatted for just a few minutes, deciding that it would be better to continue in the secured privacy of Tim's room, where we talked for about two and a half hours about each other and being gay at school. The room was quiet for no longer than five seconds when Tim rose from his desk chair and walked over to his bed where I was sitting. Then it happened. He sat down next to me on the bed and asked, "Would it be all right if I kiss you?"

What was I to say? I thought, "I've been waiting for you to do that for the last two hours." I said instead, "Yes."

It was my first kiss, and it was wonderful. The kiss was tender, yet passionate. It lasted only about two seconds, but it has set the standard for a lifetime. Our lips parted and our eyes met again. Tim asked, "Can I kiss you again?"

This time I didn't answer. Instead I brought my face close to his to be understood as an implicit yes. I was still more than a little bit nervous the second time, but I soon relaxed as that kiss developed into many more. It stirred in me what had been dormant forever before. One thing led to another and soon enough we were undressed and in bed together. That first time was very special for me. It helped dispel the ideas that even I held about homosexuality. Homosexuality was not dirty. Homosexuality was not perverse. Homosexuals do care for each other. Homosexuals can be happy. And I was happy.

That night began my longest and most important romantic relationship. I returned to my room in the wee hours of the morning and was categorically questioned by my roommates the next day. "I was studying very late, and I fell asleep in the study room." This lie was just the first of many. Lying was a fundamental part of my relationship with Tim. I did not lie to him, however. Instead, I felt forced to lie to everybody else with regard to my whereabouts and goings on. I have never been a very good liar, but I made it through my freshman year without any unwanted exposure. Such exposure was what I feared most. I was very happy with Tim as long as things were very secretive. My extreme paranoia about exposure forced me to hide my true self from my other friends. I do not blame myself for this paranoia. Instead, I blame the overwhelming ignorance of society, particularly that of the college community, with regards to gays and gay issues. This ignorance continues to instill fear in the hearts of most gays, including myself.

The beginning of my relationship with Tim seems like a fantastic blur right now. I can't even differentiate any particular evening from among the many nights we spent together in bed. I remember them all to be loving and passionate, but I also remember that I wanted more. I wanted to have more than a secret relationship which consisted of my sneaking across campus late at night to get into bed with my lover. I wanted us to be able to do things together, openly, without fear of accusation or embarrassment. I, however, was too paranoid to take that first step towards a more "normal" relationship. I was much too worried about what everybody might ask or think about me and Tim. He assured me, though, that my paranoia would disappear and we would do more together than just talk and have sex in his room.

Our first public appearance together, but alone, was playing racquetball at the gym. For a while we were playing quite frequently, at least three times a week. Other than his fraternity's parties, racquetball, and the very routine, but passionate, sex, Tim and I occasionally shared a meal together. Again, I was always afraid that someone would figure it out if they saw us together a lot. He was not as paranoid, but he, too, was concerned about exposure. Though Tim was then a senior, he did not think, as I did, that sharing a meal or playing racquetball with a freshman (even a cute one) would cause suspicion by others that one was gay. But then we began to get bored with each other, and at least we were honest in acknowledging that it was happening. As I said, the sex was very routine, and Tim wanted more. He wanted to have intercourse, and I didn't.

It really hurt me when Tim went on a trip to a gay bar in Boston with a few friends and admitted to fooling around with one of them. He said all that they did was masturbate each other. "Oh, is that *all?*" I asked, conveying the message that that was more than enough for me to be more than a little bit upset. This was the beginning of the end, I knew, and Tim must have known as well. I was still desperate to make it last though. I didn't want my love to die or to give up someone who had done so much for me. I tried to bring some more excitement to his bed, but it was very obvious that Tim wanted to have intercourse more than he wanted me.

And so our passionate love died before the end of April of my freshman year. We still share a common love for each other though. He is in California, and I am at school, but we still keep in touch. He knows that he will always be very special to me, and I like to think that I am still significant to him.

After Tim and I broke up, and particularly after I returned home for the summer break, I was very lonely. I wasn't about to jump all the way into the back of the closet from which I had recently emerged. I wanted to take some steps forward in the right direction—in the only direction which would guarantee my mental health. I decided to speak to a counselor at school. I saw her several times before I went home for the summer. She listened to everything I had to say, and explained to me why, perhaps, I was feeling the way I was. She helped me a great deal, and for that I will always be grateful. I was feeling great when the spring term ended, and with it my visits for counseling.

During the summer, I told my parents that I was gay.

My visits for counseling promptly resumed upon my return to school. I needed someone to talk to and the counselors at school listened to me. My counselor not only listened to what I had to say, but she also reassured me that I was not alone even at school in my efforts to deal with being gay. She explained to me why

I was feeling the way I was, and that these feelings were normal and healthy. She offered guidance, but she never told me what I should do. We talked about my parents and family, my relationship with Tim, and my being gay at school. I never left a counseling session feeling worse than I did when I arrived. In fact, I always felt very secure and confident that my being gay was not something wrong with me, but rather, it was a problem of acceptance on the part of others.

I found the cure for my loneliness in my new family: my friends. When I was "dating" Tim, I neglected my other friends quite a bit and did not foster much development of my relationships with them. Upon my return to campus after the "summer of my discontent," I promptly came out to Dan, who would later come to be my best friend. Dan and I got along great. We played racquetball together and had some classes together. We seemed to hit it off rather well when we first met. Dan is a very open-minded, liberal Californian. I thought that I could trust him with my secret, and I needed to share it with somebody.

I invited Dan to my room and asked him to sit down. He was more than a little bit confused. After about thirty minutes of professing my friendship and other beatings around the bush, I told him I was gay. He barely reacted at all. In fact, he made light of the tense situation by telling me that I was the third person to come out to him in the past two weeks. Apparently, he has a bisexual friend at home, and he used to live with a roommate who was gay. He also told me that there was a point in his life when he was questioning his own sexuality. Dan is not gay, however. I was not used to such a sublime reaction, but I most definitely preferred it to the more recent hysterics of home. Dan was very supportive of me and my struggle, even though he was going through a tough time of his own, as his parents were divorcing. I tried to be equally as supportive.

We grew together that term. We were almost inseparable. When we were with our other friends, we used to love to make comments which only he and I could truly understand. They were usually innocuous as far as the others were concerned, but sometimes Dan would try to put me on edge by seeing how far he could go before someone would ask, "What do you mean by that?" There was never any malicious intent—just good, sadistic fun between friends. I no longer have to hide the truth from my closest friends.

The following term, Dan and I went to Spain together on a study-abroad program. Again, we spent nearly all of our time together there. When we traveled we would usually have to share a bed because we chose to pay less for one bed than to pay more for a comfortable two. Having to share a bed with me never bothered Dan. This was a sign of great trust in me. Granted, I don't think he was worried about my making a pass at him, but his efforts to maintain a relationship where my sexuality was not the central issue was very important to me. I have nothing but fond memories of Dan and myself in Spain. We used to spend a lot of time just talking over a beer and a game of dominos in the town square. I have never been as close to anybody in my entire life as I have been with Dan. I shared my deepest secrets and innermost feelings with him. Likewise, he opened up to me quite a bit.

Dan and I decided to live together during the summer term between our sophomore and junior years at school. For the first seven weeks of the term our relationship continued to develop in the same positive way. After that things started to deteriorate. The reason for this is clear to me: Dan got a girlfriend. Stephanie lived down the hall from us. Dan and I met her at a party so wild he didn't even remember meeting her that night. Stephanie remembered Dan, though. She came by the next day and threw herself all over him. Before I knew what was happening, they were in bed together (a few days later), and I was now well in the backseat of Dan's life.

My analysis of myself with respect to this situation is twofold. First, I feel that I was very jealous of Stephanie. Secondly, I still feel that Stephanie is fundamentally not a good person. Was I jealous because I was being neglected, or was I jealous at a more fundamental sexual level? I have to admit that it would have pleased me greatly had Dan been gay as well. I think he has a lot of traits that I look for in someone with whom I would like to be involved romantically. However, I am being completely honest when I say that I really am not physically attracted to Dan. Therefore, I have concluded that my jealousy of Stephanie is due to Dan's behavior toward me, and not my sexuality.

Since they have been dating (sleeping together), I have seen Dan replace me with Stephanie. He no longer confides in me like he used to. Instead, he goes to Stephanie. He no longer has as much time for me as I am willing to give to him. These things are natural in relationships, but they hurt all the same. Since Dan gained a girlfriend, I feel I have suffered a tremendous loss. Perhaps my investment in Dan was too great, but I believe that it was reciprocal to Dan's own investment in my friendship. He, as far as I'm concerned, has chosen to invest elsewhere, leaving me feeling more than a little slighted.

I left school the next fall on pretty good terms with Dan. However, a new distance was created between us, this time geographical, when I went to work in the city for the winter months. Dan made little effort to keep in contact with me when I was in the city. I did call him occasionally, but I stopped when it started to feel like I was troubling him when I did call. My life in the city was dramatically different than it is at school, and I wanted to share it with Dan, but, apparently, he wasn't interested in hearing about it. Instead, I found others with whom to share my excitement. At the beginning of the fall term when I was at school, I came out to Jack and Paul. Jack is also from California, and even more open-minded than is Dan. He was very happy that I told him about my homosexuality and has shown a genuine interest in me and my coming to terms with it.

I was a little more concerned about telling Paul. I was worried that he might be intimidated by my homosexuality because I had suspected him not of being gay, but of being confused about his sexuality. I am now positive that he is not at all confused about his sexuality. He is perhaps one of the more "hormonal" straight men I know. I told Paul at the end of fall term after we had decided to share an apartment as we were going to be working at the same law firm in the city. I'll never forget what he said after I told him that I was gay. With a smile on his face and a slight laugh in his voice he said, "Hey, I've always thought that it's kind of hip to know someone who's gay." I almost cried. Paul is the funniest man I know. Living with him in the city, even in the close quarters of our studio apartment, was an experience which I would gladly share with him again. He will always be very special to me because he shared with me the very first period of my life in which I felt at liberty to do that which *I* wanted. With friends like these, who needs the support of an unaccepting biological family?

All of this coming out was in the context of my winter work-term in the city. I really miss the city; not only was it the arena for my coming out to three of my closest friends, but it is also where I first really lived. I secured a position at the law firm at which my sister works downtown where I worked hard and interacted well with everybody I met. My sexuality was not an issue, and I enjoyed what I was doing. If I had any concerns about my sexuality and my work at the firm, they revolved around the fear of my sister finding out about my postwork activities. I imagined a situation in which I would run into an openly gay attorney from the firm at a gay nightspot. He would talk about it at work, and through some indirect way my sister would become enlightened and freak out about it. She would call my parents, and they too would freak out. She would call my other two sisters and they, too, would freak out, until everybody in my family, nuclear and extended, all the way to Ireland and Lithuania, would be freaking out. As I am only concerned about keeping my parents ignorantly blissful, I blame them for my paranoia (and, perhaps, overactive imagination).

Of course, this did not happen, but I did meet one attorney at the firm while out for a drink in a gay video bar with two straight friends. Meeting him was special because I now had an ally in the very traditional and conservative law firm at which I worked. We would occasionally get together and have lunch. It was great to see that he was a gay man who was succeeding in the working world, the legal profession which I wanted to enter. However, it was equally as distressing to listen to him tell me how very closeted he was and how very discriminatory the legal profession is against gays, even though it has a very high percentage of homosexuals in its ranks. Apparently, image is of the essence in the legal profession, and openly gay attorneys do not help create an image of stability and competence which ultraconservative law firms demand.

My most important experiences in the city occurred outside of the workplace. Upon my arrival, I wanted to introduce myself to the gay community. I called the gay students' groups at several colleges, as well as the city's gay youth group. I went to one gay youth group meeting and found its membership a bit young for me, but I hit it off rather well with some members of another college group. By my second weekend in the city, my new friends in the student gay group took me out to the popular local nightspots. We first went to a downtown video bar. As we went in, I wasn't particularly impressed by the dark and smoky conditions of the noisy bar. My disappointment disappeared as we passed by the coat check and into the other half of the bar. Everybody in this section appeared to be college-age and very attractive. My whole disposition changed. I was like a kid in a candy store. It had been many months since I had been in a gay establishment, and that was in Spain, which is a completely different world altogether. The people with whom I came were talking to me, but I found it difficult to pay attention to anything except the dark-haired and dark-skinned gentleman standing very close to our circle of conversation. It would be a week later and in a different environment that I would meet Rob.

Rob and I were finally introduced at a gay students' meeting. I was very impressed with what he had to say at that meeting, particularly about the topic of that night's discussion: gay promiscuity. After the meeting he told me that he liked what I had to say also. We talked briefly about a dance that was to be held on Friday, and then we said good-bye. He called the next night about the dance and we decided to go together.

That was the introduction to a very important relationship for me: important because of what I learned about myself upon its dissolution. I really didn't love Rob. I even wonder if I really would find him interesting had we not gone to bed together so soon after meeting. I believe, upon reflection, that I was more interested in a relationship than I was in Rob. I lived a charade with him for over a month, therefore breaking my own rules about sexual activity. I have what some people might call an ultraliberal outlook on the topic of sex. I believe that there is nothing wrong with sleeping with anybody you want to sleep with so long as you meet a particular set of criteria. First, and most importantly, both must be consenting adults. Secondly, and following from my first criterion, one must never force another or be pressured by another to do anything in bed that one does not want to do. Maintaining this level of respect for one's partner is important if my third criterion is to be met. Nobody must be hurt, physically or mentally, by the experience. Lastly, and definitely not least of all, everything done must be done safely. It is obviously too dangerous in today's world plagued by AIDS and other diseases not to exercise the utmost caution as far as sexual contact is concerned. From experience, I would also say that sex where there is an emotional bond is incomparable to that without it, but I do not feel, as some do, that it is immoral to sleep with somebody just for fun, as long as nobody is getting hurt.

I was infatuated with Rob; he made me feel very special. It wasn't really until he came up to school with me for a weekend that I realized what the true story was. At school, I was in my element. He was out of his. I wanted so badly for him to fit in with my closest group of friends. He didn't. He didn't even try. I tried to include him in everything, but he just wouldn't get involved. I realized then that he did not meet the standards that I have for someone with whom I would like to spend, if not all, a good part of my life. When I first met him, I was impressed by what he had to say. That was the last time he ever impressed me. He just isn't an intellectual equal of mine. He isn't even mildly interesting. Again, I found myself with cold feet, and over a very long two-week period, I broke up with Rob. He didn't understand, and for this reason I feel that I have violated the rules surrounding healthy sex; I hurt him. However, I feel that I did the right thing by breaking up with him in order to avoid hurting him more. He told me that he would have liked for me to just have gone back to school and not to have told him how I felt. But I believed that such perpetuated dishonesty would be an even greater infraction of my own rules of sexual conduct.

Upon breaking up with Rob, I started to do some serious thinking about myself and relationships. I had really never had a normal, successful relationship.

I have come to the conclusion that there is nothing wrong with this, because it is not written in stone that relationships must work out. In fact, considering my relative inexperience in the relationship game, I would conclude that I have made some very responsible decisions which have helped keep greater harms from occurring. I think, though, that my standards are too high. I am never going to find someone with whom I am completely compatible. I have to learn to accept people's faults as much as I enjoy their good points, just as they must do the same for me. I'm not perfect, and I shouldn't expect anybody else to be.

My friends provide the criteria for a man to whom I would make an emotional commitment. First, but not foremost, he must be attractive. He must also be sincere and willing to share his deepest secrets with me. He must be funny. He must be intelligent and captivating. I see these traits in all of my close friends. Most importantly, he must be able to tolerate me and my quirks. Perhaps I should not be looking for a man with whom I can make an emotional commitment, but for a gay man with whom I can begin a sincere friendship. Only then, when I am his true friend, will I be able to be happy in a more intimate relationship with him. This may or may not be the answer to my romantic blues, but it makes a lot of sense to me. I still uphold my rules of sexual conduct, but I now would add another to the list. One should not become intimate with anybody one feels the potential for becoming very emotionally involved with, without first becoming their true friend.

I do have a couple of gay friends. One has graduated and the other is graduating. They, however, are not as close to me as any of my straight friends are. Why is this? The answer is twofold. First, I do not select my friends based on their sexuality. Second, befriending gays at school can be a difficult thing to do due to the lack of a visible gay community. The people who are openly gay do not seem to be the people whom I would normally befriend. Also, my fear of exposure keeps me from meeting potential gay friends. I would like to have some close gay friends, but I feel that it is more important to have true friends than it is to have gay acquaintances. I am also not willing to put my privacy at risk when I do not have the independence or support that I feel is needed to face opposition.

I have returned to school wiser but definitely more frustrated. There is a gay community, only a minute percentage of which is "out." There is a gay students group which holds weekly meetings. I went to one meeting during my sophomore fall, when I was still extremely paranoid about being exposed. I was desperate to find some people like me. I did not find them there. They were talking about marching on the Capitol in Washington. I was thinking about how exposed I was in the strange environment of the student lounge. To make matters worse, a random guy stumbled into the meeting unaware of what kind of meeting he was interrupting. He was picking up something he had left in the lounge earlier. I imagined that the first thing that the intruder did was go tell all of his friends (and mine) that he had seen *me* at a gay students' meeting. Now, more than a year and a half later, my views about this unpleasant experience have changed. I feel that it was one of the first steps I took toward trying to live my life as a gay man. True, it didn't work out, and I have not returned, but I feel that it was a step in the right direction. Indeed, it was a step in the only direction for me. I can't imagine what my life would be like now if I still hadn't confronted my homosexuality and begun to develop positively with it. This positive growth began long ago when I was just a freshman.

Where am I now? I'm very comfortable with being gay, but very uncomfortable with having to be gay at school. Why do I feel this way anywhere? I blame my parents. They will not let me be gay. They want me to be happy, but they don't want me to work for my happiness. I know that if I had the spiritual support (or even the complete assurance of financial support) of my parents, I would be, perhaps, one of the biggest gay activists on campus. Until my parents let me be what I am, I will never begin to realize what I really can do. If I had parental support in gay causes, I might feel very comfortable in the face of campus opposition. I might not fear exposure, knowing that I would always have their love and understanding. Instead, I am a member of my school's huge underground gay community. Here, my activism is limited to my close group of friends who do not need to hear my opinions about gays and gay issues. They are not the ones who need to be reached. The result is a community that refuses to come to terms with itself and its varied sexuality.

I am completing my junior year at school feeling like I am unable to make a difference in my life here or in the lives of other gays. My parents cannot possibly be so powerful! However, their financial grip remains on me. I don't want to hurt them either, but their happiness comes second to mine, as far as I am concerned. The opportunity to put my thoughts down on paper is my greatest step toward public advocacy. I feel that my experiences are similar to those of other gays, and by sharing them with them, and others who are straight, I feel that I am making an impact on others. However, I have not even been able to be honest with my parents about this autobiography project. As far as they are concerned, I am just helping a professor at school with some research.

What have I learned about myself? I have learned that I am a healthy gay man. I am happy with myself, although I could be happier in different circumstances. I feel that I am well on my way to living a productive life. I have learned that there are some things about myself which I must examine more closely if I am to live up to my own expectations. Primarily, I am concerned whether or not my dependence on my family is indeed more than financial. Do I really need their psychological support as well as their financial support? Is my love for them stronger than my resentment of their prejudices? Am I going to be the gay activist that I imagine myself being when I am finally free of my parents' grip? I will only know these answers upon graduating from college and dissolving my dependence on them. I suspect that the answers are complex. I suspect, too, that any other aspects of my dependence upon them will not be strong enough to keep me from living my life as I so choose.

REFLECTION

Being Young, Gay, and Ben

Reflections on Case 7

RITCH C. SAVIN-WILLIAMS

In his opening narrative, Ben reveals that his life has been similar to the lives of many other youths. For example, many of us, whether straight or gay, perhaps grimace or cast a knowing smile as we remember our Ben-like library experiences when we placed ourselves in a position to meet the romantic partner who would sweep us toward moments of ecstasy and stability. In this Ben is similar to millions of other youths across times, cultures, and species. Yet it has been a unique life in that a set of particular developmental dilemmas that Ben has encountered are faced solely by gay youth. Those differences are fundamental to understanding Ben; Ben did not choose them, has little control over them, and they permeate every aspect of his life. In Ben's words, with perhaps a mixture of pride and remorse: "I am gay. I have always been gay. I will most likely always be gay."

Ben's story does not—because it cannot—answer a fundamental question for developmental and clinical psychology regarding issues of sexual orientation: To what degree does sexual orientation by its very nature produce inherent effects in behavior, including social, cognitive, affective, and sensorimotor behavior? If the answer is "very little," then one assumes that differences found among those of various sexual orientations are essentially artifacts of societal or cultural influences affecting the ways in which individuals act, feel, and think. If the answer is "a lot," then biological or dynamic processes are likely causing linkages between sexual orientation and behavior. One of Ben's developmental struggles is to be like every other youth while not giving up being like no other youth. His "minority" sexual orientation, recently experienced on a conscious level as never before during his life, makes the uniqueness a relatively explicit developmental need. But Ben also longs for the "normalcy" of his peers and of fulfilling, despite his protests to the contrary, his parents' wishes. Complicating this dilemma is that Ben acknowledges not only how he fundamentally differs from his straight peers but also how he is at odds with other gay persons, at least as he conceives of other gays in a stereotypical fashion. I will illustrate these issues as well as others in the pages that follow.

There has been strikingly little research on homosexuality during adolescence. This is not because of the scarcity of homosexual behavior prior to adulthood but because as social scientists and clinicians we choose to ignore it, reflecting the wider blindness of our culture. Accounts are either retrospective (e.g., Bell, Weinberg, & Hammersmith, 1981) or limited by researching the fringes (e.g., hustlers, street kids) of gay youth (e.g., Roesler & Deisher, 1972; Remafedi, 1987a,b). Two recent large-scale studies, Herdt, Boxer, and Irvin's Chicago Youth Project and my own of upstate New York youth (Savin-Williams, 1990), are changing the portrait we have of gay youth.

But youths are also reticent to acknowledge homosexual behavior and a homosexual orientation. Only 1 out of 1,067 checked the "homosexual" box in a survey of adolescents (Coles & Stokes, 1985). More adolescents will "admit" to engaging in homosexual behavior, but their number is far fewer than estimates based on scientific sources would lead us to believe (see review in Chapter 1 in Savin-Williams, 1990). An additional difficulty is the complexity of defining terms and persons. Not all homosexual adolescents engage in homosexual sexual activity, many heterosexual adolescents experience homosexual activity, and many homosexual adolescents engaged in no sexual behavior. The synchrony between sexual identity and sexual behavior is absent for many youths. The value of Ben's story is his honest, detailed examination of how his homosexuality has affected, is affecting, and will affect his life course. This is a rarity because few youths have come forward with such insight and courage.

Ben knew his sexual orientation before he had sex. In this he is not at odds with most youths, whether gay or straight. He knew what he wanted, and he wanted Tim that freshman night in the library. But Ben was not yet prepared for anyone else to know; he had just begun the process of being able to say this to himself. Ben, similar to most males (I will not speak here of females), did not choose his sexual orientation. He longs to find happiness within the confines of that destiny.

Ben wants respect and acceptance from his parents, peers, and society—not at any cost but on terms he deems acceptable: without sacrificing his basic sense of self. He loves his parents, desires their acceptance and support, and emulates their value system, such as holding honesty as a lofty but frequently transparent ideal. Similar to many youths, Ben feels that his parents do not express sufficient interest in the real issues of his life, that they are not what he wants them to be, and that they embarrass him. Communications with his father are strained; his father acts in a sexist fashion toward his mother; and, similar to many father–son dyads in U.S. society, "the sex talk" never occurred. Ben rebels against his parents but recognizes that he needs them ("treasure your love") and does not want to hurt them. In growing up, there was an intense sibling bonding and competitiveness between Ben and his twin brother Keith. Although Ben takes some pleasure in listing their opposites (e.g., Grateful Dead vs. Beethoven), the reader should be impressed by their early attachment; they are fraternal twins, unplanned by their parents, who are "best friends and worst enemies" with fond memories of being together.

Ben begins sexual activity somewhat later than most youths, perhaps because he is, in terms of puberty, a late maturer. His first sexual outlet, a wet dream, occurred at 15 or 16 years of age and his first sex with another person is as a freshman in college. The delay may also have been enhanced by family values and Ben's desire for peer acceptance; the only sex he was interested in was condemned and forbidden by those from whom he most wanted acceptance. The former, family values, would not be unusual for most youths, while the latter is a struggle faced by nearly all gay youths. By virtue of being a late maturer, Ben is out of synch with his peers; his sexual orientation compounds this.

There are other ways in which Ben is similar to many other gay youths and not to straight peers: disliking team sports, feeling different and isolated from an early age, fearing emotional and financial rejection when coming out to his parents, feeling angry at his parents because he never felt free enough to express his true sexual identity, experiencing an inner conflict regarding the nature and social acceptance of his sexuality, being internally homophobic, having no positive gay role models while growing up, and having difficulty managing his career because his sexuality creates severe restrictions.[1] Most straight youths do not encounter these difficulties, whether because of societal heterosexual assumptions and the glorification of a "natural" heterosexual orientation or because of the very nature of heterosexuality. In either case, the outcome is the same: the noted contrasts between gay and straight youths. To understand Ben, one must recognize the developmental influence of these experiences and considerations.

Several developmental processes Ben shares with few others, whether gay or straight. Some of these occur among some gay youths, but I believe it is best to view these as residing in the intersection of Ben's homosexuality and life circumstances. In many respects they, in addition to the contradictions that Ben presents in his story, are aspects of Ben's life that should generate discussion because of their potential developmental and clinical significance. There are many ways to be gay during childhood and adolescence. Ben does not present us with a "classical" case of adolescent gayness. He is athletic (soccer, swimming) and interested in sports. His first "pseudo-orgasm" occurs while watching the gymnastics in the 1984 Olympics; his first wet dream contains athletic imagery. Ben associates primarily with other males and needs to be accepted by them. Discrepant from stereotypes, Ben is not sexually promiscuous but is a virgin during junior and senior high school. Friends in college seem surprised that Ben is gay, perhaps because he does not act in a stereotypic (effeminate) way. Ben feels he has more in common with straight than gay friends.

Yet Ben knows that he is feigning interest in heterosexuality (spin-the-bottle); he feels "abnormal." The homoerotic aspects of swimming threatened to reveal to Ben his homosexuality and so it was placed "on hold" until college. Some "pre-gay" youths assume this stance; others begin homosexual sexual activities prior to puberty and continue at a fast pace throughout adolescence. Their gay identity is firmly rooted—if not always desired—shortly after puberty when homophilia begins to make sexual sense. There is no one route to being gay.

With the first kiss from Tim, Ben's gay identity begins to escalate the internalization process. Their relationship must be secretive, not only to protect themselves from the homophobic world (e.g., Tim's fraternity[2]) around them but also from their own internalized self-derogation. Their relationship is based on lies and ultimately fails because they are unable to be authentic with each other. Ben cannot, although he wants to, perhaps because his own identity is so fragile. With their breakup, Ben feels lonely and frightened, cut off from his family and without the security of the relationship. Ben must now face himself and his "disgusting" sexuality. But he is a survivor; Ben knows how to find support. He tells the safest of friends (Dan, Jack, Paul) that he is gay, and they respond with support and humor. It is critical during this time that Ben be selective in who he tells and that he maintain control over the coming-out process. Ben learns how to build a relationship with a man (Dan) without the overt aspects of sexuality complicating the emotional, intimate bond. I will leave it up to the reader to decide whether the relationship was really asexual (emotionally and physically); perhaps the jealousy that Ben admits to when Stephanie enters Dan's life is a sexual one. In any case, the relationship with Dan raises questions for Ben and for the reader of what constitutes a homosexual relationship and attraction. If "sexual arousal" is not present, is the relationship not a sexual one? Were Dan and Ben "in love"? What is the distinction between a friendship and a romance?

Ben's gay identity is greatly strengthened when he is able to remove himself from the confines and inhibitions of college. In the city, Ben discovers the freedom, perhaps in part because of the anonymity gained, to pursue his gay identity. He is exposed to the complexity and diversity of what it means to be gay and of the forms that homosexuality can assume, from promiscuity to monogamous relationships. Through his first "out" gay relationship (Rob), Ben comes to a better understanding of his sexual self; he is more interested in being in a relationship per se than with Rob as a person. Because he could not date those to whom he was sexually attracted in high school, Ben shares with many other young gays the difficulties of inexperience in matters of love and sex.

Another issue that concerns Ben is a critical one among many gays and, I assume, straights: the distinctions among sex, romance, and friendship. In a relationship, Ben believes he wants someone who is "just like me" and who is "completely compatible" with him. Ben confuses friends with lovers. In friends we seek those who share our interests, attitudes, beliefs, and outlook; in lovers we seek those who fill our voids, satisfy our dissatisfactions, and complement our shortcomings. Ben wants a lover who is attractive, intelligent, funny, captivating, and sincere; these are characteristic of Ben and are thus characteristic of his best friends. Ben comes closer to the truth when he writes that he wants a lover who can "tolerate me and my quirks." Only in an idealized, mythic world do best friends become lovers.[3]

Ben's belief that it is "possible to have a healthy sexual encounter in which an emotional bond does not exist" is reconsidered when he wonders whether by moving too quickly to sexual intimacy with men that a relationship is precluded. Although Ben finds this may be true for him, many gay men (and straight, I assume, as well) who are in long-term relationships had sex on the first or second date. Ben does not appear to question our Judeo-Christian morality that portrays sex as the outcome of intimacy rather than as a means to that goal. Sexual encounters may be one of the best criteria for discovering whether an intimate relationship can form. Early sex does not preclude romance. I am cautious in making any general assumption[4] regarding the way in which relationships form. It is probably a very individual matter.

Ben's story contains several instances of apparent discrepancies, or at least statements that reflect disparities in thoughts and feelings. Ben speaks of inner conflict regarding his sexuality because while growing up he learned his parents' view toward homosexuality. Thus he came to self-hatred; however, Ben maintains that he is "happy being gay." In regard to his parents, Ben says he "detests their very existence. They stand for everything that I oppose." He blames them for teaching him to hate himself. Yet the story returns time and again to Ben's desire for his parents' understanding and acceptance: "Until my parents let me be what I am, I will never begin to realize what I really can do." Ben believes, on one hand, that he should be autonomous from his parents. He is fundamentally different from his family; they are racist, homophobic, and narrow-minded. On the other hand, Ben realizes that he cannot separate from them. It is as if he cares *too much* what his parents feel about his homosexuality. The reader senses that Ben speaks for a significant part of his own self when he writes that his parents will not let him be gay. When he is with friends such as Paul, he does not need the "support of an unaccepting biological family." But this is more of a statement of desire than of fact: Ben does not want his self-worth and comfortableness being gay to depend on his parents—but they do.

Ben also notes that he was never close to his twin brother Keith; they are "opposites." Feelings are frequently shared but never talked about among siblings; twins may have a need to magnify their difference in order to individuate themselves. The reality may not be so much that Ben and Keith are opposites but that Ben feels so close to Keith that he needs to distinguish himself. At some level, Ben may want to be like Keith or envies Keith because of his privileged heterosexuality. They are twins who were "accidents" in the life of their family, and in some fundamental way their fates are intimately connected. They are so close that they are competitors, and Keith has the heterosexual advantage. Ben separates himself from Keith by using his ultimate trump card: He withholds the most important, intimate facet of his life—his sexuality. I believe that these dynamics are far more important than "respecting my parents' wish that I not tell my siblings about my homosexuality" in explaining Ben's resistance to being honest with Keith.

Ben's need or desire to "get back" at someone, to punish the person for pain inflicted, is evident in his story. He harshly assesses Rob after the relationship with him deteriorated. Ben asserts that honesty is a key moral value in his life; he is honest with the people who matter to him most. Thus his most painful punishment is reserved for his parents: Because of their silence in regard to his sexual identity, he must be dishonest with them during this, the most exciting time of his life. The cost to Ben is particularly severe: loneliness and alienation. Although Ben says that his friends pick up the emotional slack, I am not convinced by the whole of Ben's story. This is not to deny that Ben's friends serve a crucial role in his life; they simply cannot fully compensate Ben's need for parental acceptance.

Perhaps the most moving is Ben's coming-out-to-parents story. It is both a typical and an ideal coming-out process that manages ultimately to fail both Ben and his parents. Ben warned his parents of his homosexuality by "subconsciously" leaving hints (gay books). His parents did not take the hint but they did display a very sensitive awareness when they asked Ben, "We know something's bothering you, and we don't want you to tell us that there isn't. We can't help you unless you tell us what it is that's on your mind." Ben at first denies and then dramatically tells them. Through tears and hugs, reassurances of love and support, and honesty the family appears to be strengthened by the event. Ben says he was "afraid of being rejected," and his father wanted to know if there was "anything I did to cause this." Ben sees his father cry and receives a rare hug. The father says, "You're my son. We're always going to love you. We could never reject you. We only want you to be happy."

From this ideal beginning, the love, support, and openness falter and Ben becomes profoundly alienated from the family. It is unclear what happened. Perhaps things were said that should not have been said ("They told me that they probably would never accept me as being gay"), and Ben began lying to them. Both Ben and his parents were far more comfortable not talking about his homosexuality; it was easier to ignore than to understand, to be silent than to discuss.

There are few "perfect times" to come out to one's parents. Ben says if he had to do it again he "would never have told my parents about me." Perhaps far more important than the initial telling is the continued need to come out to one's parents. After the initial shock, time is needed to absorb, understand, and acknowledge present and future implications. Ben attempts to make the best of this reality; it forces him to undertake self-examination and to turn to friends for support. Ben's story illustrates the consequences of an ideal beginning but a disastrous follow-up in the coming-out process. Ben went to individual counseling; as appropriate as this was, I believe the family as a unit could have prospered if they had entered family therapy at this time.

Ben's prognosis would appear to be a healthy one. He can find resources, such as counselors, books, friends, and gay lifestyles, to help him in his coming-out and identity processes. Ben does not yet have an entirely positive gay identity—he fears exposure by being around gay friends—but he is moving in a healthy direction. His humor and his insightfulness are strong characteristics in his favor. Ben understands the critical role that his parents have in his sexual identity process and that he is emotionally dependent on them. He blames his parents but wants their support; he needs to individuate from their grip without losing his connection to them. Ben understands that "homosexuality is not the cause of my happiness. My acceptance of it is." You may well ask, has Ben accepted it yet? If not, how much further does he need to go? How does he go about it? Can he accept himself without feeling that his family accepts him? Ben may already know the answers to these questions as we read his story.

NOTES

1. These and other commonalities among gay youth are reviewed elsewhere in Savin-Williams, 1990.

2. My experience has been that collegiate fraternities contain an unusually large number of homosexually inclined men, but such men are extremely closeted and homophobic—both in regard to themselves and as expressed toward others. They are attracted to fraternities as a "cover" and for the opportunities of male bonding.

3. I recognize exceptions, but I believe these to be rare among persons of all sexual orientations.

4. One example is Ben's notion that friendship must precede romance: "One should not become sexually intimate with anybody one feels that it might be possible to become very emotionally involved with without first becoming their true friend."

Ben: Eight Years Later

It is almost eight years since I put down on paper my thoughts about being gay in college and the interpersonal difficulties and triumphs connected with it. Recently, I returned to "A Step in the Only Direction" and was struck by how many of the questions that I had asked myself then have been answered during the past several years. I am not surprised that my beliefs and values have not significantly changed, but I am amazed at how the passing of time has allowed me to view many things quite differently.

One statement that I made repeatedly throughout "A Step in the Only Direction" was that I was happy. I would challenge that statement today. Certainly I was *happier,* but to say that I was happy would be a tremendous overstatement. That I still could not be myself with many people who were important to me, including my parents and my twin brother, definitely made me unhappy.

I had told my parents about my being gay, but I was quite disappointed in their lack of interest in what this meant for me, such as my relationships and my development as a gay man. During the three years of my college career that they knew I was gay, they never raised the subject except to inquire if I had changed. Likewise, I never raised the subject because I feared that by doing so I would stir things up and cause conflict. I had had enough of that already.

Strangely, it was not until my *siblings* learned that I am gay that my relationship with my *parents* began to change for the better. When I came out to my parents and they insisted that I not tell my siblings, I agreed because I was doing everything I could to avoid more conflict with them. Shortly after I graduated from college, my parents telephoned to tell me that they had told all five of my siblings that I was gay. They had not told me that they were *going* to tell them; they told me that they *had* told them. When my parents witnessed the support and positive reactions I received from my brothers and sisters, they started to deal with my being gay in a more positive way.

It was not long before my parents seemed quite comfortable with my being gay and with my relationship with another man, Luke, whom I met while in college. It is true that we seldom discussed strictly gay topics, but they manifested interest in different ways. They went to great lengths to make my boyfriend Luke feel welcome and comfortable at family gatherings. This is extraordinary behavior in the context of how my parents generally behave. My parents have not been happy with the spouses of my siblings, and sometimes their dissatisfaction is quite obvious. For them to welcome Luke and interact with him in a genuinely positive manner is shockingly unusual for them.

To this day, more than six years after meeting Luke, my parents continue to treat him with kindness and respect. I will never forget the first time my mother kissed him good-bye as we were leaving a family gathering or the first time she called our home just to speak with him. When Luke and I bought a house together, we needed a rather large loan. When I asked my parents to help, they did not let me finish explaining my request before my father interrupted with, "How much do you need, and where do we send the check?" They accepted only one-fourth of the loan in repayment before gifting the rest of it to us at Christmas one year.

My parents have come a long way since I wrote "A Step in the Only Direction." Then, I was impatient with their inability to deal with me and my sexual orientation in an instantly supportive and informed way. I was oblivious to the fact that their journey to acceptance of my being gay would be difficult and lengthy and that they needed time and education to begin to understand some of the things they were confronting for the first time in their lives. *I* needed many years to begin dealing productively with my being gay. For me not to see that they, too, needed time was immature and self-centered. The journeys, theirs and mine, continue, but we make them with love and support for one another. I am through blaming my parents for any unhappiness I may experience.

When they found out I was gay, each one of my siblings reached out to me almost immediately. They all asked the same question: Why didn't you tell me? There were varying degrees of emotion behind this question, the most intense coming from my twin brother Keith, who was clearly quite angry about not being told. I already had a rocky relationship with Keith, and the uncovering of this deception did not help. The depth of Keith's anger about not being told was revealed about a year ago when he and I were out to dinner while he was in town for a visit. Unconnected with any topic of discussion that evening, he interrupted the flow of conversation and asked me why I had respected my parents' wishes and not told him about my being gay. He was still angry six years after being told by my parents. It was an extraordinarily difficult question to answer.

Although he was angry about that element of our relationship, it is also true that my relationship with Keith dramatically changed once I was outed to him. We used to argue about everything, most notably politics. We seldom asked each other anything personal. We were twins, but we seemed utterly uninterested in each other. I am certain that my lack of interest was founded in the fear of needing to reveal more about myself to Keith. Since he became aware of my sexual orientation, I have felt less constrained about sharing my life with him and others.

Keith and I have become much closer over the past several years, and I have learned that my condemnation of him in "A Step in the Only Direction" was unfair. He is not a fundamentally bad person. On the contrary, I see in him kindness and selflessness, which I see in myself and other family members, including my parents. Keith has gone to great lengths to make me feel comfortable at family gatherings and to inquire about my life as a gay man in a different city. He routinely asks about Luke and has made him feel like a member of the family. These changes in behavior toward me developed over many months and are still developing. I, too, have changed the way I interact with Keith, and I am certain that we both view these changes as positive ones.

In my view, changes in me have facilitated changes in how I view Keith. It is clear to me now that when he did not know about my being gay, I resented him greatly. He could speak freely with our family and others about those things that were exciting to him, including his relationships and love interests. I, on the other hand, had to censor myself to adhere to my parents' wishes. Such self-censorship in the environment where Keith could speak freely and with great excitement and pride fostered in me a remarkable resentment of him and his heterosexual privilege. Since he has known about my being gay and I have been able to speak freely, that resentment has dissipated.

My relationships with my other siblings have generally been strengthened or, at worst, remained unchanged since they learned of my being gay. I was never particularly close to my older siblings, and that did not change dramatically when they learned the truth about my sexual orientation. One noteworthy exception is my sister Betsy. She has gone to great lengths to make Luke feel like one of the family. She has her children refer to him as Uncle Luke. Betsy is a physical education teacher for a public high school. She tells me that she speaks freely to her students about having a gay brother and that she confronts students who make antigay remarks. With the exception of Betsy, I am concerned about how my older siblings will handle my sexual identity and, more generally, sexual orientation issues with their children, my nieces and nephews.

My views about romantic and sexual relationships have also changed since I wrote "A Step in the Only Direction." I still believe, however, in the "rules of sexual relationships" that I enumerated in the autobiography, with one exception. I ended my list with "one should not become [sexually] intimate with anybody one feels the potential for becoming very emotionally involved with, without first becoming their true friend." To that one I now say "poppycock."

My experience with Luke confirms that this rule is simply silly. I slept with Luke the evening we met, and I feel deeply emotionally connected with him. Breaking my silly rule probably facilitated our emotional connection, as the physical intimacy of sex likely eased the way for the more challenging, in my experience, development of emotional intimacy. I wonder how much my "no sex before friendship" rule was actually a manifestation of internalized homophobia or a desire on my part to assign greater value to certain kinds of sexual relationships over others.

This is only one example of internalized homophobia I found in my essay. In another passage, I wrote that I prefer "intimacy with men over sex with women." Describing sexual activity with men as "intimacy" certainly sterilized this public statement, allowing me to avoid confronting others with my being gay and the behaviors that are part of my identity. In one short statement, I took the "sex" out of homosexuality, and I most likely did it to distance myself from what I feared would be judgment from others. What my internalized homophobia brought me instead was judgment from within.

Later in the essay I wrote that "I had really never had a normal, successful relationship." What the hell does that mean? What is a normal relationship? Part of what makes being gay exciting is that being *myself* is enough to break the conventional rules about relationships. To then characterize one kind of relationship as "normal" is to judge those who choose a different type of relationship.

Perhaps the most pronounced example of internalized homophobia is in my statement, "the people who are openly gay do not seem to be the people whom I would normally befriend." Openly gay classmates had the courage and strength to be themselves, for their own good and, indirectly, for mine, but I could not see that. Instead, I saw people who were "making waves," seeking out conflict for their cause, and flaunting their sexuality. I view those peers quite differently now and value them for their remarkable contributions and risks in an often hostile environment.

I, like all lesbian, gay, and bisexual people, must continue to battle internalized homophobia. We cannot eradicate decades of self-hate and doubts about our worth without perpetually confronting those doubts as we develop into self-loving individuals. I make it a point to be out whenever I can, even if sexual orientation does not seem to be pertinent in the setting or situation. I seek not to make others uncomfortable, but rather to make them aware of our differences and to help them to avoid making assumptions about people and their sexual orientations. If my being out does make others uncomfortable sometimes, then I hope they find some value in that discomfort. Certainly that discomfort cannot be comparable to the discomfort experienced by lesbians, gays, and bisexuals who feel that they must perpetually hide who they are from others.

I closed "A Step in the Only Direction" by wondering if my parents' financial grip on me was the only thing keeping me from becoming an activist. I suspected that their influence had a lot to do with my inability to be unapologetically myself—an openly gay man. I also surmised that the answers to these questions were complex. I was right!

My introduction to gay activism was somewhat forced upon me. When I graduated from college, I moved to Providence to be with Luke, who had been accepted to graduate school there. Luke and I were walking down a main thoroughfare in Providence during the daytime when three men attacked us. One of them leapt at me from behind, kicking me in the back; all three surrounded us, threatening to kick our "faggot asses." I have never experienced such fear in my entire life. We ran from them and called the police from a nearby restaurant. When the police responded, I was too afraid to tell them the truth, that we had been gay bashed, assaulted because of our perceived sexual orientation. The next day I contacted the president of the Rhode Island Alliance for Lesbian and Gay Civil Rights.

I became quite an active member of the Alliance. I soon became an outspoken participant at meetings and began working closely with the organization's head lobbyist and political strategist. Speaking directly with lawmakers about the virtues of statutory protections for lesbian, gay, and bisexual (LBG) Rhode Islanders was not an easy thing to do. Although lobbying and organizing others at the grassroots level was challenging, I had very strong convictions to fall back on when the challenges to our cause were particularly intense. No one was going to convince me that we were not pursuing the right thing, because I knew that we were.

I continued to work on political issues for the Alliance; eventually I was elected to its board of directors and then to the position of Vice President for Public Policy. I was privileged to be serving in this role in May 1995 when the Rhode Island legislature passed the bill. The governor signed it into law and Rhode Island became the ninth state to offer protection against discrimination in employment, housing, public accommodations, and credit.

Since the passage of the sexual orientation civil rights bill, I have stepped back from Rhode Island gay politics. Since the summer of 1991, I have been an administrator at a large university. There I have been able to be an activist of sorts as well. I took a leadership role in the university's social group for LGB faculty and staff. In 1994 I was appointed to a subcommittee of a standing committee that examines benefits issues. The subcommittee was charged with exploring and making recommendations about same-sex domestic partnership health benefits. In May 1995 the policy was approved, and I began working on implementation issues with the university's benefits office.

Not long after my involvement with the subcommittee, I was appointed by the provost to serve on the University Committee for Lesbian, Gay, and Bisexual Concerns. The committee is charged with examining and making recommendations about quality of life issues on campus for LGB students, faculty, and staff. The issues the committee explores range from academic, such as curricular issues, to administrative, such as benefits issues. I am currently one of the co-chairs of this committee.

Perhaps the most rewarding activist work I do is actually part of my job. For the past year and a half I have been working very closely but informally with a woman in my office who is responsible for supporting lesbian, gay, bisexual, and transgendered (LGBT) students on campus. She has taught me so much in such a short time about the lives of LGBT undergraduates and their needs on campus. I feel so privileged to have her as a mentor. Recently, working with and supporting LGBT students on campus has become a formal part of my job. This official role change allows me to give the important business of being a resource for lesbian, gay, bisexual, and transgendered students the attention it deserves.

My professional work with LGBT students may be the most rewarding activism I engage in, but it is not the most valuable. By far the most important gay activism I engage in is the daily activism of being myself without apology to anyone. Being out is not always easy. Sometimes it is quite difficult. I believe that if we are to make progress as a society on these sometimes complicated (domestic partnership benefits) but usually quite simple (equal treatment regardless of sexual orientation) issues, society needs to see and know LGBT people. I feel that it is the responsibility of those of us who can be out to be out. Some people cannot be out due to genuine fear of losing their ability to support themselves or out of fear of physical violence against them. I am not one of those people, so I must continue to challenge the assumptions that pervade society and the interactions between gay and straight people as they navigate through a heterosexually biased culture.

So where am I now? As I write this, I am on the eve of celebrating my seventh year with Luke. My parents support me and my relationship, and I feel closer to some of my siblings than I ever have. I am working in a field in which I feel I am making a significant impact on the lives of young LGBT students. My employer is supportive of LGB faculty and staff, and I live in a state where discrimination based on sexual orientation is prohibited. Certainly, many of these positive conditions in my life exist, at least in part, because of influences out of my control, and certainly, there is still much work to be done and progress to be made. It is also true, however, that I have made a difference in all of these areas by working hard for myself and others, and that is extremely rewarding. These successes—both those that are personal and private and those that affect institutional and public policy—are further steps in the only direction as my journey of self continues.

Loving Women

*This author describes the evolution of her sexuality from childhood sexual
play through heterosexual relationships to her present identity as a lesbian.
Rebecca was close to her father, who encouraged her intellectual interests,
until she finds that in junior high school she needs to discount her
intelligence and shun academic success in order to be popular. The resulting
breach with her father is never repaired and seems to be a turning point; if the
price of a man's love is conformity to being what he wants you to be, she can
live without it. Toward the end of high school, her troubled boyfriend
overwhelms her with his emotional needs and reinforces the sense of
emptiness and not being fully understood in heterosexual relationships. In
college Rebecca develops close platonic relationships with women in which
she feels for the first time appreciated for her intellectual and emotional
strengths. She finds that being comfortable with herself is most possible in
intimate relationships with women.*

When I think of my preadolescent years and who I was, I seem to remember
myself being much the same as I am now. I remember the same moments of standing still, listing adjectives that located me in my world. I'm sure that my list
changes, as my context has surely changed and shaped me with its changes. Yet I
have remained remarkably similar in my method of taking stock. I start by sitting
alone either in my bed with my fan or my clock, or outside on some type of rhythmically moving object—a swing or something. I like a regular beat. I first describe
in detail, to myself, the physical surroundings and the time frame that I'm in. I
guess it gets me into an observant framework.

After I establish the framework, I recount each of the relationships that are
crucial to me at the time, usually concentrating on their expectations or perceptions of me and following with expectations or desires of my own. If I'm feeling
strong joy, resentment, anticipation, or confusion, I try to list or chronicle the
events or tensions that led to these feelings. If I think that I want to cry or scream, I
definitely do it now—I find that I can't *really* cry spontaneously or in front of anyone else, unless it's my mom or my brother and I'm frustrated or angry—loneliness

or heartbreak crying happens when I decide I'm ready for it. Finally, I think about myself as a part of a bigger structure—sometimes I ask myself if I'm believing in God at the time, and that varies. If I am, I first do the Catholic prayers that I learned growing up, very quickly, followed by a very slow analysis of them. For instance, I say, "Our Father, who art in heaven, hallowed be thy name. Thy kingdom come, thy will be done. . . . Is God a father, is he like my father? Can He be in Heaven, is Heaven a different place from this one, how is it different? And is God's will what is done? Who is to know what He wills and how to do it, especially when it seems so improbable that everything priests say that God wills should actually be done?" It goes on like that, which is the only way that I can eke meaning out of it.

In the last few years, I've articulated to myself a direct challenge to my idea of God—that is, when I'm believing in God. I do not believe that God is actually a He. Now, my mother thinks that I'm crazy to be so concerned with the male-oriented language of prayers. She tells me that I can, of course, imagine a gender-less God. But this isn't really true, or at least it's not that simple. It's not just a product of intellectual acceptance of feminism and the fact that I've learned to criticize anything produced out of a patriarchal system. It's that I honestly can't pay attention to praying in any religious language that I've learned. I fall dead asleep at night when I try to pray in any form that I associate with Catholicism. And I'm sure that it's because I've incorporated the image of God as man—not a physical man like that trite grandfather image, but just someone who doesn't understand women, or at least me. Someone distant and very analytical and fair, but in a strident, formal way. I guess God just doesn't appeal much to me as "He" is constructed by the church.

My next step in the debriefing process is to bring it back into myself. I list the things that have always been true of me—most of them having to do with how I interact with others, but not all of them. I'm smart, I'm motivated, I'm eccentric, I'm honest (blunt), I'm caring. I'm high strung, I'm independent to the point (sometimes) of being selfish or claustrophobic or cold when pressured. I take stock of myself physically, describing myself as if I see me walking down the street. I end up with my mom and my dad—how I'm so like both of them and how I am also so different that they could not have anticipated how different I would be.

The first real memories that I have of myself outside of my familial role are based in what I remember of the descriptions and actions of my first best friend, Kelly. Apart from my family, who obviously contributed most to my sense of myself, she really shaped a lot of my view of me. She told me a lot about what she thought of me, but she also modeled attitudes for me, which I either absorbed or rejected. She introduced me to the idea of sex, of romantic relationships, and of physical maturation, all of which dramatically affected my own feelings toward approaching adolescence.

I met Kelly when I was in second grade, and the school that I moved into was a very small private school for girls. We had only thirty girls in our grade, and the academic and social roles were already well established when I came into the middle of second grade. These roles barely shifted in the six years that I attended the school, with the notable exception of Kelly's leading role in both areas. I don't remember how we established the best-friend-ship, but I do remember it happening almost immediately. I am pretty sure that it had to do with academic success. Kelly was the "smartest" when I got there. Within one or two weeks, I was her rival. She made the overtures, and we started an intense and very competitive relationship. We were always together, and we were always competing. We wrote plays, and we did extra math in our playtimes, racing with each other to finish the exercises.

Kelly told me once that I was smarter than she was, and it completely floored me. My immediate reaction was to protest vehemently that it was she who was the smarter, because I had always sensed a territorial tone and aggressiveness that had been the precipitating factor of our entire competitive dynamic. It seemed to me that our friendship worked on the premise that she was the dominant mind and I was her most worthy challenger. I was comfortable in the role. It was worthwhile to me to be second if it secured our friendship. A mutual friend told me that Kelly had said that she had always envied my intelligence—that she had always had to work harder than I did to end up at the same level. It made me feel displaced from the friendship all over again.

Kelly was the first person who made me aware that I was intelligent. She was the first person who showed me how dangerous intelligence, especially intellectual comparison and competition, can be to a friendship. She was also a positive precedent, however, for future friendships based on intellectual compatibility.

Kelly told me that I would get my period, which meant that I could have babies. She told me that I'd bleed a lot, uncontrollably, and that it would happen every six months and it would keep on for weeks. She told me that it would happen any day now (we were eight years old), and that when it did happen everyone would know because my breasts would get big and I'd have to wear a bra. I was incredibly distressed about all of this. I cried and cried and spent hours pressing my chest in to keep it from growing. I dreaded the blood and somehow I connected it to growing old and separating from my mom. I was too ashamed to tell her what Kelly had told me. Finally I had a nightmare and she figured out what had happened and then set it straight for me, trying to convince me that menstruation would be a wonderful event and that it probably wouldn't happen to me for a few years. I felt a little better, but never entirely confident that I would adjust to it all.

Kelly told me a lot about sex. In fact, she told me everything that I knew about it until late in fourth grade. Kelly's parents had given her some information about the actual act of intercourse early in second grade. I guess that they told her about male and female genitalia, which I already knew, but also about how intercourse actually works. They also told her that intercourse takes place in heterosexual romantic situations, and that they did actually have and enjoy sex themselves. This blew my mind.

Kelly explained to me all about the penis and the mature vagina and told me that I would definitely want a penis in my vagina, that I would have a boyfriend or a husband, and that this would be something I would do. She also explained something about being sexy, which was certainly nothing I had thought about before. She had all these old *Playboy* magazines from her dad's closet which gave us very explicit ideas about both the act of intercourse and the sexy woman. I remember being very excited about all these pictures, but very sure that all of this was a big sin. Still, my admiration for Kelly and her vast knowledge won out over religious restraint and it became our secret fund of coveted information.

Kelly first suggested that we play games based on sex in third grade. She would always act the man's part—she'd be my boyfriend. I was supposed to be sexy and receptive, and she'd seduce me. We tried to switch it around, but that never seemed to work. In retrospect, I guess it was because Kelly was always dominant in our friendship. She made up the rules for these games, and she had to be the one to control their progress. We would lock the door to our rooms, take off our clothes and try to figure out how to pretend to have sex. We were really scared of getting caught, especially me.

Kelly publicized our expertise and her magazine store. We were already leaders among the girls, so we kind of started a trend. Third and fourth grades were the slumber party years, so Kelly set forth a slumber party game which became sort of routine. We would all get dressed and made up, designate judges, put on music, and have strip shows. These became more and more elaborate, despite the risk of parents figuring it out. That was the extent of it—we never got as physically close as Kelly and I did. There were some girls who were really into it, and some who weren't, but we all did it. I never let on that it was really exciting to me; I always acted nonchalant and waited for Kelly to suggest it.

In fifth grade there was a huge turn of events. The whole attitude of the class toward academic achievement changed dramatically. All of a sudden, with the increased attention to boys at other schools, a new *type* became popular. It was not at all cool to be smart, nor was it cool to be at all involved with teachers. It was cool to be making bad grades, to be disrespectful to teachers, to smoke and to drink. The best thing to do if one was smart was to deny it. To be "modest"—in other words— I deprecated myself constantly, in hopes of remaining popular. It was a constant struggle to continue to please myself and my teachers, which I wanted to do, and to please my peers. The main connection here is that Kelly refused to deny her intelligence and she remained openly assertive about what was important to her— pleasing her parents and teachers and making good grades. Everyone turned against her, and the weapon of choice was the accusation of lesbianism, which fit conveniently with everyone's newfound interest in boys. I was incredibly relieved when Kelly switched schools in sixth grade, because I had been afraid that she would tell them what we had done. She was a constant reminder of something I wanted to forget.

My self-image, although influenced in key ways by my peers in my early adolescence, was always colored by my perceptions of what my father thought about me. Throughout my childhood, my father was my role model. I remember spending a lot of time with him until I was about 8 or 9. He was funny, interested, and challenging for me during those years. He was always intent on hearing what I had to say and encouraging me to express my ideas. It isn't surprising that I imagined growing up and practicing medicine as he did, and he certainly did encourage me to believe that I could accomplish whatever I wanted. He told me that I was very intelligent when I was about 7 or 8 years old, and I understood him to mean that I was like him, that we shared a special and elite bond. I asked him how he knew, and he told me that he could tell by my ability to converse.

For as long as I could remember, we had had intellectual play—we worked together constructing plastic models of the human body, and he would take me to the lab on Saturdays so that I could work with the lab equipment to run experiments. I remember researching and writing a twenty-page report on the cell just for fun, to give him as a present. It was understood that I was to excel in school; he certainly ascribed to a competitive model of assessing academic success. He always knew which other girls in my class were my rivals, and he was very interested in my comparative analysis of all of our performances. My mother had a problem with this, and Dad and I kind of went underground with the commentary sessions, sort of forming an alliance against Mom, who clearly didn't understand the importance of all of these measurements. I was impressed by my father's obvious intelligence, and I trusted that he was absolutely right to push me as hard as he did. I felt no resentment at that time, only admiration. I think my father picked me out to succeed, to fulfill his hopes, and this is why he never harped on the negative impact that being female would have on my chances. I'm glad of that, even if I resented the extreme pressure, since I feel it gave me strength as a female that many of my female friends never developed.

My interests started to diverge from those of my father in fifth or sixth grade, when academic success or ambition became taboo for the girls in my peer group. In our setting, a small private girls' school, peer opinion was crucial, and deviants from the accepted trend were treated very cruelly. There were no alternative social groups in our class of twenty-five, so it was adapt or be absolutely miserable. The girls devised ingenious tortures, which really scared me into line. Name-calling, mostly, but sometimes they would steal lunches, or write on lockers, or call up the boys who would be, I supposed, appalled at these academic statistics.

The only acceptable reaction was public, intense self-deprecation and real deference to the loudest ringleaders (inevitably not those making good grades) in every extracurricular group event. Sometimes, we were even required to cheat for them in tests and homework. Above all, tattling or visible signs of distress were reactions that were punishable by being ostracized from the group. I managed to stay in with the "popular" girls and, perhaps more amazing, to convince myself that I was happy at the school and in their group. I missed test questions on purpose, though never enough to seriously jeopardize my grade. I just wanted to avoid the announced list of A+ tests. I was really torn. I had always looked up to my teachers, and they liked me. And my father, of course, was fit to be tied. He sensed, as did my teachers, that I was purposefully decreasing my academic standards.

Over the course of these three years, my feelings about the kind of interaction I had always had with my father changed dramatically. Instead of enjoying the intellectual exchange, I shied away from it. I don't think my dad could understand why this happened. He's very "logical," very driven, and very emotionally distant. I never felt comfortable discussing anything personal with him; I felt he thought my friends were really silly and unworthy of his or my time. It wasn't until I switched schools in that first year of high school that we were able to reestablish any connection at all.

I had strong friendships in high school, but none of them had as much impact on my current view of myself as my first real "love" relationship. At the very end of my senior year of high school I became involved with Jason. It lasted throughout my first year of college, and it has conditioned my responses to love relationships since. I suppose, in retrospect, that it was very serious or intense, although it really crept up on me. I had always intended to avoid the dependence that eventually developed on his part, yet I seemed to miss obvious clues, or at least to avoid confronting them straight out.

Jason was two years older than me, and although I had been vaguely aware of him in high school, I never planned or even anticipated getting any more involved with him after he graduated. He initiated the dating, and when he came home for the summer, he avidly pursued both my time and my emotional involvement. Because I had just recovered from a breakup with a guy who didn't have the inclination to be committed at all, Jason's attention came as a welcomed change of pace. He was very charming, very attentive, very interested in my family, and very interested in finding out about things I enjoyed—books, plays, whatever it was that I wanted to do. Within a month we were together constantly, and he was saying that he loved me. I thought that I loved him, too, although I knew that I was attracted to him because of the way that he felt about me. He came across as very glib, witty and carefree—people were drawn to him. I felt privileged to penetrate that act—as if that was what intimacy was all about. In a bizarre way, I was really attracted to the disturbed, depressed side of his personality, which often came out when we were alone; I loved feeling as though I could help him.

I felt like I was a crucial source of positive energy for him. He would confide in me—he was angry with his father, he was worried about the alcohol and drugs on which he depended, he couldn't see any positive future for himself postgraduation, he was convinced that he couldn't be happy on his own, he would rather die than be alone. I would listen to him cry, and I would tell him that there were things worth doing—emotional and intellectual. I would tell him that we would do them together, and that then he would be okay on his own. I guess that I started feeling stifled after this scene replayed over two months, but by the time I noticed a desire to spend time alone and the need to rethink the benefits of all these pursuits, I was already inextricably involved with Jason. I worried that he needed me to help him find some self-esteem. He had mentioned suicide enough for me to feel a heavy responsibility. Probably worse, nobody could believe the seriousness of his depression, since his carefree social demeanor was so well constructed. My mother and my friends thought that I exaggerated, and I knew that his friends would never believe it. It seemed completely impossible, since he was manic in public. This increased my sense of being isolated in a relationship which was only real to the two of us. I considered it selfish of me to want to be alone or away from him, so much so that I rarely consciously articulated the desire to do so. Instead, I just felt frustrated.

I made the decision to have sexual intercourse with Jason in the middle of that summer. I decided then that the intense attachment and need I perceived and felt must be love, or the strongest feeling that I was capable of at that point in my life. I discussed this in depth with Jason and also with one of my best girlfriends. It was an extraordinarily difficult decision to make, especially because I knew that I would not be able to discuss it with my mother. Both of my parents are serious Catholics and had always taken a firm stand against premarital sex. I remember thinking that I might never be involved in something so serious again, although I don't remember thinking that I'd be involved with Jason forever. He did not directly pressure me to have sex with him, but he made it clear that he thought that sexual intimacy was a natural step in our already intensely developed emotional relationship. We went through God, sin, lying to my parents, birth control, and my fears about the actual act countless times. I went to Planned Parenthood with my best friend and cried the whole way home after the physical and the Pill lecture.

I definitely decided to have sexual intercourse because it seemed important to him. I had never been very involved in the sexual aspect of our relationship. I was completely alienated emotionally from the physical interaction, so I never really had any physical response worth mentioning. I certainly never had an orgasm, and he didn't ever ask if I had or, if not, why I hadn't. It never crossed my mind to care—I just assumed that the sexual dimension of the relationship wasn't important to me in itself. The actual act, which I had never really planned for, didn't impress me as very different from the foreplay stuff that we had been doing all along. I don't remember disappointment; I hadn't been expecting anything amazing. Intercourse seemed inconsequential compared to my reaction.

My response seemed completely bizarre to Jason, but to me it made complete sense. I kicked him out of my bed (my parents were out of town) and I started reading all of my old letters and journals from camp and high school. I played my favorite tapes and informed him that I wanted to cry alone. After he was gone, I cried about leaving my mom and my room and my high school routine. I cried about growing up, which I had never wanted to do. I didn't feel guilty then, although I knew that I had been rationalizing my way into a sexual relationship that I had learned was sinful. At the time, I just felt old. It wasn't horrible. It was just the event that I needed to release all of the separation anxiety that I was feeling before leaving home for college. It definitely didn't have much to do with Jason.

As soon as I left for college, Jason broke down. He called daily and cried on the phone; he was usually so drunk that I had to call his friends at home to tell them to go pick him up at the fraternity. So, feeling guilty about my responsibilities to Jason and the resistance it evoked in me, and simultaneously attempting to rationalize some sort of separation from him, I started in on myself with a guilt trip about my sexual relationship with him. I had nightmares about Hell and I told him that I wanted to break off the sexual aspect of our relationship, or at least the intercourse. He reluctantly agreed. The guilt culminated at Christmas time, when I decided that I should confess the whole thing before Christmas Day.

I hadn't been in a confessional since eighth grade, but I managed to drag myself in and tell the very old priest that I had had sex with my boyfriend. He said,

"Fornication!?! How many times? Less than fifty? You are very lucky that you have come for forgiveness, for you were going straight to Hell. Do you steal, too?" Needless to say, I barely made it through the prayers, and when I emerged shaking, my mom asked me why. I couldn't tell her, and that made me cry. The religious guilt served both to reinforce my sense of desperation to get out of the relationship and my anger at myself for arriving at that point. It gave me an impetus or even an excuse to leave Jason, even if it left me more confused about the place of sex within intimate relationships.

It took the rest of the year to get out of it. Jason wasn't willing to let me loosen it up at all; he definitely fought it. I told him that I would not see him until summer, when we would discuss it again. I started seeing someone else, which ended with him calling at all hours of the night to make sure that I was in my room alone. His friends called me to yell at me. I told him in May that I wasn't even willing to try to work it out over the summer. He pulled out every insecurity that he knew that I had and tried to throw them in my face. He took my confidences about my family—my fear that I was really selfish with them, even unable to move out of myself in dire situations when Mom (especially) really needed my support—and used them to retaliate. I remember him telling me that he was the best that I would ever have, that he knew that deep down I was too selfish to ever care for or love anyone, and that no matter who tried to tell me otherwise, he knew me better, and he knew the truth. I was afraid for a long time that he was right.

This relationship precipitated a screening process which is just starting to break down in my final year of college. I find myself unbelievably conscious of my own emotional independence, almost to the point of being incapable of sustaining any "love/romantic"–type relationships once they require a commitment. As soon as I detect any signs of a lover's "neediness," I start to back out of the involvement. I am reluctant to become involved with anyone who seems emotionally inconsistent; I'm very wary of tears or "melodrama." And I'm definitely reluctant to become involved with any men sexually. I like to have my physical space to myself—I have since refused any sort of cohabitation with my male lovers. I'm not sure how much of a correlation there is between my lack of interest in intercourse and the associations I have from its role in my relationship with Jason, but I'm sure that it is connected. Often that guilt which seems to be religion-based emerges in these situations. I think, though, that this guilt marks a reaction to being pressured by the men with whom I am involved, and from whom I would like to break away. I think that this guilt serves as an easier route away from oppressive relationships than confronting the claustrophobia I feel directly.

In the winter of my first year I took my first women's studies class. It was challenging, and it provided the first real professor–student contact that I had had at the college. I had been surprised at the distance I had felt from my professors first term. In high school, I knew all of my teachers well. I spoke often in some classes, depending on how the boys treated me. For my first term at my college, I hadn't spoken in class nor had I spoken to any of my professors outside of the classroom. The women's studies class was very small, discussion-oriented, and my professor insisted on seeing each of us in her office for conferences. She encouraged me to continue taking Women's Studies, and she gave me a sense of confidence about my academic work.

I also came into contact with some of the more active feminists on campus through the class. I began to be aware that there were women and some men on campus who were interested in the issues that interested me; I became somewhat involved in the countermainstream politics on campus, especially with (mostly white) women's issues groups. I also began to develop and articulate the unstated concerns, especially about stereotyping, that I had had during high school, and even before then. I learned more about feminist theory, and I developed a framework for the arguments I had always had with the way that I had been treated. I began to feel stronger, more concrete about my ability to be actively in discord with an institution or group or society that made me feel marginal. Looking back, I know that I depended a lot on rhetoric to develop this stronger stance; I don't think that issues of differences among women had made an impact on me then. But I know that it was a time of expansion for me, intellectually and socially. I knew that I had a lot to learn, but I was so excited that academics could offer me something that seemed to have to do with me and my experiences.

I still hadn't found a real group of peers with whom I felt comfortable enough to expand and act on these feminist issues. I was going to meetings, but I was still tentative and concerned about how to make personal connections with these very impressive but intimidating women. My best friend and roommate, Jane, was involved along with me, but we were both in a similar spot—reserved, shy, but very interested. The pivotal connection occurred my sophomore spring, when I took a history class on national liberation movements in Third World countries. I was grappling with issues of racism and cultural imperialism for the first time, which really complicated but expanded what I had been learning in women's studies classes that I had been taking. I remember being overwhelmed by the information; I was almost immobilized by the impact of information so radically different from anything in my world. I met Alexandra in this context. She was in the class, and she was very vocal and very intelligent. She was also beautiful, a physically engaging presence. The amazing thing about her was her ability to express all of the anger that I felt while also including all of the facts, and to make clear, pointed analyses of the situations. She clearly believed that she could channel all of her conviction into some effective action. As we were preparing to write our first paper, she asked me about how I was going to approach the question. We had an involved discussion, and we made plans to write the paper together at the computer center. I surprised myself at my own ability to debate with her; I think that I gained confidence because she obviously considered my thoughts intelligent and worth hearing.

That was the start of a very involved intellectual friendship. We spent the remainder of that class conferring over paper questions, our own questions, and questions raised by active members of the political left whom she knew. She was involved in feminist issues, but also very involved with the radical left of the international students association on campus. She constantly challenged me, and she constantly involved me in protest actions on campus. I made the transition that I had held back on for my first one and a half years—I became a visible member of the college's political left. I was nervous because it meant being recognized and often ignored or treated with hostility. Alexandra took me on as her protegé. She had such a sense of mission, and I was so impressed and awed by her, that I jumped into anything that I could be involved with.

At the end of that term, visible feminists were being harassed by "anonymous" hate mail from hostile conservative campus groups. Also, many women students had been sexually harassed in dorms, and while members of the women's issues group had heard about it through the grapevine, none of the incidents were being reported because there was no clear protocol or support system for these women. A group of us took these incidents to the college president and received little active response. So the group decided to sit in pairs, wearing gags, passing out statements about how women were silenced on campus when they tried to speak out about harassment. I was afraid to "sit in" in front of the fraternities, in the dean's office, and the ultraconservative newspaper's offices, but because Alexandra encouraged me, I did it. I remember that she told me that I was brave, and I remember thinking that it was worth being petrified and being verbally abused to be in the middle of a direct, anti-authority action with her. I felt stronger and more effective than I had ever felt.

As my friendship with Alexandra progressed, we moved out of the intellectual somewhat. I realized that I was dying to be included in her personal life. If she called me to come over and hang out, I was thrilled. I loved listening to her talk about her women friends—they were entertaining, smart, politically impressive, and always involved in some scandal or other. I liked it when she confided in me about strains or stresses in her group; she thought I was perceptive and that I offered a good perspective on what she would tell me. But I hated it when she told me about her lovers. I didn't really formulate why I hated it then; I just felt frustrated.

Sometime over the course of my junior year in England I realized that I was infatuated with her. I got used to the idea of being attracted to, even infatuated with, a woman through trying to figure out why I felt so strongly about Alexandra. I knew that I wanted to be her confidante—her intimate friend. But as I tried to imagine what it would be like to be one of her most preferred friends, I also admitted to myself that that wouldn't be enough. I knew that I would still feel disappointed. I was both emotionally and sexually attracted to her; I couldn't separate those two impulses at all in my feelings for her. It was the sexual attraction that I uncovered slowly. It had not been a conscious element throughout the process of getting closer to her. Also, I had never related personally to lesbianism. I was interested in my homosexual friends, and I had been politically involved in gay and lesbian issues at my college. But I had never felt as if the word or concept *lesbianism* had anything to do with me. Part of this was, I'm sure, that I had never had any models. I never encountered a single person who was openly homosexual until I came to college. The only contact I had had was with Kelly, who was labeled *lesbian*, derogatorily, by our peers.

I came back from London into my senior year having decided, after thinking about Alexandra, that I would be open to a lesbian relationship if someone who interested me came along. This decision was monumental, for once I admitted it to myself, I developed a resolve that I knew would back me if I did get into a situation that seemed to require it. I was scared, but I was proud of myself for making this mental step. Since Jason, I had been involved with two other men, and both of my relationships with them ended similarly to my relationship with Jason. We would start dating, and in what seemed an inappropriately short amount of time, the men would be emotionally involved to a degree which seemed unwarranted, frightening, and claustrophobic to me. Also, the sexual aspects of these involvements, although not oppressive, were not crucial or even consistently satisfying for me. I liked these men a lot before I got involved with them—both were good friends with whom I had similar political and intellectual interests. Both were sensitive about my emotional and sexual needs, but I had the same feeling of distance and constraint that I had felt with Jason, only to a lesser degree that was not frightening, only frustrating.

After Alexandra, I decided that part of the reason that these relationships were occurring was that it was always a man with whom I was involved. I thought that the emotional nurturance that I was providing and rarely receiving had to do with a communication gap or a difference in emotional expectations somewhat rooted in gender. I hadn't had trouble in the numerous close relationships that I had had with women friends. I had two wonderful women friends with whom I could consistently communicate and reciprocate emotional needs. Then, Alexandra tilted the balance by introducing in me both a sexual desire for a woman and a real drive to be totally immersed in her life. I had the resolve; the mental preparation had occurred. However, I didn't think that I would get involved in a lesbian relationship at my college. The lesbian community here was so small, so catty, and so prominent that I couldn't imagine wanting to get in the middle of it.

I met Marie fall term. I had known that she was gay, although she had graduated and was somewhat removed from the lesbian undergraduate community. She was intelligent, experienced, and wise—she had been through so much more than I had encountered in my sheltered life. I was impressed with her strength and her self-possession. She was interested in me; I suppose she sensed that I was open to the idea of a gay relationship. We talked about it extensively, and she was amazed that I had mentally prepared myself before ever making any actual steps. We got involved in a romantic relationship, although I wasn't in love or in awe as I had been with Alexandra. We developed a close bond, and I concentrated on the differences that I perceived between this relationship and my previous ones with men. I felt that I had a sense of proximity, or sexual familiarity, that I had never had before. I attributed this to the fact that we were both women. We had a much more similar approach to sex than I had had with the men I had dated. I felt that sex was much less goal-oriented, much less alienating, and much less demanding. I was more comfortable with it than I had been, and I didn't experience the guilt repercussions that I had in the past. I never felt like I should feel ashamed for enjoying it. We had an easier time relating to each others' views about feminism and, more importantly, we had a better understanding about how to talk about things on which we didn't agree than I had had in past relationships with men. Instead of defensive or aggressive counteracting of my feelings, she was able to honestly set out how she felt, and I could usually find a correlating or analogous feeling in my experience. I was looking for something which could integrate a sexually satisfying relationship with the comfortable, open communication I had had with my women friends. I got closer to this with her than I had in the past.

However, after some time I felt constricted. I tried to confront this feeling with Marie because we had established an open channel of communication. Although we tried to work with giving me space while allowing for her desire to be with me often, we couldn't seem to find a resolution. It was really hard for me to face the feeling of claustrophobia again, when I had hoped that it would not recur if I were involved with a woman. But it did, and I think (in retrospect) that I have some understanding of why it did. First, it was very hard for me to integrate this relationship with the relationships I had established with my other women friends. My friends were initially very supportive, and in theory they were all prepared to accept that I had a woman lover. But Marie's obvious attention and possessiveness interrupted the well-established dynamic. My friends, especially my two closest friends, felt sad, jealous, and somewhat displaced. Instead of asking for support as I probably should have done, or even taking more time just to talk about Marie with them, I tried to play it down for them. I was constantly trying to compensate for my relationship with Marie. Of course I ended up denying any of my own need for support and also hurting these friends as they sensed that there was so much that I wasn't sharing with them. This took its toll on my enthusiasm for the relationship with Marie.

Second, and perhaps more disturbing, I felt some of that demand for intense emotional sustenance similar to what I had felt in previous claustrophobic relationships. I didn't think that I could handle what I perceived to be serious demands on my time, space, and emotional availability. I had to acknowledge that this pattern in my relationships was entirely due to me. However, it did teach me something about my own space and time limits and the importance of my friends as they affect my love relationships. I knew that I would have to be clear from the start about what kind of interaction made me feel threatened or constrained. Anyone with whom I would get involved would have to be able to deal with my wariness, which would probably require a lot of patience. And I would have to be very careful not to compromise my relationships because of my women friends, and also not to alienate my women friends from my relationships with women as lovers. I did feel that to become involved with women as lovers was a positive move. Challenging, but worthwhile. The feeling of proximity in both communication and sex convinced me that it was an important step in ascertaining what I want in a love relationship. I know that it doesn't bypass every relationship hitch. But it makes a positive difference for me.

The only really disturbing aspect of identifying myself as a lesbian is that I worry about my family. I have not told my parents or my sister, and although I did tell my brother, he has not given me any support or feedback. This decision has been a major turning point in my life—even though I worry about my family and sometimes about my future, I feel better about myself now than I ever have. I have learned a lot about my own needs, likes, and dislikes in both love relationships and friendships. I have a new relationship now, and I feel for the first time the ability to get over this pattern that has felt inevitable at times in the past. She is the first person with whom I have been able to relax and share space comfortably, and I feel that even though there is a strong physical attraction and emotional involvement, I am not threatened or claustrophobic. I think that this ease derives in part from an understanding of my limitations and also my abilities, mostly newfound, to be comfortable in an intimate, emotional, communicative, love relationship. She is very independent, very motivated, and very concerned with listening to me and expressing herself clearly. She is able to cultivate an emotional side to a very comfortable relationship without setting up what I perceive as a need too great for me to handle. Also, I have learned how important it is to be straightforward and thorough with my women friends, especially Jane, my best friend through all of my college career. I really love her, and it has been hard to let her know that I will always be with her despite the fact that I will have women lovers. We have learned, however, that it is best to talk to each other about exactly how we both feel about our relationship and about our relationships with lovers, no matter how painful it may be. I think that the intimacy is worth the painful moments.

PART TWO

Relationships

Theoretical Overview

This section of the book focuses on relationships, specifically family and peer relationships. Psychoanalytic and neopsychoanalytic theories have yielded the most prominent and influential explanations of the processes by which adolescents' relationships with their parents and peers change from childhood to adulthood. Anna Freud and Peter Blos described the process of adolescents' individuation from their parents (Blos, 1962; Freud, 1946, 1958), and Harry Stack Sullivan wrote about the development of intimacy through best-friend relationships (Sullivan, 1953). Contemporary research has often contradicted these theories, however, or highlighted aspects of adolescent relationships that were not the focus of the psychoanalytic perspective. This introduction touches on some of the most important issues in the study of adolescent relationships that are raised by these theories and research studies and mentions some ways in which the cases in this portion of the book may be used to foster discussions of these issues.

Family Relationships

The psychoanalytic understanding of adolescent–family relationships has traditionally viewed adolescence as a time of profound inner turmoil and outward conflict—a time of "storm and stress." Explosive conflict with family, friends, and authorities was thought of as commonplace. This view was based, to a great extent, on the theoretical work of the psychiatric community in the 1950s and early 1960s (Blos, 1962; Erikson, 1959, 1966, 1968; Freud, 1946, 1958). Largely on the basis of their experience with adolescent psychiatric patients, these clinicians and theorists described adolescence as a time of extreme psychic and interpersonal stress. Emotional crisis and upheaval were viewed as appropriate responses by the adolescent to major psychological and societal tasks required during this phase of life: dramatically reducing psychological dependency on parents, separating from the family, and forming an adult identity. Adolescent turmoil was not only inevitable but necessary for subsequent normal personality integration.

This storm-and-stress perspective of adolescent family relationships is currently perpetuated by the media and widely assumed by the public. Scholars of adolescent psychology, however, are in the midst of developing a new way of understanding adolescent–family relationships. This new approach to describing and explaining family relationships in adolescence differs from the long-reigning classic psychoanalytic perspective in several ways.

One way the new perspective differs is in its contention that adolescents and their families are more likely to negotiate changes in power, responsibilities, and modes of intimacy through a continuous series of minor, although significant, daily "hassles," rather than through tumultuous, warlike conflicts. Data from empirical studies with nonclinical populations of adolescents and their families from the past twenty-five years have led to a radical revision in the psychological community's understanding of how adolescents separate from and remain connected to their families. The majority of research clearly refutes the notion that most adolescents undergo severe emotional stress and family conflict during this period of life. Although experts concur that adolescence is a period of development that requires multiple changes, the current consensus is that adolescence is not ordinarily a time of great turmoil. A variety of studies using such diverse methods as epidemiological surveys (Rutter, Graham, Chadwick, & Yule, 1976), phone interviews (Montemayor, 1983), and time sampling with electronic beepers (Csikszentmihalyi & Larson, 1984) have shown that for most families with adolescent members, serious conflict and disorganization are not characteristic states (Hill, 1987). Evidence drawn from various kinds of self-reports offered by nonpatient adolescents and their parents provides no support for an inevitable dramatic increase in family conflict from childhood to adolescence. In general, the family is not at risk for turmoil or disorganization during the adolescent years; the search for greater independence from the family is not usually played out in major battles between adolescents and their parents. Instead, current studies look for smaller, although still highly significant, and lasting transformations in sharing of power and responsibility and in the nature of family intimacy through daily renegotiations.

This new view does not claim that adolescence is a time of no conflict. It would be a mistake to conclude that conflicts between adolescents and their parents or siblings are insignificant or rare and that their presence indicates family or individual psychopathology. Any valued human relationship undergoes stress at times, particularly when the relationship must adapt to change within an individual. Adolescents have certainly been shown to value their relationships with their parents, and these relationships do change and adapt as the adolescent becomes an adult member of the family. Although there may not be striking quantitative rises in the amount of family conflict, the *number* of conflicts does rise to some degree in early adolescence and decrease when adolescents leave home. Conflicts are usually of mild to moderate intensity and are rarely about such dramatic issues as drugs or delinquency (Montemayor & Hanson, 1985; Santrock, 1990). In fact, the vast majority of conflicts in adolescence arise over mundane issues such as family chores, curfews, eating practices, dating, and personal appearance.

The case of Betsy (Case 9, "Becoming Comfortable with Who I Am") illustrates psychologists' changing ideas regarding the "normality" of conflict between adolescents and their families. This case represents the "minor hassles" picture of adolescent family life that psychologists are finding more and more often. The case describes family relationships in ways that significantly deviate from the storm-and-stress model in which developmental advances are the cause of dramatic family conflicts. In the storm-and-stress model, a temporary plateau of new independence is reached only after parental capitulation to the adolescent's demands for new levels of autonomy or after parental rejection of the "grown up" teenager. Instead, Betsy's family seems to represent a not uncommon adolescent–parent relationship that is characterized by daily, ongoing mundane conflicts and compromises that are made possible by good communication, a strong desire to maintain parental approval and harmony, and Betsy's confidence in the degree of mutual trust and respect in her family. This adolescent–parent style is exemplified in Betsy's statement that "In some ways my parents are probably the most protective parents I know, but at the same time they trusted me to do things my friends could never do. . . . I couldn't ride in a car with my friends until they had their licenses for two months, but once I started driving I was allowed to drive into Atlanta sooner than my friends." Her understanding that her parents "trusted me but were worried about the rest of the world" and that "their limits were set to protect me, even if I didn't feel like I needed protecting. I trusted them to be fair, and they usually were" is what seems to make this less dramatic style of adolescent conflict resolution possible.

Betsy's case may be used to clarify your ideas concerning what characterizes an optimal or ideal family for promoting adolescent development. In what ways do Betsy's family relationships foster adolescent independence, achievement, or intimacy goals? What problems might be associated with this low-conflict pattern of family interaction? For example, Betsy raises the question of whether she is too much of a "goody-goody" for her own development. By her own account, she senses that her strong conformity to adult expectations has been something of a constraint on her peer development. "I would like to say that . . . [a peer friendship experience] helped me relax with respect to following rules. But it didn't. . . . Even after I graduated from high school I was still conscientious to a fault." Perhaps when parents are as reasonable and fair minded as hers and a family is so close knit, it makes it difficult to justify rebelling against such seemingly sound authorities. Cases in other sections of the book may also be useful to study as exemplars of nontumultuous adolescent–parent relationships.

A second important difference in this new approach is that it seeks to encompass the description of a *wide variety of patterns* of family relationships, rather than focusing on explaining one primary picture of how "normal" adolescents interact with their families. Instead, a wide range of adolescent family behaviors is considered relevant to understanding adolescent adaptive responses to growth in relationships. This new perspective seeks to include more diversity in the adolescents and families studied. For example, not enough is known about varieties of adaptive family functioning in African American, Latino, Native American, Asian American, and other groups of adolescents in U.S. culture. It may be helpful to contrast the family pictures described by adolescents of European American descent in this section with pictures of family life described by adolescents from different ethnic backgrounds (see the thematic index on p. xx) and by other students in your class. Scholars of adolescent psychology also have an extremely limited understanding at present about adolescents' relationships with their single parents, stepparents, and noncustodial parents.

Identifying different pathways to adolescents' new levels of separation and connection with parents is possible by juxtaposing cases in this section. Betsy's family experiences can be contrasted with Chhaya's (Case 10, "Falling from My Pedestal") family experiences of major conflict and turmoil, an exemplar of the classic but less common storm-and-stress model of adolescent individuation from the family. You might ask yourself which aspects of the tumult in Chhaya's family are triggered by *adolescent* issues and which are products of a long-standing family system. Her case provides a powerful description of a family under severe stress and one adolescent's extreme strategies for coping with that stress. Clearly, some of these strategies strengthen her resilience (e.g., her perfectionism reinforces her ability to succeed at many demanding tasks, including school), while other strategies, (e.g., anorexia) eventually cause more pain than relief. Chhaya's case is one reminder of the variety of patterns that lead eventually to successful young adult adaptation and functioning. Case 13, in this section, and cases in other sections of the book may also serve as examples of a typical family situations leading to severe stress in adolescence (see, for example, Case 4, "Someday My Elders Will Be Proud").

A third distinguishing aspect of psychologists' contemporary approach to describing adolescent family relationships emphasizes adolescents' needs for maintaining intimacy and connection with parents and siblings as well as adolescents' wishes for increased autonomy and independence. Earlier psychoanalytic theories focused primarily on the process of separation from the family. Little is currently known about how adolescents establish new ways of being meaningfully attached and intimate with family members while also negotiating greater independence from the family (Gilligan, 1987).

Results from studies that have observed adolescents' interactions with their parents have indicated the importance of family interaction styles that permit conflict between members in a context of support (Baumrind, 1987, in press; Powers, 1988; Powers, Hauser, Schwartz, Noam, & Jacobson, 1983), acceptance, active understanding from parents (Hauser et al., 1984; Hauser et al., 1987), and parental expressions of individuality and connectedness (Grotevant & Cooper, 1986).

Three of the cases in this section are strong illustrations of adolescents' heartfelt need to be affectively connected to their families. Chhaya and Jen's cases present particularly significant difficulties in negotiating a sufficient level of closeness and intimacy with their parents. Their stories might usefully be contrasted with Betsy's more nonchalant assumptions of parental closeness.

Brian's case (Case 11, "At Least We Got One Right") presents a poignant example of one man's struggle to maintain closeness and connections with his parents and, at the same time, forge a new identity for himself that is not wholly based on being the "perfect son." He feels that his new identity is necessary for developing healthy peer relationships and career goals. He is unable, however, to envision a way to coordinate his developing separate self with the self he presents to his parents.

Peer Relationships

Peer relationships may include close friendships, cliques, peer groups and crowds, and romantic relationships. Many cases throughout the book discuss peer relationships, and the reader is encouraged to look in the thematic index following the table of contents for cases that can be found in other sections but include material on peer relationships. "Someday My Elders Will Be Proud" (Case 4), for example, describes the power of peer pressure when an adolescent's ethnicity and ethnic culture are different from those of the dominant culture. The sections on sexual identity and gender identity are particularly useful for examining romantic relationships.

Close friendships in adolescence may have many facets and functions, such as providing companionship, stimulation, social comparison, and intimacy or affection (Gottman & Parker, 1987; Parker & Gottman, 1989). Ann (Case 12, "No Boring Little Friends") and Rebecca's (Case 8, "Loving Women" in the Identity Section) cases present these varied aspects of adolescent close friendship and their developmental transitions throughout early to late adolescence. For example, Rebecca's description of sexual play with her close grade school friend in private and at slumber parties and the confusion that surrounds it illustrates friendship as an introduction to the sexual aspects of growing up. Rebecca and her friend Kelly show us one example of an early adolescent friendship, whereas Rebecca's friendship with Alexandra occurs in college and is an example of the meaning of friendship at a later developmental stage. Selman's (1980) theory of the stages of growth in friendships may be helpful in contrasting the meaning of friendships to these adolescents at different stages of development. Betsy's case also provides a window through which to view the importance of close friendships, cliques, and romantic relationships in high school.

Peer cliques and groups may also have a variety of functions in adolescent growth and development. Peers provide a means of social comparison as well as a source of information outside the family. Both of these functions can be seen clearly in the cases of Betsy, Ann, and Rebecca. The role of popularity—fitting in with desired cliques, being rejected or neglected by peers—is acutely felt by all adolescents included within this section on relationships. Rebecca's case in the Identity section and Ann's case provide particularly good examples of conformity to peers peaking around eighth and ninth grades and then lessening by twelfth grade (Berndt & Ladd, 1989).

Current theory and research emphasize the connectedness between the quality of family relationships and the quality of close peer relationships (Gold & Yanof, 1985; Parker & Gottman, 1989). The cases of Chhaya, Brian, Betsy, and Jen (as well as Rebecca) provide excellent material for a discussion of the impact of family relationships on the development of peer relationships.

Brian struggles to keep separate the parts of himself that are related to his friends and the parts of himself that are connected to his parents. This division of self is painful and long lasting. Brian's strategies for maintaining these separate selves go through developmental transitions as he faces this struggle from elementary school through college. Chhaya's ways of relating to her high school friends mirror the ways she relates to her family; she is afraid to show anything other than her "perfect" self.

Rebecca speaks eloquently about the strain between her father's academic goals and her own and her peers' goals for popularity as well as the influence of her parents on the development of her sexual identity. Betsy searches for friendships that stretch her growth in ways that her comfortable family relationships do not. Jen struggles to define herself and her romantic relationship with Ben differently than she has defined herself in her relationship with her father. At the same time, she works hard to understand how her conflicts and connection with her father continue to influence her romantic relationship.

Another focus for analysis might be the usefulness of Sullivan's (1953) and Erikson's (1959, 1966, 1968) theories of intimacy for understanding these cases. For example, how does Rebecca's (Case 8, "Loving Women") friendship with Kelly exemplify Sullivan's notion of same-sex "chumship"? How does friendship or romantic intimacy contribute to the development of identity? Does the research on gender differences in the development of intimacy seem to hold in these cases? (Berndt, 1981, 1982; Blyth, Hill, & Thiel, 1982; Buhrmester & Furman, 1987; Burleson, 1982; Coleman, 1987; Diaz & Berndt, 1982; Sharabany, Gershoni, & Hofman, 1981; Youniss & Smollar, 1985; Zeldin, Small, & Savin-Williams, 1982). What are the aspects of a romantic relationship that are valued by the adolescents in this book, and how do these values change as these adolescents mature? In this section, Jen may be used as an example of romantic values at the college age, whereas Chhaya, Ann, and Betsy provide examples of romantic values during high school.

9 Becoming Comfortable with Who I Am

This author presents the reader with a study of adolescence as it occurs within a happy, supportive network of family, friends, and mentors. Betsy describes her involvement in school drama as a place where she finds adult and same-age peers and a sense of self. She rarely questions her positive relationship with her parents, but her confidence in who they are and how they see her is temporarily shaken when they prevent her from traveling with friends on a carefully planned trip. She also describes her relationships with adult and same-sex friends and reflects on how these help her find or recognize another piece of herself. While her story does not fit the "storm-and-stress" model of adolescent development, it does illustrate some of the normal stressors of adolescence that are the result of developmental growth.

When I was 16, I got to sing my first solo in the school's spring musical. I also got to do my first stage kiss, which also happened to be my first real-life kiss. It took me much longer than my girlfriends to be interested in boys. In ninth grade I went to lunch with my gym class. My friend Sarah, who was in the same class, loved it. We ate surrounded by the football players, and Sarah flirted with a new one every-day. I did my algebra homework with one hand and ate my sandwich with the other. Once in a while, one of the guys would try to get me to talk to him. But I was sure that he was only making fun of me, and he almost always smelled sweaty and stale. I would answer with a shrug and a smart comment, and he would turn back to Sarah.

In ninth grade this didn't bother me. I got my homework finished during school, and this left the whole afternoon and evening to read books and write let-ters to my friends in Morocco. During my eighth-grade year, my family had lived in Morocco because my father, who was a history professor, was doing research there. My younger sister and I went to a private English school. I loved it. I hated weekends because I wanted to get back to my friends and teachers. I loved the British ritual that was a part of the school day. We started in a big hall lined up by forms. The headmaster came in and said, "Good morning, children," and we answered, "Good morning, Mr. Simmson." We stood in line outside the classrooms before the teachers came, and then they led us in. Everything was so formal and neat. The British accents were so much cleaner than the Southern drawl that I had grown up hearing. I tried to copy one, and wished with all my heart that my parents had been British.

I hated leaving at the end of the year. But I slowly began to see the merits of an American public high school, and I started to make new friends. In my tenth grade year I auditioned for the school musical. I had loved musicals ever since I saw *Brigadoon* when I was 10. Auditioning terrified me, but to my amazement and delight, I got a part in the chorus. Now I had something new to throw my enthusiasm into. I got to every rehearsal early, volunteered for every set day, and learned the whole musical by heart in the first few weeks.

By eleventh grade, I started to feel like a real part of the drama crowd. Getting to do a solo and a stage kiss made me one of the important upperclassmen. Doing the kiss on stage embarrassed me a little and pleased me a lot, but I was still not overly interested in boys. My obsession with British schools was gone, but now every spare moment of my time was spent at rehearsal, or shopping for costumes with our drama teacher, or planning activities for the drama club. I simply did not have time to devote to talking about, dressing for, and impressing the guys.

In my senior year that changed. Partly because of pressure from my friends, and partly because I really did like him, I developed a crush on Kevin, the same boy I had kissed the year before in the musical. I was excited when he offered to drive me home from the drama club Christmas party. It was my very first date, and we went to McDonald's for Cokes and then drove around town for a while. Unfortunately I spent the whole drive wondering if I was supposed to kiss him when he dropped me off. I wanted to, but I didn't know if he wanted to, and I didn't want him to know that I wanted to if he didn't want to. Being busy wondering about all this, I didn't keep up my end of the conversation very well, and soon we were back at my house. When he stopped the car, I panicked. If he did want to kiss me, I wasn't sure I knew what to do, in spite of my practice in the musical. Rather than let him know that, I decided to get out of the car fast. As soon as I got inside, I was positive that I had done the wrong thing. I should have stayed and talked to him for a while, and then seen what happened. The next day at school I was afraid to look at him and his friends because I was sure that he had told them all that I was a goody-goody and a prude. I knew that I was the laughing stock of the twelfth grade.

It turned out that he wasn't laughing, and a week later he came over to study chemistry. This time things worked out better. I was 17½, and it was the first time that I had ever kissed a boy, except on stage, which didn't count. We went out a few more times, and then the romantic part of our relationship petered out without either of us really ever saying anything about it.

I didn't really date anybody else in high school. I did get more practice kissing, though. I got the "kissing roles" in the two plays we did in my senior year, and at our drama cast parties we played spin-the-bottle and truth-or-dare. I had fun, but much to my disgust, I was never more than friends with the guys in our group. I compared notes with my girlfriends about the various merits of different boys, but the few times that I knew there was a mutual interest on his part, I was too shy to let him know, and nothing came out of the relationships except for conversations in the hall at school.

I'm not really sure why I was so late to discover boys. Maybe part of it was that it took me so long to adjust from coming back from Morocco. I had had very different experiences from the other students, and because I didn't know how to fit in, I stayed on the fringes of the crowd in my ninth- and tenth-grade years, I was convinced that my high school was not as good as the English school, and I was happier dreaming about what I didn't have than dealing with what I did. In my junior year when I did begin to fit in, I hadn't had the practice liking boys that all my friends had. Even though I wanted a boyfriend by then, I didn't really know how to go about getting one. Another part of it was that I had several time-consuming hobbies and interests that occupied me after school. In the first part of high school these included writing to friends in Morocco, taking piano lessons, playing tennis, and reading. Later I got involved with school-related activities like drama and yearbook. I didn't have time to go home after school and watch soap operas and TV sit-comedies or read *Seventeen* magazine like my friends did. Without some of these powerful reminders of how males and females are supposed to react to each other, I was happy to go about my life relatively unaware of and uninterested in boys long after my friends were involved with boyfriends.

I have always been concerned about approval. In ninth grade I received three compliments about my looks within several weeks of each other, and I replayed them often in my mind. The first was from the mother of one of my sister's friends. I overheard her telling my mother that I got prettier each time she saw me. After that, whenever she came to our house to drop off her daughter or pick up my sister, I made sure that I looked nice, and then hung around in hopes of impressing her again.

A little later my neighbor told me that I looked like a young Ingrid Bergman. I watched all the Ingrid Bergman movies I could get ahold of and looked for comparisons between us. I tried fixing my hair in Ingridlike styles, and waited to see if anyone else would notice the similarity. No one did.

The third compliment that I remember vividly from this time was from an artist mother of one of my friends who said that she would like to paint me. For a while I hoped when I saw her that she would follow through and ask me to sit for her. Then I saw some of her other portraits and was not impressed by their beauty.

Almost all the compliments that I can remember from the early part of high school were from adults. My friends would comment on a pretty article of clothing or say that my hair looked nice on a particular day, but that was the duty of friends. My curly hair wouldn't fit into the feathered style that all the girls wore, and I didn't like wearing makeup. (This was still my British boarding school stage, and the English girls weren't allowed to paint their faces.) I didn't want to look like everyone else, but I didn't feel attractive around people my own age. Adults approved of me. I was quiet and polite, I made good grades in school, and I didn't adopt the current teenage fads like listening to rock music or talking on the telephone for hours on end. I sought approval from adults as a substitute for popularity among my peers.

I was always conscious of how other people saw my reactions. It was as though there were two of me. One part was living my life—feeling happy and sad, excited and disappointed. The other part was outside of me watching and noting my effect on others. The outside part enjoyed getting sympathy, attention, and praise. It could romanticize even the worst situations. It put me in the place of the injured heroine from the movies. It was the part of me that imagined what people would say about me if I were to die, and wished to be involved in tragedies for the effect of it. The inside of me did the feelings. It was what made me grieve when my grandmother died, squirm with pleasure at getting a part in a play, and react naturally to daily ups and downs.

I don't think that in high school I could have put into words how these two different aspects of my personality reacted with each other. I sometimes worried that my thoughts didn't seem nice or proper. It seemed morbid to like the attention I got when something bad happened to me. But it wasn't that I wanted tragedy. I was generally a happy person, and I think that a part of me couldn't accept that things could get so bad that there was nothing left to enjoy. I felt a lot of things very deeply, and romanticizing what was happening to me was a way to lighten up sad thoughts.

My high school drama teacher, Susan, and her husband, Ron, didn't have any children of their own, but they have spent their lives "adopting" other people's children. I had the good fortune to be one of those children.

Susan reveled in surprises and doing special things for other people. During the musicals she would ask a couple of us to go along with her to shop for costumes. I loved these afternoons. Susan would come and pick us up in her huge old blue Cadillac. It was no longer a fancy car, but the seats were smooth and comfortable, and two people could sit up in front with Susan. There were stores near home that we could have looked in, but Susan liked to go farther afield to check out the discount outlets and used-clothing stores. The stores were cluttered and had the musty smell of an old attic. Sometimes there would be bins of old shoes or boxes of scarves for fifty cents. Some days things were sorted by style, some days by color or size, and some days there was no apparent logical order at all. We mixed and matched skirts, blouses, and jackets to create period pieces and tried on dozens of hats to find the one that would look just right. I liked Susan's approval when I came up with a good idea and the attention that was paid especially to me when looking for my costumes. When we finished with our shopping, our bags would be deposited in the trunk of the car, and Susan would almost always say, "There's a wonderful little restaurant around the corner. How would you like to try it out?" We went to The Grill, a hamburger place that still served malted milkshakes from the frosty metal cup that they were mixed in. Another time it was The Dessert Place, which served nothing but desserts. We all agreed that the cream cheese brownie with ice cream, hot fudge sauce, and whipped cream was the best. It didn't really matter where we went. There was a cozy, relaxed feeling of belonging. Susan and Ron spent hours of their free time with us. They took us to weekend-long drama conferences, and invited us all to parties at their house. Susan coached a group of us for the literary meet in my senior year and took us to the competition. Ron came to help when we built the sets for plays, and we all learned how to use a power saw and a ratchet properly.

The day before I graduated, Susan stopped by my house in the morning before school and left an envelope. Inside was a silver bookmark and a letter to me. Susan had been given the bookmark by her favorite teacher when she graduated from high school, and now she was giving it to me. The letter told about Susan's high school experience, and about her teacher who had done for Susan what Susan had done for me. Like me, Susan had been a shy, quiet student, and her teacher had encouraged her and helped her get involved and have confidence in herself. I felt very lucky and touched that Susan had decided to give the bookmark to me, and I vowed to keep it to pass down to someone special in my future.

Having older friends who weren't relatives was important to me. No matter how much I loved and confided in my parents, it was good to be listened to by someone else. They sympathized when I got into arguments at home, but they also had more perspective on how my parents felt than my loyal same-age friends. They would be supportive of me, but also helped me to see my parents' side of things. I could take suggestions from them without the resentment that I would have shown my parents.

One of my other teachers became another close adult friend. She was an interesting, extremely shy woman who had a hard time making conversation on the superficial chatty level. But she liked hearing what students were thinking. Her solution was to require a weekly writing assignment of one page on any topic that a student chose. In addition to being good writing practice, it allowed her to get to know students without the awkwardness of conversations. This is how I got to be friends with her. I was frustrated with being one of the few liberal democrats in my classes. It was important to me to have people know my political and ethical views, but I was tired of always having to defend and stand up for what I believed in when I was in the minority. There were several guys in my classes who liked to start political discussions, and when I joined in, they would all jump on me with loud, defensive arguments. Several times I came close to tears of frustration with these fruitless conversations.

After one such discussion, I wrote a passionate paper saying that I would never speak up again, because there wasn't any point in it. My teacher returned my paper with a page full of comments. She had had the same kind of experience, she said, and she knew how I felt. She went on to talk about the difference between discussions where people tried to understand others' view points and ones where the purpose was to congratulate oneself on one's own good judgment. I learned a lot from her about my own reasons for joining these arguments. I also started to realize that I wasn't going to change the views of my classmates on most issues, and that while a one-on-one discussion was often interesting and beneficial to both people, it wasn't worth it to rise to the bait of three or four people who were eager to squelch opposing views.

Whenever I most needed someone to reinforce my ideas, I would write to her, and the next day I would get an answer that agreed or at least sympathized with me. It was like having my own personal "Dear Abby." I continued to write to her when I was no longer in her class, and we became good friends. There were other things we shared besides political views. Taste in books was one, and she would bring in books for me to read, and I would lend her my favorites. Since we met by writing, it seemed most natural to keep writing, and although we always greeted each other warmly when we passed in the hall, most of our conversations were in written form.

Getting involved in drama was the beginning of the end of my shyness and lack of involvement in school and friends. Susan, my drama teacher, played a major role in this change, and the other drama students did the rest. In particular was my friend Angela. Before I auditioned for my first play, I knew Angela only as a gregarious, friendly person who was president of our class. She was always in the front row of pep rallies full of school pride and class spirit. I sat in the middle of the crowd hating the noise and thinking that the whole idea of pep rallies was stupid. Once I even brought a book and stopped up my ears with my fingers as I tried to read. I didn't like or dislike Angela. She was just another classmate, and I didn't see much in common between us.

Then we both got parts in the spring musical, and I started to get to know her. We were both drama rookies and were often grouped together for warm-up or set day. We thought that the same things were funny, we liked and disliked the same people, and by my junior year we were good friends. That ended my role as an observer at school functions. Angela just expected that everyone was as spirited as she was, and I found myself coming to school early to decorate the halls for Christmas, and making signs for the football games. And her enthusiasm was infectious. Soon I did start to get excited about the things we did. I really did care when we won a football game, or when the junior class won the spirit stick.

Angela was popular, but not in the same way that the cheerleaders were popular. She was genuinely interested in other people, and people liked her because she made a point to find out about them. She wasn't only concerned about school-related activities, and she and I went to things like the art museum and concerts together. She didn't care that my family didn't go to church. Neither did she, and that was unusual in our conservative Baptist county.

The other students in drama became good friends, too. It was a place for people who didn't quite fit into the mainstream. They were a little more liberal, and a lot more accepting of differences than the other students at school. I found a niche with them, and by the time I graduated I felt at home with them and like a leader instead of a follower.

In some ways my parents are probably the most protective parents I know, but at the same time they trusted me to do things that my friends could never do. I still had a bedtime in ninth and tenth grade, but on weekends I didn't have a curfew as long as they knew where I was. I couldn't ride in a car with my friends until they had had their licenses for two months, but once I started driving, I was allowed to drive into the city sooner than my friends.

Most of my parents' rules were based on the fact that they trusted me but were worried about the rest of the world. When I wasn't allowed to do something, it was usually because they were worried about my safety or health. I would often get furious at them for a rule that kept me from doing something with my friends, but I did know that they weren't trying to be mean, and that their limits were set to protect me even if I didn't feel like I needed protecting. I trusted them to be fair, and they usually were.

I could talk to my mother about almost everything, and although I shared some of my problems with my friends, in those relationships I was usually content to be the listener. My mother gave me more satisfactory advice than my friends, and I could count on her not to spread around what I told her. I was equally close to my father, although our conversations generally focused on discussions of future plans, political problems, or whatever we were doing together. For a long time, even into early high school, he would read aloud to me in the evenings before bed. We liked to play tennis, frisbee, or croquet together.

The biggest and most shattering argument I ever had with my parents was in my senior year. Angela's parents had a condominium in Florida, and we were planning a senior trip for the week after school was out. Angela and I and two other girls were going, as well as three guys who were friends of ours. When I asked my parents if I could go, I told them who was going and what the arrangements were. I was sure that my parents trusted me enough to know that I would be sensible and responsible. At first my parents were reluctant to give me permission, but we got out a map and found a route that was all on the interstate. They knew that Angela and Jeremy, the two drivers, were cautious, and the trip would be very inexpensive. They finally said yes, and we went ahead with the plans. For a week the trip was all we talked about. What to bring, what to wear, what we would do, where we would eat. Angela and I and Anne had study hall and lunch together and every minute was filled with plans. We'd write notes during class when an idea couldn't wait. Then one evening about half an hour before I had to leave for play rehearsal, my parents called me into the living room. They looked serious, but I couldn't think of anything that I had done wrong, and I was looking forward to rehearsal, so I wasn't concerned.

My mother said, "Daddy and I have talked about it for a long time, and we're not happy with the idea of you being away alone for so long."

I didn't get it. "What do you mean?"

"We don't want you to go to Florida."

"What? But you said I could go."

"I know, and we are very sorry. We know it's unfair, but we don't want you to go."

I couldn't believe it. It was like their words were floating around in the air and weren't reaching my brain. I knew they couldn't mean it because they had already said it was okay and my parents didn't break promises. I tried to keep my voice from shaking, "But we already planned everything. Angela is counting on me to help pay my share. And you promised." I came back to that.

"You can tell Angela that we will still pay for your share of the rent. The more we thought about it, the more we didn't want you driving that far without an adult. If something were to happen to one of you down there, it would be hours before a parent could get there to help. We are very sorry, but you can't go."

I was crying now. "Please, Mommy, I have to go. We've been planning it for weeks." And then finally shouting at the top of my lungs. "I hate you. It's not fair. You said I could go and you lied."

I ran from the room and ran upstairs, stumbling as I went. I slammed the door as hard as I could and a little piece of plaster fell off of the wall. Lying across my bed I sobbed, "I hate you, I hate you." I cried until my head hurt, my eyes stung, and my sleeve was soaking from my tears and runny nose.

I had to go to rehearsal, so I got up and went into the bathroom. Still crying, I washed my face and blew my nose, but my face was red and blotchy and my eyes were bloodshot. I drove to school and the road was blurry. I wanted to be in an accident. If I were dead or hurt, they'd see what they'd done. But I got to rehearsal without event. I was a few minutes early, but I waited in the car until warm-ups started so that I wouldn't have to talk to anybody. I finally went in, and stood in my place with my head down. I tried to keep my mind blank, but I couldn't keep the tears from coming to my eyes. At break Angela asked me what was wrong. I couldn't tell her, I didn't know what to say. I knew she would feel sorry for me, and I couldn't handle that.

For the next three days, I tried again and again to change their minds. I'd start in a reasonable voice and end up screaming at them as I saw they were truly set in their opinion. In between pleading with them, I ignored them, spending most of my time in my room, coming down to eat silently or go to rehearsal.

I still didn't tell Angela. At school when we had study hall, she'd start to make more plans, and I just couldn't tell her that I couldn't go. It got worse every day. I'd resolve to tell her, but when the time came, I'd keep quiet, and go home and plead again. Finally my mother said that if I didn't tell her, she would call Angela herself. So I took a deep breath during study hall and said, "Ange, I can't go with you guys. My parents are being jerks. They'll pay for my share, so don't worry about the money." I answered their questions as lightly as I could, trying desperately not to let them see how much I cared that I couldn't go. I said that they'd better send me postcards, and that I still wanted to hear all the plans.

It was several weeks before I spoke to them normally again, and even then when I thought about the trip, I got mad. When I look back, I can understand why my parents didn't want me to go, and I know how hard it must have been for them to tell me I couldn't. As a parent I might have felt the same way. But what was so hard for me to accept was that they went back on their word. My parents, who were supposed to be fair and trustworthy, had said one thing and then changed their minds. If they had said no in the first place, I would have pleaded to go and argued and gotten angry, but I would have been on solid ground. I wouldn't have felt as if the floor beneath my feet was suddenly gone. This argument had shaken up my trust in them, and it took a long time before I trusted them again. Even now almost three years later, when I've forgiven them and taken another trip to Florida with the same people, I can still remember the disbelief and shock I felt at my mother's words, "Daddy and I have talked about this for a long time. . . ."

Although the senior-trip argument was a major disagreement, on the whole I had a good family life. My college roommate refers to my family as a "Brady

Bunch" family. I have a little trouble with the analogy since, as my dad said when I told him, "We're not a reconstituted family, and Mommy doesn't have blond hair and wear short skirts." But I do know why she said it. My family does things together. We sing songs on car trips, and we make baskets on Easter morning to put on the doorsteps in the neighborhood. We go for walks together, and eat dinner together when everyone is home.

I don't mean to sound as if we are a wonderful, happy, too-good-to-be-true family. We aren't, and often the things we did together didn't go the way we planned them. Either my sister or I would be sullen and uncooperative about whatever we were doing, and Mommy and Daddy would end up annoyed and disgusted. Elizabeth and I got along well when we were alone together, but when the whole family was doing something, we vied for attention. We would take on opposite roles. If Elizabeth was complaining and whining, I would be interested and helpful, and if she were having a good day, I would be the one to ruin the mood. It's not something we did consciously. It's just how things worked out.

Our family does a lot of laughing and teasing. My father has a quiet, observant sense of humor. He understates the obvious, and mutters funny comments under his breath. My mother's humor is sillier—the kind that sometimes prompted her to answer the phone, "Downstairs Maid." My sister and I inherited some from each of them.

Sunday mornings were one of my favorite times, and still are when I am home. Mommy or Daddy would be cooking breakfast as Elizabeth and I trailed into the kitchen in our pajamas. The newspaper would be scattered around, and the dog and cats would be underfoot asking for food or chasing each other. After we ate, we would sit around the table for a while talking, and it would usually end up in a bout of silliness as we teased someone. It was a good time to be together. It was unplanned, and everyone was relaxed.

My family provided a good base to come back to. When things weren't going right at school, I could always tell them. We did have arguments, sometimes big ones like about my senior trip. But except for that one time, they weren't earthshattering and didn't last very long. One of the animals would do something cute, or something funny would happen and we'd end up laughing. Someone would apologize, or we'd just forget what we were mad about. I like and respect my family as well as love them, and I can count on them.

The summer after my junior year I went to the Governor's Honors Program (GHP). It was a six-week academic program for high school students, held on a college campus. I studied drama and loved every minute of it. We did trust exercises where we told other people things that we had never told anyone before. Most of our work was on ensemble pieces. The class depended on working with everyone else in the group, and we grew very close. There was no one who didn't fit in, and everyone had a place.

My roommate was a girl whose major area was drama, so we started out with a common interest. We met at the hall meeting after our first dinner, and started talking immediately. Her name was Margaret, but since there were several other Margarets on the hall, she decided to call herself "Megs," and then christened me

"Germie" because I also studied German. The names stuck, and that is how we were referred to for the rest of the summer. We got along from the first day.

It was a time of being very self-concerned, very full of the importance of our deep thoughts. Megs and I stayed up until three in the morning and talked about life. She was the first person outside my family whom I told that I didn't believe in God. We also compared experiences with guys, and hers were as negligible as mine. She too was very involved in drama, and had little time for anything else. Her family life was much different from mine, not as stable and happy, and I felt privileged that she told me all she did about it. When an old man whom she was close to died, she cried on my bed. One night when I woke up terrified from a nightmare, she was there to reassure me. At the end of the summer we cried and vowed to write forever. I wrote once, and she wrote once, and then we both just stopped.

There was something special and isolated about that summer. Not just for Megs and me, but for all the friends I made there. By the end of the six weeks I would have said that they were the best friends that I had ever had. But in the fall when school started, they seemed to fade away like the nicknames we had used all summer. I think that we all outgrew each other. That was the summer when I first solved all of life's big questions. Soon I realized that my solutions were only the beginnings of the answers.

It was a stage for all of us where closeness was vital. If you didn't tell your friends everything about yourself, you were holding back—not being honest. And so we did share everything. That may have been what made us drift apart later. When the thoughts and secrets that we had related to each other so passionately weren't important or true anymore, then the need for the friends who knew those things faded out, too. If I had met the same people in the course of my ordinary life at school, I might have gradually become friends with them. But there wouldn't have been the same urgency that there was about our six-week summer. GHP is described as an intensive learning experience, and it was. The stimulation and concentration from our subject areas were carried over into our relationships.

When I was in first grade, I came home from school with headaches because "the other kids were so noisy and bad." I hated seeing others misbehave, and I even felt responsible for them. I would try to be extra good and cooperative so that the teachers wouldn't think that it was their fault that things were out of control. On my report cards the comments would range from, "A delight to have in class," to "A studious pupil," to "Has good ideas, but needs to learn to speak up more." The slant of the particular comment depended upon whether the teacher was desperately glad to have an obedient student in a disruptive class, or whether she felt that each student should be encouraged to participate and contribute. I would try to comply with whichever behavior was valued. Luckily, over the years I had enough of the encouraging, creative teachers to overcome my shyness, and by tenth grade I was no longer embarrassed to speak out in class and express my ideas.

I still felt a responsibility towards my teachers, though, and even when they were boring and dry, and especially if they were trying too hard to reach the students by telling dumb jokes and sitting on the edges of their desks, I wanted them to know that their efforts were appreciated. It was hard work. I'd sit in the front row and smile at their attempts at humor, and be attentive and ask questions while most of my classmates passed notes or tuned out. I wasn't a brownnoser, although it may have looked to some like I was. I just couldn't stand a teacher to feel like he or she was doing a bad job. Most of my friends were also good students, and although they weren't as concerned about encouraging bad teachers, they looked benevolently on my attempts to do so. The people who I didn't know so well wrote me off as a brain and a bookworm, but they weren't people I cared about impressing.

I was also extremely concerned about following the rules, being on time, and being prepared for things. I could not feel comfortable loitering in the hall after the warning bell rang and then rushing to class at the sound of the second bell. I hated leaving homework till the last moment, and I didn't really even like holding a place in the lunch line for someone else, although I conceded to this small breach of the rules. I worried about these little things, but I didn't want to do it openly because even to my best friends it would appear too "goody-goody." I became skilled at thinking of excuses for getting my classmates to comply with the rules with me without actually showing that I was worried about breaking them. I'd think of something to show them in the classroom so that they would come in with me before the bell rang, or I'd chatter constantly while we were walking so that they wouldn't notice that I was hurrying to get us somewhere on time. I became pretty skilled at this manipulation, and although it was sometimes a strain, it was a more attractive alternative to me than breaking the rules or openly admitting that I didn't want to break them.

My conscientiousness was partly instilled in me by my parents. They have high moral standards, and Elizabeth and I were always taught that dishonesty was unacceptable. Although they were not pushy parents, they also motivated me to do well in school and in my extracurricular activities. I learned that it was important to try my hardest, and since I was capable of making good grades and generally succeeding in what I did, these things became very important to me. I liked the approval I got both from my family and other adult friends when I did well. So I followed the rules, studied hard, and did what was expected of me.

In twelfth grade, though, I met my match. It was second semester, and I had Drama I sixth period. My friend Kristen and I had both had enough experience that we were doing Drama II during this period. This meant that most of the time we were sent off to work on our own, rehearsing scenes or doing errands for Susan. This would have been fine except that Kristen had the worst case of "senioritis" that I have ever known. She was sick of school. She had already been accepted to the college she wanted to go to. And she did not want to be in school rehearsing scenes for drama class.

Susan would give us an assignment to work on or an errand to run and a hall pass, and we would be turned loose to work on our own. I liked Kristen a lot, but she intimidated me, and I was afraid to suggest that we should actually do what Susan was expecting us to do because that was obviously not what Kristen had in mind. None of my subtle tactics worked very well on her either. So I spent sixth period every day of spring semester of my senior year following Kristen around the school hoping that Susan wouldn't find out that we weren't quietly rehearsing our scenes. Kristen and I sat in the sun in the senior court yard. We went and bothered Mr. Jason, the yearbook teacher. And she wrote our initials and graduation year in magic marker on the walls outside the school! Since we were both known as good students, no one questioned our activities. Everyone just assumed that we were being responsible and mature. The fact that we were betraying their trust obviously did not make me happy. But I cared too much about being Kristen's friend and companion to protest too loudly. There was a silent struggle between us. I would tentatively suggest that maybe we should at least go over our scene once in case Susan asked to see it, or that we really should get the xeroxed copies that Susan had asked for. Kristen would concede, but would drag out the task to take the whole period so that we wouldn't have to go back to class. I tried to keep us on track and Kristen provided the entertainment.

I would like to be able to say that this experience with Kristen helped me to relax with respect to following the rules. But it didn't. My sense of duty was too deeply ingrained to be relaxed by one semester of bending the rules. Although I lived with Kristen's antics, even after I graduated from high school I was still conscientious to a fault. I now worry about slightly different things like getting papers done, studying for exams, and paying the rent. I cannot skip classes with a clear conscience, and I cannot enjoy myself if I have any unpleasant task hanging over my head. In some ways this causes me unnecessary anxiety, and I envy people who can be carefree and unconcerned all the time. But it has also given me the discipline to work hard at school and my jobs. I do have fun and relaxed times—they just come after my work is done.

In some ways I still feel very close to my high school years. I have been surprised at the amount of emotion I still feel in remembering things that I have not thought of for a long time. In other ways I am able to realize things about myself now that I couldn't see at the time. I can see the change that I went through as I struggled to find friendship and support without compromising myself and my values. I was different from many of my conservative Southern classmates since I had been brought up by Northern liberal parents. Consequently many of my basic values were contrary to those of the people that I went to school with. This made relationships difficult because I often felt that I had to choose between getting along with others and being honest about my real feelings.

In ninth grade I didn't know how to deal with this conflict, and as a result I was shy and awkward. When I got involved in drama, I met people who were also a bit out of the mainstream. They helped me to feel comfortable in saying what I really felt when it was important. But I also learned that it was not necessary to always agree with someone in order to be friends, and that sometimes concentrating on similarities was better than worrying about differences. I think that I came out of high school with a stronger sense of myself because I had been exposed to such a variety of attitudes from than my own.

I made a speech at my graduation, and as I spoke in front of my class and our parents and friends, I felt comfortable with who I was and who they were.

I was grateful that I hadn't been sent to a British boarding school.

10 Falling from My Pedestal

Living in a family characterized by disharmony and constant threat of divorce, this author traces her serious eating disorder to her attempts to compensate for her parents' unhappiness by being a perfect child. But no matter how hard she works or how perfect her grades, Chhaya's parents remain unhappy and even criticize her efforts. The emergence of adolescent sexuality creates a crisis in her sense of perfect self-control that is followed by the devastating news that despite her obsessive hard work, she will not be valedictorian. Drastically restricting her intake of food becomes a compensating obsession and means of asserting self-control and achieving perfection. Her health deteriorates and she is hospitalized. She learns that she must discover her own realistic goals and give up her "insane drive for perfection." Her recovery proves to be arduous and long, but by the end of her story she feels she has turned the corner.

So many people have asked me "How did you become anorexic?" that I'm about ready to tape-record my life story and play it back the next time the question comes up. I try to explain using the analogy of a rainbow. The entire spectrum of colors comprises the rainbow, but no single color can be extracted—they all blend together to form a continuum. The same can be said of the illness. Anorexia wasn't something that just "happened" to me—I didn't one day suddenly decide to stop eating. My problems ran much deeper than simply "not eating." The disorder was my desperate attempt to maintain some semblance of control in my life. It was a cry to establish who I was, to pick up the pieces of my shattered identity. To make sense of this insidious disease, and ultimately of myself, I must confront and examine the issues that led to my using the eating disorder as a coping mechanism to deal with the turmoil that surrounded and threatened to suffocate me.

I am convinced that my childhood represents the beginning of much of what led to the anorexia. My identity problem goes back as far as the elementary school years, and starts with my ethnic heritage. I come from what you might call a mixed background. My parents could not be more opposite in their histories if they tried—my father is East Indian and my mother is a typical WASP. As for me, I've gone through my entire life not knowing exactly what I was. I've always despised filling out standardized forms that ask for personal information, because I never know what box to check under "ethnic origin." The categories are neatly defined, literally black and white, and people who are "melting pots" like me present problems for this efficient form of classification. Technically, I'm more Indian than anything else, but I always feel deceptive saying I'm Indian when I'm really only a half-breed. Thus, I end up the perpetual "Other," an unclassifiable anomaly.

No one would guess merely by looking at me that I'm part Indian—my hair and eyes may be dark, but I'm quite fair-skinned. The one thing that gives me away is my name—my horrible, terrible Sanskrit name which I'm convinced no one on this planet can pronounce correctly without help. I have lambasted my parents endlessly for sentencing me to a lifetime with this albatross around my neck. I can't even count how many times people have completely massacred my name, either in pronunciation, spelling, or both—the number is utterly unfathomable. I'm forever giving what I call my "name spiel," explaining the origin and meaning of my name. Since such an understanding requires knowledge of my background, the subject inevitably leads into a discussion of my family, one of my least favorite conversational topics.

Even though my parents' relationship was tenuous (to say the least), they never fought in public. No one would have guessed they were anything other than normal as far as married couples go. At home, though, the masks came off, the farce ended, and the boxing gloves were donned. The match would usually begin at the dinner table. Supper was the only time we all came together as a "family," if you can call it that. It typically started with something insignificant like, "Why didn't you fix mashed potatoes with the steak," and escalated inevitably into the divorce fight. You could always tell when one was coming on. First, they'd bicker for a few minutes, then the voices would rise. The remark, "Why don't you just leave?" by either of them was the cue for my exit, for I could recite practically verbatim the arguments that would follow. Mom would snap, "You should go back to India. You haven't been happy since you left." Dad's bark ran along the lines of, "Why don't you move in with your parents?" In spite of all the fighting and all the threats of divorce that were made, though, it was always just words. Neither of the two ever acted upon their vow to end the marriage.

I think the instability and uncertainty of their relationship bothered me the most. The dark, intense fear always loomed in my mind—would this be the fight that leads to divorce? Is this fight going to be the straw that's going to break the camel's back? What if they're really serious this time? I'd be fraught with anxiety after every one of their quarrels. Within a few days, things usually returned to normal, meaning the usual strained relations in the absence of verbal brawls. Once I knew things were "safe," that divorce was not imminent and that we would remain a foursome, I could breathe a small sigh of relief, at least until the next argument.

When you're young, you think the world revolves around you. Given my egocentrism, I blamed myself as the cause of my parents' marital strife. I felt it was up to me to salvage their marriage, which I tried desperately to do. After each fight, I would ask myself what I had done wrong and how I could rectify the situation. Harboring intense feelings of guilt, I lambasted myself for not pleasing them and not living up to their expectations. Maybe if I'd cleaned my room like they'd asked . . . I wondered. If I could just be good enough, I thought, they'd love each other and, in turn, love me. I erroneously believed I could bring my parents together by the sheer force of my will. Frustration over my inability to positively influence their relationship caused me to feel completely ineffective and inadequate. My solution was to be more perfect than anyone could expect a child to be, to hide all signs of anger and rebellion, in order to deserve and gain their love.

Being achievement-oriented in school was my answer to many of the problems I faced. By making the grades, I was sure (or so I thought) to gain the love and attention I so desperately craved, not only from my parents, but from my teachers as well. Because my family life was like an emotional roller-coaster ride over which I had no influence, I turned to school for comfort and security. I knew that by working hard, I could do well—in the classroom, I could exert complete control. As the perfect student, people would respect and admire me. Only if others saw worth in me could I be truly assured of my substance and value.

Unfortunately, my plan backfired on me. The more As I received, the more my parents and classmates began to expect I would continue to do well. I strove endlessly (and fruitlessly) to impress my parents with my good grades. At the end of the marking period, I would rush home, report card clutched in hand, hoping to have glowing praise lavished upon me. Words can't begin to describe the crushing disappointment I felt when they merely remarked pointedly, "We knew that's what you'd get." Part of me was angry at having my hard work and accomplishment minimized. Whenever I mentioned my grades, all they did was preach about how "Grades aren't everything in life." Another common point they made was that "Common sense [which they felt I lacked] will get you farther in this world than will good grades." I felt I could never win with them. It seemed as though no matter what I did, no matter how hard I tried, there was always something lacking, something else I could and should have done better. I yearned for reassurance and affirmation of my worth, but because I felt that I could never be perfect in their eyes, I could never be truly convinced of gaining their love.

These traits I have described were present throughout my childhood, but no one ever recognized them as potential problems. On the contrary, my drive to be good, to achieve, to live by the rules, and to avoid disappointing or arousing the criticism of others was what made me a model child, even though I never felt like one. The severe misconceptions I held became dramatically apparent, however, with the onset of adolescence, for I was pitifully unprepared to meet the issues of this period.

As I entered high school, I became even more rigid in my interpretations. My self-doubt intensified and my self-esteem plunged even lower. I was convinced everyone else was more capable, both socially and intellectually, than I. Never comfortable with myself, I constantly devalued my abilities, thinking I wasn't good enough for anything. Striving for perfection, for being the best (and then some), became my all-consuming goal, my purpose in life, to the point where I sacrificed all else. I studied all the time, believing that if I let up in the slightest bit, I would inevitably slip up and fail. All of my flaws would then be revealed, and I would be exposed for the imperfect person and the fraud that I was. To me, failure represented the loss of control, and once that happened, I feared I would never be able to regain it.

I became petrified of showing any signs that could possibly be interpreted as imperfection. I felt compelled to live up to and surpass the expectations of my parents, teachers, and peers in order to avoid arousing criticism, which I took as a personal attack. While others may have expected 100 percent from me, I pushed for 110 percent. So driven was I to succeed—or rather, to be seen as a success—that I imposed the strictest of standards on myself. Rather than creating a sense of pride, worth, and accomplishment, however, my role as the good, obedient, successful student—the girl who had it all together (at least on the outside)—caused me to feel increasingly empty inside. Paradoxically, the more "successful" I became, the more inadequate I felt. I began to lose control of my identity more and more as I fell victim to the Perfect Girl image in all areas of my life. I had no idea of who I *was*, only who I was *supposed* to be.

I denied myself pleasure throughout high school, never allowing myself to simply have fun. To do something for the sake of enjoyment brought forth incredible feelings of guilt and self-indulgence. I think part of this conflict arose from my parents' disagreement over issues regarding my (non)social life. My mother always had a tendency to be overprotective. She tells me that when I was an infant, she used to peek in on me, sleeping soundly in my crib, and pinch me ever so slightly, just to make sure I was still breathing. I think her reluctance to let me out of the house had to do with her overriding concern with shielding my brother and me from the dangerous outside world. At the time, though, I felt she was trying to suffocate me. I would vehemently protest against her fears; what reason had I ever given her not to trust me? "It's not you or your friends I don't trust," she would respond, "it's the rest of the world." My father, on the other hand, pushed to get me more involved with my peers. "Why don't you invite your friends over here?" he'd prod. I always found that suggestion rather amusing, given the nature of our household. If I asked to do something with friends, I was always bounced from one parent to the other to obtain permission, and usually they ended up arguing over the incident. As a result, I ended up feeling guilty for being the cause of their marital strife, a position that tore me up inside. Rather than jeopardize the family harmony (or rather, lack of discord) I often didn't even bother to ask to go out. I tried to avoid the conflict by removing myself from the situation.

I had friends throughout high school, but I always kept them at a distance, scared that if I let them get too close, they would see that I wasn't perfect and reject me. Relating to my peers was extremely difficult for me as a result, because rarely could I talk about my inner feelings. I equated the expression of emotion with weakness and vulnerability, so I always remained deadly serious and kept things on a strictly superficial level. To others, I must have seemed frigid, removed, and detached. I myself felt lonely and isolated. I desperately wanted to reveal the true me, but my intense fear of exposure silenced me.

Two specific events, both of which occurred during the spring of my junior year in high school, catalyzed the emergence of the eating disorder. One of these two major happenings involved my very first romantic encounter with a member of the opposite sex. Prior to meeting Kevin, I had had no experience whatsoever with guys. My self-confidence being what it was (practically nil), I thought no one could ever possibly be interested in me. An extensive "screening" process, with stringent standards that few guys could measure up to, was a way of protecting myself from unnecessary pain and hurt. If in every guy I met I found some fault that immediately made him undesirable as a mate, then I'd never have to worry about him rejecting me. I could remain in control and would therefore be safe.

My encounter with Kevin changed things dramatically. I met him in March at a two-day science symposium held at our state university. I had mixed emotions about Kevin—on the one hand, I found myself incredibly attracted to him and excited at the prospect of what might lie ahead, but at the same time, I didn't want to open myself up for fear of getting hurt. I wanted badly to be "swept away," to experience all the wonderful emotions described in romance novels, but reminded myself I should remain calm and levelheaded. After all, I was treading on completely foreign territory. My intelligence was of absolutely no use here, and since I couldn't rely on previous experience, I had to make sure I protected myself. Despite all of my hesitance, I was able to let my guard down long enough to experience my first kiss. Kevin and I, along with another couple, parked in his car in a secluded area of the campus. As the two in the back seat started going at it immediately, I sat uncomfortably in the front, eyes focused straight ahead. I was afraid to even look at Kevin, sure I'd flush with embarrassment. He would see right through me and realize how inexperienced with guys I really was. He was definitely the one in control here, as I had absolutely no idea how to behave.

We talked for a while (with his friends in the back continuing their dalliance), and then it happened. By "it," I am referring to one of the most monumental moments in a person's life—the first kiss. I had wanted mine to be as passionate and romantic as they come. After practicing on pillows for so long, I thought for sure I'd be ready when the time came. All of my rehearsing turned out to be in vain, though, for in no way did it prepare me for the intense emotions I felt. I remember more the mixture of thrill and nervousness that jumped around in my stomach more than I do the actual physical interaction of our lips (which I simply recall as being warm and wet). Thinking back on the event, I have to laugh at how it came about. I had undone my seat belt while we were parked, and when we were getting ready to leave, I couldn't rebuckle it. As I fumbled with the strap, Kevin leaned over to lend a helping hand, but instead ended up giving me much more than just a hand.

I was exhilarated by the thought that this tall, intelligent, incredibly gorgeous guy actually saw something good in me, something more than just my grades. He validated my sense of worth, and I began to think that perhaps I wasn't such a horrible person after all. Maybe there was something inside me other than the empty space that all the As in the world couldn't fill. Whereas my academic accomplishments gave me only a transient sense of self-satisfaction, the knowledge that Kevin liked me provided a warm feeling inside me that didn't fade away. For the first time in my life, I felt truly happy just to be alive.

In addition to the positive aspects of the relationship, there was, of course, a down side. I feared losing control of myself, a worry that was intensified by the fact that I was in completely new and unfamiliar territory. The incredible power of my feelings scared me immensely. In my family, I had learned the importance of always being rational and logical, of keeping my emotions in check and exhibiting self-discipline. Now here I was being "swept away," throwing all caution to the wind and acting purely on impulse and desire. The guilt I felt was extreme.

When I related the incident to my mother (the fear of telling my father loomed so large that I never talked about the relationship with him), I was thrown totally off guard by her reaction. I had pictured her throwing a fit and saying I shouldn't be getting involved with members of the opposite sex at my age. But just the opposite happened—she was glad I had met a "nice boy." Perhaps if he had lived in our town she might have reacted differently. Given how far apart we lived, dating was never feasible, so she didn't have to worry about my going out late at night doing God knows what.

Kevin and I had been writing and calling each other on a fairly regular basis, and I began to entertain the thought of asking him to the junior prom. Though absolutely terrified at the prospect of rejection, the encouragement of my friends and mother (who actually offered to have him spend the night at our house!) finally convinced me to take the risk via the mail. At the post office, my hands shook and my stomach quivered as I took a deep breath, opened the mailbox, and dropped the letter down the chute. As soon as the deed was done, though, I thought, God, what the hell have I done?! I'm setting myself up for the biggest fall of my life! How stupid could I be to think Kevin would want to go with ME?!

I awaited his reply with nervous anticipation, checking the mail every day as soon as I got home to see if it was there. When the letter finally arrived, I was so nervous I could barely open it. My stomach was literally doing flip-flops as I began scanning the note for signs of his reply. When I read about how he would love to be my date, how he thought we'd have a great time together, and how he looked forward to seeing me again, I was euphoric. I was practically bouncing off the walls, so full of exuberance and utter joy that I thought I'd burst with energy.

Within a week's time, I found an outfit (gown, shoes, clutch purse—the whole works), made dinner reservations and a hair appointment, and bought the tickets. Everything was in place when the big night finally arrived. After I finished getting ready, I decided to risk taking a look in the mirror. I was worried that I would find a brainy nerd who was trying hard to fit in where she didn't belong. The image that reflected back at me, though, caught me by surprise. With my hair pulled up and with flowers in it, my mother's pearl choker around my neck, the teal-colored gown flaring out around my waist, and the rosy glow of my cheeks (due more to my excitement, I think, than to the makeup I had applied), I was actually not half bad to look at. I felt as though I was looking at a stranger, for I knew the elegant young woman in the mirror couldn't possibly be me, the same person who always felt awkward and ugly. I truly felt like Cinderella, transformed if only for one night.

I was anxiety-ridden about seeing Kevin again—it would be the first time we had seen each other in some months. Everyone, both family and friends, loved him as soon as they met him. They all thought he was attractive, intelligent, and an all-around great guy. I floored everyone as I made my entry with him—not only had I myself been transformed, but here I was with a gorgeous date at my side. Finally my feelings of inferiority melted away. I had always been recognized as smart, but now on top of that, people saw me as attractive. The culminating event that evening was my election to the junior prom court. Normally a popularity contest, I never dreamed of standing among the four couples who flocked the king and queen. When my name was announced, I arose from my seat, mouth agape, as everyone around me applauded. Again I had stunned everyone, especially myself—smart people simply did not make the court. Proving them all wrong gave me a sense of uniqueness that I cherished. I reveled in my now complete blossoming from a former ugly duckling into a beautiful swan.

In spite of all its magic, the prom experience stirred up the same mixed bag of emotions I had felt when I first met Kevin, only to a much greater degree than before. At the dance, Kevin's open display of affection bothered me tremendously. I felt uncomfortable expressing my emotions in public, especially since I wasn't even sure exactly what I was feeling. I had no idea how to behave, and so I distanced myself from Kevin. If he moved his chair closer to where I was sitting, I moved in the opposite direction. If he tried to hold my hand, I would fold my arms across my chest. I wouldn't even let him kiss me in front of everyone. He was probably totally baffled by my behavior—I know I myself was, but I couldn't help it. Since I felt out of control and didn't know what to do, I turned to the only defense mechanism that I knew from previous experience had worked—isolation.

After the weekend of the prom, Kevin and I stopped writing and calling each other. To add to my confusion, my mother and friends expressed their disdain for my handling of the situation. They reminded me that I had had the chance at a relationship with a wonderful person and had blown it, big time. My mother, who had thought Kevin was one of the nicest, most polite, handsome young men she'd ever met, laid the worst guilt trip of all on me. She made it seem as though he had done me this enormous favor, for which I should feel some sense of undying gratitude and obligation. "Here this nice boy drove all the way over here just to escort you to your dance, and how do you treat him? Like dirt." As a result of others' reactions to my behavior, I became even more miserable and disgusted with myself. This relationship represented the first time in my life that I had tested the wings of independence and trusted my own feelings, and I had failed. The incident reinforced my belief that I was worthless and incapable of making decisions on my own.

I mentioned before that the prom was one of two important events that helped catalyze the emergence of my eating disorder. The second event, which occurred within a month after the prom, was my guidance counselor informing me that I was not ranked as first in my class. My very first reaction was that some terrible mistake had been made. There was absolutely no way I could be anything but number one. I was the only person I knew who had maintained a 4.0 GPA, with nothing less than As on all of my report cards. Becoming valedictorian had become my life; every aspect of my identity was in some way wrapped up in it.

When I expressed my disbelief to my guidance counselor, he assured me that no mistake had been made—I simply was not first. That's when the shock set in. I sat in his office thinking, "I have to get out of here NOW." The walls were closing in on me and I felt as though I was suffocating. I quickly mumbled something about having to get back to class and practically ran out of his office and into the nearest bathroom, where I let the intense pain that had been welling inside me burst forth. My heavy sobs shook my entire body, and I was hyperventilating so badly I could barely breathe. I leaned up against the wall and slid slowly to the ground, clutching my knees to my chest and pressing my hot face against the cool wall tiles. "How could this be happening to me?" I screamed in my head. Why? What had I done wrong? Hadn't I sacrificed everything for the sake of the almighty grade? Wasn't I the perfect student? How could I pretend everything was normal when inside I was falling completely apart? Afterward I fought desperately to keep up my false image of control and stability, stuffing my pain down further and further inside me in the hopes it would somehow magically disappear. Everyone expected me to be number one—what would they think when they found out I wasn't? If only they knew. . . . I felt duplicitous and deceitful, as though I was projecting a false image that was just waiting to be debunked. I was falling from my pedestal, and I knew the fall would be a long and hard one from which I might never recover.

The fall was even more profound than I could have ever anticipated. It devastated my life to such an extent that now, five years later, I am still trying to put back the pieces and recover. An eating disorder, however, was the last thing I expected. In my mind, I had imagined people losing respect for me, devaluing my abilities, and seeing me for the incapable fool I felt I was. That didn't happen. The only person to turn her back on me was me. I was truly my own worst enemy, endlessly berating and cursing myself for being so stupid. Gone was the radiant, smiling teenager from prom night, so full of life and exuberance. In her place was an ugly, sullen person who could barely drag herself out of bed in the morning because she saw no purpose to her life. The change was dramatic, but no one ever commented on it, perhaps because I was so good at putting on a happy face, and perhaps because they felt (or maybe hoped) I was just going through one of the low points that characterize the average adolescent's life. What others didn't realize was that this was not simply a phase that would pass in time—it was to become a deadly disease that would grab me by the throat and nearly choke the life out of me.

I don't really know when the anorexia actually hit me. Thinking back, it seems to have been more a progression than an event whose full impact hits all at once. Why I turned to food as a means of establishing control in my life, I honestly have no idea. I had never been concerned with my weight prior to this time. I was always thin, but ate whatever I wanted—in fact, I was the ultimate junk food addict. Chocolate, candy, cookies, chips—if it was bad for you, I loved it. These items were, of course, the first to go when I started my downward spiral, and as time went on, the list of "forbidden" foods grew while my food intake gradually but steadily diminished.

The earliest recollection I have of anorectic behavior involves its isolation more than the self-starvation. During the spring of my junior year, I began skipping lunch. My friends and I usually sat together during the lunch period, eating and chatting. Instead of going to the cafeteria with them, I starting holing myself up in the library, where I could be alone with my pain, as I felt I deserved to be. My friends immediately noticed my absence and commented on it. I told them I was simply doing my own research into the different colleges that interested me. I wasn't completely starving myself at this time, but what I now know were the early signs of my eating disorder went unnoticed at the time.

It wasn't until that summer that the disease began to intensify. With the school year over, I no longer had to deal with my teachers and peers on a daily basis. Thus, it became easier to isolate and confine myself to my own internal world, a jail cell out of which there was no escape. I felt I was divided into two separate personalities—one jailer and one prisoner, simultaneously beating myself up while begging for mercy. I would lie on my bed, behind the safety of my locked bedroom door, crying endlessly. One part of me was saying, "I hate you—you're stupid and worthless," while another part was pleading, "Please don't hate me— I'll work harder to make you like me." It was a no-win situation, though. There was no pleasing the jailer, no matter how hard the prisoner inside me tried.

As the prison walls began closing in on me, I fought desperately to hang on. I got a job waitressing at a nearby restaurant, and tried to keep busy by working as much as I could. My work schedule made it easy to hide my eating patterns from others. Since Mom and Dad worked full-time, I was safe for most of the day. "I ate something before going to work and then had dinner on my break," I'd lie. If anyone at work asked about my eating habits, I'd say my mother was saving dinner for me when I got home. I was really clever about deceiving others, as most anorectics are, and delighted in the thought that I was able to pull the wool over everyone's eyes. No one would be able to figure me out, I vowed. By keeping to myself, I'd be safe and protected and could get back some of the security that I felt had been brutally snatched from me.

I started cutting back on my intake with the initial goal of becoming "healthier." I'll look and feel better if I get toned up and shed a few pounds, I told myself. After a period of restriction combined with exercise, I lost between five and ten pounds, and did in fact feel better about myself. The source of my improved self-image wasn't so much being thinner as being able to accomplish something with tangible results as reinforcement. I could step on the scale and watch the number drop from day to day, just as I could feel my clothes getting baggier around my waist. Here was something I could do successfully! Maybe I wasn't good enough to be first in school, but I certainly seemed able to lose weight, a task that presents enormous difficulty for many American women.

I read every article on health, nutrition, and weight loss I could find. I sought the diets that offered the quickest route to losing weight, pulling together bits and pieces from each to develop an elaborately detailed plan of my own. I learned what foods were "good" and what foods were "bad," and became a careful label reader, comparing caloric and fat content for a wide variety of foods. Going to the grocery store was a big production—I would spend ages in each aisle, trying to hunt out the products that would give me the most food for the fewest calories. Almost paradoxically, food became my obsession, the center of my world. Pouring myself into losing weight became a substitute for pouring myself into my schoolwork.

As with all other areas of my life, I gave 110 percent to the illness (when I commit to something, I do a thorough job). My insane drive for perfection, however, once again turned on me, in the same way it had done with my schoolwork. Losing that first bit of weight left me feeling good about myself for a little while, but then I began to question the greatness of my accomplishment. After all, I told myself, five pounds really wasn't that much—anyone could lose that amount of weight in no time with minimal effort. Now, if I could lose ten pounds, *that* would be something—shedding that much weight requires more commitment and dedication. If I could do that, I'd really feel capable of doing something important. Thus, longing desperately for that feeling of self-worth, I readjusted my target and continued in pursuit of my new goal.

Of course, once I reached this new weight, the same thing happened, and a vicious cycle developed. No sooner would I finish patting myself on the back than a little voice in the back of my head would squelch my pride, saying okay, maybe you achieved that goal, but I bet you can't meet this one. . . . I found myself getting caught in a cycle of self-destruction. Even though I craved success, I would go out of my way to ensure it eluded my grasp. As soon as I reached one goal, I'd set a new, higher standard. I was doing to myself the very thing I hated my parents for doing to me. Whereas I could detach myself from my parents, however, I couldn't escape myself. I internalized the frustration of not knowing how to please them, to the point that I was unable to recognize and meet my own needs and desires. Because I didn't even know how to satisfy myself, I was forced as a consequence to look to outside indicators of my value. My life became dominated by the numbers of the scale, which governed all of my feelings and emotions. If the number fell, I was secure and happy (for at least a little while). If it moved in the opposite direction or not at all, I panicked and tried frantically to think of a way to regain control of my body. I based my every mood on my weight, not realizing that in doing so I was setting myself up for failure—though I didn't realize it at the time, self-worth comes from within, and can't be found outside oneself.

As I continued my quest for a "wholeness," an identity I thought thinness would provide, I failed to recognize the self-destructive path I was following. My body became more emaciated, but all I saw in the mirror was excess flab that I had to be rid of. I rejoiced when the skirt of my waitressing uniform became so big I had to use safety pins to keep it up. One day while going through my clothes (which were becoming baggier with each passing day), my eye caught a glimpse of my prom gown, sheathed in plastic and hanging at the very back of the closet. I decided to try the dress on, just to see how it fit. As I removed it from the plastic, I thought about how far away the dance seemed—almost like another era, even though in actuality only a few months had passed. I pulled the dress on and zipped it up, only to have it fall past my bare and bony hips to the ground. Gone was the elegant gown that had transformed me into Cinderella. All that remained now was a mass of teal-colored satin lying in a pile around my feet. Though somewhat wistful over my inability to recapture the magical quality of prom night, I comforted myself with the thought that at least I wasn't fat like I had been then. Thinness was the one measure I could grasp hold of to convince myself I was better now than I had ever been.

I deluded myself into believing I really was doing fine. Though I experienced all the telltale symptoms of the eating disorder—constantly feeling cold (especially my hands and feet), hair falling out, problematic bowel movements, insomnia, amenorrhea, dizzy spells, skin discoloration, and the gnawing hunger that penetrated to the bottom of my stomach—I brushed them off in denial. I can recall only one instance that summer when I was forced to face the gravity of my illness. I remember getting out of bed and heading for the bathroom to take a shower. As I reached my bedroom door, I got a swift, overpowering head rush that nearly bowled me over. The room started spinning and I had to clutch the door frame just to keep from collapsing. My heart started palpitating and I felt as though my chest was going to explode. For the first time in my life, I truly thought I was facing death. I leaned against the door frame and let my body go limp as I slid to the ground. Stabbing pains pierced my heart so sharply that they blinded me. Oh my God, I thought, what have I done to myself? I prayed to God to please let me live. I'll eat, I promise I'll eat. . . . I won't try to lose any more weight. . . . I'll go back to eating normally. . . . Just please make the pain stop and don't let me die!

Being faced with the all-too-real prospect of death shook me up enough that I did fix myself something to eat. The frightening impact of the incident faded rapidly, however, and within a few days I was once again back to restricting. I passed off this danger signal, reassuring myself that since I survived the episode, I must be fine. When I tightened my grip over the food, I was in control—I was invincible, and no one could touch me. The eating disorder gave me an incredible feeling of power and superiority, a sense of independence. I could prove that I had control, that I could accomplish something on my own.

You may wonder where my family was in all of this mess. Didn't they see me slowly wasting away into nothing? I vaguely recall them nagging me from time to time to eat. I don't feel any resentment towards them for "letting" me become anorexic, for not catching me before I got as bad as I did. They were, I'm sure, in as much denial as I was. Acknowledging my disease would (and eventually did) open a Pandora's box full of problems, ones that went far beyond my not eating to include the entire family. My mother did get worried enough towards the end of the summer to call my pediatrician. When she explained my situation, his advice was to get me to take vitamins (just the solution to an anorectic's problems!). His failure to recognize the severity of my illness made it easier, I think, for my parents to gloss over the situation. Having a doctor's reassurance probably put their minds at ease. The family problems could stay safely locked away, at least for the time being.

I somehow managed to make it through that summer, and the beginning of my senior year in high school soon arrived. My mother tried to warn me of the reactions people at school would have to my emaciated appearance, but I could see no difference in how I looked now as opposed to how I looked at the end of junior year, when I was at least twenty pounds heavier. She was right on target in her assessment of the situation. I'll never forget the looks I received from my class-mates and teachers that first day of school. Their eyes bulged and their mouths dropped in horror as they stared at the withered, drawn figure before them. Three months earlier, I had been a healthy teenager and now all that remained was a skeleton covered with skin. I was incredibly self-conscious walking through the halls, certain all eyes were on me and that the topic on everyone's mind was my dramatic weight loss. Feeling like a queer anomaly, I tried desperately to cover my twiglike arms and hide my body under baggy clothes. My answer to the stunned looks was that I had been sick and was run-down as a result. Though I found it per-fectly plausible, my explanation was met with skepticism. No one pushed the issue, though, probably due to my unwillingness to discuss the subject, evident by my curt responses to their questions.

Within the next few days, the nurse called me down to her office. Apparently, nearly all of my teachers had voiced their concerns regarding my health. I offered the same excuse to her as I had to everyone else—yes, I had lost some weight, but would be fine once I had a chance to recoup from being sick. She was skeptical at my insistence that everything was okay, but I promised to work hard to get back my health. I was, of course, lying through my teeth. I had absolutely no intention whatsoever of returning to what I considered my grossly fat previous weight. Did people think I was going to abandon my quest for thinness just like that, simply because that's what they wanted me to do? No way was I going to let all the hard work I had poured into this project over the past three months go to pot! I was annoyed with others meddling in my life. Rather than seeing their concern for its genuineness, I was convinced they were trying to undermine me. They just wanted to see me fail at something else so they could laugh in my face. Well, I wouldn't let that happen! I'd show them that I could achieve! They would marvel at how well I could shed those pounds and admire me at least for that, if nothing else. I thought that perhaps by being successful at losing weight, I could somehow make up for my intellectual flaw of not being valedictorian. I was knocking myself out to impress others for no reason, though. The only one who cared that I wasn't first was me, but ironically, that was the one person I was unable to satisfy no matter how hard I tried.

I remember one key experience that clued me in to the severity of my prob-lem. While going through candid photographs for the yearbook, I discovered two of myself. I picked them up to examine more closely and gasped in horror as I looked at the ghastly image captured on film. Her face was as white as a sheet, her eyes sunken, and her cheeks severely drawn. The blue veins bulged out of her sticklike arms, and her clothes hung limply on her fragile frame. She looked mor-bidly depressed, a pathetic creature who seemed ready to snap at any moment. Surely that person couldn't be me! Tears started welling in my eyes as I looked at that picture. What had happened to the smiling, vivacious teenager of the previous spring? She was like a rose that had bloomed and then withered away. I bawled uncontrollably as I realized I was falling apart. The life was being slowly sucked from me, and I was growing increasingly weak and helpless. Please God, help me get my life back together, I prayed. I don't want to die!

You may think that, having recognized myself as having this disorder, I would be well on my way to recovery. I know that's how I felt—now that I really *wanted* to get better, to get back to a normal life, I would. I tried to convince myself and everyone else that I could tackle and overcome this problem on my own. The solution was simple, I thought—all I have to do is eat and gain back the weight I had lost, and I would be fine. Unfortunately, it wasn't quite that easy. Anorexia nervosa had come to symbolize 17 years of emotional instability, psychological turmoil, shattered dreams, and bits and pieces of my fragmented identity. There was a lot more that needed fixing than simply my diet—all of the issues that permeated my entire life needed to be confronted and dealt with before recovery would be possible. It took everyone—my family, friends, teachers, and even myself—a long time to realize this and to recognize the full, devastating extent of the disease.

Though I really did want to get better, I was unable to regain the weight my body required. Having gone beyond the point of no return, so to speak, I continued to lose poundage. The nurse finally suggested my mother take me to a specialist, someone who might offer the assistance I needed to get better. I became absolutely irate at the very mention of the subject. "I am NOT crazy, and have no intention whatsoever of seeing a shrink!" I hollered at my mother. But she was adamant. The psychologist I went to see was unable to help me, though. My disease had progressed much too far by the time she intervened. About a month later, she told my parents there was nothing more she could do for me, and recommended I be evaluated for admission into the Eating Disorders Service at a nearby children's hospital. Though I strenuously resisted the idea of hospitalization, my mother calmly but forcefully put her foot down: "We can commit you without your having any say in the matter." My parents were finally taking charge.

In terms of my treatment in the hospital, Mom and Dad focused more on the outer me—my body and its weight—than the evolution of my inner self. Whenever I spoke with them on the phone or whenever they visited, the very first question was always, "How's the weight doing?" My recovery became framed in terms of numbers, the very thing I was trying so hard to get away from. I had based my entire identity on tangible indicators of my worth—grades, class rank, weight—at the expense of my true inner being. As a result, I never established a self-directed identity. My work in therapy to evoke an awareness and understanding of the impulses, needs, and feelings that arose within myself was incredibly difficult and emotionally draining.

Before my admission, I had been closer to my mother. She was always the more reliable one. If I had a problem or needed something, I always went to her first. My father, on the other hand, was a lazy bum. I couldn't count on him for anything except for material objects. When I was in the hospital, this changed dramatically. Mom was like an ice woman. All the other parents felt guilty, thinking they were in some way responsible for their child's eating disorder. Not my mother. She staunchly and promptly informed me that she was not going to take the blame for my problem. At the time, I saw her as cold and heartless. I *wanted* her to feel sorry for everything she had ever said or done that caused me to be the way I was. She *deserved* to feel guilty for creating the sham of a family life I had to endure. My father, on the other hand, was easier to deal with when I was heavily dependent on him, as I was when in the hospital. I think he needed to feel needed by me, to feel in control of my life. He called me every night, just to find out how my day had gone. On his frequent visits, he would always bring fresh flowers, and we would sit and talk, watch TV, or take a walk. I remember on one occasion, we even made the bed together. It was times like these when I felt closest to him. I wanted to be taken care of, and he seemed willing to do the job. The combination of my not wanting to grow up and his wanting me to stay daddy's little girl helped to sustain this dependence. Though at the time I saw his behavior as a form of care and affection, I now recognize it for the power game it was.

Paradoxically, our weekly family therapy sessions failed to reflect these newly developed interactions. During that one hour, the family roles reverted to their usual prehospital form. At first, I actually looked forward to family therapy, thinking it would expose some of the important and volatile issues that had always been buried underground. Finally, we would be able to resolve our problems and, I hoped, become a loving, cohesive unit, the perfect family I longed to be a part of. Unfortunately, this miracle transformation didn't occur. Our problems ran much too deep for even a therapist to tackle. The sessions became as much of a sham as our family itself was. Every week it was the same thing. Everyone, with the exception of myself, shied away from the real issues, the potent problems we faced as a group of four individuals collectively termed a "family." My parents always wanted to discuss specific aspects of the Eating Disorders program, details that were "safe" for them—for example, "Why isn't she eating any red meat?" or "When is she going to get back to eating normal foods?" Getting them to recognize that food was not the main issue, that the eating disorder cut far deeper, to the very core of my identity (or lack thereof), was the most difficult task I faced. I would try to bring up a particular aspect of our home life—for example, my parents' marriage or my brother's attempt to shut himself off from the rest of the world. Before I could even finish my account, though, my father interjected, shaking his head and protesting, "She's making too much of this and blowing things way out of proportion."

The dismissal of my emotions as trivial wasn't nearly as bad as what came next. "Our family life may not have been wonderful," Dad admitted, "but it was relatively normal until she began this whole mess and disrupted all of our lives. She's the one with the problem, not us." I sat dumbfounded, not believing my ears. How could he possibly lay the entire blame on me? Did he honestly believe I had planned on becoming anorectic, that I set out on some mission to destroy our family? I refused to just sit back and let him heap any more blame on me. I had meekly taken all the denouncing for so long that I had internalized and turned it back on myself, resulting in incredible feelings of guilt and self-doubt. I couldn't stand the torture any longer. "You're wrong if you think I'm the cause of everyone's problems," I told my father point blank. "We had problems long before I got sick." To my surprise, my mother then spoke on my behalf, saying to him, "You can't blame her for everything. We're part of the problem, too." Finally, someone was taking my side! I looked over to my mother with gratitude in my eyes, silently thanking her for saving me from drowning in a sea of guilt and self-worthlessness. At least she was beginning to recognize my problem encompassed much more than a simple decision to stop eating. Throughout this entire scene, my brother remained isolated and detached from the rest of us. When confronted, he would usually just shrug his shoulders. He had a grand total of two standard responses to the therapist's questions—"I don't know" or "I try not to think about it."

After six weeks in the Eating Disorders Service, I returned to the real world—back to my home and family and to my teachers and friends at school. Everything was pretty much the same, though. My parents still fought and my brother still shut himself off in his room. I was still obsessed with food. Though I had gained weight and was now eating more, I still kept a meticulous log of every (measured) bit of food that entered my mouth. I refused to touch red meat, junk food, or any kind of fat whatsoever.

Eventually, I had to resign myself to the fact that I alone cannot repair the immense damage that exists within our family. Without the cooperation of others, my endeavor is doomed to failure. I have relinquished my role as the family savior, realizing I am unable to control the behavior of my parents and my brother. I can, however, change my own actions and reactions within the family structure. An important, and difficult, part of the recovery process has been extricating myself from the dynamics of the family in order to develop and accept my own independent sense of self.

I can't believe I'm almost through with my college career. So many things have changed since I was a clueless, teary-eyed freshman. Now I'm half through my senior year. Within the past year alone I have undergone a complete metamorphosis, beginning with my revealing my anorexia to the world. I had wondered for so long whether I would ever be able to overcome this wretched disorder, and finally, I have reached the point where I can eat when I'm hungry and stop when I'm full. My recovery has been due in large part to the drug Prozac, which has also made me less obsessive and less high-strung. My recovery, however, has had its ups and downs. This past summer I fell into a deep depression. I felt like my life was spiraling out of my control, that everything I had worked so hard for was falling apart. I spent most of my days crying and mulling over things. I didn't even want to go back to school in September to finish my senior year, but everyone convinced me to do so. I got treated for the depression, and finally decided to take medication for it. I had adamantly refused to do so in the past, though an antidepressant was recommended by two of my previous psychiatrists. When I think back to how bad I was this past summer, I'm so thankful that I got help in time and was able to turn things around before they got completely out of control. I'm finally starting to feel good about myself, comfortable with who I am, and actually happy!

A big part of the change in me is due to LOVE. Yes, I finally met someone who was as attracted to me as I was to him. He has stood by me through some of the worst times of my life, through fighting the eating disorder as well as depression. I started seeing him nearly a year ago. Things were rough at first, mainly because of my inexperience and the issues I was having to deal with about myself. I was freaked out about sex and mostly about opening myself up to someone. I had been so egocentric for so long that it's been hard to give some of that self-centeredness up. I also had my first sexual encounter with him. That was another issue I had a hard time dealing with at first, but now, after having lived with him for the summer, it seems pretty silly.

I thought for sure that we would spend the rest of our lives together, deliriously happy and in love. But this past summer really put our relationship through the wringer. We've been fighting a lot, but more than that, I think we've been starting to pull back from each other. We pretty much both know that June will bring with it not only graduation but the end of our relationship. It's been really hard for me to accept that what I thought was an infallible, perfect romance is actually not immune to problems. I really wish things had worked out the way we planned them, but I guess I should have learned by now that life doesn't always follow the plans you make for it.

So, you might ask, what happens next? Well, I have moved ahead, and after four long years, I have finally beaten this disease. I feel as though an enormous weight has been lifted off my shoulders (no pun intended), and that I am finally ready to move ahead with the rest of my life—to "live, laugh, and love," as they say. I'm optimistic about the future, for if there's one thing I've learned, it's that I'm a fighter. . . . And, more importantly, I'm a survivor.

11 At Least We Got One Right

In this case, Brian describes his close, intense relationship with his parents. The third of three children, he is the "perfect son," the one who will fulfill his parents' dreams of academic, social, and economic success. Even as Brian appreciates and responds to his family's love and support, he finds that he must hide a great deal from his parents in order to explore friendships and relationships in school and later at college. Catholic school contributes to his sense of the conflict between the ideals and illusions people maintain and the realities of his own life and the lives of others. Brian struggles to live up to his parents' and siblings' expectations, to maintain the stable family environment, and to figure out who he is and who he will become.

It is Christmas. I am 19. My brother, 33 years old, is crying alone in the next room, his old bedroom. My father is not speaking, has been stoking the fire for the last hour, his face burning from the heat. My sister, a bruise on her left arm, is trying to explain things, screaming so loudly at my mother that her voice starts to scratch and fade. My mother's face is wrinkled with tears. Choked from crying, she barely has enough breath to tell my sister to get out of her sight—she says if she hears any more about it she will throw up.

My brother has just told us he is gay. For me, it is not really a surprise, more of an explanation, a confirmation of something I had already known for some time. A reason, almost, for why he has always seemed so closed-off and passive. I feel many things—scared and sorry for him, confused and happy for him, repulsed and empathetic—all at the same time. I would like to express these feelings, but I hold back. I don't let anyone see. Because I have always been the responsible one in the family, the flawless one, it suddenly becomes up to me to fix the crying and desperate silences that are now invading all the rooms in the house. I will have to start to calm people down, to change people's minds, to pull the family back together. It's simply the way it's always been.

For a while, even I thought our family was lucky, that somehow we had been blessed. Looking back now, after all that's happened, it is easy to see how we thought this, how comparing our own little family to our extended family and to the families we watched on the news or saw on the talk shows made us feel virtually untouched by life's tragedies. Sure, there were minor arguments (my sister spending too much money, my brother spending too much time away from home), but these were usually smoothed over before they got out of hand. Never were there any of the chronic troubles, any of the violence or drugs or pregnancies that rooted themselves into so many families we knew, problems that lingered and eventually tore them apart. We prided ourselves on the fact that these kinds of things had not happened to us and felt almost consciously that we deserved the peace we'd been granted. For this reason, my mother and father and older sister and brother and I considered ours the luckiest family in the world. We thanked God every day and threw that word—lucky—around without a second thought, always saying things like, "I'm so lucky to have a mother like you," or "You're the greatest sister anybody could ever want." We were always hugging each other, and we never left each other or hung up the phone with each other without saying I love you. In these very sincere words and gestures we professed how much we cared; there is no doubt in any of our minds that we all love each other deeply and with all we have. But beneath these words and gestures and love lay all the things we were all either too scared, too embarrassed, or too proud to say. Beneath it all lay the addictions that we kept to ourselves, the private pain that we hid for so many years and for so many different reasons. Today, provoked by a single night and a single announcement that forced us all to confront what we meant to each other, my family is just beginning to realize the cost of keeping too much inside. But in spite of all this and in spite of the soul-searching and sharing my family has been forced to do, there are still secrets that I find myself clinging to. There are still some illusions of myself I can't afford to shatter.

Here was the American success story, the stuff of miniseries and Fourth of July specials: A man and his young bride fled war-torn Europe for America, settled down in the poorest area of the city, and began to make their lives. The husband, my father, worked seventeen-hour days on an assembly line. The wife, my mother, got a job at a dry cleaners that she had to walk an hour to and from each day. Once, walking home, she was thrown against a wall and beaten up for the change she kept in her stockings. To get out of this area, they saved up money and began a succession of moves into increasingly nicer areas until they reached one secure enough to start a family. This theme characterizes their whole lives: the quest to move up and out. They sacrificed everything and anything to make sure that their children would have a more stable and comfortable life than they did. It became an obsession, not just a goal or a hope, to keep climbing this imaginary ladder. And if they couldn't climb it themselves, they would climb it vicariously, through their children.

They had a girl first, my sister, then my brother the year after. My sister married at 19 (not because she was pregnant, of course, but because she was in love with a man with a good job who came from a wealthy family). She got a good job and gave birth to two athletic and bright boys who are now breaking records in their respective grade schools. Together they live in an area at least five rungs up from the area my parents settled for, in a house we used to gaze at from the road and only dreamed of living in. For a while, we were able to blame her husband's temper on his Italian blood. We called it part of his "color," and my sister laughed right along with us.

My brother never married or went to college or had very much money but did live the life of the swinging single, having the looks and the charm to do so. For a while, watching his age increase, his energy sink, and the women decrease in number, we feared his true love would never come. In his company, though, we called him the family Casanova and pretended we weren't worried. My parents saw education and marriage as the ways to climb the ladder and so my brother grew up constantly pressured to concentrate in school and date girls seriously even though it was obvious that he simply didn't have the knack for school or the commitment to a steady relationship.

I was born 15 years after my brother, when my mother was 41. I am what my parents have come to refer to as "the best accident they've ever had." It is said that from the minute I was born I was something astoundingly special, that I lifted my head up instantly when my mother first held me, looking around at the world with a fierce curiosity and excitement. It is said that I was reading the *TV Guide* at two, that by the age of three I was already writing my name and entertaining visitors with little shows and stories that I would create in my head. In grade school I won countless academic and service awards and never got a grade less than an A. In high school I won national writing awards and even spoke on national television. I'm not only the first in our extended family, one as far-reaching as Sicily and as numerous as seventy members, to go to college, but the college I attend has an internationally known and respected name.

In direct contrast to my brother, I did everything right. If my parents were always harping on my brother for screwing up even the smallest things, they were always praising me for even the smallest things I would do right. An example of this is how they took my sister and brother to Europe when they were in grade school. My brother cried the whole time he was there, clung ferociously to my mother's side, refused to do anything, and basically ruined the trip for everyone involved. When they took me when I was roughly the same age, I was "an angel." It's a wonder my sister and brother don't hate me for being the perfect one. I always felt guilt for the constant praise I got and shied away from acknowledging it when I was in their presence. It used to embarrass and anger me terribly when, in their company, my parents would lavish praise on me and simply smile at my brother and sister as if to say, "at least we got one right."

I can't remember one single time when our family sat down together and talked about anything important, any problems any of us were having. No Brady Bunch family meetings were ever called in our house. It was simply assumed that no one was having problems and there was nothing to talk about. Whenever one of us did something good, got a raise, a good grade, a new stove, we all talked about that for hours, praising each other and saying how happy and lucky we were. But never the problems. It has been easy for my family to think that because I am "a genius" in school, popular socially, and stable within the family, I am able to handle anything. It's not true, never has been true, and much of the control I may have been assumed to have has been an illusion. It is an illusion, however, that I have created myself and that I still persevere. I have let them see only my brightest pieces and have successfully covered up the others.

I was always a very lonely and morbid child, in spite of (or should I say because of) the academic success I had in grade school. Everyone knows the class brain is no fun, and boy was I no fun. I swear I used to wear three-piece suits to the second grade (there are pictures!), and my hair was always combed and parted so severely you'd think I was from Transylvania. And I was too mature for my own good, excited not by the things little boys should be excited by (mud, frogs, cars) but by fun things like what the last chapter in our math book was about and could the teacher promise we would get to it? Once, a month after our first grade teacher had randomly mentioned that no word in the English language was spelled with two consecutive *i*'s, I found a 45 by a singer named Amii Stewart in our stack of albums. I was excited to the point of shaking that I had proved my teacher wrong and actually brought the 45 in for Show and Tell. I got booed. I think even the teacher booed me. From then on, I was labeled as the geek.

Because of my geek status, I had no friends until the sixth grade, when I befriended the other weirdest kid in the class, Richard. We spent our recesses walking around the playground singing songs, and everyone called us fags. When I wasn't with him, I was at home making up math problems to solve or watching television. On Friday nights, instead of sleeping over at friends' houses or playing moonlight football in the neighborhood, I would sit up with my mother and watch soap operas. Many of my conversations with my mother centered around these soap operas, what would happen to J. R. or to the Ewing ranch, and we used to laugh and joke and pretend we lived in a huge house with servants and fancy cars. During the sex scenes, though, all conversation would cease and we would look stone-faced at the screen, not breathing, hiding every emotion, pretending it wasn't happening. When they were over, she'd laugh guiltily and say, "if your father knew I let you watch this . . . " and that was the extent of any discussion of sex that ever went on in my house. Any hint of sexuality outside of "doesn't your sister look pretty?" or "look how handsome my sons are!" was never expressed. As a result, I learned everything about sex from *Dallas* and *Dynasty*. I learned that it was dirty and unspeakable.

On those Friday nights my mother and I would sit in the family room with the windows open and I remember that I could hear all the neighborhood kids yelping outside, riding their bikes and making mischief. I remember feeling two conflicting ways: very sad and sorry for myself, sure that I had some kind of disease that made me an outcast and a weirdo or that, maybe, I was *so* special that I was too good for those boys. I know I was most convinced that there was something wrong with me, that there was some reason why no one talked to me in school and I spent my recesses helping the teacher clean the classroom, but what was it? I concluded that, fundamentally, I was an awful person. Or was it just that I couldn't swing a bat or catch a ball to save my life? Or were they just jealous of my academic prowess (my parents' explanation)? Or did I just need to be more friendly, more receptive? I was plagued with self-doubt and self-loathing, the fear that I was a freak. But I had also bought into my parents' notions that all of my hard work, all of my concentration on school, would pay off later and that I just had to wait. I was a mass of contradictions, sure I was headed for greatness but convinced deep down that I didn't deserve it, that I wasn't good enough, that I would be found to be a fraud.

I know that my parents noticed how unpopular I was, that no one ever came to the door for me, but they considered this a necessary sacrifice. I realized later that they were happy that I was unpopular, glad I wasn't associating with anyone who would expose me to interests outside of school. I think that they were lonely, too, my brother and sister having moved out, and that they were counting on me to keep them young. They wanted to keep me all to themselves, and in grade school I grew fiercely attached to them. I considered them my best friends in the whole world, and I loved being with them. I have fond memories of driving in the car with my father, playing games with street signs, him teaching me jokes and me trying to say them back. We would test-drive expensive cars we could never afford just for the fun of it and watch cartoons in the afternoons that he had off from work. He taught me card tricks and jokes and prayers and laughed when I could never get them right. I remember trying to teach my mother how to read English, using the old blackboard we had downstairs, giving her tests and quizzes and hamming it up as the teacher. I would put old 45s on the record player in the basement and practice little shows for her, then call her down and dance and sing my little heart out for her. I would bow at the end and she would clap and clap and say that one day I would get an Oscar, and I believed her.

My mom and dad would always say, "Friends will always let you down, but your parents will never leave you. We are the only ones you can ever count on in this world." Though I know that they meant no harm in telling me this all the time, that they were just trying to express to me that they loved me with all their heart, it is an example of the distrust they instilled in me, one that stays with me yet. They both always had a fundamental distrust of anyone who wasn't a member of the family or at least a member of the same ethnicity. I understand this distrust and paranoia and know that it is attributable to their own upbringing and the hardships they had in escaping the war and fighting prejudices in America, but I still resent the fact that even today it is very difficult for me to trust people. Even today it takes a lot for me to be convinced that my friends are really my friends.

My attachment to my parents, I think, is the cause of virtually all of the problems I am having today. As much as my parents came to depend on me (to keep them young, to fulfill their dreams, to fix all the minor problems), I came to depend on them to an unhealthy and ridiculous degree. After all, they were all I had, and they needed me. I have never felt so needed by anyone as I have felt needed by my parents. Because they are from a different country, they are very naive. To this day, my mother cannot read or write and my father can just barely get by. By the fifth grade, I was balancing their checkbook, filling out insurance forms, addressing letters, and writing birthday cards to their friends. A very interesting dynamic began to form: I treated them as children, and, as far as certain things went, they treated me as an adult. No wonder I acted so mature in school! I worried about my parents all the time, terrified I would lose them. Once, in Bible school, we learned that when someone contracted leprosy they were taken instantly from their home and never heard from again. For a while I lived in a paralyzing fear that my parents would contract leprosy. In school I would find myself short of breath, heart racing, worrying about returning home at the end of the day and finding them gone, my only friends in the world gone. Those, I think, were the first instances of the panic attacks that would recur later in high school. I was always conscious of the fact that my mom and dad were older than most parents and convinced myself that they would die before I got a chance to grow up. Still today, every time my parents are five minutes late I am convinced that they are dead in a car accident. I am always snooping in my parents' room for their medical records, making sure that they aren't hiding the fact that they have cancer. These fears are more rational than they sound. My parents are the type of people who won't tell their kids they are sick until they are on their death bed. When my mother was going into labor with me, she told my brother and sister she was going shopping. When, two years ago, my father went in the hospital for a minor but pretty risky operation, my mom said he was working late. I can't even count how many different nightmares I used to have about going to their funerals.

I have always been a TV junkie. I think that I watched so much TV growing up that I sometimes find it difficult to separate what really happened to me during my childhood from what happened to characters I saw on television. Growing up, my greatest longing was to have the boyhoods I saw on TV. I wanted to track mud in the kitchen, to catch frogs with my bare hands, to race matchbox cars up and down the walls. I wanted to step up to the plate and, for my teammates and the crowd around us, hit the winning run. I wanted to be carried home on their shoulders. I wanted to get in trouble with the neighborhood boys, to come in late, to skip school; to be one of the guys, to break the rules and risk the consequences, and then have my parents find out, get angry, but then laugh it off and chalk it all up to "boys will be boys." This, I knew, would never happen. Any rebellious action, any action that didn't involve bettering myself or bettering my academic career, would mean disappointing my parents and taking away their dreams. I refused to let myself do that, and so I never let myself get caught doing anything remotely wrong or making any sort of a mistake. Instead, the times when I did get caught were devastating to me. Once, in the fifth grade, I got a 58 percent on a social studies test, which meant that I had to have it signed by my parents. I was white as a ghost the whole day, barely able to eat or speak. I remember handing the test to my mother and crying uncontrollably. She called my father into the room and, after their initial anger and confusion (how could this have happened?), they began to *console* me because I was completely out of control. When I finally stopped crying, they told me that it was okay, that I could always make the test up, and that they weren't mad. But I was inconsolable. They asked me why, and I had no reason for why I was so upset. Now I know it is because that small failure, that fifth-grade fluke, was a chink in the armor that I had so painstakingly fashioned for myself. It was a mistake I couldn't cover up, and it meant that I wasn't perfect. How upset I was symbolized that I would never be brave enough to rebel, never brave enough to let them know that I was not perfect, that I was just like the rest, just like my brother; that not only did I have no friends, but that I wasn't even as smart as everyone thought. I always knew that I wasn't as perfect as I'd always been told I was, but that didn't matter as long as my parents didn't find out. I know that it is all still true today, that because I never let them see me make a mistake from the beginning, it's impossible to start now.

As a kid, I felt I had to protect my parents from the bad things going on in the world, the things like bad language, breaking rules, and sexuality that I was beginning to notice in grade school. These things were brought to me courtesy of a group of friends that I remarkably gained late in my grade school career. It came slowly, and it started with one person: Mark. He was the class clown, the most popular person in the class, and he lived down the street from me. He was one of the kids I used to hear from my window, and I would have given anything to be his friend. We had walked home from school together in the same "Walkers" group since first grade, but it wasn't until the seventh grade that he struck up a conversation with me and, to my amazement, invited me over to his house. I was beside myself with joy. I couldn't believe it! We hung out, watched TV, lit off firecrackers in his back yard. Soon we were walking home together every day, spending hours sitting on the curb in front of his house talking. It was a dream! I helped him with his homework and he taught me how to be "cool," how to dress, how to play sports. He introduced me to his friends, the cool crowd of my class, and assured them that I was all right. Acceptance from them came more slowly, but eventually it came. Suddenly I had a group of friends who called and came over, and I began to look at myself differently. There were people who admired me for how smart I was, and thought it was funny that I was too scared to be as rebellious as they, to go pool hopping or steal condoms from the Rite-Aid. Of course they didn't know that I was scared of disappointing my parents, but that was okay for then. The times I spent with Mark and my new friends were times I cherished and replayed over and over in my head. But the joy I got from these times, from the water fights and stickball games and popularity, was not enough to commit me to giving up my role as the class brain and family treasure. My parents disapproved of Mark because he was the dumbest kid in the class and because he had introduced me to sports. They didn't like me hanging around with him, but felt I was mature enough to pick my own friends and they didn't forbid me to hang out with Mark. My times with him, though, began to be plagued with guilt because I was always told by my parents that "You are only as good as the company you keep," and that Mark was not good enough for me. The crazy thing was that I believed them! I actually thought that I was somehow above Mark when I actually had so much to learn from him: how to get along with friends, especially boys, how to let loose, and, ultimately, how to enjoy just being a kid. I was trying so hard to uphold my perfect image to my parents that I learned to lie about everything I did with Mark. Instead of playing or riding our bikes across the highway, we were doing homework. I got to be a very good liar, and, since my parents were so naive and trusted me so much, they believed me. I felt incredible and irrational guilt. Here I was trying desperately to be the perfect kid, and all the time I was lying! Here my parents were supposed to be my best friends, and I had abandoned them for the dumbest kids in the class! I wanted so desperately for my parents to think that everything was great, that I was great, that my friends were great but that they didn't compare to them, and that they didn't have to worry. I lied because I didn't want them to worry, because I feared not their punishment but their disappointment. I wanted punishment! I wanted to be sent to my room without supper! The funny thing is that the things I was doing—climbing trees, sneaking down to the creek—weren't even that bad! They were "normal" boy things to do, according to TV at least. I didn't understand why my parents would be so freaked out by them if they knew I was doing them! The truth was that I never knew what their reactions would be because they never found out about them. I told them only the good things and they never found out about any of the bad things I did, with the exception of that 58 percent.

I went to St. Joe's for high school, a notoriously strict and athletics-oriented Catholic boys' institution that also had a great academic reputation. I was terrified of this place from day one. The Catholicism didn't scare me, since my grade school had also been Catholic. It was all those guys: 1,500 of them roaming the halls next to me, guys three times my size who traveled in packs and spoke with the deep voices I still hadn't acquired. Where was the tiny grade school where I was a star? Where was the softness of all those girls in their plaid skirts? All of my grade school friends were gone, the beloved group it took me eight years to win, and I had no vocabulary for these Cro-Magnons I now found myself with.

Mark was my only friend from grade school who went to St. Joe's and I clung to him as much as I could. But because he was tracked much lower than I was, I never got to see him during school time. I banked on the fact that because he still lived down the street from me, we would still hang out and he would ease me through all the parties and dances and football games that we went to together. It took me a while to realize that high school friendships are defined by the quantity of time that you spend with someone and not by the quality of that time. Because we spent the bulk of our time in school in classes with different kinds of people, the amount of time we spent together was cut short and we began to grow apart. We still got together and chatted every once in a while, and we still told each other things we would never have told anyone else, but outside of these times, I simply didn't feel comfortable with his jocular friends guzzling beers in the backs of jeeps, and he felt uneasy with the "smart people" whom I slowly began to befriend. We still considered each other "best friends," though, and somehow at the time just that label was enough. But our relationship was often tense: At the random party when we would run into each other, we were both conscious that the "geek" was talking to the "jock." Groups of friends on our respective sides would stare us down as we spoke, or at least that's how it always felt.

Those first two years were very lonely ones, surpassed only by my first year of college. I spent most weekend nights writing in my journal, writing angst-ridden poems about the fleetingness of happiness and the burdens of being young and alone. I wrote fake suicide notes to myself and dreamed of how horrible everyone would feel when they found out how disturbed I was. I would call in to those radio shows where people dedicated songs to their significant others and give fake names, pretending I had someone, feeling overwhelming bouts of self-pity. I wasn't doing as well as had been expected in school, either, getting my first grade ever lower than an A on my report card: a C in algebra. I was a wreck showing this to my parents, who promptly scheduled a meeting with this teacher and myself. It quickly became apparent that math and science (I was getting a B in Biology as well) weren't my things and that English was where I really shone. My parents were very relieved by this, assured that an interest in English would turn into an interest in law (I don't know who they got that idea from) and that I would make lots of money as a lawyer someday. I had a fabulous English teacher who encouraged me and inspired me to love literature and writing. At parent-teacher meetings, he would tell my parents I was one of the most talented students he had ever had, and my parents would glow for days. They convinced themselves that if I really wanted to, I could do well in math and science and that, if I had to, I could always go to medical school and become a doctor. It was simply a matter of putting my mind to it. I just shook my head, letting them believe what they wanted. What was the point in disappointing them?

It wasn't until my junior year in high school that I found a group of friends that really affected me, a handful of guys who seemed both winnable and exciting. These were the "alternative" guys, the ones who wore black and painted peace signs on their bookbags, who smoked pot and memorized Allen Ginsberg poems. They fascinated me and I felt a real kinship with them. Like me, they didn't really fit in with the rest of the people in school. Like me, they also seemed to think they were too good to hang out with the "cool guys." I made a conscious decision to become a part of their group. Since they were all smart, they were all tracked in the higher classes with me, and one or two different members of their group would be in all of my classes. I campaigned unabashedly—desperately—for their friendship, sitting next to them, striking up conversations with them, dressing like them, and saying things in class that they would agree with. I remember kissing up to their hippie contingent in my history class by asking, "Could you tell us more about the peace movement in the sixties?" It was very blatant, but it worked, and soon Gabe, the ringleader of the group, began talking to me. He invited me to sit at their lunch table (an absolutely crucial and risky first step), loaned me some of his tapes, and invited me to hang out with them on the weekends. Again slowly, and again with the help of one guardian angel, I had a group. I knew I was one of the gang when I roomed with them at a weekend retreat we were all required to go on our junior year. We smoked pot and did whip-its in the bathroom and I was in heaven. Here was real rebellion! Never mind the unbelievable guilt I felt doing drugs on a religious retreat, I had finally found a group of my own in high school. Now I was ready for Happy Days.

I began to drink and smoke pot regularly with Gabe and his crew, lying to my parents all over the place. Though they waited up for me every night no matter how late I came in, they were too naive to notice that I was drunk or stoned. My grades didn't suffer—they actually improved, I think—and things were relatively easy and fun. I was frightfully insecure about my group, though, no matter how much I was accepted. It came back to the learned mistrust I had gotten from my parents. I was constantly afraid my new group would discover I was a geek in hippie clothing and send me back to the abyss of nerddom. Even though they respected me for my talent in school and my eagerness to "try anything once" (as long as I could do it before curfew), I still held on to these fears. I would panic every weekend that they wouldn't call. When they did, the high from that renewed acceptance lasted for days. My insecurities came from the first six years in grade school and the first two years in high school when I had no one except my parents and a couple of Friday night DJ friends. I would do anything to keep from returning to that.

My senior year of high school was the best in my life as far as friends were concerned. There were parties every week, and I gained popularity with all different types of people. Though I still maintained the same group, which I by then was co-leading with my new best friend Gabe, I made other friends who were "cool" and, through them, even started to hang out a little more with Mark. I entered short stories and essays in contests and won national recognition, trips, and money for them. I read in a nationally televised ceremony in front of an audience that included ex-presidents, Nobel Prize winners, and published writers. I was accepted on scholarship to a top-rated school and my parents and family radiated pride for a whole year. "It was really happening!" they thought. I had the whole world open for me, and my family was convinced I was going to be a millionaire. By the time I graduated, I had gained a new security within my group of friends, which by then included girls from our sister high school, St. Anne's, and during the summer before college we spent every moment we could together. We were all going to different colleges, and we knew things were going to end, so we clung to each other as tightly as we could.

So much for friends. What about those other complex entities called girlfriends? The fact is that girlfriends, at least the gaining of them, has always come easily to me compared to the gaining of guy friends. It might have been because I was always told by my parents and family that I was very handsome and attractive to girls, which helped me to maintain some self-confidence when it came to talking to them or going to dances. More likely, though, it had to do with the fact that I have always been a little confused about my own sexuality. Though I have always been attracted to women, and still am, I have always felt an attraction to men that was stronger than merely wanting to be their friend or a part of their group. I didn't want to admit it then, mainly because I didn't really understand it, but I did know there was something different about me, a reason why when the other boys called me and Richard fags in the fifth grade it affected me more deeply than it should have. I had crushes on the most popular girls and the most popular boys in grade school, wanting to kiss them and touch them and be as close to them as I knew how to be at the time. Though I knew this about myself in grade school, and knew it clearly, I refused to believe it and waited for it to pass.

I never had a crush on Mark or Gabe, but there were plenty of opportunities in an all-boys school for these kinds of crushes. I mostly had crushes on the cool and popular guys, on the rich, clean-cut ones with the nice cars and beautiful girlfriends. I think I had a crush on heterosexuality, on the strong man who knew how to handle a woman, on the guys who seemed more slated for the life that was expected from me by my parents than I ever seemed. More than wanting to be close to these guys, though, I wanted to *be* them. I longed for their strength and confidence, their coarseness, the sure movements of their hands. I was too sensitive with the girls I dated in high school, too cautious, and always scared I was offending them or pressuring them. Though I was incredibly and frustratingly attracted to them sexually, I was too "nice" to try anything more than kissing. I wanted to have my way with them and not care about their feelings, to treat them badly and have them love me anyway. I wanted to tell the guys in the locker room what I got off them. Just like in grade school, though, I wanted to want to do these things more than I could actually bring myself to do them. I was too uncomfortable with my attraction for the guys in the locker room to ever discuss girls with them and too uncomfortable and confused about my sexuality to ever be very aggressive with a girl, afraid that she would somehow figure it out if we got too close. Again, I didn't understand why the "normal" youth experience was denied me, why my life wasn't a sitcom, why I wasn't one of those skirt-chasing guys with a great smile and a whole lotta heart. Everyone around me, including the members of my group who everyone considered the hippie fags, seemed to be having fabulous heterosexual sex and wild experiences while I was stuck on first base.

I had a stream of steady girlfriends from the beginning of junior year when I first became accepted by Gabe's group. I went on dates with girls and had month-or-two-long relationships with them that included drunken explorations of each other's bodies and passings of notes that expressed the love we said we felt for each other. I dated Kim my whole senior year and we proclaimed our eternal love for each other. We even came close to sleeping together, but she decided she wanted to wait. We broke up before she could decide, and I left high school a virgin, the only one, I thought, to come out of there since St. Joe himself walked the halls. Though I did tell Kim I loved her, I never felt the kind of love I had come to expect from all the movies and TV I'd seen. There were none of the Bobby Brady fireworks, none of the puppy love I'd expected. Romantic love, to me, meant not being able to eat, sleep, or breathe without thinking of the person you were in love with. It meant that your mind was always consumed with thoughts of her only, that you'd rather be with her than anyone else in the world at every given moment. By those rules, I had never been in love with any girl, even, as it turns out, the ones I dated in college, and again I didn't really understand why I was being denied. I began to get scared that I would fall in love with another man. I hid my frustration and confusion over this from absolutely everyone and didn't even write about it in my journal in case anyone found it. I was waiting for it all to pass. I was waiting to wake up as the Fonz.

Now that I have had more time to put things in perspective, I realize that going to Catholic schools all my life has had a lot more to do with my adolescent difficulties than I originally thought. I think both schools I went to were fundamentally unhealthy environments because of the hypocrisy inherent both in the Catholic doctrine they taught and in the codes of discipline that were built from this doctrine. Both schools seem to have had a deliberate agenda: to establish a community of unquestioning believers through strict discipline, guilt trips, and discrimination against those who didn't fit in. Grade school, I think, is survivable because all the crucial questions about one's self haven't yet come to the forefront, and it is a time when you are still completely trusting authority. High school is the time when all these questions come to the surface and demand attention, and so it is the Catholic high school that has a responsibility to address these questions and help its students become strong individuals.

St. Joe's and Catholicism in general say they build themselves on one fundamental maxim: Love your neighbor as yourself. My earliest memories are of hearing this phrase over and over and believing that it was possible. At St. Joe's, we heard it every day and learned to feel guilty when we couldn't live up to it. The problem was that the school itself couldn't live up to it and yet would never admit it. Catholicism, a religion that stresses love and acceptance in its teachings, couldn't be more intolerant when it is put in practice. St. Joe's was a very sexist, racist, and homophobic place, a school that encouraged regarding women as objects (all the whistling and grabbing of the St. Anne's girls in the halls that was laughed at by the administration) and that favored its white majority by discriminating against its black students. (If you compared the percentage of detentions and expulsions given to the handful of black students at St. Joe's with the percentage of those given to white students, you'd find a frightening imbalance.) Heterosexuality was taught as the only way of life besides celibacy; homosexuality was evil and sinful. The school's goal was to combat the turbulence of adolescence by providing a regimented and strict set of rules, to provide a stable and reliable backdrop to the instability of the teenage years. It worked for the students who couldn't see the discrepancies in the church teachings and who didn't recognize the appearance-orientedness of the discipline code: the fact that it was OK if you harbored hate for a certain group as long as your hair wasn't too long or you were wearing a tie. I still clung to the beautiful parts of Catholicism—Christmas, Easter, all the pretty rituals—but was forced to reconcile what I liked about it with what I found disgusting: its hypocrisy and intolerance. Catholic school taught me the importance of keeping things hidden, the stakes of being different: losing your god, your family, your well-being, your peace of mind. This only fueled my crises of personal and sexual identity. The school that was supposed to love me condemned me and my brother, and swept us under the rug.

The Catholic religion, in spite of all I did to combat its hypocrisies, did manage to ingrain some very conservative views in me. I hate feeling this way, but a part of me still believes we were better off when mothers stayed home and gender and societal roles were held firmly in place. This comes, I think, from my years of TV (all those fifties shows) and from my longing for a stable environment that mirrored those families where everything was always resolved, where no one was divorced or gay or on drugs. Of course I know these families were fantasies, that everything that goes on today went on then as well, but that doesn't seem to make a whole lot of difference. In spite of the fact that I believe in equality for all people and tolerance of virtually every difference, in spite of the fact that I vote that way and do what I can to combat ignorance and intolerance on a personal level, these conservative feelings and wishes and expectations still creep up. I fear that I am just as racist, sexist, classist, and homophobic as I have accused my church and family of being.

My first year of college was a nightmare. I cried every day for the first two weeks I was there, going home every opportunity I got (my house was only an hour away and my parents were more than happy to pick me up) and feeling lonelier than ever. I missed my parents terribly, scared that without me they would grow old, grow sick, and die. All my kid fears resurfaced. I missed the everyday routines of home and neighborhood, the kids playing stickball in the street outside my window, the lulling landscape of suburbia I had taken for granted. I was paralyzed by nostalgia. I couldn't believe anything in the future could compare to my high school experiences and the friends I had there. I was forcibly detached from my parents, and I couldn't deal with the fact that my childhood was over, that I was no longer their little boy. I didn't think I could survive without their protection and stability, and I missed the babying and unconditional love that I had grown accustomed to. Who would love me like they? Who would be as committed to me, as believing? No one, I thought. I was a wreck.

Everyone seemed to be so well-adjusted, comfortable with all these new, incredibly intelligent people. The same way I was scared of all those guys in high school, I was terrified of the leagues of geniuses who weren't just in my classes but living right next door to me. I was scared of all the issues and all the melodrama that surrounded them, all the anger and hostility of activism. There was not one stupid person on campus, no dumb jocks or flitty girls to feel superior to. It was now time to prove myself, to really rise to the occasion, and I was sure I couldn't do it. I had always believed my smarts were a fraud because they came very easily. I hardly ever studied and I always managed to do extremely well. I relied on my talent in writing to get me through and distinguish me from those who could use both sides of their brain equally brilliantly. Mostly, though, I felt like the dumbest person at school and convinced myself I would never fit in. I was silent in all of my classes, scared to open my mouth, thinking my insight was juvenile. I rationalized that these geniuses around me were nerds who needed to get a life, who weren't as cool as I found I could be. I told this to someone on my hall—someone who would drink with me when I asked her—told her how I thought college would be, all keggers and one-night stands and hangovers. She flatly stated: "You're at the wrong school." I wanted to do all the college things I saw in the movies, all the constant partying and practical jokes. Instead, everyone seemed so serious, so into their academics that they had no time for fun. They acted like I did in the third grade. I started drinking more than ever to escape from it all, and, as is common to too many college experiences, that's when I started making friends.

By the end of my first year, I had established a set of friends that I loved, and I was very happy in that regard. I managed to find people with similar backgrounds to me and strike a balance between hard work and hard partying. I dated several women, but the kind of love I had always expected never happened with Jane or Hannah or Maria. Though Jane, the woman to whom I eventually lost my virginity, told me she loved me and I told her I loved her back, it never felt to me like true love. It always felt pretend. Though I had a very good sexual and emotional relationship with Hannah for a while, I never felt the all-encompassing love for her that I so desperately wanted to feel. We broke up amicably after three months, knowing we were meant for different people. I started dating Julie soon after Hannah and I broke up, and we had a sexual relationship instantly, but nothing outside of that. We enjoyed each other's company, but our relationship was mostly physical and we didn't pretend to try and stay together after she graduated. Through all these relationships, my feelings for men increased, especially after I found out about my brother and heard all those statistics about genetics and environment. I am terrified these feelings will eventually take over, in spite of the fact that I have never had a semblance of a romantic relationship with another man. Every recent relationship I've had with a woman has been a comfortable one, one I have settled for but not initiated, one I've sort of fallen into and gone along with until it was obvious it couldn't go on any further. There was always something missing from these relationships, something that prevented me from feeling truly happy about them and about the women attached to them. So many times after being intimate with Jane or Hannah or Julie, I would be overwhelmed with a tremendous sadness and guilt; sadness for my inability to give myself totally to them the way I had always wanted to give myself up, and guilt for my unwillingness to be completely truthful with them.

I grew to love college life, the freedom of it, but I still needed to go home every Sunday. I needed a break from all the intensity and I needed to see my parents, to make sure they were okay. My mother cried every time I pulled into the driveway and every time I left to go back to school. My not coming home, though, would have killed my parents, who centered their weeks on these Sundays, preparing feasts made for kings on my arrivals and pampering me shamelessly. It made me feel guilty; guilty, I think, for growing up, for moving away from being their baby into becoming my own man. I regressed in their presence. I didn't want them to think I was having any growth experiences, and so I, of course, lied about what I was doing in school. According to my parents, I did nothing but study and go to the occasional movie. They knew none of the real stories, none of the drinking or drugs or the men I was fantasizing about or what I was doing with the women I was seeing. Again, this was my fault. How were they to know if I didn't tell them? And how was I to start? How was I going to sit them down and say that this had been going on for years, that who they had known as their son for twenty years was someone completely different, someone with desires and faults and addictions?

What does a family do when its tradition of lies and covering up starts to break? What does a family that has never let the word *sex* come over its lips do when one of its members says he is gay (i.e., a disgusting pervert, a demon, doomed to hell?). Mine reacted with tears and anger, and it was up to me, the one who supposedly had no secrets, to patch things up.

My brother apologized to me, said he couldn't help the way he was. He said he hoped I wasn't embarrassed by him. My sister hugged me, said she knew I would understand, because I was the only one with his head on straight. My father shook his head, then said, "Thank God I still have one real son." My mother clutched me so tight that my ribs ached, crying into my shirt. She managed to say, "You are the only one who has ever made me happy."

But they were talking to a stranger, someone they didn't know. I wanted them to know me, and I wanted to say to my brother: "You don't have to apologize. More and more I am being convinced that I am just like you. Despite all the pretty girlfriends I've had, there has been an inkling of something different about me, something I refuse to acknowledge. You are not alone, and my head is not on as straight as they think." I wanted to say this, to assure him that he was not alone in this, but I was too scared. Instead of saying what I wanted, I hugged him and said, "Everything will be all right. Mom and Dad will understand because they love you, and I understand because I love you." He hugged me back tightly, tears of relief streaming down his face. He hugged me as if I was the last person on Earth, and I envied him because he had the courage to begin to free himself.

I wanted to tell my sister that it was time to follow my brother's lead and come clean with the problems she was having in her marriage, to leave Bill and get out of that situation. I wanted to tell her that I understood how badly she wanted us all to think she had the perfect family, how it was the only thing she had ever been appreciated for and that she didn't want to screw it up and seem like a failure. Instead, I took her arm and said: "Stop yelling at Mom; you're not making things any better. She'll be okay; I'll talk to her later. But now you should just go home." She said she trusted me to calm things down.

To my father, I wanted to say: "Don't count on me to make things right because I'm terrified of life and of my future. You have two sons, and you should remember that more often, because I won't be able to cover my tracks for much longer and you'll see that I'm just like the rest—not smart, not talented—that I'm just as bad as the rest." But instead, I told him in the deepest voice I could muster: "He's going through a rough time right now, and he needs us. Sure, you don't have to worry about *me* (I can't believe I'm saying this, digging my hole even deeper), but *he's* your son, too, and he needs you. Don't abandon him this way." He considered this, because my words carried weight, and kept stoking the fire.

To my mother, I wanted to say: "Don't you know how many times I've made mistakes, how many times I've come home stumbling, driven the car drunk; don't you know I've stolen things from stores, had sex with girls, fantasized about men, lied about grades; don't you know how sad I've been, petrified of my future, how I've wanted to get out of this house and this area of the world for so long, to break free of you and Dad, and yet have been too scared to leave you by yourselves? Don't you know how I have been paralyzed with fear that I would lose you and yet, sometimes, I have wished for that very thing? Don't you know I'm not as innocent as you think?" But instead I said, stroking her hair, "Shh, it'll be okay, I'm here, Shh, things will work out, I love you, Shh, stop crying now, there's no reason to cry, I'm here, Shh."

I played the part like the actor I have grown up to be.

Today, it is disturbing to me that I am still wearing the same masks I have worn since the first grade. The stakes have risen, though, now that I am about to graduate from college and begin to make my way in the world. There is a lot that's expected of me, and the overwhelming feeling that I have as I think about the future is guilt: guilt for the lies I've told and the people I've betrayed into a false hope. I know that what I want to do with my life—write—won't be enough for my parents. I know they are expecting more than I will ever be able to deliver, from the amount of my paycheck to the structure of my lifestyle. Scarier than how well I know that I can't keep all the pretending up for long is how much keeping my perfect image intact matters to me. I won't let myself disappoint them—I can't—because with every chink in my armor a little love will be lost, a little respect taken away. I won't settle for anything less than the hyperbolic love I've received from them throughout my life. I knew it as a child and I know it now: There is no one else out there who will love me the way my family has loved me. Unlike my family, others are not blinded by any happiness or hope or expectations that they have invested in me over these many years; therefore, others see my mistakes and faults and realize that I am nothing special.

I do consider myself lucky for the love I have received from my family. There are some people out there reading this who have never felt or will never feel the strength of such a love. But it has been a mixed blessing: It has given me support and protection and many happy memories, but has also stifled me from being all that I could be. To fit it into a popular cliché, the love of my family has given me roots, but no wings. For now I am desperately holding on to my roots, scared to shake things up any further, playing the role of the perfect son with however much pain and deceit it takes.

Brian: Three Years Later

It is Memorial Day. I am 24. My brother has invited me to a barbecue at his partner's house; he never misses a chance to spend time with me, hopeful that this will be the summer we finally connect. My sister is organizing a party of her own to celebrate the sprawling stone mansion she and Bill have just bought. Bill is calmer now since being promoted, but my sister has spread herself thin with the worry of a forty-something working mother; her physical bruises have been replaced (as far as I know) with intense anxiety and the panic attacks we've both inherited. My parents, still in the dark about any of their children's anxieties, have never been happier. I've chosen to spend a month with them before returning to grad school; they've fixed up my old room, cooked my favorite meals, and treated me like a movie star forced to lay low a while. Sometimes I catch them staring at me, starstruck, amazed at their luck at having me home. But when they stretch their arms to hold me, bury their heads in my chest (I'm taller now and can rest my head on my father's when he hugs me), I feel mostly grief, a profound longing for the life we've never had. We are still strangers.

My relationship with my family has always been defined by longing. I have lived six hours from them for the past three years, but I still speak with my parents every day on the phone, mainly for us both to make sure that we're still alive. We never discuss anything beyond the weather, what we've made for dinner, or how we're doing at work and in school. I experienced a minor victory when I convinced them that I didn't need to talk to them on Thursdays or Fridays, that I was just too busy to call, until Thursdays and Fridays would come around, and I'd feel that same fear I felt when I was younger—that while I was off living my carefree, selfish life, they were somewhere in danger, dying, in pain. I braced myself every Saturday morning when I called them, and when I heard both of their voices, I'd relax and settle into the pleasantries of conversation, feeling guilty but thankful to have them in my life. During our conversations, the longing would always mount: I'd want to tell them about my life, have them share in my worry and confusion, but instead I'd keep silent, focusing on my honors and intermittent happinesses; after I hung up, the anxiety would rebuild until Sunday morning, when the cycle would begin again.

My friend Gail told me recently that I was unhealthily obsessed with my parents. At first I took her comment the way I took it when my ex-girlfriend Hannah years ago accused me of not being close to my parents—I refused to believe either comment was true and vigorously defended my family's unique understanding and abiding, if blind, love. Now I know both women were right. I am not close to my parents because they don't know me, and though I'm obsessed with the fact that they don't know me, I'm completely unable to make myself known to them. Though my therapist maintains that my parents never allowed me to express myself openly to them, that they carry the bulk of the blame for our shared inability to be honest about our mistakes and fears, I take on most of the burden. I feel that my parents raised me the best way they knew and that, if I were stronger, I would be able to be honest with them, and we could enjoy each other for the rich, complex, beautiful, flawed people we are.

Though I feel I have come a long way since writing "At Least We Got One Right," in the presence of my family I am still the same high-achieving, peacemaking, jolly savior I described then. If anything, because of my graduate school and work experience as both a high school and college teacher and my ability to live independently in a distant city and yet keep close ties with friends and maintain an active social life, they view me even more as a hero. I have since learned that no one in my extended family has ever lived more than two hours from their original home (not counting emigrations, of course); one of my cousins, for example, attempted to attend college across the country but dropped out only three months later. She returned home emaciated and depressed, apparently malnourished on a life away from her overprotective family. Within, I am like this girl—seething, scared, lonely, anxious, dreamy, vaguely hopeful, and constantly waiting for my life to begin, yet I have somehow been able to hide all of these conflicting emotions under an elaborately detailed mask of control, reason, and satisfaction.

I am amazed at how much I both knew and didn't know about myself when I was 19. As you can already tell, the same issues are still as salient now as they were five years ago—a fact that is even more startlingly disheartening when I remember they are the same issues that plagued me as a child—and I am impressed that I was able to isolate these issues as clearly as I did in that piece. That I was able to recognize my constant fear of being found a "fraud" (still a major fear today), my inverted relationship with my parents, and that "my attachment to my parents . . . is the cause of virtually all of the problems I am having today" convinces me that adolescents are all too aware of the nature of their needs and fears, and that they may even know how to address them. Though isolating these issues (then and now) has not prompted me to actively improve my family dynamic, I believe it has allowed me, over time and by much risk taking, to be more honest with myself. Most important, it has given me the courage to make myself known to others (to friends, co-workers, etc.—anyone not related to me).

Three major issues have marked my past five years: the remembrance of sexual abuse I endured as a child, a continued conflict with my own sexual orientation, and the treatment of my panic disorder through therapy and anti-anxiety medication. Though I have taken decisive steps to deal with these immense issues, I still have a long way to go to achieve some sense of peace with them and to integrate them healthily into my family and social life. Attempting to separate these three issues from each other, to order them or arrange their cause and effect, is as difficult as distilling the subtleties of my identity development down to ten thousand words or less. Yet, mercifully cathartic, writing this essay helps me to see that certain issues remain broader and less unique than I once suspected. I know now more than ever that I'm not alone, and it helps somehow that you the reader are sharing a part of my life with me.

I spent an anxious and lonely year living at home after college, teaching at a local high school and attempting to salvage a social life out of the few friends left in the area. That Christmas my parents and I vacationed in Europe in the country from which my parents emigrated, and though I felt connected to my heritage there, identifying strongly with the passionate esthetes in my mother's family, I was distanced by language and oppressed by my parents' constant presence and attention. They were literally the only people I could talk to; we ate every meal together, slept in the same rooms, and packed ourselves tightly into tiny cars on endless sightseeing tours. Midway through the trip, I began having inexplicably gruesome nightmares of being chased, trapped, or smothered. One day toward the end of the trip, as I was peacefully writing in my journal about watching my grand-mother with my mother and enjoying a rare moment to myself in the early morn-ing, I began to think about those Friday nights I wrote about so nostalgically in "At Least We Got One Right," when my mother and I would watch soap operas, and I would listen longingly at the window for the neighborhood boys playing outside. It's true that I learned that sex was "dirty and unspeakable" on those nights but not only from the soaps we watched and my mother's dubious censorship. I came to remember, simply by writing it down during that day amidst the beauty of my ancestral home, how, after the soaps were over and before my father got home, my mother and I would crawl into her bed together, and she would sexually mistreat me. There was never any physical penetration, anything that could have been con-strued as rape, but mostly a lot of inappropriate touching that seems now a lot like wrestling or horseplay. At first the details were very vague but real; unfortunately, since remembering them, they have become more and more real, and they are clear, damaging, and frightening. I was so young, so trusting, and so entranced by my mother (she looked like Audrey Hepburn and acted with as much style and sophistication; she was my best audience for all my silly stories; and she was my best friend) that I never thought twice about expressing affection to her then, about touching her and letting her touch me. Our family was always very physically affectionate, so this did not seem extraordinary at the time.

In the last few years, dealing with these memories in therapy and on my own, I have felt a range of emotions both all at once and in stages: intense confusion, dis-belief, anger, guilt, sadness, embarrassment. I have felt like damaged goods; I have felt betrayed. Writing this feels like another betrayal. I still love my mother, but I will never forgive the physical, emotional, and metaphoric ramifications of her actions—my inability to trust anyone (especially the women) I've dated or see them in any way other than as suffocaters (there is always the image—and sensation—of my mother's body on top of me, crushing me; it's as real as if it were happening to me now); my fear and intermittent repugnance of women's bodies; the feeling of fear at the end of every night with a woman or a man that I will be forced to please them. In the four years since I have remembered those nights, I have not been able to maintain an intimate (sexual and emotional) relationship with a woman or a man. Every time I am with someone romantically, I am 8 years old again, and he or she is my mother, and I am being seduced against my will, forced to do what I feel duty bound to do, not what I actually want to do. I don't really know what I want to do or whether I even want to do anything except feel safe. I am left lying next to my boyfriend or girlfriend, ashamed and heartbroken, scared and embarrassed, pouring my heart out to him, trying to explain, telling her the whole story (I don't lie to anyone except my family). Everyone I have dated has always been patient, kind, and understanding—with few exceptions anything but suffocating, demanding, or sexually aggressive—and offered to see me through my problems, but I don't let them. I've rejected and broken up with all of them, hoping that with the next person I'll be okay, I'll be over it. I'm still waiting, longing for that next person. I am most afraid that my mother's abuse has ultimately denied me the capacity to love anyone fully, that her systematic betrayal has forever prevented me from achieving what I've always regarded as my highest goal: a family of my own to love and care for, to whom I would be devoted. I spend hours alone in restaurants and coffee shops now writing in my journal, looking around, glancing shyly at attractive strangers, hoping for some glorious revelation in his or her eyes, hoping to be rescued by them.

Of course no one in my family knows about the abuse; I have only told my therapist, two close friends, and the three people I have dated since my trip to Europe. I can't bear my own shame in reliving it again, but I especially can't bear the look of pity in their eyes that says, "how awful for you; you must really be fucked up." The only way I've found to coexist peacefully with my mother is to mythologize her, to find reasons for what she did. I know she was lonely; I know she thought she was doing nothing wrong, that we were just "playing"; I know she has always been a very seductive woman, taking pride in—and using—her beauty and personality to get what she wanted; I know those nights were her way of letting me know she thought I was just as beautiful as she and that she loved me. I also know I was desperate for attention and that I must have enjoyed feeling "special," yet I can't determine whether my lifelong need to be the best in everything began before those nights or after. These days, I can barely hug my mother without shuddering, though I do it anyway. It's difficult for me to tell her I love her, though I do it almost every day and though I'm constantly—without reserve or hesitation, with only boundless affection—telling my father that I love him.

Before and after my trip to Europe, I believed that being with a man would be the answer to my fear of intimacy and my inability to truly enjoy sex or feel comfortable in a relationship. I had convinced myself that my biggest problem was my inability to accept my homosexuality and that once I came out, I would (like my brother) finally achieve peace. I had a short, secretive, and purely sexual fling with a man during my last year of college, and though at first it felt exciting, instinctual, and good, I eventually began to fear him and distrust him, afraid not so much that he would tell people (I had already begun that process, coming out as bisexual to my friends) but that he expected more from the relationship than I could give him. He was talking love, but I wanted only to feel physical closeness with a man; I didn't see that the two could go together. Eventually, I turned him into my mother and avoided him. I had a similar experience with a female housemate a year or so later: We drank, we had sex, we talked, she wanted more, I turned her into my mother, she betrayed me, I fled.

My most significant relationship has been with an older man named Mark who I met in grad school. At first the relationship was all very romantic, like something out of a movie. We met at a party (my first all-gay party) and talked the entire night on the couch, unable to get enough of each other's company. He was a doctor (a real catch!) and handsome, if not exactly the boyish type I always desired. We went on a few dates, taking it slow, revealing ourselves to each other soberly, jumping into bed with clear, informed heads, one eye on safety in this age of AIDS, the other eye on pure excitement about sleeping with someone you knew and were beginning to fall for. This experience in itself was new: None of my relationships had begun so maturely. Most were stereotypically "college romances," where the sex and alcohol came first and the questions later. For that reason, I think, I was happy the first few weeks I dated Mark; I felt grown-up, honest, balanced, and protected. I was in control of my own emotions in a relationship that was a true partnership. I hated my inability to tell my parents about us, but since lying to them has always been second nature, covering up our relationship proved easy; if all worked out, I told myself, I would stop lying and present Mark to them saying, "love me, love us," or some equally dramatic gesture.

But soon, not really surprisingly, the pattern reemerged. Mark talked of the future, of love and destiny, and I grew repulsed by his sentimentality and uncomplicated approach to such immense possibilities; I was afraid of his clinging, of his expectations that I could never fulfill. I grew to feel trapped and put upon; every moment with him felt like a chore I had to perform before gaining permission to seek fun somewhere else, with anyone but him. I told him all of this, along with what I believed to be the origin of these feelings, and he was patient and understanding—so patient that I began to lose respect for him, thinking him needy, desperate, and of questionable taste (I am, of course, one of those who would never belong to a club that would have me as a member). We are friends now, despite the last few weeks of our relationship when he painfully attempted to reconnect with me, and when I—guilt-ridden but with equal force—pulled away, shutting him out of my heart, mind, and social life. I look to his friends, as I look to strangers in coffee shops, as potential lovers now. The answer lies always in whomever I haven't yet chosen; then when I choose him or her, the answer lies in someone else. My most enduring fear is that no one will ever prove good enough—that there is no real answer. I fear that that awful, repeated, physical and metaphoric violation of will and desire I experienced those Friday nights will blind me to any "answer" in a man or woman that I might one day love and feel safe with.

I have called these fears my "ugly" side and noted that the reason my immediate family never talks to each other about anything substantial is because we are all afraid of making our true selves known; we are afraid to show our "ugly" sides to each other, choosing instead to believe that we are all perfectly happy, in perfect control, and on the straightest paths through life. Showing our ugly sides means disappointing, scaring, and upsetting each other; it is much safer to appear happy and to suffer in private or with our friends. I have learned that I am not the only one who is hiding; this house is filled with expert pretenders. Like bluffers in a poker game, we hold our cards to our chests pretending we've got royal flushes, but no one will call anyone else's hand. We just sit around the table staring at each other, edgy but professional. When we lose a hand—i.e., say "I'm gay," lose our temper, admit we are sad, cry in frustration—we rush to each other's aid immediately, feeling guilty that we had such a better hand and never knew it, guilty that we didn't realize how lucky we were. But soon enough another round begins, and the stakes are raised. . . .

Constant hiding implies constant fear of exposure. No time is ever your own. Something always threatens to expose you, to force you to show your hand, to hold you under the lights. Always on edge, you never feel safe from discovery. As I described before, I grew up with a constant, irrational fear that something would disrupt my life, take me or my family away. The fear started to surface in late high school in the form of panic disorder: short (but overwhelmingly powerful) attacks of sheer terror striking without any apparent warning, cause, or signal. I'd be driving in my car, and suddenly my heart would race, my stomach sink, my skin tingle, and my hands shake, while a burning sensation ran up and down my legs and spine. Or I'd be in bed reading or talking to my friends or waterskiing—I was never safe. The aftershocks of these daily attacks lasted nearly the rest of the day, so that just as I was getting over an attack, a new one would begin.

I lived this way for seven years. Then one weekend several years after college and after writing the original case, after taking allergy medication that (unbeknownst to me) aggravates panic disorder, I had a panic attack that didn't go away after a few seconds. It lasted all day and into the night until, sitting in a restaurant the next night surrounded (safely, I thought) by all my friends, I jumped up and said I had to go to a hospital because I was going crazy—finally, I believed, my lifelong fear of going insane was coming true. A friend calmly walked me to his apartment and called the campus police, who put a therapist on the line. Hearing her reassuring voice explaining the disorder to me clinically but empathetically, rationally but warmly, I settled down, and the fear subsided. We talked for hours, me spinning countless family stories. She convinced me to seek professional help, informing me that panic disorder is common, treatable, and beatable.

The psychiatrist I met the next day, who prescribed me a very low dosage of pills that I still take, told me the story of my life, as if the details of my complex and seemingly unique childhood were merely bullets in a textbook: He asked, having never met me, questions such as "Did you feel when you were younger as if you were the parent and your parents were your children? Were either of your parents sexually inappropriate with you or your siblings? Are you struggling with your sexuality? Do you have strong separation anxiety? Is your mother or father overly anxious?"—questions that, though commonly asked by the stereotypical psychiatrist, defined the core of my identity. (I remembered once looking through my mother's medical records and finding the one-line diagnosis scrawled in the corner: anxiety. I didn't understand it then.) I took immeasurable comfort in knowing that I was not alone in my distinct brand of anxiety disorder, finally understanding that my problems were part chemical and part environmental. My psychiatrist and

I agreed that to mitigate the disorder, I somehow needed to merge the many lives I was leading and piece together a cohesive identity for myself—with the help of the medication (that, much to my relief, eliminated the panic but did not diminish my everyday neuroses) but, most importantly, with the help of talk therapy. I arranged to meet with the woman I talked with on the phone, and I have been seeing her for the past two years. Slowly, we are devising methods to deal with my life's stubborn patterns and to work through my conflicted feelings about every member of my family (not just my mother). And though it is difficult to keep up the energy and summon up the courage, and though I fail constantly, I work every day to be honest with myself. There seems to be simply no other path to sustainable happiness for me and no path more difficult in my family.

I can see the pieces of my life before me, how easily the pattern fits together: the precedent of lying (and anxiety) set long before I was born, the disruption of safety early in my childhood giving way to a longing for "normalcy" during those crucial early years of adolescence, the panic that ensued from that early violation coupled with growing awareness of ("abnormal") sexuality. Threading through it all is my vigilance to maintain order and peace, to transcend my history, to beat it and come out the victor—a vigilance that places immeasurable weight on my conscience and spirit and that leaves me always guilty, put upon, unsafe, and scared. I am, of course, still 8 years old, putting my parents' needs (to see their children happy) before my own (to be honest, to be happy). I am still constructing finely detailed masks at so quick a rate, one of top of the other, that I've lost the original face beneath them. When I look in the mirror, a cast of strangers stares back. I long to meet somewhere among them the boy I never got to be. I imagine him more beautiful than the many boys who have taken his place since, masquerading, performing, protecting, passing for him. They have done a great job covering for him, but their work is done—the boy needs his own chance.

12 No "Boring Little Friends"

This writer describes the key high school friendships that helped her deal with issues of control, identity, and sexuality in early adolescence. Despite her role as the oldest and most responsible in a family of eight and her success in school, Ann finds herself looking for friendships and adventures that will help her rebel against the comfortable and known sense of self these accomplishments gave her. She and her friends hang out in bars, sneak out of their houses at night, and fantasize together about men and sex. Her actual love life consists of many unfulfilled crushes early on, masturbation that makes her feel guilty and sinful, and eventual experimentation with men who return some of her feelings. Ann's early adolescent years seem full of unmet desires: The words "I want" appear again and again in this case as she reflects on the role of male and female friendships in her life.

I was funky. Dana was sophisticated. Liz was crazy. We walked to school together, went for bike rides, cut school, got stoned, talked on the phone, smoked cigarettes, slept over, discussed boys and sex, went to church together, and got angry at each other. We defined each other with adjectives and each other's presence. As high school friends, we simultaneously resisted and anticipated adulthood and womanhood.

Seven years later I am still a little funky, living in New York City, and working and writing. Liz is still a little crazy—she lives in London now with her Portuguese rock-'n'-roll boyfriend, and works at a hotel. I think Dana is in the Army, but we have lost touch. She was never that sophisticated, but she was a model and incredibly beautiful and went out with lots of boys. So she seemed sophisticated to Liz and me, who were busy clunking into each other in front of our lockers.

Today I am in love with a man I have been seeing for over two years. I love him and he loves me. Simple—and yet incredible and unexpected and as wonderful as I had hoped. At age 15 I never thought a man that I loved would ever love me. All my personal experience had proved quite the opposite.

What was possible at 15 and 16? We still had to tell our parents where we were going! We wanted to do excitingly forbidden activities like going out to dance clubs and drinking whiskey sours. Liz, Dana, and I wanted to do these forbidden things in order to feel: to have intense emotional and sensual experiences that removed us from the suburban sameness we shared with each other and everyone else we knew. We were tired of the repetitive experiences that our town, our siblings, our parents, and our school offered to us. The realization that *our* world was actually a very small part of *the* world hit us when we were 15. The real world looked bigger, brighter, and much more fun.

The friendship between Dana, Liz, and myself was born out of another emotional need: the need for trust. The three of us had reached a point in our lives when we realized how unstable relationships can be, and we all craved safety and acceptance. Friendships all around us were often uncertain. We wanted and needed to be able to like and trust each other.

In the following story, I talk a lot about myself as a high school student. I call myself a "good girl" a few times. To me that means I didn't get kept after school for talking in class. I didn't fail classes. I was not fresh to my teachers or to my mom and dad. Mostly, I didn't do any of those things because I was successful and happy when I was a "good girl." I got good grades, didn't get hassled too often by my folks, and had a bunch of friends. I really wanted to go to college, and go away to school, and I knew my parents didn't have much money, so I figured that I'd need a scholarship if I wanted to go someplace challenging. With that understood, I resolved to do well in school.

Although I was "good," underneath the surface I felt wicked, or at least hypocritical at times. I smoked in the bathroom, but I made sure I did not get caught. I had a fake ID, but when I went to bars I did not get drunk or into trouble. I had a few drinks and laughed with my friends and looked at boys. I was a pretty cautious teenager.

I was also responsible, partly out of caution, and partly because I really wanted to get things done the right way and not fool around with failing or losing out on an opportunity. I have a pretty competitive streak (I think from growing up with siblings all very close in age), which pushes me to do things even when I'm not that inspired to do them. Like if I thought I might win an essay contest, I would write something. Just to do it.

I think the other reason for my responsibleness is that I was brought up to be aware of other people's needs. I was/am the oldest girl (woman) in a family that continued to grow and change while I was in high school and college. As new kids were added and little ones grew up I think I developed the aptitude to see what needed doing. Then I would do it, often just to cut down on household strife—or to help out my mom, who I am very close to and sometimes felt bad for because she was so busy. I liked helping out. It always felt good to contribute.

My parents' lives are not carefree. They have money worries, and worries about my other siblings, and worries about their own private lives. I was always reluctant to add to their burden. On the other hand, they sometimes seem especially good at making me feel that that is just what I am doing. Most of the time I get along well with my parents. Most of the time everyone in my family tries to be supportive and giving to other family members. But my parents seem to have a fear of losing control over me and my two younger sisters. My older brother has almost always done what he wanted to do whether my folks liked it or not. I was always more obliging. I liked it when they were proud of me.

In the suburban area where I grew up, many people are extremely conformist and preoccupied about money. My family really went against this money-as-most-important model. We didn't have a lot of money. I didn't always have the right kind of jeans or sneakers. I wore clothes from thrift shops before it was cool and trendy.

I went to East Middle School, which had the reputation of being run like a Catholic school—very tight control. The kids from West had reputations as loud-mouthed rich kids. Many of them lived not in town but in the Harbour, where there were no sidewalks or 7-Elevens. Many of the West girls wore designer jeans and expensive sweatshirts. These girls also talked extensively about who they had fooled around and gone out with, what guys liked them, how far they had gone with guys, and how many times they had gotten drunk or stoned. Most of the West girls weren't like that; but the cliques from West were much stronger and less fluid than the cliques from East.

At the beginning of ninth grade it was amazing how quickly it was established that the "cool" West girls and the "cool" East girls were supposed to somehow be friends. It was also quickly established that the West girls were really the coolest. They were the richest and the toughest and the loudest. I was a "cool" girl in East, but not because the guys liked me, or I was really pretty, or because I had great clothes. I was the editor of the newspaper, the valedictorian, friends with all the teachers, and on basketball, volleyball, and softball. So I was cool for basically unexciting reasons—the girl people could refer to when their parents weren't going to let them do something; "Ann's going. . . ." I was also pretty perceptive and evenhanded for a junior high school kid. So people usually trusted me, telling me things about themselves and their lives and other people because I either gave good advice or could keep a secret.

I was always pretty insecure with the "cool people," though. I saw so much backbiting and lying and name-calling and dropping of friends that somewhere inside I was always nervous that I would be pushed out; maybe people would stop calling me or inviting me to parties. When I entered high school, my preoccupation with the "cool people" heightened. Suddenly there were so many more people to keep up with, and new ideas of what was in or out. In the first two years of high school I was quite popular—mostly for the same reasons I was popular in junior high school. I was cool enough not to be a geek, nice to lots of people, and was also productive. I could run for president of the class, or chairperson for sports night, and get elected. My "popular" friends really pushed for my election (making posters, etc.), probably because they would get some "fringe benefits" out of it, too; they would get to be on committees where they didn't have to do anything, but could still get out of going to class. I guess I felt like an outsider because my popularity always seemed quite precarious—it seemed so connected to external factors. I remember feeling that others were inherently popular—while I had to work at it.

In ninth grade I worked pretty hard at being popular. By the end of the year I felt smug about my popularity, but by tenth grade this smug attitude turned to impatience. Popularity was not always fun; it was often unsettling—or boring. Tenth grade was a year filled with Sweet Sixteen parties that were actually competitions: who had the best party, who wore the best outfit, who bought the best gifts, who got invited to the most parties. One time a girl hated another girl because she had bought an identical outfit to wear to the same Sweet Sixteen party. I remember being down in someone's basement during tenth grade (a whole bunch of girls were hanging out after school), and the girl who got the outfit first got on the phone to "bawl out" the other girl for buying the same outfit. Then all the girls there took turns getting on the phone to say nasty things to her, telling her she was a slut, or stupid, or that they never really liked her. I sat there for about a half hour getting angry and embarrassed. I was ashamed that I was actually *debating* about leaving. Finally I did get up and said, "This really sucks." And I left.

I walked out. I kissed them all off. I walked home, in the rain I think, really mad at them for hassling/demoralizing Donna about a stupid outfit. I was also incredibly nervous all night that my phone would ring and they would be on the phone bawling me out for something. I was also afraid that I would be labeled uncool and idiotic and blacklisted from parties and lunch tables and weekend plans. When I went to school the next day I found out that the girls decided they "respected" me for leaving.

The phone call was made from Liz's basement. She had been much more "in" than me in junior high and grade school. Short, cute, and incredibly funny, Liz was a daring loudmouth. When I had moved to town in fourth grade, on the first day of school Liz asked me if I was a boy (because I was tall, had short hair, and a pencil case with my brother's name on it) and I hated her for months. Liz and I had become really good friends during freshman year. She and I hung out with the same kids and walked home from school together almost everyday. During the walk we moaned about boys and school and popularity and the pressures we felt from our parents and our group of friends. We reassured each other. I confided in Liz my multitudes of crushes.

During ninth and tenth grade I constantly fell in love with older boys I knew only slightly and shy boys my own age I knew well. I never went on dates with these boys; I just thought about them a lot. I knew some older guys from school government and committees. They were nice to me. Some flirted quite a bit with me. But I never went on dates with the older guys because they never asked me out. They usually had girlfriends who were seniors. The shy boys my own age were not quite ready for dating. While I was thinking about true love and romantic walks through the park, I think they were thinking about video games, Pink Floyd, and sex with girls from Budweiser ads. I never quite felt much like "dating material." I was tall and liked school and talked a lot in class. I wore weird clothes and wrote articles for the school newspaper about local political candidates. Sometimes bizarre boys who wanted to be comic strip heroes or felt as stifled as I did by our relatively small town would confess their true love for me. These incidents never led to sexual relationships with these boys. I would tell them that I knew how they felt, seeing that I had a few unfruitful crushes of my own. I never liked any of the boys who liked me.

Perhaps Liz and I became good friends because we were both incredibly sensitive to the propensity of the "popular group" to just drop people, to turn on them for no apparent reason. We were both afraid and angered by this possibility. Perhaps we bonded because we walked home the same way, or because we were in the same confirmation class in seventh grade, or because we put each other into hysterics, mimicking people we knew and writing sordid letters back and forth about teachers at school we pretended were having illicit affairs with each other. We loved to talk about Dr. Ruth Westheimer. Neither of us had any sexual experience (beyond kissing) until eleventh grade, but we both had dramatic imaginations.

I also unburdened my family problems on Liz as we walked home, stopping to sit on the curb before we parted. I was the oldest girl in a family of eight. My two baby brothers drove me crazy—I was responsible for them quite often. I had an older brother and two younger sisters too. It sometimes embarrassed me to have so many siblings. People always seemed so surprised and compelled to say rude things about birth control and ask if my family was Catholic. We were, in fact, Catholic. I went to religious instruction until eleventh grade or so. So did Liz. We hated it sometimes, but enjoyed getting out of our houses on a school night. Liz, my brother, and I would go to lectures at church and then go to Carvel and hang around for another hour and laugh or talk about our lives. Liz told me about her family problems, too—about her cousin Susan who had died of cancer the previous summer; about her "perfect" older sister; and about her older brother who was emotionally disturbed—he was four years older than Liz, but lived in his own world where he was king and spoke his own language.

I think high school and her changing body crushed Liz's spirit. Suddenly she was supposed to stop wearing painter pants and start blow-drying her hair. She was supposed to wear makeup, start French-kissing guys, and stop being loud and crazy, because, "God, Liz, you really intimidate guys when you act so crazy like that. . . ." A gymnastics accident forced Liz to be relatively sedentary, and she gained weight as she started developing breasts and hips. I remember her period was (and still is) terribly painful. She took the Pill for a while, too, and hated the side effects of bloating. We talked about it a little bit in a joking way—how she ought to find someone to have sex with while she was "protected." I think taking the Pill was really embarrassing for Liz. It seemed premature in light of the rest of her life. Womanhood was like one big punch in the face to Liz—it really spoiled her fun.

By the end of ninth grade, my friendship with Liz had solidified. We each trusted the other's loyalty. We probably began hanging around with Dana out of a desire for other solid, loyal, caring friendships. Liz and I both knew Dana from grade and junior high school. She had always been incredibly prissy, cute, and quiet. She brought tuna fish and crackers to lunch every day because that's all she would eat. Boys and teachers loved her. She wore cute little skirts and had blond hair and blue eyes. I had been friends with her off and on, and so had Liz.

The three of us had gone through the same religious instruction, and Dana and I each had a brief connection to a Catholic youth group. Liz stopped going to mass when she got her period. I think she must have felt that there was no God, or that God was abandoning her—since growing up seemed so difficult. Painful and unattractive bodily changes like cramps and pimples, coupled with her sadness about her cousin Susan's death, made Liz lose faith. Soon the youth group made me want to throw up; it was as cliquey as high school, except here it was cool to be depressed and pathetic. In my opinion, the youth group was less interested in spiritual growth than group therapy. Dana stopped going after all the guys there were in love with her. Although I continued to go to mass and believe in God, by the time I was in tenth grade the admonitions of the nuns and religious instruction teachers to think holy thoughts began to fade from my conscious thoughts, which were filled with boys and sexual fantasies and worries about school.

In ninth grade Dana was itching to emerge from her circle of (as Liz and I nastily had characterized them) "boring little friends." She began to model in high school and the "popular crowd" was suddenly eager to embrace her. It didn't hurt that many beautiful senior guys were in love with her. The popular crowd believed in coolness by association. By the end of tenth grade the three of us knit together in an effort to be "real" friends for each other. The "popular crowd" became less and less important as we became more important to each other, depending on each other for support and social life.

I think it was our personality differences, as well as our common desire for true and loyal friends, that made our friendship initially exciting. Dana was somewhat devious, manipulative, daring, and exciting. As a professional model she enjoyed the attention her appearance got her. But sometimes she despaired over her "looks" in melodramatic evenings where she would sit on the floor of her room, stuffing her face with pretzels and ripping up her modeling pictures. Liz was "the clown," always the loudest and funniest. (Later, in eleventh and twelfth grade, Liz had weeks of depression where she wouldn't come to school or answer the telephone. In tenth grade, however, Liz was still able to put on the act of crazy woman without too much strain and inner contradiction.) My personality was not as overtly extreme as Liz or Dana's. I always felt boring in comparison to the two of them. They were always getting into trouble at home and in school, while I was getting good grades and having a relatively peaceful time at home. I always got along pretty well with my brothers and sisters. I got along well with my parents overtly, but I spent much of ninth and tenth grade lying to them about where I was going and what I was doing.

My days were full of fantasies. I wanted to get out of my town, my family, and my life. They were all so boring and safe. I wanted to go on trips, live in England for the summer, and have a love affair. I really wanted to fall in love. More than that, I wanted someone to fall in love with me. I wanted a taller, older, smarter, more worldly boy (more everything than the boys I knew) to be in love with me. I wanted that kind of boy/man to help me experience the world more fully. I read a lot of books, which no doubt perpetuated my idea that a relationship would complete me and increased my desire for a boyfriend or a love affair. Reading always reminded me of the worlds that I was not part of. It reminded me how boring my life was. Magazines like *Seventeen* and *Teen* helped me to connect self-worth to whether I held a man's sexual attention. My father and brothers paid attention to me. So did my uncles and grandfathers. And my male friends. But I wanted to feel sexually desirable. I wanted everything right away and simultaneously felt as though it would never happen. I wanted to go and see and do and experience the world. Instead, I was in Eastview, babysitting, riding my bike, and going to the beach.

I was always much taller than everyone in my classes until high school. By junior high school I was even taller than some men teachers, which embarrassed me greatly. My body size influenced me in two important ways. I think people felt that I was very mature and responsible, and they treated me that way—so I did assume a lot of responsibility from my teachers and my parents. At the same time, I think my physical body did mature earlier than other kids' did, and this seemed to be a social drawback to me. I never felt cute or desirable. I always felt too big, too much like a boy. I think I missed out on the girlishness of adolescence. At least I never felt that I was desirable to boys my own age, although I was comfortable with them socially, to be friends and hang out and talk. Sexually I always felt out of place. I was the size of a woman, but not the age of a woman. I had the life of an adolescent without the right physique or mentality.

I remember intense waves of desire as early as seventh grade—sexual feelings I didn't know what to do with. Perhaps it was due to my early-developed body. I remember distinctly the first time I masturbated—the night after a sleepover party in seventh grade. Though I consciously had crushes on "nice boys," I fantasized that night about a boy I felt was really sleazy and sexy. Sexiness and sleaziness were completely interwoven to me—as indoctrinated as I was by my religious instruction classes: "Don't read your horoscope! Abortion is always killing a baby! Sexual desire is bad news! Feel guilty if you start to think lustful thoughts! Repent if you are looking at dirty magazines or reading dirty books!"

During seventh grade I said my rosary every night before I went to sleep. I got up every morning to go to mass before school during Lent. I also masturbated at least once a day. It was during seventh grade that I became a part of a dirty book swap, where girls I knew and I would find books loaded with sexual passages and trade them before volleyball practice. One of my friends had two brothers in college and we found *Hustler* magazine in their room. The pictures, and more than the pictures, the stories, sexually excited me. The images and words in the magazine were so strong and enticing. The pictures showed naked men and women having sexual intercourse. It was incredible to see nude bodies. It was amazing to see a man's penis. I was very curious. The stories were filled with images of women who were weak and submissive. They loved the sex that was forced upon them by overpowering men. Many of the stories told of once innocent women who suddenly became nymphomaniacs after being raped. The magazines were an unending source of fascination. I thought about the stories and pictures even when the magazines were not in front of me.

It is amazing to recall that all this sexual turmoil coincided with playing volleyball, singing in the chorus, writing for the newspaper, and getting awards when I graduated from middle school in eighth grade. I felt incredibly guilty about masturbating until about the eleventh and twelfth grade, when I began dating, and began to debate about whether or not to have sex with the boys I went out with. Suddenly masturbation seemed innocent when compared to my new, more horrible and dangerous desire to actually have sex.

During the tenth and eleventh grade, the friendship I had with Liz and Dana made me happy, but it never pushed me to explore these incredible contradictions within myself. Liz, Dana, and I were sympathetic to each other. We encouraged each other to feel what we were feeling. However, in retrospect, we were not that honest with each other. I had these incredible contradictions in my life about who I appeared to be, and how I actually felt inside; but on the outside I was tame compared to Liz and Dana. Both were frequent class cutters, school skippers, family haters, and shoplifters. In contrast, I went to my classes, didn't steal, and didn't have screaming matches with members of my family. It may have seemed as though my confusion and despair did not reach the depths of Liz or Dana's, but it did. I didn't act like Liz and Dana because it really was not my style. I could not judge their actions as bad because I really didn't think they were. I agreed with them that their family life was hard. I didn't care that they stole. I just didn't want them to get caught. The manifestation of my confusion was perhaps more internally directed. I was enormously confused by the contradictions I experienced. I desperately wanted someone to help me break out of my boring life. I wanted someone to fall in love with me. I realize now I wanted a boyfriend during early high school so badly because his presence would somehow validate the sexual urges I was having. I know I felt my appearance would be validated if someone else appreciated it—I felt that if someone liked my face and my body, perhaps I could, too.

I realize now that for the years I was in high school I was pretty obsessed with my weight. In almost every single journal entry I have written, "I need to lose at least five to ten pounds." Sometimes at night before I went to sleep, or if I couldn't sleep, I would eat. I would eat much more than I needed to, more than I even wanted to, sitting at the kitchen table at two o'clock in the morning. I just kept eating because somehow the food did comfort me, fill me up, helped me to relax and sleep. Often I would go on a diet. In ninth grade, when I was planning to get pictures taken to bring to a modeling agency at my aunt's suggestion, I dieted strictly for four solid months. I would eat a slice of bread with no peanut butter and drink a glass of water with it for lunch. I exercised in the basement every day. I lost at least fifteen pounds. I remember being pretty skinny, but never feeling like I was thin enough to look good.

When my mother told me I couldn't model and be a chairperson for class night (a position to which I had just been elected), I went immediately to the bakery and bought two chocolate-covered custard donuts and ate them one after the other. My attempt to get away from my house, to get away from the control of my mother and dad, to live an exciting, non-high-school-ish life, which I thought having a modeling career would accomplish, was foiled. I wanted to be grown-up. I wanted to be an adult, to divorce myself from my parents, to not care about what they thought or said.

During the summer before eleventh grade, Liz went on a bike trip to the West Coast. While she was gone, Dana and I hung out almost every day. We went to the beach one day with three boys we knew. I was in love with Randy, and Tom was in love with Dana, and Bill was this weird guy we didn't know (who has ended up being one of my best friends from high school). I remember feeling that Randy liked Dana and not me, and I painfully remember coming home on the train and seeing him rub Dana's calf "because it was so smooth." It made me feel dead inside that he was attracted to her. She was so much more sexually appealing than I was.

Being with Dana made me want to be more desirable and made me actively confront the importance of appearance. Dana and I would go into New York City; Dana wanted to take me to her modeling agency so I could model, too. Sometimes we went to the city dressed in her modeling clothes. We went to bars and got propositioned by old men. It was simultaneously gross and exciting. Only now do I realize what it must have looked like, two 16-year-olds in low-cut sweaters hanging out in seedy bars too close to Penn Station. But then it felt exciting and even slightly dangerous.

When Liz came back from the West Coast, the three of us hung out together. We lied to our parents regularly. If we got dropped off at the movies we went around the corner to the Ticktock Cafe and used our fake proof (bought in the city) to drink whisky sours and Tom Collinses. We smoked pot in the bathroom of the movie theater before we saw *The Muppet Babies.* When Dana's parents went away to bring her older sister to college, Liz and I slept over. We pulled down the shades, drank beer, smoked cigarettes and pot, and took the train into the city at 2 A.M. to buy pretzels on Seventh Avenue. We also rode our bikes to the Bay almost every night after dinner, pretending we were on the shore of France, or England, or Spain. Liz and Dana would take off their shirts in the twilight and ride with just their bras on, though I was never that nervy.

While Liz and Dana were similar in rowdiness and spunk, Dana and I shared a common interest in men. Since we were both tall we were often mistaken for being older than we were. Liz was much shorter and cuter—most of the time she could not pass for anything over her age, 15. Dana and I were competitive about attracting men. I think this was a phase propelled partially because Dana was a model and had met a lot of people who informed her about the power of her appearance. This mindset, along with the images thrust upon us by *Seventeen* magazine, made us all think a lot about how we looked. Boys did like Dana more than they liked me, and it made me jealous, and I think that also put a competitive edge to our friendship. At that time Liz was not interested in flirting. Dana and my barhopping adventures in NYC made her feel excluded. She *was* excluded, to the extent that we were interested in men on a level that she was not—or could not be. Liz looked and acted too "childish" to even toy with going to bars and flirting with older men, and I know this bothered her even though she thought Dana and I were idiots to be so obsessed with appearances and men.

Dana actually had boyfriends. I didn't have a boyfriend until the middle of eleventh grade. During ninth and tenth grade my "love life" consisted of crushes. I can't believe now how many crushes I had on boys during junior high and high school. Reading my journal from that time period is amazing. I entertained thoughts of three or four boys simultaneously, and would write about my "progress" with each of them, in my journal: "Harry danced with me four times at the party. I always thought he was stupid, but maybe he's just shy." "I talked to Donald in Spanish. He gave me a piece of gum." "Sonny keeps touching me in lab." "I think Dan has a girlfriend." During ninth and tenth grade I didn't "go out" with anyone. My crushes on older, inaccessible guys always faded away after a few months. My crushes on guys my own age never amounted to anything either—perhaps because my crushes were on guys who were not yet interested in dating. I felt, however, that no one was interested in dating me because there must be something wrong with me. I was too tall. I was too fat. My hair was ugly. I was too loud. I wore weird clothes. Maybe I smelled.

I often felt uneasy about always "being good" when Liz and Dana went on stealing sprees or cut school, but I consoled myself by thinking that I was often the only thing that stood between them and juvenile court. It did not make me feel too "out of it" when Liz and Dana were "bad" together. Men were much more intriguing and powerful than theft by the time we were 15 and 16. Because Liz felt she could not participate, or in a sense, win, when she competed, she often felt left out of conversations and men-meeting sprees. I think that Liz began to resent both Dana and me, and thought that we were silly and stupid for "acting like 21-year-olds." Often Liz would remind Dana and me of our age and complain that we were no longer any fun. Liz began to resent men as well. For her men became adversaries who challenged her for (and often won) Dana's and my attention.

Liz, Dana, and I differed greatly in our rebellions that summer. Liz and Dana waged all-out wars, fighting daily with their parents, running away, and stealing. Although I participated by lying to my parents, smoking pot and cigarettes, and going to bars, my "rebellion" was actually a period of intense internal confusion. On one level I felt good about my schoolwork and social life and friends, and on another level, I knew I was an unattractive loser doomed to be controlled by my parents forever. I wanted so many things: to have fun, to be smart, to be free, and to be desired. It was a dramatic time of life—it was difficult to feel and want so much and to actually be so limited.

New friendships with women which I developed in college did not replace or mimic the relationships I had with Liz and Dana, but there are elements of sameness. I see my relationships with women as continuing to be places where I develop and define myself, where through interaction and shared experience I become more and more comfortable with who I am, where I have come from, and where my life is going. I am supported in these relationships; in them I feel comfortable and safe and loved.

In eleventh grade, I started really dating guys. My first boyfriend was an exchange student from Greece. He was very good-looking and charming—he brought me roses, champagne, and perfume. In some ways I loved to be with him; we went out to dinner and basketball games and movies. We took bike rides and made out. But after a while, his height (he was a whopping two inches shorter than me) and our lack of communication began to bother me. He really didn't speak much English—and I spoke no Greek. So we broke up. Even while I was going out with Evan I had a huge fixation on a guy a year ahead of me who just wanted to be friends, but he (I felt at the time) really led me on, led me to believe he did want to go out with me. By the end of eleventh grade I was pretty sick of having pointless crushes on guys.

During the summer before twelfth grade I met lots of guys and went out on a few dates here and there. At the end of the summer I started dating a friend of a friend's brother. He was older, very handsome, and smart. He wanted to have sex with me, and he quickly moved (away from me) when he realized that I was not going to sleep with him. At the time I didn't really see this. I thought there was something wrong with me. Later that year I met another "older guy" at a dance club who I then dated for over a year. I really fell in love in that relationship. Don was very good for me and to me. He came from a background similar to mine, and was able to help me through difficulties with my family and friends. He was very understanding and sensitive. He did not push me (very much) about sex—he was pretty good about waiting until I was ready. We had lots of fun together, I think because we were both open and giving. We broke up mainly because he wanted a big commitment (like marriage) and I was still in my first years of college. I was learning different things. I wanted to become a person at least a little different from our parents and I felt that although he wanted to, he was just too hung up about life and his family. It just got too hard to reconcile what we both wanted.

In college lots of guys had crushes on me. I think it was because I was nice and friendly. I have a warm personality. This was fun for a while, and then it got to be a hassle to tell guys I only liked them as friends, etc. I actually felt, at times, eager to be in a relationship with a man to avoid having guys telling me they liked me. Perhaps the crushes reminded me too much of my own painful crushes—that I had begun to see as immature and selfish.

Now I am involved in a committed long-term relationship that really might go anywhere. . . . My wariness in this relationship (I think) stems from not wanting to "waste time." I guess I have learned lots of lessons about men and relationships through the difficulties I have had with them; but for a long time I felt pretty humiliated by my propensity to feel so much unwarranted feeling for guys who didn't *really* care about me.

My high school years seem incredibly far away. I feel as though I have grown a lot since high school, and I'm sure my growth has a lot to do with leaving home and making my life at college my own. Moving away from home has helped me to make decisions without needing my parents' approval. I have learned that they love me even if they don't agree with my decisions to live away from home with my friends for a summer, or go on a trip with my boyfriend. I think I've learned a lot from friends in college who have had family experiences very different from mine. I have also learned about myself, my identity, through the actual process of making decisions.

Because I have graduated from college this year, I am at another extended moment of indecision and anxiety about who I am and what I am going to do with my life. So maybe I shouldn't be writing about my adolescent feelings as though they are something of the past. I am still in the process of defining myself as my own person. However I now see this "self definition" more as a lifetime process that involves what I will do more than who I am. I feel confident that my life will straighten out. I don't spend days lying on my bed listening to the same song over and over. I've been through it all before. Life and love and sex are no longer great unknowns.

13

Love Me for Who I Am

In this case, the author describes the conflicted relationship she had with her father throughout adolescence. Jen is the youngest of three daughters, all of whom struggle in different ways with their father's demands that they be high achievers and show the filial obedience expected in a traditional Chinese American family. Jen's academic and athletic successes provide her with a strong, independent sense of self, but she continues to fight with her father, never believing that he truly values her for who she is. In college her involvement with a man who loves her provides a new kind of relationship, one that helps her reevaluate both herself and her relationships with her parents.

I loved to be alone when I was little, to have no one around me and be able to escape to an imaginary land with no other people. One spring day when I was 5, I was playing out my favorite Barbie scenario: Fake Barbie was pretending to be sweet and kind and befriend Real Barbie, who was good and kind. Fake Barbie then revealed her true evil nature and beat up Real Barbie. I suddenly heard piercing screams echoing down the hallway as my parents fought. I snuck over to watch them; both were out of control and screaming at each other at the top of their lungs. My dad was shouting at my mom for making "stupid" mistakes on the tax forms. After arguing for a while, my mom grabbed a pair of gleaming silver scissors, whipped the flowered bedspread off the bed, and began destroying it in broad, zigzag strokes—destroying the cloth and the memories it held of me playing and talking with my two older sisters. I rushed into the room in shock and tried to wrestle the scissors from her before she decided to hurt herself. The fight ended with my mom soothingly assuring me that she would not hurt herself.

I looked at my dad angrily, blaming him for making my mom so upset. It became a habit for me to take my mother's side in these fights because my hot-tempered dad often lost all control in his rages. Though he rarely hit my mom, he often threw or broke things in his anger. My dad looked like the very image of the devil to me right then with his angry eyes and the curl of his mouth. Eventually, my parents' relationship deteriorated until they could not live together anymore, and my dad moved from our home in the South to a midwestern city. For three years, my dad continued to support the family financially, while my mom took care of us three girls, my grandmother, and my cousin from Asia who was studying in the United States. Though my dad would often joke about divorcing my mom for some reason, I never realized until recently that he was actually serious. I knew that the welfare of the children came first, though, and this prevented my parents from actually divorcing.

My father never became too involved in rearing his children. I didn't mind that too much when I was little, for I was stuck to my mom's skirt like dried-up sticky rice. I tagged around everywhere she went—to the bank, the supermarket, shopping malls. She was my beautiful mother with warm, twinkling eyes, who sometimes got mad at me and said mean things but who always hugged me and let me know that everything was okay. I must have chatted her ear off. My dad, on the other hand, struck awe and fear in me. He was this big, unknown entity when I was little. He had a quick temper and very low tolerance for screeching little kids. Being willful and hardheaded, I would throw temper tantrums whenever I didn't get what I wanted. My sisters told me countless times how childish and immature I was, but I didn't understand what they meant.

After deciding to live together again, my entire family moved back to where I was born on the East Coast. I gave my dad plenty of reasons to get upset with me. One time, my mom, two sisters, and I had just gotten home from an outing. While I was looking with wonder at the pinkish red balloon flying in the air, my dad picked up the ringing phone and began chatting in the background. Just as I was thinking how awful it would be if I let the balloon touch the spiky ceiling, my hand let go of its yellow curlicue ribbon. As soon as I heard the loud pop, I started howling. Being an attention-loving child, I started crying harder because no one had noticed that I had lost my toy. My mom came over and tried to shush me, explaining that my dad was on a very important phone call and warning me that if I wasn't quiet soon, he was going to be extremely angry. I just cried harder since I wanted to be more important than some stupid phone call. As soon as the receiver clicked into its cradle, I shut up in total trepidation. My dad began shouting at me for being so stupid, selfish, immature, and spoiled. Shouting back at him only made his anger get the best of him, and he grabbed my right wrist and my right ankle and used his boiling anger to throw me around in the air like a discus. I was hoping that he would not launch me into the kitchen table or through the patio doors; luckily, he threw me onto the sofa. Another time my dad became incensed by my lack of respect for him, and he pushed me down the stairs from the second floor because I disagreed with something he said. These situations solidified my fear of my dad.

My father dominated the family physically and mentally with his short temper and his self-righteousness. It wasn't until several weeks before my 11th birthday that I remember replacing my fear of my father with hate. I was playing with stacks of towels and sheets in the dark, narrow hallway outside my room when my dad pulled me aside and informed me, "You have to change yourself because most people won't like you when they find out who you really are and what you're really like. Soon you will be turning 11, and I read somewhere that when you turn 11, it becomes very hard to change your personality. It's possible, but it gets harder as you get older. Some nice people might be your friends, but that will be rare. So you better change who you are." My face felt hot with shame and confusion. I didn't understand what he meant when he said I had to change. Did this mean I was a bad person, unacceptable, and doomed to fail? I'd never had many friends, but that was because I didn't want to get to know anybody really well. I always thought that kids were mean; they liked to pick on each other to make themselves feel better. After this talk, I didn't know if I was supposed to cry or not. My dad gave me this talk several times. The only thing I understood was that I must be utterly worthless for him to think this of me.

By middle school I understood that my dad said this to me because he believed I thought too highly of myself. For "my own good," my dad was trying to deflate my self-esteem to compensate for my numerous character flaws. I believed what he said, though, and I decided that if my character was so awful, at least I could be a good student and thus try to pass as a good person. Nothing seemed good enough for my dad, though, as he constantly criticized me for everything— for not being popular, for not being able to multiply polynomials in sixth grade, and especially for not being able to think in a logical, organized manner. He would then say that this was okay, I just had the brain of an artist, rather than a mathematical brain. This comment didn't console me, because I knew that mathematical thinking was necessary to be doctor, and my dad thought being a doctor was only for the brightest people. All occupations outside of the sciences were for those who weren't smart enough. Little did I know that he also told my two sisters, "How can you be so stupid?" all the time.

When I was 11, we moved to a rapidly growing midwestern city. I would finally attend one school for the next six years after going to three different schools in three consecutive years. In middle school, I began to study five or six hours a night in order to exceed the accomplishments of my perfect older sister and gain my dad's respect so that he would despise me less and stop criticizing me and everything I did. I thought that if my dad respected me and was proud of me like he was of my oldest sister, then he wouldn't treat me as contemptuously as he did my middle sister, and he would love me for who I was. This drive forced me to obsess over getting As on tests and papers.

After school I would eat lots of cookies and milk while my mom prepared dinner. I loved dinner because it meant more good food to eat, but it was also the time when my dad would sometimes be tired and grouchy after a hard day. I don't remember the content of the fights we had when I was in middle school, but I always initiated one whenever I took the slightest offense to one of my dad's comments. By this point, I realized that I really could not be the awful person my dad thought me. I had many friends, and I was at the top of my class. As I realized that I wasn't really the horrible, incompetent person he made me out to be, I lost any respect I held for my dad, and everything related to him was fuel for my simmering cauldron of contempt for him. At this point in my life, I began to strike back, usually with a vicious or sneering retort whenever he made any sort of comment about me. He always said, "Can't I make a single criticism of you?" and I often retorted, "Nothing I do is good enough for you. You criticize me on everything: who I am, what I do, how I think." He would then tell me in his condescending way to "stop getting so excited." His attitude and self-righteousness riled me even more. We fought over everything: misunderstandings of language, disagreements of opinion, the way in which we talked to each other. It drove me crazy that I had to respect him simply because he was older, when he did not respect me. I thought this belief was stupid, along with the Asian culture that shaped him and his treatment of me.

I became quite the tactical sprinter during these dinner conversations, when most of the fights would occur. Our arguments followed a pattern. First, one would be suspicious that the other was slighting the other in some way. That person would then make an obvious comment criticizing the other. The other would then raise his or her voice, with voices echoing louder and louder through the house. I made a pact with myself that I would never leave the table until I hurt my dad more than he hurt me. This meant, though, that I would have to make him so angry that he would lose his temper. Then the chase would begin. I rose when he stood up from the kitchen table in anger. We would continue to argue as we began to circle the table like two boxers waiting for one to throw the first punch. Horrible comments were made that hurt both of us even more. When I knew he was on the threshold of losing his temper, I would begin to scream louder. He would then start chasing me around the table as I tried to stay out of his reach. I would then make a run for the hallway and the foyer, which led to the stairs. This required good timing or I wouldn't have a large enough start to outrun my father. I would then sprint up the steps of the curving stairway two at a time, something that I practiced often, and make a dash for my room on the right. My dad would never catch me as I sprinted up the stairs, but sometimes I wouldn't get the door shut and the lock pushed into place before he would shove it open.

Other arguments would explode when I would storm out of the breakfast room and up the stairs and then slam the door of my room behind me. My dad was never fond of door slamming. He would try to open the door with a bobby pin (I had already stored away the little fake keys that could unlock the doors to prevent him from getting in too easily). I made sure that I kept my thumb firmly pressed on the push-lock, but sometimes my dad would win after all. By this point, his temper was long lost. He would storm in with that devil look on his face, hand raised ready to slap any exposed part of me. I would usually end up in a fetal position to protect myself until his anger dissipated. One time I remember being cornered on the floor between my bed and the closet with him towering over me. I began kicking out of fear, which only made him kick me. After he spent his anger, he would always leave for a few minutes, come back, and then lecture me on something. I never remembered what he said, but his tone was always calm and controlled. I hold all these vivid images and memories of the fear generated by the punishment but no memories of the lessons the punishment was supposed to teach me. The same thoughts would just hammer themselves over and over in my head. What had I ever done to deserve so little respect from him? Why couldn't he just love me for who I was and support me even when he disagreed with me? Did I really mean so little to him? This only made me angry and willing to do anything to defy him and make him suffer for how he made me feel.

That screeching voice and his devil-like mien made me feel so alone. It was worse when I couldn't reach any of my friends on the phone. I didn't know what to do or how to feel. The only thing I knew was that I had to make him hurt more than he hurt me. At these times I would beg God to take my life away from me. I was too much of a chicken to take my own life, but I would sit there and wallow in the pain of existence. It was also during these times that I would reflect that my dad and I argued and annoyed each other so much because we are so alike: stubborn, strong-willed, and opinionated. I hated myself for being just like my dad.

My grandmother used to tell me to behave better and to keep my voice down, explaining that my dad had had a horrible temper since he was a little boy. Sometimes she would get angry at my dad at dinner when she felt that he was getting mad at me for no reason. Because she didn't understand any English, my grandmother often would miss the subtle taunting that occurred prior to the fights. My mom would not say anything when she felt that I had caused the fight, but she did try to reason with him when she thought he was getting mad for no reason.

The problems with my parents extended beyond the common disagreements which often occur between parents and adolescents. All problems became arguments about making the other person wrong. Simple disagreements over things such as curfew often blew up into battles that stemmed from opposing cultures and personality differences. My parents wanted my sisters and me to take advantage of the good aspects of American culture and society while maintaining the good aspects of Chinese culture. This was never stated explicitly, though, and so for years I was confused about with whom or what I was supposed to identify. They never told us any stories, and the only traditions we ever participated in had to do with food and paying homage to my ancestors at my grandmother's mini shrine. Part of my confusion about my identity and how to accept myself came from the conflict between the two different cultures, one stressing community and selflessness and the other stressing individualism and self-sufficiency.

By the time I got to high school, my dad finally awoke to the carnage his child-raising tactics and temper had left behind when he saw how unhappy and unstable I was. Not only did he stop criticizing me, but he stopped taking his anger out on the family. Despite his new parenting style, I became increasingly critical of my parents and the manner in which they supported me. I started criticizing them whenever they did not support me the way I wanted them to. One of my biggest complaints was that they would not come to any of the games I played throughout high school. Their reasoning was simply that sports were a waste of time.

Over the next six years, my dad attempted to do penance by allowing me to say and do anything I wanted. One major conflict during these years occurred when my parents threatened to disown me in my sophomore year because I refused to stop dating an African American. In addition, they refused to explain their reasons. Who knows if they really meant their threat, but I asked them very carefully to consider what they said, because no way in hell did I want to be a part of a racist family. I took their silence to my comment as yet another insult and basically lost all regard for them. I continued to date my boyfriend without their knowledge for another five months.

I was convinced that my dad deserved to suffer while he was "changing." Why should I forgive him when he had hurt me so much? I wanted him to fail and realize how imperfect *he* was. I wanted to make him suffer for all of the constant criticism of everything and anything I did, his constant undermining of my confidence through these comments, and his total lack of faith in me. I always thought my dad was using culture as an excuse so that he could blame his behavior and his flaws on something other than himself, like I wanted to blame all my problems on him. I would not listen to his excuses, his explanations of why he did what he did. I did not even bend when my father started crying when I would not even try to accept his apology for his treatment towards me. He was so sorry that he had made me hate him so much.

My mom did not usually intervene while my dad and I argued. She would, though, when she thought my dad got angry at me when I had not done anything to purposefully provoke him. My mother's inaction during the times when my dad got angry at me made me think of her as weak. I never got as angry with my mom because I felt sorry that she had to be married to my dad. She once said that she would have chosen a different path in life if she had known what being married to my dad would be like. "This is life," my mom commonly says. To me this statement reflected her acceptance of the role of caretaker, one she has been raised to fulfill. My mother's view added to my resentment of the hierarchical roles and lack of choice for women in traditional Chinese society.

I also felt sorry for my mother for having to live with a mother-in-law who despised her. My mother and father married out of love, but my grandmother came along with the wedding package. Harsh and critical of my mother, my grandmother greatly disliked her, especially because my mom did not produce any sons. The gossipy society my grandmother lived in provided a wonderful audience, and she spread falsehoods about my mother's character and meanness. Though I had problems with the way my parents dealt with me, I always thought that they treated my grandmother exceptionally well and with great deference. My grandmother, however, continued to complain about my mother to everybody even after the family moved to the States. After years of telling stories, my grandmother was diagnosed recently as having Alzheimer's disease.

My grandmother's claim about my mother's meanness was obviously false to those who knew my mother. Whether it be tailoring the long legs of a new pair of pants so I could wear them that Saturday night, or making lots of spaghetti just for me because I had a big game tomorrow, my mother did almost anything I asked of her. I never appreciated this demonstration of love because to me such a demonstration was a sign of weakness. I felt sorry for her that she grew up in a culture which limited her to just caring for others in the family. However, during my college years I became increasingly aware of and disgusted by my lack of appreciation and respect for her. This disappeared for good when I saw the selfless way my mom took care of my helpless grandmother every hour of every day for over a year until my grandmother reached the point where she could not even sit up in bed unassisted. Despite the horrible stories my grandmother spread about my mother and the nastiness my grandmother displayed to my mother daily, my mom took care of my grandmother with great humanity and love.

Though my parents did not openly compare one daughter to another, saying that we were each unique and different, I felt myself attempting to live up to the standards set by my oldest sister and trying not to live down to the standards set by my middle sister. My oldest sister Joey was the brilliant, well-behaved one who always helped my mom around the house and who graduated early from high school and began college as a sophomore. Growing up, I saw Joey as my guardian angel. I would tag along after her whenever she was around. Though I did not always understand what she was saying, my sister always shared all of her insights and opinions with me, including reasons why my parents treated me the way they did. We moved to the Midwest at the same time Joey went off to college. Writing me long letters, she tried to convince me to ignore what my parents thought of me and to do things for my own happiness, not for the approval of others. I was stuck, though, on blaming my dad for my low self-esteem and unhappiness.

Katie, on the other hand, was the mystery sister who locked herself in her room at all hours of the day. No one ever knew what she did or what she thought. Being a member of the popular clique at school, this sister lived a lifestyle that my parents disapproved of. Sacrificing pleasure and happiness in the present for the sake of the future was not something Katie practiced, nor were academics ever Katie's top priority. My parents would mock her intelligence and lecture her on being selfish. When I hit adolescence, I began to respect Katie and understand why she had removed herself from the family. Her "selfishness," along with her strong, independent sense of self, allowed her to survive my parents' disapproval and degradation of her. Despite her "stupidity," Katie attended an excellent university. My dad grew to respect her for her strong sense of independence and the quiet strength and confidence with which she went about her life. I wonder if he is aware of the pain Katie endured silently as much as he is of mine.

The private, all-girls school I attended validated my righteousness in hating my dad. I was taught to fight for what I believed and act on these beliefs. Knowing this gave me the strength to deal with my dad. I was incredibly studious in middle school, trying to prove to everybody that I was smart. I then discovered the joy of playing sports and being part of a team. From these experiences, I saw that I earned respect and friendship by being myself.

I feel that the impact of school on my sense of identity was strongest in high school, where I embraced the messages the school threw at us. I believed that being anything less than a superwoman would be compromising my potential. By the time cliques had disappeared during junior year, I was respected by peers and teachers as a student, an athlete, and an active member of the student community. My school was the perfect environment in which to fight against my father's views. It gave me a chance to develop into an independent, capable woman who did not need to answer to anyone but herself. Though I dated a few people here and there,

I joined my friends in the "guys suck" movement and prided myself on not wanting or needing a guy in order to affirm my sense of self. I also attempted to be as emotionally independent of my parents as I could. Unfortunately, the more I denied needing my parents' support, the more the support became painfully necessary.

When Katie left for college, I was afraid of having to deal with my parents alone. My sisters worried about me throughout high school as I was constantly depressed and angry whenever they came home from college. They would engage me in these marathon talks late at night where they would try to get me to be happy, but I always found something to be bitter and resentful about.

In addition to dealing with the stress of growing up at home, school was another source of stress, as I had to get into the best college possible and do more than Joey so that I could prove to my parents that I deserved as much respect as they gave Joey. I liked receiving my report cards because they were proof that I was successful and good at something. My parents would only say, "You don't have to prove yourself to anybody; you should be working hard for yourself and not for others." I did not understand my parents. Though they were never proud of my grades, they would laugh at the Cs and sparse As on my middle sister's report cards. By senior year, I was dying to get out of the house.

In retrospect, senior year was often a blast. My mom, my dad, and even my grandmother came to my last volleyball game, where we ended our season undefeated. This was the only game my family had ever seen me play in, and I was ecstatic. School was fun and friendships deepened, while the entire school year was a celebration of my class. I thought the emotion of the year would peak at graduation or at the graduation parties, but it actually climaxed during the upper school awards ceremony. I had already been inducted into the cum laude society, which was one of my biggest goals because this was something Joey had achieved. At the awards night, which my parents attended, I received two subject awards, a goal that had burdened me for almost ten years. Later that night, my father actually looked at me with respect for the first time. He said, "I didn't realize your teachers thought so much of you and how successful you were in school. You should think about being a doctor." Only a week earlier my dad had told me I didn't have the intelligence or the right kind of thinking to be a doctor and suggested that I go into psychology because that field was more at my ability level. When I got angry with him for his insensitivity, he told me to grow up and learn to face reality. I found it interesting that these awards actually created such a change in his perspective, and I wasn't sure how I felt about this occurrence.

None of this mattered, though; I was about to begin living a life of freedom and peace at a great college far away from home. I entered college wanting to be independent yet with a low self-esteem. I was also confused about the Asian part of my identity, the result of living in places with few Asian Americans. Despite my personal cultural differences with my parents, I was proud of being Asian American and didn't mind letting people know it. But I didn't know very much about Asian culture or the Asian part of my own identity.

I was insanely gleeful when my parents left for home after helping me move in, but I wasn't really looking forward to doing schoolwork and expanding my intellectual horizons. Knowing I was burned out from high school, I had wanted to take a year off from school. However, my parents would only pay for college if I attended immediately. I thus floundered through my first year surrounded by incredibly motivated and high-achieving students, while I did as little work as possible.

Happy to escape stressed-out students and my evil roommate (along with her piles of dirty clothes, rotting food, and possessed Chucky doll), I returned home that first summer with relief. The physical distance college created between my dad and me allowed us to talk to each other as human beings now. Our relationship was relatively smooth until an August evening when my dad was using the computer to work on his finances. Because I had lost three papers the last semester, I strongly suggested that my dad back up his important files on a floppy disk. As soon as I popped a disk into the drive, my dad became angry at me for imposing "my way" of doing things on him and for looking at his financial information. I tried to explain lightheartedly how ornery computers had screwed me over several times, but my dad just ignored me. I exploded at him, which in turn ignited his anger. Another ugly fight ensued. Afterwards, I sat dejectedly on my floor, gripped by the familiar sense of desolation and reveling in the pain, wishing to be zapped out of existence.

The idea of being in a serious relationship has always freaked me out. I did not want to depend on someone else, because I would be making myself vulnerable to hurt. I threw out all of these fears at the very end of sophomore year when I began dating my hallmate Ben.

Our relationship blossomed out of nowhere; he had been involved in a serious long-distance relationship which began when he and his girlfriend were classmates back home in East Asia. Because Ben drove sixteen hours every other weekend to see her and had daily phone calls and hour-long e-mail marathons with her, his friends and I thought that their relationship was more than stable. We all thought they were going to get married, at least we knew that Ben wanted to. I had not gotten to know Ben very well until the last month of school. As soon as we started to get to know each other, though, I felt that I had known him forever.

At the same time, Ben told me that his relationship had been shaky for many months. Discovering that she had wanted to break up with him several times, I found myself "knowing" that I would be a better girlfriend and much more appreciative of someone as devoted and kind as he. It soon became obvious over the next four days that Ben liked me by the physical contact he initiated and the things he said. I wasn't sure what to do. While I felt very comfortable around him, I didn't find myself bowled over by his looks or his personality. After consulting with friends, I decided that commitment and a relationship with Ben could be pretty neat. Ben conveniently broke up with his girlfriend around this time. Two days later, I found myself in over my head in a situation I never thought I would voluntarily be in.

If you had asked me at my high school graduation three years ago what I thought about marriage, I would have shuddered. Serious relationships and marriage were things to be done only after I had established myself as a confident woman cognizant of her identity, of her strengths and weaknesses, and of her goals in life. Being in a serious relationship would prevent and compromise this development. Before my relationship with Ben, I prided myself on being an autonomous person, someone who could relate to others yet not have to trust them. In this relationship my identity changed in a number of ways. I swayed from wanting to lavish Ben with all the care in the world to being completely disgusted with my desire to do things for him while ignoring my own wishes.

Ben stayed at my house for a few days soon after I returned home for summer vacation. My parents accepted the statement that we were "just friends," and I didn't tell them until September that we were dating. Being a thoughtful, intelligent, and compassionate person, Ben had my dad marveling at what "a good boy" he was. In a matter of weeks, I found myself marveling that I wanted to depend on Ben for the rest of my life. It didn't matter that I wasn't particularly attracted to him or that he was shaped by the same culture as my parents, because here was a person with whom I felt connected like never before. I ended up living with Ben near the college that summer because I could not comprehend being without him for a second.

Ben was unquestionably the most devoted and supportive friend I ever had. I was going crazy the first semester of my junior year. Being a dorm counselor for a problem-filled hall was stressful enough, and it didn't help that I was taking birth control pills that were making me extremely unstable and depressed (although I didn't realize this at the time). Ben helped me unfailingly through it all, always intent on making me happy.

Our relationship basically consisted of him supporting me (or me being totally dependent upon him) and us sitting in my room studying or having sex. One thing he loved was the sex. For both of us, the act was symbolic of the love and care we held for each other. For Ben it was also an act of great passion, but it wasn't for me, unfortunately. There were times Ben got caught up in the throes of passion and entered me without any protection. Sometimes he stopped when I told him to, but often I forcefully had to shove the idiot away. He was then apologetic and remorseful, but this happened more than once. I also ended up thinking that I was pregnant more than once. While the thought of being pregnant made me stressed, at the same time I entertained the thought that if I was pregnant, at least it would be an impetus to get married to Ben sooner rather than later. After the second pregnancy scare, I finally found a brand of birth control pills that didn't have such negative effects.

While I loved Ben for the wonderful person he was, the rest of our relationship was not so great. When Ben visited my home again during Thanksgiving break, I was surprised that my mom expressed her concern that though I cared for him deeply, I seemed very unhappy in the relationship. I didn't realize I had been complaining about him so much. Automatically I responded that my unhappiness had nothing to do with our relationship; school was just overwhelming me, and the few glitches in the relationship were resolvable.

Having grown up in the same country and culture as my parents, Ben believed in many of the same customs and traditions my parents believed in. One of these traditions is having deference toward elders. Ben had never communicated to his parents how he felt about them or implied that he had any problems with them. Even if Ben disagreed with his parents, he did anything they told him without a word of resistance. It bothered me that he would never disagree with them or offer any suggestions because he believed their age gave them the experience and knowledge to know what they were doing. He insisted that he finally did rebel by choosing to go to college on the East Coast instead of the West Coast, which was his parents' wish.

Ben dedicated himself to playing the role of the ideal boyfriend. He wanted to be the most appealing guy in the world to me, to be the only person I ever needed to be happy. Ben knew I liked spontaneity. Thus Ben planned occasional "spontaneous" things such as a night at a bed and breakfast. These occasions felt unnatural for both of us, and we never had as much fun as Ben wanted. He would then feel bad and apologize for being "so boring." We had been spending so much time together without getting any work done that we were both suffering from sleep deprivation while in the heart of our sport seasons. One of the things Ben did that was natural to him was to set up the rule that on weekdays, we could only see each other between 5 P.M. and 7 P.M. and after 3 A.M., which was when both of us would usually get our work done. For the most part, we followed this schedule.

Though Ben was not always the most scintillating company, he really irritated me when he would try to be someone he was not just to please me. Ben even told me when he was doing this, so I didn't understand why he was doing it at all. I knew he wanted to be the man of the house, to pamper his loved one who, in turn, would make him feel like the most essential and important person in the world. Did he play these roles as a way of entreating me to love him, if not for himself then for what he did for me? Friends around me were shocked at how his activities annoyed me. They felt that I was supposed to appreciate how devoted he was to me and his demonstrations of how much he loved me.

Thankfully, the infinite number of hall problems essentially disappeared the second semester of my junior year. I finally had time to relax by myself and read my *Sports Illustrated*. Our relationship began to sour as I found myself wanting to spend this extra time by myself. I just wanted to have some space, to be able to sleep by myself for one night. Spending time with him was beginning to lose its appeal because we never did anything but work and enable each other with our constant complaining. As co-captain of the water polo team, Ben was heavily involved in his beloved sport. Unfortunately, his team only had two home games that season. Missing the first one due to my lacrosse game, I was supposed to go to his other home game. When that game day arrived, I had been suffering from bronchitis for several weeks and was sacked with a pound of overdue papers. I decided that I had to finish one overdue paper, which to my mind was ridiculously late. Ben was disappointed, but he said he understood. I had been working on the paper for several hours that night when a hallmate of mine, with whom I had become very good friends, crashed into my room looking for food. Wanting a study break, I convinced him to throw the ole pigskin around for a few minutes before I returned to tackling the paper that was stagnating on my hard drive. As we were throwing in the hall, Ben appeared at the other end of the hallway. He took three steps forward, saw me, and went immediately back downstairs. "Shit! Shit! Shit!" I knew he was upset, especially since he wouldn't trek sixty-three stairs to my floor just to turn around. I immediately went down to his room to explain what had been going on. Expecting him to mope and be reluctant to reveal what was bothering him, as was his usual response, I was surprised to find him out of control with anger. The usually quiet and reserved Ben started *yelling* at me because he couldn't believe that though I couldn't go to his water polo game, I could play football in the hall with other people. Understanding his anger as a misinterpretation of the situation, I replied that I had simply wanted to take a five-minute study break and that I had only thrown the ball once when he came on the hall. Ben then yelled back at me, "I'm so unimportant to you that you couldn't come to my game for five minutes?" Shocked by this statement, I realized that Ben was still insecure about my feelings for him. I was hurt because I still couldn't believe how important he was to me. I thought that if he truly loved me and I loved him, our love shouldn't be so tenuous that one incident would demonstrate otherwise. When I told him this, Ben said I was just making an excuse for myself. The whole conversation was so ridiculous that I left him to mope in his room and think about what he wanted.

Ben later apologized to me for becoming unreasonably upset. I wanted to know where all this anger suddenly came from. Ben revealed that he had just gotten extremely jealous. I thought he was just being insecure about me loving him. We talked about how he got jealous easily whenever I spent time with my male friends and that he felt bad that I needed to be entertained by other male friends. Ben also was jealous over my spending "excessive" amounts of time with one of my hallmates who had become a good friend. He was afraid that I liked my hallmate better than I liked him because my friend was an awesome athlete and really funny. I assured him that his concerns were unjustified and that I just wanted a little more time for myself. After he apologized to me, there was an uncomfortable moment of silence as Ben looked at me expectantly. I knew he was waiting for me to apologize to him, but for once in my life I felt that I had absolutely nothing to apologize for. Telling him this was not what Ben wanted to hear. He immediately left the room.

I didn't know what to do: I thought that I was selfish and unappreciative for not wanting to spend time with someone who cared for me so much, yet I was beginning to feel trapped in the relationship. The guilty feelings won out. Even though I didn't want to at all, I kept having sex with him because I didn't want him to think that I didn't care for him any more. Thinking that he was losing me, Ben responded by trying to squeeze me even tighter in his grasp, by doing things for me, buying me things, and trying to support me better than anybody else. He believed that these things would keep me going out with him.

Never having had a strong identity as an individual, Ben depended a lot on our relationship to reinforce his self-confidence. As my annoyance with Ben persisted, I began to feel increasingly guilty about not being there for him as he had been for me and for not appreciating him for who he was. I was also spending lots of time with my friends and not in my room because I was getting tired of seeing only Ben and nothing of my friends. I would ask Ben if he wanted to do things with me and my other friends, but he never would. In fact, Ben only wanted to socialize if it was just the two of us.

Spring vacation soon arrived, along with the annual sports team trip to Florida. The hall was filled with gleeful people whose joy was highly contagious. An absolutely exhausted Ben was resting in my room after pulling three consecutive all-nighters. Ben kept falling asleep as I was packing for my trip, so I suggested he take a nap. Being drawn to the excitement on the hall, I ended up raucously frolicking until the wee hours of the morning. I felt guilty for not spending my time with Ben, so I kept checking up on him periodically, asking him if he would rather rest or spend time together. He opted for the former, so I let him rest. My best friend later came to visit as I was finally packing for my trip. With the halogen lamp dimmed low, we chatted in the silence of the room while Ben rested in the shadows of the bed. I expressed to Yvonne that it felt so good to be able to spend time with other people without feeling guilty. I expressed to her the annoyance and guilt that I had been feeling. Both of us kept trying to see if Ben was awake, but he lay there totally asleep.

Or so I thought. Several days after the end of spring break, Yvonne told me that Ben had heard our entire conversation. I was so incensed that he had pretended to sleep for almost three hours as Yvonne and I talked about me and him that I confronted him immediately, demanding an explanation. I had told him over spring break how I had felt that night, and Ben had not revealed that he already knew. In a condescending and self-righteous tone, Ben replied that he hadn't told me because if he was important to me, I would have wanted to spend time with him and not my hallmates. As he said this to me, I suddenly found myself disgusted with him.

I knew I had to break up with him, but despite my feelings of disgust, I was afraid of crushing him. In order to make the breakup easier for both of us, I told Ben that I wanted to take some time away from the relationship. Ben began asking me all these technical questions about exactly what I meant, as if I had decided to propose a new legislative policy. Ben said he had been waiting for this moment ever since the water polo incident, which by this time was weeks old. I blamed him for not trusting me and thinking that I was slipping away when I wasn't.

Irritatingly enough, Ben continued to visit me once a day after this talk. Feeling stalked and constantly watched, I was even more unhappy and annoyed than before. Yvonne made it clear to me that Ben was still "desperately in love" with me. After an invitation to the spring formal dance appeared under my door one morning, I broke up with Ben permanently. I finally realized that it wasn't Ben I loved; I loved the knowledge and feeling of being loved.

The summer after the breakup was unlike any other summer before. Thinking back over my experiences during the past couple of summers, I realize that my understanding and existence as an independent individual have continued to evolve over the years. Now I am more able to be objective and realize when I define myself in relation to others versus when I define myself as an individual without the need of others around me. I am more conscious of when I make decisions based solely on my own desires and needs and when my decisions are influenced (hampered or enhanced, depending how you look at it) by the opinions or wishes of others.

Now I am figuring out what *I* want out of life. Ben supported me unfailingly and accepted who I was. In a Freudian way, I wanted him to be the male figure in my life who was everything my father was not. This was the first time I believed that someone truly loved me for who I was, and it hurt desperately when I broke up with him. I worried that I was throwing away this kind of love, and perhaps a wonderful husband, because I felt I was losing my independence and ability to do what I wanted to do. But I could no longer do things for someone else while losing myself in the process. I was starting to feel truly secure and wanted to do my own thing again (like in high school) uninhibited by someone else's wishes.

After years of conflict with my father and a lack of respect for my mother, I find that, once again, I long to have a solid relationship with them. I finally understand that my dad has always loved me, and I have begun to accept his way of supporting me. My dad sacrificed everything to make sure we always had enough money to live a comfortable, upper-middle-class life. I went to private schools my entire life because this was the best thing that he as a parent could provide for his children. I thought this was just his way; I didn't tie his caring to any sort of cultural behavior, and thus I was as ungrateful as I could be since I didn't understand why he couldn't just give me moral support and accept me the way I was, like any other "normal" American parent. While I was so intent on proving to myself how independent I was of my parents, I relied on all of my friends. Only now that I am beginning to feel complete with my parents do I find that I need to have less of these deep connections with my good friends or anybody else that I know. With my relationships with my parents healing and growing, I find myself not needing the care and support Ben was providing for me.

The anger and pain are almost entirely behind me now. I care for my parents very much and want to make them happy, to show them how much they do mean to me. Though people's opinions still affect me greatly, I feel that I need less and less the approval of everybody and can focus on doing things for myself. I am incredibly happy living by myself this summer without any obligations to do things for other people unless I choose to do so. Having this choice and freedom of not catering to everyone's needs gives me this exalted feeling. I find myself embracing life with an acceptance and freedom I never thought possible. I can't pinpoint exactly the factors leading to this happiness, but I know that who I am has nothing to do with external circumstances. It truly comes from within.

PART THREE

Challenges

Theoretical Overview

There exists within the field of adolescent research a debate over whether adolescence is typically a period of storm and stress, of alienation and separation, or a more harmonious evolution in which positive feelings about self and family are extended into the larger realms of peers and society. Each of these perspectives has merit and accounts for the different individual circumstances and coping styles of a complex period of human development. One point of agreement in this debate is that, stormy or halcyon, adolescence is a period of radical transformation of the physical and psychological self. Even under the best of circumstances, adolescents travel an exquisitely poignant journey through difficult developmental terrain. Finding one's way would be challenge enough. But when the ground is continually shifting with the ongoing physical, emotional, and cognitive growth of this period, the journey becomes full-time work for most adolescents. When the normal and inevitable stresses of adolescence are overlaid with extraordinary additional stresses, important risk factors for healthy development emerge. The cases in this section explore both the dangers and strategies for coping with such challenges.

Our notion of "challenges" implies obstacles or special difficulties that must be negotiated in addition to all the more "typical" preoccupations and developmental tasks of adolescence. Challenges are important both because of what they tell us about adolescent coping strategies in general, and because many adolescents face such circumstances at some point. If we add up all the adolescents who must deal with such challenges as physical disabilities; serious illness; divorce; the death of a parent, sibling or close friend; physical or sexual abuse; unwanted pregnancy; racism; substance abuse; or mental illness, we can see that significant challenges, whether acute or chronic, represent, if not the norm, at least a sizable subsample of all adolescents. An autobiographical exploration of adolescent challenges also provides a window on resilience. It allows us to learn which coping strategies and character traits appear to be most protective and even promotive of adolescent mental health.

Each of the three cases included in this section represents a distinct challenge to healthy psychological growth at three different developmental periods: (1) a severe stutter and serious sexual abuse in early childhood, (2) the emotional crisis surrounding an abortion in adolescence, and (3) a journey from war refugee to immigrant to the United States and gradual acculturation. Taken as a whole, these cases highlight both what is unique and universal, at least for Western culture: unique, in terms of the specialized issues these problems raise for adolescent development; universal, in that the cases highlight the way in which the tasks of adolescence remain relatively constant even in the face of powerfully destabilizing events. The emergence of adolescence represents both a difficult context in which to bring preexisting problems and a new opportunity for overcoming some of the more debilitating psychological effects of these issues.

Self-understanding is one of the more important aspects of emerging adolescent abilities for overcoming serious challenges. Prior to adolescence, childhood is characterized by the embeddedness of the child in his or her family and the profound tendency, whether for better or worse, to identify with important persons and norms within the family. The increasing importance of the peer world and the simultaneously evolving capacity to see parents as less powerful and more fallible are conducive to a loosening and diversification of earlier identifications. This evolving capacity for perspective can facilitate healing through important substitute relationships such as teachers, mentors, peers, families of friends, and others. Such healing may be necessary when families have not been sufficiently nurturing, protective, or enhancing of self-esteem. While these relationships may also be important at earlier periods, the adolescent can increasingly see herself through the eyes of these important others. This fresh perspective allows the adolescent to take a more autonomous approach to creating a self of her own choosing. There has long been recognition that this emergent ability to gain self-knowledge and perspective through interaction with others—this "looking glass self" (Cooley, 1902; Mead, 1934)—helps explain why positive relationships can have such a restorative effect on the damage of earlier events. This "mirroring" becomes especially salient in peer and romantic relationships during this time (Erikson, 1968; Sullivan, 1953) as the adolescent learns to take a perspective on herself by means of gradually modifying the self she sees reflected in the eyes of peers.

Self-understanding has been shown to be an important "protective factor" (Beardslee, 1989) in ameliorating the risk to healthy psychological development from serious life stressors. Ideally, self-understanding should lead to action that transforms one's adaptation to circumstances or changes the circumstances themselves. It is only when insight leads to new and better means of coping with life's challenges that we can say the individual is rising to the challenge. Indeed, insight without action can reflect a profound sense of hopelessness. The cases presented here all reveal the adolescent biographers to be reacting to significant stress by first developing insight and then taking steps to make things better.

An important emerging field within developmental psychology is devoted to studying individuals who are resilient or seemingly invulnerable to serious risks and stresses that have been shown to affect negatively the mental health and long-term adjustment of many children. This new field represents a significant historic shift from studying almost exclusively those individuals who succumb to developmental risks to studying those who are equally exposed but who overcome the risk and remain healthy. Among factors shown to place children at risk are serious mental illness of a parent, physical or sexual abuse, serious marital discord, poverty, emotionally unsupportive relationship with parents, foster home placement, and parental alcoholism (Rutter, 1975, 1979; Werner, 1989). While different studies find differing degrees of relative risk for each of these and other factors, it does appear that no single risk factor is determinate. Rutter's studies mentioned here found that, when only a single risk factor was present, the probability that a child would suffer from a psychiatric disorder was no greater than that for a child in a family without any of these risk factors. However, two risk factors produced a fourfold increase in the chances of a psychiatric disorder in the child; four risk factors produced a tenfold increase in risk. It would seem that most children can cope with a certain amount of stress stemming from these risks, but when overloaded with multiple stressors, they become exponentially more likely to succumb. Many children and adolescents, however, do not succumb even under such stress. And therein lies a hopeful avenue for understanding how some children are protected, or protect themselves, against the vicissitudes of serious stress. And we might speculate that, whatever these protective coping mechanisms are, they are promotive of good mental health in general and could be helpful even in low-risk individuals.

Three of the most important protective factors appear to be (1) personality features such as self-esteem, (2) family cohesion and lack of discord, and (3) external support systems that encourage and reinforce the child's efforts to cope (Garmezy, 1985; Masten & Garmezy, 1985). Protective factors are not fixed attributes; they are subject to development or reduction over time within the same individual, and those that may aid in coping at one time may not work at another. Thus these factors should be seen as dynamic; the resilient individual is one who can adapt his or her coping strategies to changing situations. In this sense, protective factors should not be seen as fixed traits of the individual or circumstance but rather as interpersonal and interactive. This is what Rutter (1987) refers to as protective *mechanisms* or *processes* that the individual may apply or modify as needed.

The cases in the section that follows reveal a variety of risks and developmental vulnerabilities, as well as a number of protective coping mechanisms. These mechanisms are employed to secure important emotional needs, and with development these needs themselves undergo transformation. In the case of our sexually abused adolescent, "The Simple Beauty of a Conversation," we read how a severe stutter during childhood and adolescence (which may or may not have been related to his abuse) devastated his self-esteem and his relationship with his parents. This devastation had a profoundly negative impact on his social relations.

But the functional needs and possibilities of adolescence propelled him into new relationships—warm mentors at work and an accepting and affirming girlfriend—that gave him belated self-confidence to overcome the more debilitating effects of his stutter and abuse. In this sense, the functional tasks of adolescence became for this young man more than something merely to be achieved on the road to adulthood; they became his single most important opportunity for redressing the developmental damage incurred in his childhood. Each phase of life, therefore, not only provides extra obstacles for adolescents with special challenges, but also represents a fresh chance to redirect the inexorable movement that phase will require. His ability to seek and use the support and encouragement of adult mentors, as well as his self-understanding, are the protective mechanisms that may account for his resilience against the vulnerabilities from his abuse and speech problem. These mechanisms and the developmental task of romantic intimacy that emerge in adolescence combine here in a powerful protective partnership.

The case above represents a long-term challenge, whereas the case concerning adolescent abortion, "Proud of the Strength I Had," involves an acute crisis that results in an extended period of depression, anxiety, and guilt feelings. The resulting effects on this autobiographer's self-esteem, attitude toward sexuality, and capacity for intimacy represent risks to her healthy transition to adulthood. A variety of studies find that many women who undergo abortions experience periods of depression, regret, and guilt (Cvejic, Lipper, Kinch, & Benjamin, 1977; Ford, Castelnuovo-Tedesco, & Long, 1971; Smith, 1973), but that these feelings are typically mild and abate in the short term without negatively affecting general functioning. Other studies have found that the primary response to abortion is relief (Adler, 1975; Ewing & Rouse, 1973; Monsour & Stewart, 1973), and that in the case of adolescent abortion in particular it "is neither psychologically harmful nor in other ways damaging to the patient" (Olson, 1980, p. 440).

In comparison with adult women, adolescent females are found to have somewhat more negative emotional responses to abortion, though not severely worse (Adler, 1975; Bracken, Hachamovitch, & Grossman, 1974; Margolis, Davidson, Hanson, Loos, & Mikelson, 1971; Payne, Kravitz, Notman, & Anderson, 1976). This seems to reflect the experience of our autobiographer, who describes somewhat more lasting negative feelings, perhaps because as a middle-adolescent at the time, she was unable to fully anticipate her sense of loss and to prepare for it psychologically as older adolescents appear better able to do (Hatcher, 1976). The inherent stress of an unwanted pregnancy in adolescence was exacerbated by her sense of betrayal and isolation; her former boyfriend offered no support other than to pay for the abortion, and she felt unable to tell her parents or even her twin sister. She describes how this crisis led later to her participation in a college support group for other students who had terminated pregnancies. The emotional catharsis and gradual understanding of her feelings led to active participation in reproductive-rights events and close friendships with other women who shared the same experience. We can see here the integration of self-understanding and action as central to her eventual success in managing this stress and recovering from her depressed feelings. This emerging insight also brought into focus her family's inability to communicate emotionally and her determination to redress this constriction of her own emotional openness. When her younger sister thought she might be pregnant, our author took this opportunity to soothe her own feelings of isolation and abandonment by providing the type of support she wishes she had. Thus the opportunity to reflect on the linkage between how she became pregnant—"not being able to talk about sex and contraception" with her boyfriend—and her family's emotional silence—"I grew up in a family that stuffed their feelings and never talked about anything, including sex"—led to an important self-understanding about the ways she wanted to change. This crisis illuminated an underlying and ongoing challenge to her happiness—her family's dysfunctional emotional communication.

The developmental vulnerability of an unwanted pregnancy is itself reflective of the adolescent tasks of balancing intimacy, identity, and sexuality. In this case, we can witness the painful beginnings of learning how to develop and employ protective mechanisms—sharing intimate feelings with trusted friends, providing the type of support to others she now knows she needs, searching for an ideology that gives meaning and purpose to her experience, and actively identifying with other women who assert their feelings. Her moves in this direction are tentative, but she seems to have a solid understanding of the cause of much of her unhappiness and the means of redressing it. Similar to the lessons of the other cases, the challenge to her emotional development is met by the interaction of protective mechanisms and developmental tasks.

In the case "Seeking the Best of Both Worlds," the adolescent tasks related to separation and individuation become especially poignant in the context of an immigrant family having fled a war-ravaged Vietnam. The traumatic experience of emigrating under such circumstances understandably can have profound effects on both the individual and the nature of family relationships. In this case, the author describes feeling both great loyalty to and respect for his mother's heroic role in rescuing the family from an impossible situation, and feeling shame and contempt for her unwillingness to allow him to adapt to the U.S. culture to which she had exposed him. He wants acceptance and permission from his mother to live in both worlds—the Western world to which she brought him and the traditional world of his family. Though he is willing to accept the dichotomy and to live according to the rules of family when at home and of society when outside, his mother seems unwilling to make any such accommodations for herself and thinks he should not either. The result is that he chooses to segment his self into dutiful but resentful son at home and "Americanized" adolescent in school and the larger world. He must resort to constant lying and other subterfuge to keep his mother from knowing his other self. This stress of a double life and the alienation from his mother leaves him emotionally isolated and increasingly depressed.

In addition to all the normal preoccupations of adolescence, and beyond the typical parent–child conflicts of the period, this author demonstrates how hard it can be for immigrant adolescents to integrate the best of both cultures if their family demands exclusive loyalty to the native culture. His strategy of alternating his behavior to whatever culture he finds himself in is often effective for immigrant adolescents (LaFromboise, Coleman & Gerton, 1993) and is even associated with positive mental health (Rogler, Cortes & Malgady,1991). In the case reported here, however, we can also see the tremendous emotional stress and developmental risk this form of adaptation can cause. At the same time, the case also illustrates how his increasing competence and validation in the larger culture gradually creates for him a new and respected role in his family as the intercultural go-between. By the time he writes his autobiography in college, he describes ways in which he has been able to influence his mother in rearing his two younger siblings so as to lessen some of the pain and conflict he experienced.

These three cases reveal much about the opportunities of adolescence for growing stronger through challenge. Unfortunately, not all such challenges are met so successfully. These autobiographies do, however, represent the fortunate fact that most adolescents who face such circumstances do somehow find a path to productive lives. The following cases give us an intimate look at how it might be done.

14 The Simple Beauty of a Conversation

This author's shocking discovery of his speech impediment in first grade leads him to feel insecure and self-conscious regardless of academic and social accomplishments. Ray's "identity as a stutterer" makes him give up in school, because it is "easier not to attempt something than to fail at it." He plagiarizes and cheats his way through high school without being caught, as much a rebellion against his parents as a way of getting by. His religious faith, a close friendship, and his work in the library help him through some of the most difficult years, providing support and contributing to a growing sense of himself as a valued person. Ray experiences a setback when, early in college, his girlfriend is raped, an experience that causes memories of his own early sexual abuse to surface for the first time. He feels like a stronger person now, "standing on his own two feet." His stutter reappears only occasionally, reminding him of the difficulties each of us has in our lives.

As I started high school many teachers and friends held high hopes for me, but by the end of my senior year there was a question as to whether I was going to graduate or repeat the year. My academic problems did not all stem directly from my learning problems. The most accurate description would be to say that I was burned out. I desperately wanted someone to recognize that I was having problems and to offer help. That never happened and I continually failed at all attempts to get myself on track. It became easier not to attempt something than to fail at it. I could see no future for myself. I never even tried to think about what I wanted to do after graduation. I couldn't handle the present, so trying to plan my future was an impossibility.

I got by the best I could. High school was very painful and difficult for me, and as a way of protecting myself I pretended that I didn't care about the school or my classes. If I had let myself feel that high school could be a very positive experience for me if I was successful, then the pain would have just been worse. I did very little homework, cheated on almost every test, plagiarized all my critical papers, and skipped school as often as I could get away with it.

I need to go back to my early childhood to explain all the problems I had with school. At the age of 5, I went through kindergarten. I enjoyed it and as far as I knew I was just like all the other kids. However, I found out that while all my other friends were going on to first grade, I was going to go to another kindergarten class. No one ever explained to me why I was repeating kindergarten. When I got to the new class I was with a bunch of other kids who were pretty normal. For one hour a day, however, I was taken aside with a special teacher who came to the class just to work with me. I didn't mind because I remember thinking she was pretty. She would show pictures and ask me to tell her what I saw. For example she would show me a picture of a dog and I would say, "dog."

"No, that's not right. Try it again," she would often say.

I had no idea what I was doing wrong. The picture was very obviously a picture of a dog and as far as I knew I was saying the word "dog." This would happen with pictures of trees, cats, farm animals, and many other simple items. I would tell her what it was and she would say, "No, try again." She never told me what I was doing wrong.

The other kids in class must have picked up on what was going on because pretty soon they all started calling me names like "retard" and "moron." I didn't understand this either. I went home crying to my mother one day and asked her why I was being called these names. I can remember the most pained expression I have ever seen come to her face and she said simply, "Because they're not very nice children."

I made it through that year in pretty good shape, all things considered. In first grade the same teacher came to see me every day again. We would go to a small office in the basement and do the same things we did in kindergarten. I know it was unintentional, but one day she did one of the most cruel things I have ever experienced. I went to see her that day and we went through the same routine. This time, however, she had a tape recorder. She recorded the answers I gave to the pictures. Then she rewound and played the tape back to me. I'm not even sure how to describe my reaction to the tape. I was about 6½ years old and like every other little kid I wasn't all that self-conscious or worried about the differences between myself and other kids. But that tape crushed me. The voice I heard was absolutely unintelligible. The voice was stuttering terribly and all the pronunciation was completely off. I couldn't even recognize what it was saying. The voice didn't even sound human. I was sure that I had said "dog" but when the tape got to the point where the word should have come, something completely foreign, not even resembling "dog," came out. I started crying and screaming, "That isn't me! You put another tape in there! That isn't me!" She couldn't calm me down.

I guess everybody assumed I was aware of my speech problems because they were so severe. At the very least I must have been aware of my stutter. But I wasn't aware of it at all. As I've said, no one, my parents included, had ever talked to me about it before.

That tape had an immediate effect on me. I became very withdrawn and would hardly talk to anybody. I particularly avoided talking to my parents, both because I didn't want them to hear me speak the way I did and also because I felt betrayed; I wanted to hurt them with my silence. That might sound like a lot for a 6-year-old but it is very true. Everything that had happened—staying back in kindergarten, the special teacher, all the kids making fun of me—became clear to me and I became very bitter towards my parents for having never talked with me about it. I really hated them. Over the next ten or eleven years I spent much of my time finding little ways that I could hurt them and get back at them for the way they had failed me.

My relationship with school didn't fare much better. Soon after the tape was played to me, the special teacher told me that she was transferring and that we wouldn't be working together any more. I have no idea if the tape incident had anything to do with her decision, but I am sure now that it did play a part in my parents' decision not to get any more help for me. They couldn't deal with the pain, and I think they felt that the best thing to do was to ignore my problems and hope they would disappear with age. So I no longer went to any special classes. In the regular classes I did everything I could to keep from having to speak in front of the class. I didn't want the other kids to hear how I talked. Through the rest of grade school every teacher I had just about killed himself or herself trying to get me to apply myself more. They all felt I had great potential if I would be more outgoing. I resisted all these efforts. While my pronunciation improved somewhat, my stutter had not improved at all by the time I entered junior high.

It is very difficult to discern how much my stutter affected my image of myself and how much it affected others' image of me. Trying to look back objectively, I would say that for the most part it had its greatest influence on my own self-image. When I was growing up it sometimes seemed that everybody was laughing at me and pointing me out, when in reality probably only a few did so. There are some events that make me realize now that my friends and classmates must have held me in fairly high regard. In the fourth grade I was elected class president. In sixth I was given awards for sportsmanship, leadership, and math ability. In the seventh grade I was chosen as the "Most Intelligent" out of a class of about 150. Still, these did very little to raise my self-esteem, so sensitive was I about my stutter. The effect of these positive reinforcements was minimized to the extreme by my self-consciousness. The only identity I had for myself was as a stutterer. None of my other accomplishments came close to having the effect on me that the fear of stuttering and speaking incorrectly in front of others did. I felt that no one else knew who I really was because I had become so proficient at hiding my speech problems. I saw myself as hiding who I really was from others. To some extent this was true.

In junior high my self-esteem reached its lowest point. My outlook on everything was dictated by my view of myself. I built a reputation at school for being able to get away with cheating, skipping classes, forgery, and other things like that. During lunch at school a lot of kids would come to me looking for help. I'd make a cheat sheet, sell an essay, or do whatever the occasion called for. This was my first niche in junior high and freshman year. It was fun at first because it was novel and it got me a lot of attention. Sometimes it was more innocent and sometimes it was of a much more serious nature. For example, I went through the honors English sequence in high school and plagiarized almost every critical essay I was assigned to write. Some other students were caught doing this but I never was. I learned how to choose obscure, yet valid, sources and how to change things around just enough so that there was very little chance of getting caught. I cheated on almost every test I took and spent a minimal amount of time on homework.

I was shy with girls and doing things like this created opportunities to talk with them. This was very important. I've been attracted to girls as long as I can remember. My first kiss was in kindergarten—the second year that is. I was embarrassed afterwards and I was afraid the girl would start telling the other kids that I had kissed her, so a couple of days later I went back to her house and beat her up, which sounds worse than it was. I had my first opportunity to have sex when I was in the sixth grade. The girl was in the eighth grade and I'm pretty sure she was drunk. We were behind some bushes in the church playground across from my house. She came over to me and took off all her clothes. She kept saying, "Come on over and lay me." I had never done more than kiss a girl at that point and I didn't know what "lay me" meant. I went over to her and she stuck her hand down my pants. I ejaculated as soon as she touched me. She laughed at me and said she wanted me to do that again but this time while I was "porking" her. I didn't know what that meant either. To be honest, I had no idea what to do at all. We fooled around for a while but we didn't actually have sex because I didn't know what to do. She kept laughing at me the whole time. I put my clothes back on and left her lying in the bushes. Immediately after this experience and for the next few days, I felt awful. I was cold and shivering all the time and I couldn't stand to have anyone closer than a few feet away from me. I didn't understand why I felt this way but then I didn't understand anything to do with sex at that time.

I went through puberty at an early age. By the end of the sixth grade I had had a couple of wet dreams and I was masturbating often. The incident with the first girl made me curious about and interested in girls. A friend and I used to climb trees in our backyards together. It started a few years earlier as an innocent childhood pastime and we just kept on doing it. One late afternoon during the summer after sixth grade, we were sitting up in the tree talking quietly when we saw a light go on in my neighbor's house. It was the bedroom of a girl who was about a year older than we were and who was my sister's friend. My friend said to me half jokingly, "Wouldn't it be awesome if she changed and didn't pull her shade down?" I agreed, of course, but we really didn't expect anything. But then she did change into her bathrobe without pulling down the shade. We sat for a while without saying anything. I think we were both embarrassed to talk or to move because we both had erections and didn't want the other to know.

One day later in the summer the girl we spied on, Jean, stopped by to see if my sister was around. I was home alone that day and told her so. She came in for a while anyway and we started talking. I got an erection and since I was wearing my bathing suit it wasn't long before she noticed, although I tried to hide it as best I could. At first I was embarrassed, but pretty soon we started talking dirty. We kept daring each other to say dirtier and dirtier things and to shift our clothes around to reveal more. Eventually we went into the shower and I lost my virginity. I think it was her first time also, but I'm not sure.

The time in the shower felt pretty good to me but I don't think Jean enjoyed it very much. She looked like she felt very guilty. Nevertheless she started coming over often when I was alone. We fooled around and tried a lot of things. She must have known more than I did because I really didn't understand how girls got pregnant, but after the first time in the shower she never let me penetrate again. Instead we did other things. At the time we did it I liked it, but I always felt dirty after she had left. Every time we fooled around she would ask for a few of my father's beers to take back home (he never kept track of them). One day she came over with a *Penthouse* and read some of the letters to me. She said she would try those things if I could get her a full bottle of wine. My father had one and I gave it to her. I had heard about prostitutes in church and what it meant if you got into that stuff. I started thinking that what we were doing was almost the same thing. I had a terribly guilty conscience, but every time she came over the same thing would happen.

There was something more than just a guilty conscience though. I couldn't bear having people being physically close to me. If I ever was in a crowd, such as in a mall, I would get lightheaded and have dizzy spells. I also hated to have anyone stand behind me. If I was in any line I would stand a little off to one side to prevent people from being directly behind me. I thought that maybe these feelings had something to do with what Jean and I were doing but I didn't understand them.

When school started again, Jean stopped coming over. We never talked about what we had done again and I think both of us really wanted to forget it. I have never bragged about these experiences to anyone. There are just too many painful feelings and too much confusion connected with it for me to be able to talk about it lightly. As a Catholic I felt what I did was morally wrong, and then there were all those other feelings which I couldn't figure out. In college I told the first girl I slept with that I was a virgin. She said she was, too (and she was probably telling the truth), and that it made it more special because it was the first time for both of us. I've only slept with one other girl since, and I told her that my only experience was with the other college girl. Right now I just don't feel comfortable letting anyone know about what happened.

After the summer with Jean I entered junior high school. That's when most kids start dating, but I became very shy with girls. I knew what sex was like but I had a lot of trouble talking to girls. Each day I was becoming more and more self-conscious about my stutter; I felt that no girl would ever go on a date with a guy who talked like I did. As a result I didn't have any dates in junior high or high school, although I did begin to talk to girls more. I had other problems then as well. I've mentioned what my academics were like. My grades were respectable but they were not earned honestly. My parents and I were moving further apart. About the only time we ever talked was when we were fighting.

As a result of my problems with my family and in school, I needed to find a place I could find some solace and security. Actually, I found three areas: religion, friends, and work. I was raised in a fairly strict Catholic manner. My mother took me to church every Sunday and we fasted before and after mass. I went to classes preparing me for all the sacraments and attended service on every holy day. Sometimes the tedium and monotony of these rites would get to me but overall I have always been a religious person. Often prayer and hope for the future has been the only outlet I have had when times have been really bad. I have never had a serious question about my belief in God and the scriptures, and for most of my life I have prayed every day. While my religion is and always has been an important part of my life, I have often questioned the attitudes of the Catholic Church itself. Nevertheless, I do have strong faith and I try to follow as best I can the teachings of forgiveness, forbearance, and humility. I take pride in my faith.

When I was a sophomore in high school, a priest in my parish, a person whom I really admired, came to me and tried to convince me to enter the priesthood. I actually considered this for a time. In the end I decided against it. But that is not the significance of that incident. This was the first time that someone I really admired let me know he saw some value in me. He was seeing good in me that I couldn't see myself. It had a profound effect on me. I didn't turn myself around in a day because of it, but I did have my first thoughts of where I was going and the person I was as opposed to the person I was capable of being. These were brief, very scattered thoughts but the seed had been planted. It was the encouragement of other people like him that helped me learn that many people saw me in a better light than I saw myself. I had very little self-respect so I had to get it from others, most of whom have been very religious. At least they are religious in my estimation of how the religious should be; they practice their faith and they show their belief in how they treat other people rather than by preaching to them. And they are secure enough in their faith that they can accept faiths that differ from their own. I have a lot of respect and admiration for these people. I learned from them that a strong belief in the self often goes hand in hand with a strong belief in a set of principles and precepts.

The Catholic Church requires public worship and professing of faith, but I was always very private about it. In that sense I made a poor Catholic. In fact, along with most of my friends, I denied holding any beliefs. I made jokes about the church and about older adults who were very religious. It's also true that I outwardly denied my faith because my mother was Catholic and worship was an integral part of her life. I didn't want to be anything like my parents, and it was a form of rebellion. But, still, inside I found it a source of comfort and hope. As I grew older I started understanding the readings at Mass more and saw that they could be applied to my life. I often looked at myself as a modern-day Job. I suffered through trials and hardships as a test of my faith. Not only my faith in God but also my faith in myself and my ability to keep hope alive in my breast and work for something better. I had occasional thoughts of suicide, and three times I made concrete plans to go through with it, but there was always something inside that wouldn't let me give up on myself. Religion helped add to my sense of identity, but that still wasn't enough. There was only so much I could get through my private contemplations and beliefs; I needed experience on a more social level.

This leads to the other two areas—friends and work. I had enough friends that I didn't feel like an outcast, but I had only one really close friend, the one who was my peeping-Tom partner. The two of us had met when we were 5 and had been best friends ever since. The strength of our friendship cannot be overstated. We never pressured each other into doing anything (like trying drugs) and we could share our secrets and problems. My friend, Bill, had a much better relationship with his family than I did, so I adopted his family as my own in a way. I didn't look up to or respect my parents, but I did his. Their opinions had more weight with me than my own parents' opinions. I don't mean to imply that my mother and father were failures as parents, but I held hard feelings against them and looked to Bill's parents for guidance.

Bill and I did everything together. We liked the same shows and music and hung out together all the time. In fact, it wasn't uncommon for teachers and other kids to get the two of us mixed up. There was a great amount of security in that relationship for me. I felt that Bill accepted me for who I was; he was the only person who I wasn't afraid to stutter in front of. Bill and I were (and still are) blood brothers. When we were very young, probably 7 or 8, we slit our thumbs with a knife and rubbed our bleeding fingers together. I assume that isn't done much today. We took everything from swimming lessons to guitar lessons together.

Our parents all worked and much of the time we were left to ourselves. During the summer we spent most of every day unsupervised. Some of our activities were questionable. For example, there was the summer that a moose was spotted in our town. A moose had not been seen in our town for over a hundred years so the news stirred up some fear along with the curiosity and fascination. Only a handful of people had seen the animal, and it was assumed that it had just moved on out of town. One afternoon Bill and I came up with a brainstorm. Our local paper had carried a picture of the tracks left by the moose so we cut that out. Next we got some wood and cut out models that resembled the prints. We tied the models to the bottom of our sneakers and walked in the backyard. Sure enough, we left tracks in dirt that were very similar to those in the picture. The next few nights we snuck out of our houses and went to the swampier areas of town. We put the moose feet on the bottom of our sneakers and walked in the mud of several backyards. A couple of days later we read in the paper that the moose was back and, the paper said, it was possible now that there was more than one. The police had been placed on alert. Aside from our terror of being found out by the police, we loved the whole episode. We had fooled the adults again.

The two of us did everything together and continually made future plans. In the long run this may have come close to hurting me; I relied too much on Bill's friendship and didn't try to be more outgoing and build my confidence. On the other hand, if I hadn't had Bill and the security of our friendship, I never would have learned how to function well socially.

The summer before high school I got a job at the town library, and I was excited about starting work. I had spent a lot of time at the library (it was very close to my house) and I knew several of the librarians. My immediate boss, Mrs. Johnson, turned out to be one of the most special people I have ever met. She was kind, friendly, intelligent, always quick to praise but also ready to point out mistakes in a constructive way, and an all-around lovely person. She could discern everybody's personality. She must have known that I needed a place where I could feel I belonged because she soon gave me many important responsibilities that were within my capabilities. This helped my confidence tremendously. I felt everyone there wanted to see me succeed, and when I made mistakes they treated them as very minor in comparison to all the other things I had done right. It wasn't long before I was working very hard at my job. I would do everything they wanted done—and more if I could find other little jobs. If they needed someone at an awkward time on short notice, I always volunteered. At first it was simply that I wanted Mrs. Johnson and the others to keep giving me praise and that their good opinion was very important to me. Eventually, though, I began to realize that to do a task with integrity and diligence was important and was its own reward. Before working at the library I had never felt what it was like to accomplish something that I had spent much time and effort doing. There was great satisfaction in it. It was a long time before I applied this to schoolwork, but that would come.

I worked at the library for about six years. It's hard to summarize all I learned and all the feelings connected with the library and the staff, but there are a few key points. First is the dedication of the staff. Many of the full-time employees held a master's degree in Library Arts and yet were making under $22,000 a year. They unfailingly did their best to work for the community in what was often a shamefully thankless capacity. I admired their dedication. I felt I wanted to emulate that, and often now when I feel I'm unfairly overloaded with work and responsibilities I think of those people and remember that I should appreciate what I have going for me. The other staff—the part-timers, custodians, and such—were the same. They all did their jobs well and created an enjoyable atmosphere for everyone. Sometimes I wondered how so many good people could be concentrated in one small place. Maybe I'm a naive optimist but I came to the conclusion that it was the atmosphere, the congenial and supportive feelings around us all, that was responsible for it. Most people have it in them to be their best but the circumstances surrounding them are not as favorable. And where did this atmosphere come from? I think it came from Mrs. Johnson and a couple of others there who were much like her. They were very supportive, generous, and kind to everyone, and so everyone else began to emulate and encourage this attitude. I don't know how well I have succeeded, but I have tried to hold this attitude and to project it to those I come into contact with. I've learned that how you treat people can really make a difference. Sometimes a kind word from the right person at a certain time can make all the difference in the world.

Another aspect of the library that was very important to me were the patrons, whose questions and requests for help had a great influence on me. I felt I held a certain power. If I knew the answer to a question, then I could solve a person's problem. Perhaps if a person was particularly nasty I could purposely misdirect that person (I never did that but I was aware that I held the power). It really built my confidence. I was given certain responsibilities and I was living up to them. This was something I couldn't find in school.

After a couple of years of working at the library, I noticed that many people recognized me outside of the library. For a very shy person this really fed my ego. One of my favorite memories happened right in the library. A mother brought her little girl to check out some children's books. The girl was no more than three and a half years old. She could walk and talk only a little bit. Her mother sat her on the counter as I checked out her books. I was talking to the girl like I usually did with little children; I asked if she enjoyed reading or if her mother read her stories at night. When I was done checking out the books and the mother was taking her off the counter she smiled and said, "He's a nice man, isn't he, Mommy?" Her mother agreed. I felt about ten feet tall the rest of the day. I knew from my experience at the library that I wanted to work in some capacity with people.

The problem was always that I couldn't seem to apply myself to anything outside of working at the library. I matured a great deal while working there, but I needed to extend that to other areas. I continued cheating on tests and papers throughout all of high school, but after freshman year I stopped advertising it. I quit helping my friends cheat and bragging about my crooked accomplishments. I wanted to become a more serious student, but I wasn't secure enough in my abilities to give up cheating. I felt I needed to cheat to get good grades. It was also partly force of habit; I was accustomed to cheating—not studying—and that was hard to break. I was still very withdrawn in class and did not participate. I avoided all high school social events. Overall, high school did not have a great effect on me because I put so little into it. What I did outside of class was of greater consequence.

When I wasn't working and my friend Bill wasn't around, I spent most of my time by myself feeling very lonely. Only those who have experienced extended periods of loneliness know what it can do to you. Fortunately, I had enough interests to occupy some of my time. For example, I was very interested in astronomy, and early in July there is a meteor shower that appears every year. One summer I decided to get up in the middle of the night to watch it. I had never seen a meteor shower before and I was not expecting it to be anything too spectacular. I got up around one in the morning and went outside the house. It took a while before I could discover the section of the sky in which it was taking place, but when I first saw it, I was frozen in place. Every few seconds a bright streak would shoot across the sky and disappear. Each one couldn't have lasted more than a second, but the power they seemed to display left me awestruck. They sped over the sky so quickly that they were hard to follow and I got dizzy from turning my head so quickly.

Then I decided I wanted to enjoy this more. I went inside and made a couple of sandwiches and got a drink. On leaving the house I caught a glimpse of my father's old pipe. It was a big, awkward thing but it seemed to match the moment perfectly. I had never smoked before—I had never even considered it—but I grabbed some tobacco and some matches and went outside with my little package. When I got outside I wasn't satisfied with my view. My house is on a hill but the house next to mine was taller and was blocking my line of sight. Nothing was going to get in my way of enjoying this show so I decided to climb up my neighbor's roof. I had scaled the side of their house several times before a few years earlier (to peek in their windows) but I had never been on the roof. The house had a fairly sturdy drain pipe so I tied my things in a bundle around my waist and climbed up to the roof. It was an old house with a lot of nooks and crannies in it so I found a good comfortable spot which couldn't be seen from the ground and sat down to rest. Lighting up the pipe took a few tries, and when I did light it at first I felt sick from the smoke. After a while I got used to it and started on the sandwiches. There was no moon that night and the sky was very dark. I looked upward and watched the lights streak from one side to the other.

I was all alone. I could see no one and no one could see me. The darkness of the sky was very soft and deep and the warm yellow streaks painting a path across the backdrop every few seconds were both magnificent and calming. My troubles were all below me and the show I was watching seemed to put everything into its right place. This was so much larger than anything else I had ever seen. How many trillions of miles and billions of years had these meteors travelled only so I could watch them burn out in flame? Everything else seemed insignificant. There were no happy families, no unhappy families. No good students and no bad students. There were no words locked inside my head refusing to come out right. All of us were little and of no importance to what I was witnessing. A quote from Dickens floated over me and didn't seem as harsh as when I first read it: "The universe makes a rather indifferent parent." I stayed on the roof for a couple of hours and for that time all was right in the world. Unfortunately, that was only a passing moment—no matter how good it made me feel, it didn't help me deal with everyday life.

After barely graduating from high school, Bill and I went together to a community college. It was something of a joke academically; my high school classes were more difficult. In spite of skipping a lot of classes we ended up with As and Bs and decided to transfer to a technical college. A couple of weeks into the semester I realized engineering was not for me and decided to transfer again in order to become an English major and live at school. It meant separating from Bill the next fall, but I felt it was time for me to try going out on my own.

That summer I met a girl named Ellen and soon started dating. Everything seemed perfect—almost too good to be true. We understood each other's feelings and problems and were able to give support to each other. For example, one day we were talking and I stuttered a little bit. She asked me directly about my stutter. No one had ever done that before. People had avoided mentioning it because they thought it would embarrass me. That attitude carries the implication that there is something wrong with having a stutter. Ellen asked me about it very straightforwardly. I realized that she accepted it as simply a part of me—just like my hair is brown and my eyes are blue. It had a great influence on me and I felt myself falling for Ellen. I took her to her prom and we saw a lot of each other during the summer.

So much happened that summer that it's hard, even in my own mind, to organize it all. Most was due to Ellen's influence and the nature of our relationship together. She was the first girl I ever developed an intimate and supportive relationship with. We shared our secret hopes and dreams and could rely on each other if we wanted to talk over problems we were experiencing in our lives. We each knew that we could depend on the other. We took things very slowly as far as a physical relationship went. When I think back to the time we shared, I think my favorite memories were when we went to the park and had a picnic. We would lie on the grass, sometimes I would lay my head on her lap, and talk or just sit quietly. There was something very special about being able to spend quiet time with someone as close to my heart as she was. All the days we spent together seemed to be sunny, happy, and fulfilling. I'm probably romanticizing our time together, but that is the quality of my memories of Ellen. Being able to build a relationship like that, particularly since Ellen and I were so well matched, resulted in my maturing a great deal.

I can't give a surefire explanation for it, but my stutter was decreasing markedly. By the end of the summer, stuttering had become a rare incident whereas before it had been the norm. Perhaps it was because I was at the age when men finally stop growing. My metabolism may have changed slightly. Maybe it was because I was maturing mentally and emotionally. By the end of the summer I was almost speaking normally. I am determined never to forget, however, what it was like having a problem such as that and what it was like to have people judge me and put me down for something over which I had no control. I'm very fortunate to have experienced that and to have had it corrected for whatever reason. I work with the mentally handicapped now, and it's always surprising to see how far they can go beyond what is expected of them. I've learned never to place restrictions on the abilities of other people, and more important, on my own abilities.

Ellen was going to a school about 1,500 miles away. We could have made a commitment at the end of the summer, but we both thought that we should go off to school with full freedom and then see how we felt. It was difficult because we were both very much in love by that point. It was a good decision though, and we promised to keep in touch. Without Ellen's support, I don't think I would have had the confidence to leave my home and all my established friends and go off to an unfamiliar environment. She was never even aware of that. It was one of the ways she helped me without knowing it.

We left for school and, as promised, we kept in touch. I wrote her every day, and she called me often. After three weeks we found it very hard to be apart. We kept on saying how much we missed each other. Towards the end of September, Ellen said that she was coming home in a couple of weekends. She wanted to get together and spend a day with me. I'm pretty sure we were both ready to make a commitment—we were going to become engaged, so to speak. Ellen hinted that she felt ready to begin a sexual relationship. We started talking on the phone more often, and Ellen began thinking about transferring to a school in my area so we could see more of each other. I was on top of the world.

Friday night around 11:00, about a week before Ellen was to come home, I was in my room studying when I heard the phone ring. It was Ellen and she sounded upset. She said she had been assaulted that afternoon and described what happened. When she had finished, I said, "Ellen, you keep saying that you were assaulted but I think it's important that you admit outright that you've been raped."

It was a painful phone call for both of us. We talked for an hour or so; I said I knew a place I could call to get some information and I would call right back. I called a rape crisis hotline and found out all the medical, legal, and physical aspects I could. I called Ellen back and we decided to fly her up here, take her to a hospital, and see what she wanted to do as far as pressing charges. She felt she couldn't tell her parents what happened, so I had to help her on my own. I did what I could for her, but I don't know how much help I was. I was very upset. It was an extremely difficult weekend. She went back to her school in a couple of days, which was probably the hardest thing of all. I wanted to keep her with me and protect her. But she had more courage than I did and went back to finish the semester.

I was in a bad state after she left. I didn't eat for a total of six days and when I did start eating, it was only in little bits. I couldn't sleep, and when I did I was having terrible nightmares. I would dream of people chasing me and then setting me on fire; people surrounded me and hacked at me with knives. The nightmares were bad, but I wondered why they were always about me. Ellen was never in any of these dreams. I felt very selfish, like I didn't really care about her. This brought on a tremendous feeling of guilt.

Soon the dreams started to change and seemed to reflect something that had actually happened. I couldn't put my finger on it, but each time I woke up I seemed to be close to recalling something I hadn't thought of in years. Bits and pieces started coming together, and it just got worse and worse. I began calling back memories in my waking hours. For over thirteen years my mind had withheld these incidents and blocked them from coming forward. However, now with Ellen's experience, it all came back. I remembered being a small child and a man I knew brought me into a bedroom. I remembered him laying me on my stomach and his hot breath on the back of my neck and the pain as he pushed down on me. It happened more than once; he did things that I didn't understand then but I understand now. I can't say how many times he did this because they are all blurred together. The experiences had been locked in my memory for years—I had never recalled or spoken about them to anyone before. I must have been afraid at the time to tell anybody, including my parents, what was going on.

By the end of the semester, I was a mess. I was in a crisis situation and my grades were horrible. I did pull through it, but the next semester I decided to get counseling. I started understanding a lot of things. I understood now why I hated crowds and having people stand behind me. I understood why the experience with sex brought up so many confusing emotions. What I have never learned to understand is why some people will use other people weaker than themselves to satisfy their own selfish wants. I still know the man who did the things to me and it really seems he doesn't remember it at all. Maybe he does and is suffering with a terrible conscience, but I don't think so. I have been watching him since to find out if he has been doing it to any other child. I don't think he has. If I find out that he is, I'm not exactly sure what I would do. Most likely I will kill him if I think I can get away with it. I don't have violent feelings towards most people, but if someone like him keeps hurting innocent people in that way, I don't think he should live. I want people who do things like that to know that they are in a lot of danger.

The relationship between Ellen and me was never the same. We stopped dating. She wasn't able to continue a physical relationship with me, or start one with anyone else at that time. It wasn't a complete loss because we developed a very strong and supportive friendship. I eventually told her what had happened to me as a child, and we helped each other in many ways. Our friendship became something very important to each of us, and we have both benefited from it. I learned from her what love and generosity in the face of pain really is. Since then we have both gone on to date successfully and are both happy and contented people. We both had something horrible done to us, but neither of us is guilty of ever hurting another person.

I have found a role for myself. It was very painful growing up, but through the pain and all my mistakes I have learned a lot. I do very well in school, and I'm working my way towards studying counseling psychology in graduate school. I earn As and a few Bs now, and I'm finally the student that I've always wanted to be. In fact, I'm more successful in college than anyone else in my family. I'm not spiteful and bitter and don't rub it in my family's face, but I do like the feeling (and the place in the family) it gives me. I find that even now I tend not to participate in class discussions as much as I could, but that is more from old habits than from shyness. I date girls, but I haven't dated steadily since Ellen. I guess I'm guilty of comparing every girl to her and the quality of the relationship we had. A friend who is studying for her doctorate in psychology and knows my history with Ellen would like to see me get into counseling men who physically and sexually abuse women. I can't consider that right now because I still have very violent feelings toward these people and I know that is wrong. Maybe sometime in the future I'll be able to think about it.

Some days I go through mood swings. In the morning I can be the most cheerful optimist and yet come back in the evening seeing red with rage. However, it has been a long time since I've experienced any sort of depression, and I think that is the important thing. I simply write off my mood swings to my Irish temperament. Besides, these mood swings are so minor compared to my former depths of depression that I can joke about them.

Recently I became very ill and spent several days in the hospital confined to a bed and connected to an IV tube. For the next several weeks I was very weak. During this time my speech regressed terribly. It made me realize that my problems had not gone away, but rather I had learned to compensate for them. When I was weak and fatigued I didn't have the concentration necessary to maintain my methods of compensation. I was at first upset and felt once again that I was very different from others. Soon, however, I came to the conclusion that it was a good thing. It would come back every once in a while to make certain that I didn't forget where I came from and how far I've come. I would be reminded from time to time that we all have our strengths and our weaknesses and it is important to accept both from all people. I would be reminded of the simple beauty of a conversation.

Altogether, I have been very fortunate in my life. Some terrible things have happened to me, but then I have also been lucky enough to come into contact with many wonderful people. These people have shown me what it means to be a caring and responsible person. They've allowed me to make all my mistakes without placing any judgments on me. I have learned from them that the way you treat other people really can make a difference for the better. Treat everyone with the dignity and respect they deserve and it will always come back to you. Stand by others when they're in need because when you're in need you'll find you have a lot more friends than you thought you had. But most of all, learn to stand on your own two feet. If you can't help yourself, there is little that others can do for you. Everyone is going to experience pain and hardship at some point in their life, and that is when we learn the depth of both our own strength and of our relationships with others. If we have planted strong roots, we should be able to withstand much of what comes our way. At the library, there was a saying on the bulletin board which I have always liked: *Be optimistic even when you feel desperate.*

Opportunities for Recovering

Reflections on Case 14

ROBERT KILKENNY AND GIL NOAM

This life story is a compelling portrayal of the emotional and developmental after-effects of psychological trauma in childhood. From the beginning there is a central question of why an apparently popular and intelligent child would feel so hopeless, insecure, and unworthy. Ray describes a childhood marked by self-imposed isolation from both parents and peers. His despair seemed to grow worse with time, eventually causing him to plan several suicide attempts in adolescence. The indigenous psychologist in us all searches to know the cause of so much pain and wasted potential; we seek clues to solve the central mystery of why a life so promising should prove so unsatisfying. But our author takes pains to make clear that for him there is no single explanation for his unhappiness. Our analysis here will emulate Ray's approach by slowly and carefully peeling back the layers of shame, guilt, and depression that protectively cover the truth.

As we struggle to understand another's life, we want to account for why it has progressed in one way and not another. No single course of development is strictly inevitable; there are too many variables and opportunities for overcoming. So in looking at this case there is no simple cause and effect between experience and outcome. Many other children with severe stutters do not experience the same degree of shame and despair, which is not to say that it isn't an additional burden to maintain self-esteem in the face of so apparent a handicap. Something has happened to destroy Ray's childhood but he won't reveal exactly what. Clues are dropped (he has a bad stutter) and hints given (his parents let him down) but the mystery remains until he reveals his sexual abuse at the hands of an adult male known to him. But even then Ray does not make an explicit link between his childhood problems and his sexual abuse. So it is left to the reader to decide what, if any, connection his abuse had to his symptoms of depression, alienation, and poor self-esteem, and most importantly to the course of his overall development. The temptation in such a case is to attribute to the most serious trauma the causation of all subsequent difficulties. This line of analysis might lead us to speculate that some symptoms have symbolic value, that is, that his stutter represents an inability to speak the unspeakable truth of his sexual victimization. And though such an analysis would elegantly tie together many loose ends, it may not be what is really important here. What matters more is listening carefully to what meaning the author constructs from his experiences.

Initially, our author offers a two-part explanation in which his stuttering is described as the main problem. First he says that his shock at discovering his stutter through a tape recording of his speech therapy led to feeling "bitter toward my parents for never having talked to me about it. I felt that I really hated them. Over the next ten or eleven years I spent much of my time finding little ways that I could hurt them and get back at them for the way they had failed me." Though that serves to account for the seeming lack of closeness with his parents, it is such a prolonged overreaction (6-year-olds don't typically hold ten-year, all-consuming grudges against their parents) that we wonder what else might account for a rage and alienation so severe that he would cut himself off from the most likely source of love and comfort in his life. However, it does offer the important insight that he felt his parents had somehow failed him in their obligation to protect him from devastating emotional pain. It raises significant questions about the nature of his relationship with his parents and indicates an ambivalent attachment at best.

When Ray finally relates the fact of his having been sexually abused, we see the trauma that shaped the troubled outlines of his development, either as primary cause or as a corrosive catalyst to an already shaky self-esteem. Research on the effects of child sexual abuse reveal that there is a wide variation in its developmental effect (Van der Kolk, 1987). Risk factors thought to affect outcome include age at which abuse occurs, physical force or violence, threats to the child, age difference between victim and perpetrator, length of abuse, closeness of relationship between victim and perpetrator, whether the abuse is disclosed and the circumstances under which it is, whether the child is believed, reaction of parents, consequences for the perpetrator, and availability of expert professional services for the child and family. In general, children's vulnerability to psychopathology is magnified by multiple stressors so that, typically, no single factor is determinate. As one would expect, the more severe and numerous the stressors, the greater the risk of lasting psychological impairment. The relative contribution of each risk factor to psychological outcome is not yet fully understood and is probably complexly mediated by individual, cultural, gender, and other differences. Risks can be counterbalanced by protective factors that buffer the stresses (Garmezy, 1987). These may include (1) personality features such as self-esteem, self-understanding, and social competence, (2) supportive relationship with parents and lack of family discord, and (3) external support systems such as adult mentors, school experiences, and peer support.

In Ray's case, what information we have on his risk factors is not hopeful, though he appears to have a number of protective factors. We know that he was repeatedly subjected to forced anal intercourse by an adult whom he knew. Though we don't know the nature of the relationship with the perpetrator, he apparently knew Ray well enough to have ongoing access to him, which at that age implies someone he probably trusted. And since Ray stated he is still in a position to observe this person closely enough to determine whether or not he is abusing other children, it seems plausible that the perpetrator could even have been a member of his family. The popular notion of child molesters as strangers is not supported by research. Most studies find that the majority of sexual abuse is perpetrated by either relatives or other adults known by the child (Finkelhor, 1984, 1987). What this points to is an increased likelihood that Ray was abused by someone close enough to him to cause him to feel betrayed and to have subsequent difficulty in forming trusting relationships. The combination of force, betrayal, apparent silence, lack of timely professional help, and so forth, all conspire to create a constellation of vulnerabilities that go a long way toward explaining the serious nature of Ray's sense of shame, isolation, and depression. It makes his subsequent success and movement toward recovery all the more remarkable and important to understand.

The efforts to overcome the aftereffects of childhood trauma often reach far beyond the early years, as we have seen in Ray's case. This fact raises the question of how adolescents and adults experience traumatic events differently from how children do, and how these different developmental eras produce new opportunities for recovery from traumatic events. In this case, Ray uses his emerging adolescent abilities and desires for intimate peer and romantic friendships, vocational exploration, separation from family, and intellectual development to full advantage in addressing and undoing some of the damage to his self-esteem and social confidence in his childhood.

Instead of focusing only on the maladaptive aspects of repeating trauma, our theoretical perspective (e.g., Noam, 1988) emphasizes how each revisiting of the traumatic event always has a "healing intention." Each time old anxieties and symptoms are reawakened, there is an implicit hope that the effects of the trauma can finally be overcome and the painful thoughts and feelings can be put in a new perspective. Though some theorists take a similar approach to trauma, we have found one key to the potential recovery from traumatic events in the normal sequence of social, cognitive, and emotional development (e.g., Noam, Powers, Kilkenny, & Beedy, 1990). Many clinicians report—and we have found this phenomenon to be consistently present in our own clinical work—that those forces that produce hopelessness and despair can become the seeds for future opportunity and vitality. We think the best approach to understanding these capacities for psychological recovering is to begin with a framework of normal developmental transformations and to explore within each transformation a new opportunity and strengthened ability to rework some of the debilitating effects of psychological trauma.

Before returning to Ray, we want to address briefly two developing capacities, evident in our own adolescent research, that can contribute to overcoming trauma: (1) the development of intimate relationships, and (2) the continued evolution of self-understanding or insight into self and relationships. These two capacities define in essential ways that we are social beings who cannot achieve our full humanity without interpersonal bonds and that we are all essentially epistemologists in that we give meaning to our experience and our relationships. Gaining insight into painful relationships of the past has the potential to modify the power of the traumatic experience. But thinking, without strong feelings, remains shallow

and intellectualized. In intimate relationships, where it really counts, we make ourselves vulnerable, and thus the earlier hurts inevitably reemerge. It is only in the
context of relationships that the capacity for insight has the opportunity for trans-
forming feelings and behavior resulting from a self-protective reaction to trauma.
Full recovery requires that new insights somehow transform old behaviors and
feelings. Important relationships are the context within which this can happen—
indeed, where it often must occur to preserve the relationship.

There is, in fact, a great deal of evidence for these ideas from research with at-
risk children. Those children who successfully master their development in the
face of grave adversity (e.g., schizophrenic or depressed parents) are the ones who
have had some positive and sustaining relationships (e.g., Garmezy, 1985; Rutter &
Quinton, 1984). It is these important relationships that form the backdrop against
which later relationships can be formed. But even when these resiliency-producing
relationships do not exist, adolescent and adult intimacy can provide new opportunities for recovery.

With this brief theoretical background we will return to Ray. On both
counts—a history of intimate relationships and an ability to generate insights
about these relationships and his life—Ray demonstrates great strengths. In terms
of the former, he has had enduring friendships in childhood. His childhood chum
was a source of continuous strength and support. Ray tells us: "Bill and I did everything together. We liked the same shows and music and hung out together all the
time. In fact it wasn't uncommon for teachers and other kids to get the two of us
mixed up. There was a great amount of security in that relationship for me. I felt
that Bill accepted me for who I was. . . ." His ability to make such a friend is an
important sign of psychological resilience, or ability to maintain aspects of health
in the face of serious stress. He was able to reach outside his family for the nurturing he needed, despite the fact that he had been so deeply and consistently hurt by
important people in his life. His ability to maintain this long and strong friendship,
or in the terms of Harry Stack Sullivan (1953), a "chumship," is an important factor
in buffering the damage done to his self-esteem and ability to trust others: "We
could share our secrets and problems." It was his primary means for staying connected to the world of peers and finding validation in the process. Significantly, his
best friend's family became an important resource for trusted support: "I adopted
his family as my own. . . . I didn't look up to or respect my parents but I did
his . . . and as a consequence I looked to his parents for guidance." He views his life
path as one great attempt to escape the nonnurturing experiences with his parents
and teachers, who harmed him deeply. We are not concerned here with what they
actually did, but with his experience of them as most unhelpful and even undermining of his emerging self-esteem. For many people, life becomes the attempt to
overcome these early hurts.

Turning to the second protective process, the development of insight or self-
understanding, Ray gives us many examples of his strength in this area. In the
process of his development, Ray begins to define himself in opposition to the people he does not respect or trust (parents, teachers). We can see his chronic lying and
cheating as manifestations of his alienation from adult authority and as a prob-

lematic assertion of his own will and autonomy. In a positive sense, it is his way of being less of a victim of incompetent authority. His own abuse had, after all, occurred within the scope of his parents' own, at best, ineffectual authority. Instead, he is beginning to build his own identity, asking himself who he is in the face of all the experiences that shaped him. This case itself is a beautiful example of a developmental shift to a greater degree of personal, ideological, spiritual, and professional complexity and commitment. Throughout, Ray is introducing his voice and making sense of the relationships that have been important. And in the process he is asserting his own power over his life—a very important step in undoing the feelings of helplessness and powerlessness that come with being victimized as a child.

We often identify this search for self with adolescence. But we forget that depending on the cognitive, social, and emotional developmental level, adolescents pursue these goals quite differently. At earlier developmental levels, adolescents tend to blame others for their fate and are quite impulsive and self-protective in their responses. Many of those adolescents who remain at these less mature developmental positions for prolonged periods of time have been abused or come from homes impoverished on a number of levels.

The developmental shift described earlier is from what we call the *mutual-inclusive* level to the *systemic-organizational* level (Noam, Powers, Kilkenny, & Beedy, 1990). At the mutual-inclusive position, the self is defined through important identifications with significant others. A self so tied to external sources of validation is particularly vulnerable to the actions of others and feelings of inadequacy and responsibility for problems in the relationship; for example, "People would treat me better if I were a better person." If these important relationships are abusive or nonsupportive, a negative self-concept and/or social isolation may result. On the positive side of this equation, however, Ray's ability to form warm mentoring relationships with adults at the library where he worked is a positive example of his ability to meet these crucial developmental needs for building trust and confidence in himself through other means. He tells us what he needed in the relationship with an adult: support, care, encouragement, but also an honest guidance and critique based on the firm foundation of acceptance. Some people are lucky enough to receive this kind of treatment from their parents, but many people have to find these relationships with mentors and friends outside the immediate family.

Further development is no guarantee of positive self-experience. But in the move toward the systemic-organizational perspective the person can stand back somewhat from his or her identifications and begin to question and thereby modify them into a new sense of identity. It allows one to think of oneself in biographical terms, as a life with multiple influences and turning points. Influences are seen as formative but not necessarily deterministic; the self can reshape itself if it knows what and how it has come to be. With this multiplicity of perspectives on the self emerges the potential for mourning the injuries afflicted by trauma in a new way: The trauma does not need to define self and relationships anymore. Instead, the traumatic experiences can be objectified and be given the proper place in development. Ray provides us with excellent descriptions of how the evolving abilities for self-reflection at the systemic-organizational level provide a means for recovering. Simplifying our developmental account considerably, we view Ray as describing a fundamental shift of perspective about himself and important relationships. Statements such as "I had very little self-respect, so I had to get it from others" demonstrate hard-won psychological insight and the development of a complex understanding of human motivation. At many points, he takes a biographical point of view, tracing how the past has shaped the present (e.g., "I need to go back to my early childhood to explain all the problems I had with school. . . ."). In fact, this autobiography would not be nearly as interesting or informative were it not for these abilities to reflect on the manner in which otherwise disparate influences converge to shape his life.

In spite of these evolving protective processes, there remain unresolved thoughts and feelings that cause Ray to operate simultaneously on less evolved psychological levels. When Ray talks about the man who abused him, the complexity of cognition and emotions collapses. He states; "If I find out that he is [sexually abusing another child], I'm not exactly sure what I would do. Most likely I will kill him if I think I can get away with it. I don't have violent feelings towards most people but if someone like him keeps hurting innocent people in that way I don't think he should live. . . ." It is perfectly understandable that Ray feels like killing the man who abused him, but in other areas he has demonstrated considerably greater abilities to explore the consequences of his ideas and actions. We can feel the pent-up rage he still feels and also realize that he has not had the fifteen years since the event to process these feelings and gain some emotional distance from them, because he has only relatively recently allowed these facts to reemerge to conscious awareness. So his insight and ability to integrate these feelings into the rest of his thinking and feeling is still limited by his reawakening and reliving of his trauma and its effects. This is a phenomenon we call "encapsulation," in which certain developmental aspects of the self, often connected to previous trauma, lag behind the general psychological development of the individual in other areas.

Overall, Ray provides us with an excellent example of how present experiences evoke unworked-out issues from the past, and how they can be readdressed with new information and emerging developmental abilities. Here, his girlfriend's rape is an assault on him as well. He is extremely upset, as anyone would be whose intimate friend were attacked. But in Ray's case, it leads to a return of many memories that had been hidden from consciousness. Having described nightmares of being chased and hurt, he relates the coming into conscious awareness of his own rape.

> Soon the dreams started to change and seemed to reflect something that had actually happened. I couldn't put my finger on it, but each time I woke up I seemed to be close to recalling something I hadn't thought of in years. Bits and pieces started coming together and it just got worse and worse. I began calling back memories in my waking hours. For over thirteen years my mind had withheld these incidents

and blocked them from coming forward. However, now with Ellen's experience, it all came back. I remembered being a small child and a man I knew brought me into a bedroom. I remembered him laying me on my stomach and his hot breath on the back of my neck and the pain as he pushed down on me. It happened more than once; he did things which I didn't understand then but I understand now. I can't say how many times he did this because they are all blurred together. The experiences had been locked in my memory for years—I had never recalled or spoken about them to anyone before. I must have been afraid at the time to tell anybody, including my parents, what was going on.

The agony of the return to those feelings that he had carried with him for so long and that have made him so vulnerable are quite typical for any person who has the courage to readdress the trauma "head on." With the help of his girlfriend, Ellen, he can now gain some control not only by working on his own abuse history but by giving her support. It is this "passing over," helping others with what has been most dangerous to the self, that creates a grammar, a language, for what before had been unspeakable. To make one's own vulnerabilities the source of helping others is at the heart of most clinical practice. Most therapists have experienced some trauma or problem that they were able to work through. It is also at the heart of intimate friendships. It is not the vulnerabilities that are the problem in relationships—they are to be expected; it is the shared willingness to work on them and move beyond them that distinguishes productive from stagnant relationships.

Ray's relationship with Ellen served as both the stimulus and the means for his courageous confrontation with his own past that some precocious part of him had kept secret even to himself until the circumstances were right. His closeness and deep empathy for his girlfriend made her rape such a powerful emotional provocation that his own rape experience broke into consciousness. However, this relationship served as more than the mere stimulus for his reawakening. It also helped him recover to the point that he now had the strength and courage to finally address his own trauma. Prior to this he understood his stutter to have been the core problem around which his life had revolved. But this understanding of the problem would face a new challenge, as his stutter virtually disappeared in the context of his girlfriend's love: "[S]he accepted it as simply a part of me—just like my hair is brown and my eyes are blue. It had a great influence on me and I felt myself falling for Ellen." Whatever the underlying cause of his stutter, one psychological purpose it served—the primary explanation for his depression and alienation from his parents and peers—was no longer serviceable. Because he no longer stuttered, he would have no explanation for the lingering feelings from his own rape. His improved speech did undoubtedly ease the burdens on his self-esteem. But it couldn't also be expected to address his own rape-induced feelings. His conscious understanding of his unhappiness as solely based on his stutter was being destabilized by the press of his own healthy development in the areas of intimacy, self-confidence, and self-understanding.

Also at this time, just prior to his breakdown, his relationship with Ellen was about to become sexually intimate: "Ellen hinted that she felt ready to begin a sexual relationship. We started talking on the phone more often and Ellen began thinking about transferring to a school in my area so we could see more of each other. I was on top of the world." Though part of him was on top of the world, his other sexual experiences with girls had left him feeling dirty and ashamed, a frequent outcome of sexual abuse. The unfinished business of his own past meant that he was not yet ready for a sexually intimate relationship with someone he truly loved. Their love for one another led to the prospect of sexual intimacy, and that same love made her assault his assault. Their relationship had boosted his confidence in himself as an attractive, sexual young man who was now strong enough to face the major source of his enduring anguish. It was love that empowered him: his love and empathy for her and the effect of her love on his own belief in himself. This is an example of using the developmental opportunities of adolescence for forming intimate romantic attachments to redress the damage done in an earlier developmental period to that same ability for attachment.

Ray's story illustrates two important features of human development, one discouraging and the other heartening. First, we can see the devastating effects of sexual abuse in childhood. It is worth each of us contemplating how utterly devastating an event would have to be for us to expend daily the energy required to totally suppress something that was having such an effect on our lives. We all know the simple phenomenon of trying to put a tune or phrase out of our minds; the more we try to suppress it, the more forcefully it jumps to consciousness. If that is true for something of no consequence, imagine the psychological energy Ray had to expend, unknowingly, to keep from awareness this most influential event in his life. This suppression reflected the devastating strength of the trauma and affected the suicide-tinged ruin of his childhood. The recognition of despair that he states at the conclusion of his autobiography—"Be happy even when you feel desperate"—represents an ongoing challenge to his recovery. And if we extrapolate Ray's suffering and despair to the prevalence of child sexual abuse, we have a sobering view of the developmental struggle of many children and adolescents.

More optimistically, however, we also have an example of the way in which life presents opportunities at each developmental level for healing and transformation. Ray demonstrates that one can find important parts of what one needs in close relationships and other contexts for learning. His chumship and "adoption" of his best friend's family, his willingness to be mentored and nurtured by his supervisors at the library, his eventual openness to intimate, romantic relationships—coinciding with the remarkable disappearance of his stutter—and even his ability to allow his empathic reaction to his girlfriend's sexual assault to break his suppression of his own abuse, are all powerful examples of relationships as the primary developmental context for healing. But not all such cases show such progress toward psychological recovering. An important part of the reason for Ray's success is Ray himself—his thoughtfulness, ability to reflect on himself, and courage to face the truth. This combination of his predispositions to self-understanding and to seizing the developmental opportunities for relationships explains Ray's impressive progress. These two forces for healing—relationships and insight—are at the center of our clinical–developmental theory and are poignantly captured in Ray's description of his reaction to the parish priest asking him to consider the priesthood:

> This was the first time that someone I really admired let me know he saw some value in me. He was seeing good in me that I couldn't see myself. It had a profound effect on me. I didn't turn myself around in a day because of it, but I did have my first thoughts of where I was going and the person I was as opposed to the person I was capable of being. These were brief, very scattered thoughts, but the seed had been planted. It was the encouragement of other people like him that helped me learn that many people saw me in a better light than I saw myself.

These are important words of reminder that for most people the process of recovering from serious psychological trauma happens not in the clinic but in the context of warm and caring relationships. Ray demonstrates courageously the possibilities that exist within us and around us.

15 Proud of the Strength I Had

This writer describes her experience of teenage pregnancy and how she copes with its effects on her emotional and social development. Without the support of her former boyfriend or the knowledge of her parents, Connie decides alone to have an out-of-state abortion soon after her high school graduation. She shares her struggle to find meaning in her actions and to redefine her own identity. In college, Connie finds support from a campus women's group that helps her make sense of her experience and understand herself better. She begins to examine her family life and the impact of those relationships on her feelings about men and the coping styles she has developed. Connie also comes to acknowledge her own strength and courage in dealing with this extremely difficult adolescent experience.

It was a week or so after high school graduation. The air was musty and the cement floor was cold. I played nervously with the phone cord and traced its path to the door with my eyes. The garage was the safest place, but I prayed that no one could hear me. It's funny how you suddenly believe in God when you think something bad might happen.

The woman on the other end of the line finally found my records. "Let's see," she said, "Oh yes, your test came out positive!" She sounded excited. I wasn't. I almost dropped the phone. My stomach felt like lead. I couldn't believe her.

"Are you sure?" I barely managed to utter. "Yes, isn't that what you wanted to hear?" Was she stupid? She had to look up my name for the results, didn't she know I was only 17?

"No," I said. She gave me the name of some abortion clinics and I hung up the phone.

On August 18th I had an abortion. In September I left for college. My grades were never affected; in fact, I got a 4.0 my first semester. Studying kept me from thinking too much. Six months after my abortion I saw a sign for a support group for women who had had abortions. I knew that I needed to go. Shaking, I called the number, and they told me where and when it would be.

In this group I began to let out some of the feelings that I had kept bottled up for months. Listening to the other women taught me that I was not alone, although many told stories and expressed feelings that were different from my own. Sometimes I left the group aching with the pain I felt from reclaiming all those feelings I'd pushed to the back of my mind. Other times I was amazed at how well I connected with these women, how much I learned from them, and how much I looked forward to this meeting every week. In the journal I kept, things came out on paper that I never could have said aloud.

March

My boyfriend and I had just broken up when I found out. He wouldn't even speak to me so that I could tell him, but eventually I cornered him. He didn't care, and he didn't want to help. All he could say was, "Jesus Christ, are you sure?" I reminded him that it was his problem too, and he said he would give me the money, but he wouldn't go with me. He assumed, as I did, that I would have an abortion. My Mom would hate me for it. She had always condemned abortion, saying that it was killing a baby. Maybe it is; maybe I did.

After a few phone calls I found out that you have to be 18 to get an abortion in my state without parental consent. I was just four months too young. Eventually I made an appointment with a clinic in a nearby state. The woman I spoke to was very supportive, but I had to figure out how I would get there. A week went by before I asked a friend to take me. Then a few more weeks of wishing I could tell someone and trying to hide the hurt and tears. I guess I did a good job, because no one noticed. The worst part was when I saw my half-brother, an adorable 3-month-old. I couldn't hold him or look at him without thinking that I might as well be killing him.

April

I live constantly in two worlds. One is where I can talk or write about it and show my real emotion—when I'm alone and cry, when I'm with the few friends who know, or when I'm with the support group, the only people who really understand. The other world is all the other times. Then I have to pretend that I am okay. I have to conceal my feelings. If someone reminds me, I can't share the hurt inside. Nor can I when some guy makes a joke or comment about a girl who had an abortion, when Amy eats a peanut butter and banana sandwich and Jean asks if she's pregnant, or when everyone giggles at the jokes, even me, but they don't know what's going on in my head. The pain is when there is an editorial in the paper about abortion and Mary says, "My friend at home had one—I'll never forgive her. She could have given it up for adoption; I was adopted." If only she knew. The pain is when I walk by a poster advocating reproductive rights that someone has scribbled "Fetus-Bashers" on in red magic marker. I want to scream at the person who did it, but they aren't there. I want to rip the poster down, but I don't. I want to tell the person I'm walking with how upset I am, but she won't understand.

May

Mom,

I know you'd hate me if you knew. To you it's disgusting, it's killing. I'll never be able to tell you. Maybe I'm hurting myself or our relationship by not telling you. I would have liked your support. I needed your help, but I couldn't tell you, and I still can't. I never wanted to hurt you.

Sometimes I wish you had guessed somehow. But you would have wanted me to have the baby; you wouldn't have let me make my own decision. Maybe it was a bad thing to do, maybe it wasn't the "right" thing to do. But I don't want a baby, and I don't want to give birth to one only to give it away. I wanted to go to school and learn and have fun, not be trapped in my own body for nine months. I didn't want to be stared at by mothers who warn their teenager at their side: "She can't be more than 16; I hope you never do a stupid thing like that!" I didn't want my sisters to be ashamed of me. I didn't want my friends and teachers to think I was a bad person. Because as we all know, girls who have sex are bad, and girls who get pregnant are stupid.

When I read these journals over again, I remember feeling so isolated and scared that everyone would hate me if they knew. When I did start telling people, I felt terrified of what they might think or say. But the more people I told the less it hurt to retell and the more confident I felt that I was right. The decision I made was a good one, and it was mine to make. I felt proud of the strength that I had to make it through this crisis on my own and stick to what I really wanted to do.

Experiencing for myself the inaccessibility of abortion for teenagers and going to the support group both pushed me to explore feminism and identify with it. I joined a pro-choice group on campus, went to protests against Operation Rescue, and wrote an article for a women's newspaper. I told my closest friends and even some not so close. My experience with abortion was becoming an integrated part of my life. But I also felt disillusioned by "the feminist movement." The political group I joined talked about "rights," and I didn't feel comfortable talking about my abortion, or talking at all, for that matter. It was hard for me to talk about abortion without including my own experiences. But I continued going because I had to make sure that abortion didn't become illegal, or in my case, more illegal. Being involved politically made me feel like maybe I could make a difference.

The pro-choice group organized rides to Boston for the protest against Operation Rescue, which was trying to close down clinics there. I rode down the night before with Sarah, another woman in the group, and we stayed at my dad's house. I don't remember when exactly I met her, or if we knew before that ride that we'd both had abortions, but for two and a half hours we talked about our experiences. It was amazing how close I felt to her; she made me feel even stronger. We found that we both felt alienated from the political group, and we talked about it a lot. She told me that she was in the support group that I had been in the semester before. I realized how much I missed talking about my abortion with women who understood.

It was an emotional weekend and maybe one of the best ones in my life. Talking with Sarah and being with her at the protest made it seem that much more important to me. I felt so good and real and so passionately involved. This was something I believed in like I never believed in something before. It was an incredible feeling facing, inches away from me, the people who believed I was a murderer and wanted to take away my right to control my own body.

After the protest I saw little of Sarah outside the pro-choice meetings until another semester later. She called and asked if I wanted to help her start a support group, or what we later decided to call a consciousness-raising group, for women who had had abortions. We both missed and needed those discussions. We put signs up and met the people who answered in a café on campus. Soon we were a group of eight, and the first night we met I found myself in tears, realizing how much I still needed to talk about it and how much was still left unresolved. I wanted to piece my life together. Why had all this happened to me? Can I go on hiding it from other people, from my family? At the fourth meeting I decided to tell my whole story. I didn't just talk about my abortion, I talked about my whole life. I was trying to make sense of it all. I began to identify some reasons behind my getting pregnant. One was my family. I told the group; "No one ever talked about anything in my family. My dad left when I was 13 and my mom told us not to tell anyone. My twin sister and I never said a word to each other about it. When my dad told us he was leaving we cried. Actually she cried, I didn't. I went upstairs to my room and closed the door. And that was the end of it, no one ever talked about it again."

The second explanation that I alluded to was my early sexual relationships with men. I described myself during that time as very insecure: "In school I wanted desperately to be liked, and boys actually seemed to like me. When some guy asked me out, I couldn't believe it. I'd say yes. I didn't know what else to say, even if I didn't like him. I dated a few guys and each time one of us got scared off and then avoided each other. Then Rick asked me out." I had difficulty talking about him even with this group of women. I tried to describe him and our relationship. "God, I don't know why I ever went out with him. He was . . . so awful. And we had a nine-month 'relationship.' After the first month I just wanted to break up with him, but I couldn't do it. I didn't want to hurt his feelings and I was afraid of what he'd do. He was always trying to get me to sleep with him. I was only 15. He ended up basically raping me."

Rick said he wanted me to be his girlfriend. There were guys I liked a lot more than him, but no one had asked me out before like that. He was nice and funny and said he loved me. Though I soon found him annoying and pushy, I couldn't break up with him, even after he raped me. I was scared that he might kill himself. I was afraid he might freak out and hurt me. I was attached to him and the attention he gave me. And I didn't even know I had been raped. "I just thought I was a horrible person because I couldn't keep him from touching me. I felt horrible, but I didn't know why. I thought I'd done something wrong. I just cried. I didn't even think of saying anything to anyone; I wouldn't have known what to say. I couldn't believe that I'd just had sex with someone; I couldn't even say the word. My parents never talked about sex either, except my mother's little innuendos about it being bad. So I thought I was the worst person in the world."

I finally broke up with Rick, but I often felt pushed into later sexual experiences as well. I said to the group, "I slept with Chris, too, or he convinced me to sleep with him. That's what it always seemed like. I didn't want to do it, but I would give in. It was always like the guy was trying to convince me and I never really wanted to, but I always would." With Chris, part of me did really want to sleep with him, but I was unsure and I didn't know how to talk about it. I think most of the time I didn't want to was because I was afraid of getting pregnant, and I didn't know how to talk about birth control either.

Chris and I broke up when he went to college, partly because he was going away, and partly because I was interested in someone else. I was 16, almost 17, and a senior in high school. Darren was a junior, but I thought he was the greatest. He drank a lot and did some drugs, and I hated both. But for the first time I really felt comfortable sleeping with someone. To Sarah and the other women I said, "Birth control was just never an issue for us." It was the first time I had admitted it, but it wasn't completely true either. It was an issue, but we never talked about it. I didn't ask him about it and he didn't ask me about it. It was really strange because I was terrified that I was going to get pregnant. I always thought about it, worried about it, but I couldn't do anything about it.

Although we didn't use contraception, and we didn't talk about it, I thought about it constantly, and I was scared. I even wrote a paper about teenage pregnancy for a psychology class. I remember working on it, thinking, "This could be you, you have to do something about this." I remember having this feeling that I HAD to talk to him about it, but I couldn't. It seemed easier not to say anything and put it out of my mind, to try to forget about it.

At one point I thought I was pregnant, and I told him. He couldn't believe it and he said something about me being on the Pill. I said, "No, I'm not, where did you get that idea?" But inside I felt relieved that the subject finally came up. He said that he just figured that I must have been, since I never seemed worried about it. It seems almost funny now, but it wasn't then. How could he have thought that all this time, when for me it hurt so much to pretend it wasn't a problem?

It turned out that I wasn't pregnant. He was so happy and I was relieved. We talked more after all that, we started using condoms "most of the time," and I worried about it less. Then he started to drink more and got more into drugs, and he wanted to be with his friends and not me. He tried to break up with me, but I took a fit. "You can't leave me, Darren," I cried, "I love you, I can't believe you are doing this to me, you said you loved me!" Finally he gave in and said he still did, but he kept away from me and finally he broke it off completely. I was still hurt, but I knew I didn't like the drinking and our disagreements around it, so I didn't argue this time. Two or three weeks later I worried that I was pregnant again. I tried to call him. He was never home, and his brother once just said, "He doesn't want to talk to you." Finally I got in touch with him and told him. He just said, "Jesus Christ, I can't believe this!"

My mother is totally anti-abortion. I knew if I said anything to her, I would be having a kid. I only told one of my girlfriends; she was the only person I thought I could trust. I did one of those home pregnancy tests; I hid it behind the books in my bookcase because you have to let it sit for a couple hours. I totally freaked out when I looked at it and it came out positive. My friend was more clueless about what to do than I was. I turned to another close friend, this time a guy. I asked him to drive me to the hospital so that I could have a real test done. I didn't tell him why I was going, and he drove me, no questions asked. I was convinced that this test was going to be negative, that the first test was wrong. I was sure of it. The next day the woman on the phone told me it was positive.

Meanwhile I started getting involved with someone else. Todd and I started spending a lot of time together. We weren't going out yet, but we were close. One night I told him about it. He said he'd been through it with a girlfriend, but she turned out not to be pregnant. He said he'd take me for the abortion appointment. I was so relieved. I told my mom and my boss that we were going shopping for the day; Mom even let Todd take her car.

When we got there he just dropped me off, he didn't come in with me. At the time it was exactly what I expected, but now it seems strange that I didn't want him there for support. It didn't even occur to me to ask him to come in with me. I think I felt that it wasn't his responsibility and it was something I wanted to do on my own. I am still in awe of the idea that I went through this all by myself.

I walked in alone with my $250 check from Darren. I was nervous, but I felt better once I was inside. The woman on the phone warned me that there might be picketers, but no one bothered me. Most of the people in the waiting room had someone with them, but it didn't bother me too much at the time. I was so relieved to actually be there. I started to get scared waiting, but I still couldn't believe that I had made it there and that I was going to be okay.

The first thing they did was counseling, or at least that's what they called it. It's just when they describe the procedure in detail. I went into this room with the counselor and a 30-year-old woman who was there for the same reason but seemed totally relaxed. The counselor started to explain to the two of us exactly what happens with the doctor and the instruments.

Suddenly I was terrified and I started to cry. I couldn't help it. I was scared of how much it would hurt, of what it would be like. The counselor and the other woman were like, "Oh my goodness, what's wrong?" as if there was no reason whatsoever for me to be the least bit upset.

What bothers me about the whole thing is that no one ever talked about it, I mean really talked about it. They were all robots, just doing their job, describing the procedure, taking blood, giving out pills, acting like it was no big deal. It seems like it wouldn't have been so scary if we could have talked about it more. If someone only said, "I've been through it, too. It's okay to be scared, but you will be okay."

Someone sent me to get changed and directed me to the next waiting room. I was there for two hours in my gown. Or maybe it was just an hour, or only twenty minutes, but it seemed like forever. There were around five other women there, and a woman came in to call a name once in a while. The chairs were arranged in a circle around the room. We sat there facing each other and no one said anything. Everyone seemed scared except the older woman who flipped through a magazine and made comments here and there. But the person who really stuck out in my mind was a girl who looked no older than 13. I felt so terrible for her—she looked so scared. I just wanted to reach out to her, and tell her everything was going to be okay.

Finally they called my name and I followed a woman to another room. Another woman was there to talk to me and to hold my hand during the abortion if I wanted to. The doctor said, "So you are going to college in the fall? So what's your major?" I couldn't believe he was asking me about college; I could barely answer, I was so terrified. But I guess it was better than him not saying anything at all. It was so painful. I remember screaming and crying, literally. Afterwards I wondered if anyone heard me. They said it would hurt some, but this was the most painful thing I had ever felt. It hurts to think about it.

Afterwards I went into a room with other women who were recovering, lying down with blankets and eating slices of oranges and crackers. After about fifteen minutes I felt a lot better, so they said I could leave even though you're supposed to stay for longer afterwards. I started to get cramps after about fifteen minutes driving home. We stopped and bought some pain reliever but it kept getting worse. They said that cramps were normal, so I didn't really worry about it. I didn't realize how bad it was until the next day when I got up and got ready for work. I was still bleeding heavily. I knew I should call the clinic. According to the information sheet they gave me I should have called them if this happened. I thought about it, but I knew they'd want me to see a doctor. I don't know if I was more scared that something was wrong with me or that my mother would find out. For three days I was in agony and then finally it stopped.

My experience with abortion and the support groups I've involved myself in have allowed me to experience a great level of intimacy with other women that I never felt before. But it also seemed to pull me away from my family. It was something I couldn't go talk to any of them about, something I hid from them. I hate that they can't really understand a part of me. The people I'm closest to don't know my deepest secret, my deepest hurts, and the greatest motivation for some of my interests. Sometimes I feel guilty about not sharing it with them. I'm afraid that one of my sisters may have to go through the same thing one day and she wouldn't tell me either. She would have to deal with the same silence I did. But last year I realized that I hadn't hidden everything from them. One day my 17-year-old sister called me at school. She was scared that she was pregnant and didn't know what to do. Even though she didn't know I'd had an abortion, she knew how I felt about it. She said, "I can't have it. School and field hockey, I just couldn't." I told her it was okay and she didn't have to do anything she didn't want to do. I told her where she could go for a test and that she could call me anytime she wanted. If she was pregnant, I told her, "I'd know what to do, it's all right." I was scared for her, but I was happy that I could be there for her. It made me feel good that she wouldn't have to go through it alone.

I know I will never tell my mother, and that's okay now, but sometimes it still makes me sad. We are still very close, though. I'm probably closer to her than any of my sisters. We talk a lot about boyfriends (both of ours), school, jobs, and my dad. I know she's not the best listener in the world, but I like to be there for her. Sometime she really surprises me and gives me good advice, but she has trouble just listening. One of my greatest fears is that she will find out and it will ruin the relationship we have. I think she'd hate me for a while, and she'd feel guilty, too.

I'm sure her love for me would overcome it, but I just don't want to put her or myself through it.

I want to tell my twin sister. It is absolutely bizarre to me that she doesn't know this about me. Although we fight and still compete, we've shared a lot more since we've been at school and I feel pretty close to her. I told her about being raped and we talked about that often. But I can't seem to tell her about my abortion. I want to. I'm not afraid of what she will think of me anymore because I've had one, but I'm afraid of what she will think of me for not telling her. I'm afraid that she will really freak out. That she wouldn't believe me anymore or she'd hate me for not telling her. I'm afraid of totally shocking her.

Recently my mom said to me while looking at an old picture of the four of us kids, "You were always so happy as kids, laughing all the time, having fun." I had a really weird feeling when she said it. I never remember being happy as a kid. Scared of my own shadow might be a better description. I couldn't bear to tell her that; I just nodded and smiled.

I remember all of us kids fighting a lot. I remember my mom yelling a lot. I don't remember my dad being home much. I remember him coming home at 1:00 in the morning. I remember them yelling a lot on weekends. We bought a sailboat, but it was mostly just another place to fight. I remember a teacher who I loved in seventh grade. We wrote in journals in her class. Once I wrote about one of our boat trips, only I left out the bad parts, the fighting. When I got the journal back she wrote, "Sounds wonderful!" I felt like she liked me and what I wrote, but I also felt horrified. I had a sick feeling in my stomach, like I knew it wasn't true; it wasn't wonderful.

In the autobiography I wrote my senior year in high school I identified my dad leaving as one of the two events that had the greatest effect on me (the other was being a twin). The hurt was fresher then, and I was angry and jealous. Those feelings certainly haven't gone away, they just aren't so strong. Then it seemed I wanted so badly to believe that my family was perfect before the day he destroyed it all and left. Now I tend to think of the bad times, all of the fights, and I can't remember the good stuff. Now I see that something was very wrong with my family before he left. No one communicated, but everyone fought. I guess my dad just wasn't happy, and he spent less time at home and more at work, and then my mom became unhappy. Or maybe it was the other way around. I don't know how it really happened or whose fault it really was.

To me then it was all my dad's fault; he did everything that hurt me. But sometimes I think my mother's reactions, as well as our own, made things worse for us. No one in the house talked about it, except my mom, who was an emotional wreck. She'd try to pry information out of us after we'd been to my dad's. She told us, begged us, to ask him to come home and to tell him that we loved him. She said he'd come if we did. We couldn't tell him how much it was hurting us; we just went to see him and tried to be "good." But mom telling me this made me feel even more like it was all our fault. She also told us not to tell our friends; she didn't want anyone to know. Until we moved two years later, I told my friends he was on a business trip when they came over.

I don't blame my mother for any of these things, even though they hurt me. I feel thankful that she survived and didn't just give up. As for my dad, I try to see him as much as I can. We can have fun together, but I feel like he can't ever be there for me emotionally. It still makes me sad. For the most part, I'm not bitter anymore. But he still tries to get away with giving my mother as little money as possible and he pays almost nothing toward our college bills. Though they've been divorced for years, the hurt still seems to drag on. Mom still makes comments about his wife and kid. I understand her hurt, but I'm still caught in the middle.

I have tried here to explain my inability to deal appropriately with sexual relationships as being the result of my not having been able to talk about sex and contraception. The feelings from the beginnings of my adolescent sexuality were of being scared, not having control, and not having a choice. I now know that this is related to having grown up in a family that stuffed their feelings and never talked about anything, including sex. My family always avoided subjects that were upsetting, embarrassing, or controversial. So when it came to talking about contraception with my boyfriend, I had no basis to deal with it and felt it was beyond my control. My way of coping with the inevitable crisis of a pregnancy was not to practice contraception, but to put it out of my mind. That was easy; I had practiced that all my life.

This is the story of a harrowing emigration from Vietnam to the United States as part of the "boat people" crisis after the war. The author describes his struggle to be both a good son to his very traditional mother and to find a means to belong and succeed in the culture to which his family fled. As he enters adolescence, he begins to feel that his mother's many troubles and unbending ways are harming both him and his siblings. When he discovers that his stepfather is abusing his younger brother and that his mother will not intercede, he experiences a turmoil of shame, guilt, and powerlessness. His mother's insistence on traditional child rearing forces him to live a double life as an increasingly "Americanized" teenager on the outside while playing the role of dutiful son at home in spite of numbing sadness and overwhelming rage toward his mother. Eventually, it is his success in the world outside his family that allows him to gain his mother's respect and thereby influence how she raises his younger siblings.

"*Con không biết mạ đã trở qua bao nhiêu là nỗi khổ để đem con qua nước Mỹ nay*—You don't know how much I went through to bring you to this country," my mother said in a soft voice as she lay staring at the ceiling. A continuous stream of tears flowed from the outer corner of her eye down into her pillow. At times like this, I would sit next to my mother on our torn carpet while she recounted the tragedies that had happened to her in her previous life of misery, the life she left behind in Vietnam. My older sister Chau, on the other hand, could never stand to listen to our mother's repetitions. She would usually brush her teeth and go to bed or go to our other bedroom, close the door, and delve into the imaginary world of her romance novels. I remember praying at the start of the episodes that I wouldn't end up crying myself (because my mother instilled in me her belief that "*nam nhi đại trượng phu đổ máu không rơi lệ*—real heroes never show tears even if they are bleeding to death") as these painful stories entered my mind. However, no gods or spirits answered my prayers, and after each occurrence I would feel low and unmanly because I had let tears fall even though I wasn't bleeding to death.

"*Dạ mạ*—Yes, Mom (respectfully)," I said. In Vietnamese a child must always acknowledge his or her parent with a polite "*Dạ*" (pronounced "ya"). It matters not that the parent did not ask the child a question; any less respectful response could very well lead to a beating! I learned this lesson soon after I learned how to talk (being polite was much better than being hit).

"When I was your age living in my village, I never had a full meal to eat," my mother continued. "Most days we would only be given one small bowl of rice and a dab of fish paste for flavor. I wasn't as lucky as you are today. I could never eat meat every day like you can." As far as I can remember, my mother would, without exception, start her stories by establishing that her youth was utterly miserable compared to my life of luxury. To this day I still am not sure whether by stating this she merely wanted me to feel grateful that I had enough food to eat or whether she was actually pitying herself as she realized the vast contrast between her childhood and mine.

"I was cruelly beaten daily by your grandmother and often for no good reason. She had fourteen children, but I was the only one who ever got punished. I don't know why. She'd beat me if I didn't fetch enough firewood for cooking. Or if I didn't cut up enough food to feed the pigs. Or if I stopped fanning her during those scorching summer days because my hands felt like jello." As my mother went on, at this point in her talk I would have a difficult time understanding her because her nose was plugged up from crying so much. Sometimes I tried to pay closer attention so that I could catch everything she said; other times I would not bother since I more or less knew by heart all that she wanted to say.

"The worst period in my life was after I married your father. I had just given birth to your sister when your father disappeared without a trace. I tracked him down finally in Hanoi. I found that he was living with his first wife, a woman that he never told me about. I was more than shocked that the man I loved and trusted lied to me."

After hearing my mother describe my father's deceit, I simultaneously felt resentment, sympathy, guilt, vengefulness, incredible sadness, and, oddly, joy. I resented and even hated my father for ruining my mother's life. The anger I felt inside was so overwhelming that I would often tremble while gasping for air. Sometimes I sat there and wished that he were standing right in front of me so that I could pick him up by the throat and slam him against the wall as hard as I could. I'd scream at him, "You damn asshole! How could you treat your wife like that? Don't you have a conscience? Is this the model that you want your children to follow? I am ashamed to be your son! But don't worry, I won't turn out to be like you, you piece of shit!" At the same time, I felt sympathy for the incredible pain that my mother must have endured since that episode. She did not do anything wrong; her only mistake was falling in love with a lying womanizer. Yet mixed with my negative emotions was a slight ripple of joy. I felt happy to see that my mother was courageous enough to take her children and leave him behind in his poverty-stricken home. I was shamelessly content that he still has to live in filth with his first wife while our family, although poor compared to others in America, has enough to eat everyday.

Throughout my early childhood, occurrences like the one above were commonplace. Almost anything could provoke my mother into telling those stories:

seeing happy couples walking together in the park, seeing my sister and me not doing our chores, watching television shows that depicted any aspect of Vietnam, and especially having her children do badly in school (i.e., not getting straight As). Those nights I would cry myself to sleep thinking of how much I should hate my father and how much I should love and respect my mother. I racked my brains wondering how my father could have consciously treated my mother with such inhumanity. "How could he? How could he?" I hollered silently to myself over and over. "There must be some reason for what he did. My mother must be leaving a lot of details out. I should not listen only to her side of the story." I convinced myself that I could not make final judgments about him until I heard what he had to say. Thus, for years I wondered what his story was.

My first memories are of escaping Vietnam and landing in Hong Kong on the way to our final destination, America. I only remember random scenes of our journey; the rest of what happened my mother has filled in through our conversations over the years. Thus, I have a fairly detailed knowledge of what happened in those few days that drastically altered our lives.

In the spring of 1981, my mother, then fairly wealthy thanks to a prospering business, decided that she wanted to give her two children educational opportunities that her country could not offer. I was only 4 years old and my sister just 6 when one ordinary night my mother told us to say good-bye forever to our homeland. . . .

A blinding flash of light snatched me from my restful sleep. Five seconds later the inevitable boom of thunder crashed on our little boat and sent everyone into a state of panic. When I peered out at the darkness, I saw rushing at us some of the largest waves I'd ever seen.

"*Ma, con sợ qúa*—Mommy, I'm so scared," I cried. However, the raindrops on my face camouflaged my tears, and the roaring thunder drowned my attempts to communicate with my mother. I finally caught her attention by pulling on her sleeve as hard as I could.

"*Con đừng sợ nhe*—Don't be afraid, son," my mother comforted, "It's just a little storm. It'll be over real soon." She covered us with a plastic bag, and we huddled so close that I could feel her heart pounding against my cheek.

"*Chị Hong, Chị Hong*—Sister Hong, Sister Hong," my uncle Oanh approached us from out of nowhere and said in a disconcerting tone, "There's too much weight on this end of the boat. We need more people to move to the bow. If we don't do it fast, the waves'll flip us right over."

"What do you want us to do?" my mother answered calmly.

"You put Phuoc on your back and I'll put Chau on mine. Then we'll slowly walk up there."

"Okay, okay," my mother approved. I did not realize what was happening. All I knew was that I wanted to cling to my mother for dear life. "Phuoc," she spoke directly into my ear because at any other distance the thunder would drown out her voice, "We're moving to the front of the boat. I'm gonna give you a piggyback ride, so you grab on as tight as you can, okay?"

"*Dạ*," I acknowledged and quickly climbed onto her back while the storm blanketed my body with what felt like a thousand pebbles every second. Without thinking, I immediately locked my arms around my mother's neck and grabbed each of my wrists with the opposite hand. Just as instinctively, I wrapped my legs around her waist and also bolted them in place. As we began inching toward our destination just a few meters away, my awareness of the surroundings increased tenfold compared to when I was sitting with my mother. I saw every wave as it crashed on the boat's side, I anticipated the direction of impending thunder, and I felt the blowing raindrops on my skin as if they were needles piercing all parts of my body. Another acute awareness was of my body's position in space. Because I did not budge, it seemed as though I became an extension of my mother's body. When she lifted her left foot to take another step, I felt the entire left half of my frame move accordingly.

"*Gần tới rồi con à*—We're almost there, son," my mother said, "Don't worry." When I looked up, I saw the bow just a few steps away. However, I did not feel as though I could breathe a sigh of relief because a few steps is still a few steps. I kept my tight lock around my mother's neck and waist. It turned out that this choice saved my life, because just then a huge wave slammed into the side of our boat with such force that it threw her off her feet and sent us plunging into the freezing water of the South China Sea. I do not recall feeling scared. When I was under water, instinct made me hold onto my mother as tightly as I could, shut my eyes to avoid the stinging seawater, and close my mouth so that no saltwater entered my system. I do not know why I didn't panic. I just didn't. Fortunately, the two of us avoided staying in the water long enough for hypothermia to set in. My uncle, who was following closely behind us with my sister, dived in after us when he saw us fall.

Following our dramatic rescue, the heavens blessed us with sunshine and peaceful waters. The gods also bestowed another miracle on us. Several days after our departure, just when we had almost depleted all of our food supply, we came across a cargo ship headed in the same direction we wished to go: Hong Kong. A year later in April 1982, my mother realized her dreams of raising us in a land where more opportunities and fewer obstacles lay before us. What my mother did not realize was that she herself would become the major obstacle in her children's future.

Throughout my early adolescence, I wished I had a better, more understanding mother. To this day I still believe that most of my "growing pains" could have been alleviated or missed entirely if my mother had also experienced these same "pains" when she was an adolescent. She did not know how best to assist me through my tough times, because she had no understanding of the cultural and social pressures facing teens growing up in America. She was often insensitive and apathetic when I came to her with an adolescent issue such as schoolmates making fun of me.

Puberty started rather simply for me in the sixth grade; there was no big event that announced its arrival. I remember exactly when I knew that I had entered this period of change. One evening while I was showering, I noticed that I had started growing pubic hair. At first I felt confused. "What's this stuff?" I asked myself. Thinking that it was just dirt or something, I tried rubbing it off. After a few unsuccessful attempts, I realized, "Oh, yeah, this is what my sex education class last year taught us. I'm supposed to start this business at my age. Don't worry about it. It's just puberty." I thought about telling my mother to make sure it *was* just puberty, but after some thought I decided against the idea because these topics were not spoken of in our household. Subjects such as sex, love, human genitalia, and rape were taboo in my family because they were supposedly "impure" things to talk about. We were not to adulterate our minds and hearts by bringing them up in conversation. Consequently, many issues that "normal" families in America talk about were never brought up in our household. This lack of discussion forced me to learn about them from other sources, such as television.

At first I did not think that puberty was going to be the time of tremendous psychological change that the sex education videos at school had depicted. I felt like the same little kid I was before, going to class in the morning, coming home to do homework and watch television in the afternoon, talking to my mother before going to bed, and then repeating this same monotonous routine. The only other difference was that my voice started cracking when I spoke, but that did not bother me because I understood that was a natural part of human development.

Although I was only aware of my physical changes, I was also changing mentally. I remember my sudden self-consciousness, low self-esteem, new found interest in girls, and awareness of my lack of peer relationships, all of which started in junior high. Now when I look back, it seems that my experience was nothing out of the ordinary for children of that age. Yet my life then had an additional, *extra*ordinary factor. The conditions under which I interacted with others my own age were, culturally, American conditions, while at home I confronted a Vietnamese cultural environment. On the one hand, my mother did not understand American culture and disapproved of the American beliefs (such as gender and racial equality, free speech in the family, etc.) that I had adopted. On the other hand, the children at school who were not Vietnamese did not accept the culturally Vietnamese side of me, probably because they saw it as strange and not "normal." (Back then it was a dream of mine just to be normal like everyone else.) I shall illustrate my point with a few examples.

Before the sixth grade, I never thought about how physically different I looked. I knew that I was Vietnamese, but I never felt that I was an outsider in school because of my skin color. When I began adolescence, however, I became acutely aware of my bodily characteristics. In grade school I was your stereotypical skinny, short, brainy Asian kid with a bowl haircut. When kids made fun of me by calling me "chink" or "nerd," I usually never paid any attention to them. This was true until the day I received a disciplinary referral and was sent home. During music class, a Caucasian classmate of mine, Eugene, was getting upset because Mr. Marmastein told him he was out of tune. The entire class giggled as Eugene squeaked the words to "Yankee Doodle Went to Town." I, being a wiseguy, said loudly, "No more, Eugene, please!" With a frustrated look, Eugene quickly turned to me and yelped, "Shut up, you damn *chink*!" The old me would have just laughed it off without giving it a second thought, but that day a rush of anger swept through me, and I wanted to beat him up right there on the spot. The only thing that restrained me from doing so was my music teacher. I did not want to disrespect him by disrupting the class; I decided to wait till later. When recess time came and we were all let out to the grass field to play kickball, I only had one thing on my mind. As soon as I caught sight of Eugene, I ran over and tackled him onto the ground with all the might that my eighty pound body could conjure up. We wrestled around on the grass throwing blind punches at each other until the recess supervisor pulled us apart and gave us both referrals. The principal sent me home because I was the one who started the fight. Eugene's words somehow triggered a highly reactive area inside me, an area that told me that I was not the same as everyone else, and this made me feel inferior. At the same time, though, the fight made me proud and confident because this time, unlike previous times, I had stood up for myself when others thought I would be weak and passive. However, my raised spirits received a powerful blow from my mother's reaction.

"What? You got in a fight because he said you were Asian? *Sau con ngu qúa vậy*—Why are you so stupid, son?" my mother said, as if she didn't believe that "chink" was a derogatory word. Maybe if I told her again, she would understand.

"But, Mom. That word is racist! He wasn't just saying that I was *Asian*," I repeated, "He had a different meaning."

"Who cares what he meant," she replied. "It's just a word. Those white people are all racist anyway. Next time he says that to you, just ignore him." Ignore him? *What*? How could I do that when Eugene insulted me? And how could my mother say that *all* Caucasians are racist? Didn't the fact that she uttered those words brand *her* a racist? "And they're bigger than you, you know. I don't want you to get hurt again. We're smaller than they are, so we just have to act our size. So next time he makes fun of you, just turn your head and laugh." I did not know how else to persuade her. My mother did not seem to understand that in America, equality is cherished and prejudice is not tolerated. Wasn't that why she decided to risk her life and the lives of her children to come here in the first place? My mother's words directly conflicted with what my teachers had taught me in school all these years. How could I reconcile this? I could not believe what she said nor do as she ordered, because the morals I had acquired in school were too strong. This incident posed yet another problem for me—when should I listen to my mother and when should I not? In the past, she had always taught me how to be a good person, including the do's and don't's of life and the difference between right and wrong. It was simple—Mother was always right no matter what. Thus, I always listened and took her words to heart. Now that I recognized a flaw in her beliefs, I did not know what to do or who to go to.

Another example of my mother's lack of empathy was how she laughed at me when I told her that other kids made fun of my name. For as long as I can remember, almost everyone I met has mispronounced my name at least twice before getting it right. It was such an embarrassing scene whenever I met anyone new that it made me wish I did not have to meet new people at all. The worst part of it was the name-calling I endured all my life. Through elementary school and beyond high school, my name was the subject of a laundry list of teasings. It may be difficult for others to understand how my name can be so damaging to me psychologically. However, it was not as if I had a name like "Jaime," which everyone pronounced "Himee." People can easily turn my name into vulgar words if they want to (and I believed that everyone around me wanted to). Here are a few of those hurtful teasings: "Fok," "Foo-ook," "Pook," "Fuck," "Phuoc you!", "What the Phuoc!", "MotherPhuocer." In my high school junior yearbook there is a picture of me playing volleyball (I was on the team). Underneath it the subheading reads, "Phuoc 'U' Nguyen spikes one!" Those kids did not realize that every time they poked fun at me I wanted to crawl into a cave and not come out until everyone was mature enough to accept my name.

The only person who understood my agony was my sister because she too has an uncommon name, but hers had less potential to be the butt of everyone's jokes than mine. On occasion when she and I went somewhere together, we would temporarily change our names to make the experience a lot more pleasant for ourselves. For instance, when I was a sophomore in high school and Chau was a junior, she wanted me to accompany her to a meeting of students interested in applying to college. She was sure that no one we knew would be there, so we decided to become "normal" for the evening. When the hosts asked us to write our names on those "Hello, my name is . . ." stickers, we picked random "American" names. As it turned out, we both found it easier to meet people when we weren't feeling self-conscious.

Whenever I told my mother about people making fun of my name, she would usually laugh and say, "Fuck? Ha, ha . . . isn't that a bad word? Ha, ha . . . That's kinda funny." At times like those I thought my mother was the most insensitive and uncaring person in the world. How could she sit there and laugh at her son when he had just told her that everyone in school was already laughing at him? Did she think that it would make me feel better if she laughed as well? Of course I did not voice those questions. Thinking about it now, I believe that my mother's concept of emotional pain was completely different from mine. The physical pain and agony she endured for most of her life in Vietnam was probably ten times more intolerable than mine. That's probably why she couldn't understand the emotional pain I felt when kids made fun of me.

My mother also hindered my healthy adolescent development by refusing to let me associate with girls. I recall one incident in junior high when a seventh-grade girl wrote me a letter. Minh, a Vietnamese girl who played in the orchestra with me, sent me the first "I like you" letter I ever received; in it she expressed her admiration for me because I was smart and musically talented. Frankly, I did not have the slightest inkling what to think of the situation. No one had ever taught me how to initiate intimate relationships. The guy friends I had at school were all uncool "nerds" like myself who did not have any experience with girls either. I did not even consider asking them for help. I never had an older male role model to turn to with questions; the only older men I was in contact with were my uncles, and they were unlikely candidates because they did not grow up in America.

Asking for my mother's advice about girls would be tantamount to suicide. She always forbade my sister and me to date or see any members of the opposite sex until we were college graduates. One may think that she was just joking—no parent can be that strict, right?—but believe me, she wasn't. She strictly enforced her commands with severe actions. For instance, one day after school when I was waiting for my mother, one of my female acquaintances came up to chat with me. We were talking about how Mrs. Sloboda's world history test was too difficult. But when my mother drove up and saw us standing there together, she thought the subject of our conversation was something less than innocent. She immediately rolled down her window and screamed at the girl, "*Ây, đồ con quỷ sứ kia, mày làm chi với con tao rứa*—Hey, demon, what are you doing with my son?" My friend asked me whether my mother was yelling at her; I told her that she was just telling me to get in the car (this was one of the perks of having a mom who does not speak English). When I stepped into the car, my mother started chastising me for talking to the girl. She did not listen to my explanation and warned me that if she ever saw that scene again, I'd end up in an orphanage. That was the last time I stood next to girls after school.

There I was holding my first love letter in my hand, but I had absolutely no idea what to do with it. I did not understand my role as the male figure; was I supposed to ask her out first or wait until she made the first move? Should I talk to her just as a friend or try to flirt with her? My mind was filled with confusion at the time. The only places I could think of to turn to for direction were Hong Kong mini-soap operas. These translated productions were usually set in ancient China, where a gentleman was one who followed the Confucian code of conduct and women were innocent and supportive. Honestly, I learned more about relationships from watching those shows than from any other source. They taught me that real men were brave, polite, chivalrous, confident, and independent, while women were caring, sensitive, nurturing, and passive. Of course I am much wiser now, but back then I embraced these ideals. However, even though I knew from those movies how I *should* have acted towards Minh—who I thought was pretty and intelligent—I did not put that knowledge into practice. Instead of initiating any type of conversation, I tried to avoid her. Whenever she walked up to me to talk, I would turn around and walk the other way. Finally, after realizing that I seemed repulsed by her, Minh gave up on me and started seeing someone else. Later on I felt like such an idiot for letting her go. "Why didn't I go for it?" I asked myself repeatedly. "Am I not a guy? She liked me! She really did, and I just let her go." I thought that I did not possess the qualities that a "real" man had, those qualities that the Hong Kong mini-soap operas presented to me. It was not until my last years in high school that I realized what "manly" qualities actually were. It was also then that my self-esteem gradually rose to a level where I was confident enough to look people in the face when I was talking to them. These changes came slowly and originated from an incident that was a milestone in my life. This incident served as the beginning of my long and successful struggle to break free from my mother's emotional influence.

The changes took place shortly after my mother allowed her ex-husband, my stepfather, back into our family. A few months following his return, I learned with horror what kind of man he really was. My half-brother Tai, a vibrant 4-year-old, told me that his father liked to pinch and bite him just for fun; he also liked to fondle Tai's genitals for prolonged stretches of time.

Something like this was not easy to accept or deal with, especially for a 14-year-old. I trembled at the realization that this beast of a man, this perverse monster, sexually abused his own son, my innocent brother. And all of this occurred right beneath our unwitting noses for weeks on end. "This cannot continue," I resolved. "I *will* not allow him to hurt my brother any longer!" Never in my life had I been more sure of what the right thing to do was. Although I knew that this could potentially hurt everyone else in my family, particularly my mother, I did not falter for a moment. I was willing to destroy my mother's happiness to protect Tai.

My method of expressing my frustration was to slam doors. Every time I saw my stepfather touching Tai's genitals, I would walk to my room and slam the door behind me. Our home only had two bedrooms, so Tai's father definitely heard and understood my signal. He understood all right, but he did not change, and the abuse persisted. However, my stubborn-headedness kept me from giving up. I wanted to reach a standoff, a sudden-death situation. That day came about two weeks after my initial resolution to fight. Thoughts of me being courageous or honorable never entered my mind; everything I did was by gut instinct.

It was a windy Saturday afternoon, and everyone was at home except for Chau, who was at work. My mother and stepfather were talking in their room while Tai and I played *Civilization* on my computer. All of a sudden Tai's father summoned him to their room. The inevitable happened, and again a rush of rage crashed into my body. I breathed hard as my heartbeat shot up like a bottle rocket. Shoving my chair behind me, I stepped out into the living room and looked into their room as I walked by. The scene did not differ from the ones I had witnessed over the past few weeks. After standing in the living room for a moment, I went to my room taking loud, heavy steps along the way and, upon reaching my destination, slammed my door with as much force as I could conjure up. I did it! My mother had to say *something*. I wanted to confront him that very moment; I wished that deep inside me there was a courage that would manifest itself now by giving Tai's father the hardest punch on the jaw. I waited for them to come in.

"Phuoc, what the hell are you doing!" my mother screamed as she raced over to my room and gave me a slap on the left side of my cheek. I still vividly remember the physical and emotional pain I felt the instant her hand landed on my face. "He's his father, and he can do whatever he wants with him. It's not like he's killing him or anything, he's just playing. And besides, it's none of your business! Now if you don't want to live here anymore, then I can always put you into an orphanage!" I knew then that my mother cared more about her own selfish needs than about the welfare of her younger son. My respect for her started fading behind a curtain of disappointment. What could I do? Everyone around me could not see what I saw, and after trying fruitlessly to expose the truth to them, this was what I received. Fear and alarm overwhelmed me at that moment, and I did not, could not, fight any longer. I had already drained myself of all the fortitude I possessed, and no matter how deep I searched, my well of courage was dry. At that time, fear—the emotion I detested most and the emotion I constantly encountered—took control of my mind. I didn't want to end up in an orphanage, a ward of the state. I didn't want her to put me in a foster home. No. No. I couldn't let that happen. "It was the wind, Mom," I responded innocently. "The wind slammed the door." And that was that. I was tired. I didn't want to feel any more emotions. I just wanted to lie in bed and pretend that none of it had happened.

I had never been more disappointed with my mother in my life; the time she ignored my pleas for new shoes, the time she made fun of my name, could not begin to compare with this. I wished she was not my mother. I wished that I had never been born into this backward family.

Two months later my mother kicked her ex-husband out. Apparently, he emptied her bank account with his gambling habits. While he had been staying with us, he constantly took her money to play cards at the local casino. Eventually my mother had no money left to pay the bills. This time his leaving was for good, she said. His departure left me with a feeling of relief for my brother because it released him from constant victimization. Yet I knew that what he went through might leave lasting psychological effects.

The problems between my mother and myself did not spontaneously disappear when my stepfather left. I remember not feeling anything at all for her; it was as if my stepfather had taken with him all of my emotions about my mother and left only a void. I did not speak with her for half a year following his separation from us. I constantly asked myself how my mother, whom I regarded so highly—a woman who had risked and sacrificed everything for the sake of her children—could ignore the obvious abuse of her child by her husband. This inner questioning led to my emotional isolation from her. Withdrawing from my mother's world allowed me to step back and reevaluate from a different perspective my perceptions of her and myself. With the help of this new vantage point, I painted a new picture of myself and my relationship with my mother.

"*Thưa mạ con đi học*— (Respectfully) Mother, I am going to school." "*Thưa mạ con đi học về*— (Respectfully) Mother, I am home from school." These eleven words, which tradition forced me to utter every day, were the only words I remember saying to my mother during those silent six months. How did I do it? What did I feel? What did I use to replace my relationship with my mother?

My first few weeks of silence I attribute to hatred. I loathed being in my mother's presence. When we were together in the same room, I never looked at her face or even positioned my body toward hers. At the dinner table, I swallowed my food without tasting it as fast as I could to shorten the torture of sitting near her. When we had company over and she asked me to come out and greet them, I stayed only long enough for them to see my fake smile before returning to my room. I did not think she deserved to be a mother, thus I did not treat her like one. I regarded her like a distant relative—with respect, but with no warmth or emotion. At night when my mother slept with Tai in her arms, so much anger welled up inside me that one time I released my rage by biting on a pillow with all my strength. "How could she go on like nothing happened?" I asked myself. "How could she not feel guilty?" Those nights I stayed up until two or three in the morning feeling sorry for my brother, furious at my mother, and disappointed in myself. I did not talk to anyone about my problems. Chau had isolated herself from the rest of our family, so she and I did not communicate, and I did not feel close enough to any of my friends at school to share with them my inner emotions. I also felt too ashamed to tell anyone about the unhappy circumstances in my family. Consequently, I existed for weeks like a walking balloon full of negative emotions just waiting to burst when I could no longer contain them. But I did not burst. I needed to appear strong, stolid (like the heroes in the Hong Kong movies). I needed to show my mother and myself that I did not depend on her for my emotions. The way I subdued these feelings is similar to what happens when a chemist immerses a helium-filled balloon into a vat of liquid nitrogen. Like the helium in the balloon, my emotions underwent a condensation into a colder, less active state.

For the remaining months of my silence, hatred and anger no longer played a large role in my reluctance to communicate with my mother. I figured, "Why should I torture myself with all these bad feelings? They don't do any good. I can't go on living so miserably." Convinced that emotions only hurt rather than benefited me, I gradually suppressed them. Soon I replaced those gut-wrenching feelings of guilt, sadness, and animosity with apathy and insensitivity. I no longer felt uncomfortable sitting next to my mother, because I had no feelings for her. Although I still remembered the events that occurred several weeks prior, it ceased to cause pain and anguish. My indifference made it easier for me to sleep at night, increased my ability to concentrate in school, and lifted the midnight clouds that hovered over me. In retrospect, I can understand the attraction of this defense mechanism; it was an easy escape from emotional pain and dependence on my mother. The side effect of my remedy, however, was that I lost the ability to feel other types of emotions as well, such as sympathy, sadness, and joy. I felt like a machine. When I watched inspirational movies, I did not have warm, fuzzy sensations. When I was elected president of the sophomore class, my only reaction was, "Good, this'll look good on my college applications." When my friend Vu made a full recovery after undergoing chemotherapy for lymphatic cancer, I never felt ecstatic, just relieved for him. Now I realize the price of indifference, and I have been trying hard to gain back— with little success—my ability to feel deep emotions.

In the months following my isolation from my mother, I found numerous ways to convince myself that she had absolutely no influence on me and that I had completely and irreversibly broken away from her. I guess this was the rebellious stage of my adolescence. However, I did not rebel in the typical demonstrative fashion, like screaming "I hate you" to my mom or getting drunk. Instead, I rebelled in a passive way so that only *I* knew I rebelled, while everyone, including her, still thought I was the perfect son. One of my defiance strategies was to achieve top grades in my classes without putting in any effort. I cheated in almost every subject. After school, when my mother asked me if I had any homework, I always replied, "No, Mom, I'm already done." She never asked me to show her my completed work because she could not read a word of it. I also started lying a lot to my mother. One time I told her that my friends and I went to the library to study, but actually we drove to San Francisco and spent the day playing volleyball on the beach. I cannot count all the times that I lied to her and she never found out the truth. I felt much satisfaction knowing that I had some control over her; it raised my self-confidence and esteem and felt like sweet revenge for her dominance over me when I was younger. I simply wanted to believe that my mother had no part in my success in both academics and life. Yet I allowed her to continue assuming that I was the model son and that without her I would have been nothing. I figured she deserved at least that much because of the sacrifices she made in bringing me to America and raising me in a strange land.

What did I use to replace my mother's absence from my life? Certainly not other relationships! I found it difficult to make close friendships in high school for several reasons: my school environment, my inability to share feelings (mostly because I had no emotions), and the fact that I thought close friends were unessential for my well-being. The school I attended had the lowest SAT score averages in the country. Fifty percent of the student body was black, while about 90 percent of the faculty was white; the remaining students consisted mainly of Hispanics and Asians, with a few token white students. Almost everyone came from poor households; I once read an article about our school that revealed that over 70 percent of the students' families depended on welfare as their sole source of income. I witnessed gang fights almost every week, mostly between black gangs—the Bloods versus the Crips. But sometimes I also saw some action from the smaller Asian gangs like the Oriental Boyz. The extraordinarily high incidence of violence and drug abuse in my school forced the government to establish a gun- and drug-free zone around the school and the nearby housing complexes. Fortunately, I participated in the school's magnet program, called the Academy of Math, Science, and Engineering, that better prepared me for college. I limited the group of friends I hung out with mainly to other Vietnamese students from the Academy, and I stayed away from most of the black students because I was afraid of being associated with any of the gangs. My friends and I had lunch together, copied homework from one another, and joined the same clubs. However, outside of school we did not go out on a regular basis or call each other to have heart-to-heart conversations. Even when my friends did call me, we never discussed my family problems or feelings, probably because I didn't want to admit that I had any troubles at home. I also never developed strong companionships in high school because I did not feel that I needed them to make me content. I felt satisfied that I had friends to turn to when I wanted to copy homework from someone; other than that I had no burning desire to have best friends.

Relationships with girls also did not fill the void left by my mother's absence. In my high school years, a number of girls wrote me love letters, asked me out to proms, or tried to get to know me, but not once did I take the initiative to pursue a relationship with any of them. Sure, I went to their proms, but I only did it because I did not want to turn them down. It wasn't that I didn't find women attractive or that I didn't want a steady relationship; rather, I think that the combination of my mother's strict rules and a lack of male role models contributed to my nonaggressive behavior. As I stated before, my mother adamantly forbade me to have girlfriends, and although I wanted to establish my independence from her, I still needed to abide by her rules because I was living under her roof. The other reason I wasn't able to tell girls that I liked them was because I didn't know how. No one ever taught me the correct procedures for getting to know women, and what I saw on TV seemed too straightforward for my tastes. My closest male friend in high school, Vu, never had any experience with girls either. Thus, even if I wanted to go out with someone, I did not know how to approach her and ask.

I do not believe anything replaced my relationship with my mother. Her dominant presence simply disappeared as a result of my ability to suppress my emotions. How she felt no longer dictated how I felt. When she cried, I no longer cried; when she laughed, I no longer laughed with her; and when she told her disturbing childhood stories, they no longer affected me emotionally. It may seem heartless, but that was how I felt. I did not need anyone to take her place; what I *did* need, however, was to fill up the free time I had now that I wasn't spending it with my mother. I kept myself busy in high school by joining numerous clubs, volunteering at nursing homes and hospitals, playing on the tennis team, participating in math and science competitions, working, attending Vietnamese school on the weekends, and enrolling in night courses at the closest community college. I occupied my days with so many activities that on a typical day, I would not return home until eight or nine in the evening, and by that time my mother would be in bed.

In other ways, I came to understand my mother at a deeper level. In junior year I had a history class in which we learned about ancient China; we discussed Confucius's philosophy and how his ideals still permeate East Asian culture. One of the most important aspects of Confucian theory is its emphasis on role-playing in the family and in society. I remember writing a report on Confucian influence on contemporary Vietnamese society and realizing that my family performed the parts that he outlined centuries ago. Observing my family as a source for my essay, I learned that Confucius dictated our use of verbal and physical affection.

To this day I cannot say "I love you" to my mother, older sister, or younger brother. The only person whom I *do* verbally acknowledge my love for is Carol, my 4-year-old half-sister. It may seem strange, but Carol is also the only one that I hug, kiss, or show any other form of affection to. The same is true for my mother, Chau, and Tai—from an outsider's perspective it may seem as though all of us love only Carol. I also hear Chau verbalizing her love for Vinh, her fiancé, and it seems perfectly natural. What would be completely *unnatural* and unprecedented is if she said "I love you" to me, my mother, or brother.

During elementary school my mother nurtured and cared for me as if I had just learned how to walk. One of the ways she made me state that I loved her was by asking, "Phuoc, where do you put your love for me?" My rehearsed answer was, "Mom, I put my love for you on my head!" (She considers the head the most important part of the body, so putting my love there meant that it was the most important love.) We kissed and hugged one another all the time and without reservation. By the time I started junior high school, however, we suddenly yet intuitively stopped being physically affectionate. Even though I missed my mother's touch, especially when I witnessed her affection for Carol, I knew that its cessation was appropriate for my age. Thinking back, the start of my adolescence and newfound need to break away from the nest, particularly when kids at school filled my head with the notion that kissing your mom was "sissy" and "gay," influenced the shift in our relationship. A change in my mother's attitude also contributed; she no longer asked me where I put my love for her. Instead, she asked Tai, who was 2 at the time, this question, which I thought she had reserved just for me. It was as if the game had age limits, and I had already passed them. My mother now expected me to show my love for her by obeying her and bringing home the As. Accordingly, she showed her love by feeding and clothing me.

"*Con không cha như nhà không nóc*—Children without a father are like houses without rooftops." My mother never failed to remind me of this Vietnamese proverb whenever she wanted to show off how she had disproved the old saying. She was correct in her claim, because we never grew up with a father, yet our house definitely has a "rooftop." My mother played the roles of breadwinner and caring mother at the same time. She disciplined us while bandaging our wounds, taught us how to ride a bike and then cleaned our scrapes and bruises, encouraged us to succeed in the real world while wishing we would never leave her side. In December of my last year before entering college, I unwittingly replaced my mother as the rooftop and the foundation of my home.

The news jumped at me out of the blue. "I'm going to Vietnam next month to visit Grandpa and Grandma," was all my mother said. "I'll leave some money for you while I'm gone. I'll be there for a month." She never discussed with me the possibility that I did not want to take care of 1-year-old Carol and 8-year-old Tai for an entire month, especially December, when I had so many things to do in my senior year. She never taught me how to cook dinner, potty train Carol, comfort her when she cried, and keep the house clean all in one day. Yet I never raised a single objection to her vacation plans. The only thing I recall telling her while we said good-bye at the airport was, "Have a safe trip, Mom. Don't let anyone con you over there, okay? Let me know when you want me to pick you up." For the next thirty-one days I enrolled in a crash course in parenting in which the teacher and student were one—me.

The most difficult part of the day came after Tai got home from school. During those few hours before bedtime, I ran around my two-bedroom home like a madman in nerve-racking attempts to prevent my hyperactive sister from hurting herself while also trying to complete multiple tasks. Within a two-hour stretch, I made dinner, did the laundry, mopped the floors, took out the garbage, changed Carol's diaper when I forgot to remind her about the mini-toilet, helped Tai with his fractions and long division, answered phone calls from friends seeking advice on how to fill out college applications, and played with Carol to keep her from wrecking the floors I had just mopped!

Every night I longed for nine o'clock to come around so that I could put the two children to sleep and actually attend to my own affairs. This was the time during my senior year when the college application deadlines loomed. In addition to completing seven or eight college applications, I worked on finishing nearly a dozen scholarship applications, all of which kept me up late every night. Luckily, I did not have trouble finding a topic for my personal essays; it was easy to write about my experiences performing the duties of a parent and how much I learned from them. This topic proved productive; the following spring I was accepted to a prestigious college and also won a full scholarship to the school of my choice.

Looking back on that month, I recognize now the richness of my experience and just how much it contributed to me as a person. During that time I learned what qualities an ideal man and woman should possess. My firsthand knowledge replaced my archaic notions of men as chivalrous protectors of passive, caring women. Another new concept I developed was that there weren't any obvious differences between the required traits of a man and a woman. I no longer divided the genders and designated specific attributes each should acquire. It was as if I took my culture's gender role assignments and synthesized them into one person, and that was who I became. Whether it was hugging Carol to sleep when she cried in the middle of the night, explaining fractions to Tai, cooking, cleaning, or fixing the door handle, I did not feel as though I switched roles when I performed them. I never thought to myself, "No, I can't do this because I'm a man. That's not what I'm supposed to do. But, since Mom's not here, I *have* to do the woman's work." Those thoughts didn't cross my mind. What I did think, however, was, "Of course I'll do this. I'll do it because I love my sister and brother. No other reason."

Ever since my sister went away to college, my role and responsibility in my family has changed dramatically. I have much more say in household affairs than before. Now whenever I am at home I take care of all the bills and paperwork that my mother has accumulated over the months while I was in college. If there is a decision to be made, I usually make it and then tell my mother why I did so. I think she finally realized that I was old enough to make the right choices for our family. Along with my added responsibility, the weight of my word has increased markedly since high school. Again, I think my mother takes my opinion more seriously because I am old enough now to play the role of an influential person in our family. Knowing that what I say has a more profound influence on her than ever before, I have not wasted an opportunity to help my little brother and sister. Whenever I have a chance, I persuade her to change her ways toward Tai and little Carol so that they can have a smoother childhood than I did. By this I mean that I encourage her to allow them to make friends within and outside of the Vietnamese ethnicity, let Tai talk to girls his age because he can benefit from them and vice versa, and most importantly discipline them with words instead of whips. I believe my words have not gone unheard, especially those dealing with punishment, because since I started college I cannot recall ever hearing about her spanking Tai or Carol.

My years in college have allowed me to develop a new, more equal relationship with my mother. I think the time I spent at school three thousand miles away has made us both appreciate and respect one another (although she would never admit that she respects or appreciates me). She now sees me as an independent individual, and I see her as both a mother and a friend. I know that she takes much pride in seeing me succeed in my academic life, but even though I want to make her proud of me and hope that she gains the proper admiration she deserves from those in Vietnam, I do not base my goals and aspirations on pleasing her. If in the process of attaining my goals I also make her happy, then I will have lived up to both my American and Vietnamese ideals—doing things for myself and doing things to show respect for my parents. I praise my mother when I see the improvements in the way she is raising Tai and Carol compared to her raising of Chau and me. I think she knows that she cannot apply every aspect of Vietnamese culture to children she is raising in America. When I go home for vacations, I still function as the man in the house, the person who takes care of the bills, fixes doorknobs, and attends the parent–teacher conferences. At the same time, I am also the only male figure for my brother, which puts pressure on me to be the best role model I can. I play these roles willingly and with satisfaction.

As for my search for the culture that suits me best, I have come to the decision that neither Vietnamese nor American culture alone can fulfill my needs. Thus, I chose to pick out the best aspects of each culture and synthesize them into one. For instance, while I believe in the American ideal that every person is equal, I also disapprove of children not treating their elders with respect and proper manners. I do not consider myself Americanized or Vietnamized; rather, I'm enjoying the best of both worlds.

What are the issues that I am still struggling with? As I enter my senior year, I'm still trying to inflate the emotional balloon that I've suppressed for so long. Recently, my girlfriend Jennifer has been helping me recover my ability to feel strong emotions again. Last month she and I cried together, something I haven't done since my sophomore year in high school! However, I find it much more difficult to bring back the emotions than to tuck them away, and so far I haven't made much progress.

From the academic success my sister and I have earned, it may seem that our family is living out the American dream. We escaped from a war-scarred country that offered us few opportunities and arrived in a land we knew nothing about. My mother worked hard all her life to provide her children with a home that was conducive to learning. She created such an atmosphere by using the whip, along with guilt-provoking stories to encourage us to learn. Now that two of her children are excelling in their respective postsecondary institutions, my mother feels that she has done an admirable job of raising us. However, her feelings of pride come at a high cost to the relationships in our family. Maybe she did not know any other way to raise us than by using her native culture's means. She did not realize that most families who bring up successful children do not use the switch as their tool of support. I believe that practicing Confucian ideals in the family will lead to decreased communication and ultimately to feelings of isolation similar to those that Chau and I felt and are still experiencing. Fortunately, after seeing her family structure crumble because of her, my mother realized that her rearing methods needed improvement. She knows now that her children will inevitably become "Americanized" to some degree. Accordingly, she now allows Tai and Carol more freedom; hopefully, they will also live up to her ideals. I can sense that the relationships in my family are becoming more intimate. We all can hug and kiss each other now, and I am optimistic that in the near future my mother and I will be able to say "I love you" to one another.

Differential Acculturation: Negotiating Two Different Worlds

Reflections on Case 16

MARGARET STEPHENSON

Adolescents face a number of developmental tasks, and confronting these tasks leads to a stable, continuous sense of self. How an adolescent goes about negotiating these developmental tasks is dependent in part on cultural norms, the ways in which a culture defines normal behavior for a specific developmental period. Immigrants and children of immigrants who become adolescents in the United States must confront these tasks along with the added challenge of negotiating two different cultures whose norms and values may conflict. Phuoc's compelling story of his childhood, adolescence, and young adulthood demonstrates the numerous challenges faced by children of immigrants. His story affords us a glimpse of their struggle to integrate two different worlds while developing a sense of self that reflects and validates both worlds.

Before we can address these challenges, it is important to consider the issue of acculturation that takes place after immigration. Acculturation, very broadly defined, consists of the changes that occur in individuals and groups when they come into continuous, firsthand contact with a different cultural group (Redfield, Linton, & Herskovits, 1936). As people immigrate to a new country, they undergo change in order to adapt to the new environment and culture. These changes occur in a number of different domains. For example, changes in language use occur as an individual learns the language of the new culture, or norms and values change regarding acceptable and unacceptable behaviors. Although acculturation occurs in the mainstream group as well as in the immigrant group (the mainstream group also adapts to and adopts some customs, dress, and language of the immigrant group), the immigrant group changes more quickly in order to function in the new culture. Adaptation to the new culture is not a single event but a prolonged developmental process of adjustment that affects family members differently depending on each member's developmental phase (McGoldrick & Giordano, 1996).

Immigrants who become adolescents in the United States often experience intergenerational clashes of values with parents and grandparents because of fundamental differences between what the adolescents may want for themselves and what parents want for the adolescent (Baptiste, 1993). Although intergenerational conflict may also occur in nonimmigrant families, immigrant adolescents experience not only cohort differences but also cultural differences. Immigrant adolescents may undergo acculturation to the new culture more quickly than their parents and therefore adopt the norms and values of the new culture while their parents do not. Contributing factors to this differential rate of acculturation may be the adolescent's malleability and increased contact with schools and other mainstream social institutions.

While some of the more traumatic aspects of Phuoc's immigration experience are not shared by many immigrant children, the challenges he faced after immigration due to living in two cultures are shared by many immigrant adolescents. Phuoc provides several striking examples of this *"extra*-ordinary factor" of having to interact in American and Vietnamese cultures simultaneously, and of the subsequent conflict between what is taught in mainstream culture and what is taught at home.

One cannot help but feel the social and emotional isolation and the loneliness embedded in Phuoc's story. Whereas many adolescents experience both types of isolation, for many immigrant adolescents acculturating at a faster rate than adult family members often leaves them without role models, such as family members who have successfully negotiated both cultures and who can guide and advise them. In fact, often the roles are reversed, with the adolescent becoming the family guide and serving as spokesperson or intermediary between the family and the larger society. Parents may lose expert power when their children's knowledge of the language and culture surpasses theirs. They may lose referent power, which is derived from children's identification with their parents, as children may experience alienation from their culture of origin or even shame due to their parents' lack of facility in the new culture (Giles, 1990). This situation itself causes family conflict because the adolescent may lose respect for the adult family members, and adults may resent this role reversal that leaves them feeling ineffective as parents. In families where there is a more rigid hierarchy, the intermediary may be treated more harshly than other children in order to insure elder respect and obedience.

Depending on immigration and preimmigration circumstances, adolescents' experiences may be quite different from their parents, leading to increased feelings of loneliness and shame or guilt in engaging in normal adolescent concerns. As in Phuoc's case, issues regarding personal appearance, being made fun of, and emerging sexuality and how to approach the opposite sex may be perceived as trivial by family members who have experienced considerable hardship during or prior to immigration.

Adding to feelings of isolation or confusion are the mixed messages that adolescents often receive from the different cultures regarding their emerging roles and identity. Whereas in many non-Western and non-European cultures parents are expected to be authoritarian and children obedient, and the family rather than the individual is valued, in traditional American culture autonomy, individualism, and authoritative parenting is valued. For example, children of immigrants often receive the message that they must fit in and perform well academically, which entail embracing a more autonomous, individualistic, and competitive cultural attitude. Yet at home they are expected to adhere to prescribed cultural roles that entail cooperation, interdependence, humility, and obedience. Likewise, they receive conflicting messages about their emerging racial and ethnic identity from mainstream institutions. On the one hand, they learn the value of equality and tolerance, yet they are often the victims of individual and societal racism and prejudice that devalues their culture of origin.

Many family rules and values that were effective in the immigrant family's country of origin may be less adaptive in the new culture and can create a degree of confusion and alienation in the family (Sluzki, 1979). For Phuoc, a great source of conflict was making sense of the traditional beatings he received from his mother throughout his childhood and early adolescence. On the one hand, American culture taught him that physical punishment is barbaric, traumatizing, and against the law; on the other hand, from his mother he received the message that such actions were evidence of good and caring parenting. Although it is difficult to assess whether the ritualized beatings represent cultural or individual child rearing practice, research with some immigrant and migrant populations suggests that corporal punishment is seen as a time-honored and essential disciplinary tactic of child rearing (Bibb & Casimir, 1996; Garcia-Preto, 1996; Mague & Stephenson, 1997). An even more striking example of conflicting values is that presented by Phuoc regarding the abuse of his brother Tai. How do adolescents negotiate such conflicting values within a range of acceptable cultural behaviors?

For many immigrant adolescents, traditional mainstream options and resources are often not available or viable. The support of an extended family nearby, which could provide other adult family members who might intervene in resolving such conflicts, may not be available, because immigration often involves leaving behind extended family and support (Leung & Boehnlein, 1996). Phuoc, for example, did not have a network of related people with whom to speak about the ritualized beatings or the abuse of his brother. In the case of Vietnamese refugees, there are countless isolated families throughout the United States. American government officials have in many cases deliberately dispersed Vietnamese families throughout the United States, precluding the development of ethnic enclaves that would provide support for or reinforce ethnic values and identification (Matsuoka, 1990). Similarly, in many cultures, involving outsiders as agents of conflict resolution is often not an option. Potentially shaming the family in this way would very much violate the cultural expectation of filial loyalty and result in being outcast or, as Phuoc was threatened, being placed in an orphanage. For many immigrant families, family matters are private and should not be scrutinized by outsiders (Bibb & Casimir, 1996). Children are expected to obey and honor their elders, and the family's welfare takes priority over the individual's welfare. Traditional American strategies based on individuality, self-expression, and self-disclosure may also not be viable options for these adolescents. Talking things through and trying to resolve issues within the family, for example, may violate acceptable parent–child roles and expectations (Leung & Boehnlein, 1996). For a child or adolescent to speak of certain issues to his parent or to question the parent's wisdom or authority would be disrespectful and violate the family's code of conduct. Like Phuoc, many immigrant adolescents are faced with choosing a course of action that is both appropriate given their emerging sense of what they know to be right and inoffensive or disrespectful given the family hierarchy.

Phuoc chooses a course of action that is psychologically healthy in some ways but that places him at risk in other ways. He undergoes a period of rebellion within the confines of his role as a dutiful son. He engages in some rebellious behaviors such as skipping school and cheating, and he also detaches emotionally, becoming a workaholic and suppressing his emotions of disappointment and anger. He acknowledges the hardship and possible damage he sustained in using this particular coping strategy, which enabled him to both continue an outward show of respect for his mother and acknowledge and validate his own moral code. Although this strategy cost Phuoc the ability to experience his full range of emotions, it did preserve a connection to his family, which is thought to be psychologically healthy for adolescents as they become more autonomous. This strategy also eventually led him to a greater understanding of and appreciation for both cultures. Continued connection with his family allowed him, as he gained more prestige and respect within the family, to intervene on behalf of his younger siblings. Phuoc eventually comes to a place both in the family hierarchy and emotionally where he can simultaneously appreciate his mother's strengths and help her to overcome her shortcomings and adopt child-rearing behaviors that are more adaptive to raising children in the United States.

Phuoc's strategy of suppressing his emotions while maintaining some connection to his family seemed to help him cope at a time when he had few viable resources. However, many adolescents acquire an array of strategies for dealing with the dissonance between the two cultures. Many adolescents, for example, forge a close relationship with adults outside the family such as teachers or other community members. If these surrogate extended family members share an understanding of, respect for, and appreciation of the adolescent's culture of origin, they can guide and advise the adolescent within the range of acceptable cultural behaviors and expectations. Adolescents who have this option report feeling less lonely and have the opportunity to explore their emotions and validate their emerging identity within two cultures (Mague & Stephenson, 1997). Phuoc eventually found such a resource in his girlfriend Jennifer, with whom he is struggling to share and explore his emotions.

Another strategy many adolescents use is to alternate their behaviors to fit into whichever culture they are currently involved in (LaFromboise, Coleman, & Gerton, 1993). The adolescent develops an understanding of and appreciation for both cultures and, depending on the demands of the social context, may use different interaction or communication styles. Researchers have suggested that people who are able to alternate their use of culturally appropriate behaviors exhibit higher cognitive functioning and mental health than those immigrants who are monocultural (Rogler, Cortes, & Malgady, 1991).

Phuoc seems to be headed in a healthy direction as he explores his cultural identity and his emotions. Culturally, he describes himself as "Americanized and Vietnamized," choosing and enjoying the best aspects of both cultures. Many immigrants who were socialized in the United States chose this integrated mode of acculturation, which has been found to be most positively correlated with mental health (Berry, 1986; LaFromboise et al., 1993; Rogler, Cortes, & Malgady, 1991). Schiller (1987) examined academic, social, psychological, and cultural adjustment in Native American students and found that bicultural students were better adjusted than nonbiculturals and that biculturals perceived their Native American heritage as an advantage. Biculturals hold each group in positive regard, allowing them to experience a sense of efficacy within the dominant culture and a sense of pride and identification within their ethnic culture (LaFromboise et al., 1993). Maintaining a connection to the culture of origin also serves as a buffer or support system, particularly for minority adolescents.

In addition to the integrated mode of acculturation Phuoc chose, there are three other primary modes of acculturation: assimilation, in which the culture of origin is rejected and there is only meaningful immersion in mainstream culture; separation, in which mainstream culture is rejected and there is only meaningful immersion in the culture of origin; and marginalization, in which there is no meaningful immersion in either culture. A number of factors can determine the mode of acculturation individuals choose, ranging from individual psychological factors of the acculturating person such as education, age, gender, cognitive style, contact experiences, coping strategies, expectations, and migration motivation, to societal factors such as the degree of tolerance or discrimination in the larger society (Berry, 1986; Berry, Kim, Minde, & Mok, 1987; Berry & Sam, 1996). A society with multicultural ideals—a society that values cultural diversity and that encourages positive attitudes among cultural groups—will foster an integrated and assimilated mode of acculturation, whereas societies with less tolerant ideals will foster segregation and marginalization, which are thought to be the least adaptive modes of acculturation (Berry & Sam, 1996).

Overall, immigrants and children of immigrants who become adolescents in the United States are remarkably resilient. Like Phuoc, they confront these challenges courageously, and many are able to master and integrate the two cultures. Apparently, weak rather than mixed cultural identification may create problems for immigrant adolescents (Oetting & Beauvais, 1990–1991). Without positive regard for both groups, adolescents may be unable to feel good about interacting with the group that is the target of negative feelings, and they may display negative behavioral and educational outcomes and negative self-concept (LaFromboise et al., 1993). Although Phuoc continues in his struggle to better understand and integrate both worlds, he appears to have been successful in negotiating the developmental tasks that lead to a stable and continuous sense of self.

> I know that she [his mother] takes much pride in seeing me succeed in my academic life, but even though I want to make her proud of me and hope that she gains the proper admiration she deserves from those in Vietnam, I do not base my goals and aspirations on pleasing her. If in the process of attaining my goals I also make her happy, then I will have lived up to both my American and Vietnamese ideals: doing things for myself and doing things to show respect for my parents.

Phuoc has emerged with a sensitivity, tolerance, and appreciation of cultural differences. Phuoc and others like him are perhaps the bridge that will facilitate the continued emergence of a multicultural ideal in American society.

CONTRIBUTORS

Andrew Garrod is Associate Professor of Education and Chair of the department at Dartmouth College, Hanover, New Hampshire, where he teaches courses in adolescence, moral development, and educational psychology. His recent publications include a book, *Preparing for Citizenship: Teaching Youth to Live Democratically* (written with Ralph Mosher and Robert A. Kenny), and a co-edited volume, *First Persons, First Peoples: Native American College Graduates Tell Their Life Stories* (with Colleen Larimore). In 1991 he was awarded Dartmouth College's Distinguished Teaching Award.

Carol Gilligan is the author of *In a Different Voice: Psychological Theory and Women's Development* and director of the Harvard Project on the Psychology of Women and Development of Girls. She holds the Patricia Albjerg Graham Chair in Gender Studies at the Harvard Graduate School of Education and works collaboratively with students, colleagues, clinicians, and teachers. Two of her recent books are *Meeting at the Crossroads: Women's Psychology and Girls' Development* (with Lyn Mikel Brown) and *Between Voice and Silence* (with Jill McLean Taylor and Amy M. Sullivan).

Robert Kilkenny is Instructor in Psychology, Department of Psychiatry, at Harvard Medical School and Research Child Psychologist at McLean Hospital. He has published an article in the Life Span Development Series with Gil Noam, Sally Powers, and Jeff Beedy on adolescent relationships in a life-span perspective. His current research interests include delinquency, moral development, and adolescent relationships.

Gil Noam is Director of the Hall-Mercer Laboratory of Developmental Psychology and Developmental Psychopathology and Assistant Professor of Psychology at the Harvard Medical School. He has published widely on adolescent development and clinical developmental life-span psychology and teaches courses at the Harvard Medical School and Harvard Graduate School of Education in child and adolescent development. He is currently working on a longitudinal study of the process of recovery in the development of adolescents and adults.

Sally Powers is Professor of Psychology at the University of Massachusetts, Amherst. She has published numerous articles based on her research on family interaction and its relation to adolescent development and psychopathology. She teaches courses in adolescent development, psychopathology, and child and adolescent psychotherapy and is currently investigating the relation of interpersonal behavior, neuroendocrine indices of stress, and gender differences in adolescent depression.

Ritch Savin-Williams is Associate Professor in Human Development and Family Studies at Cornell University. He is the author of *Gay and Lesbian Youth: Expressions of Identity* and *Adolescence: An Ethological Perspective.* His research interests include exploring the diversity of developmental patterns that gay men, lesbians, and bisexuals undertake in achieving a gay, lesbian, or bisexual identity, with a particular focus on the adolescent years.

Lisa Smulyan is Associate Professor in the Program in Education at Swarthmore College, Swarthmore, Pennsylvania, where she teaches courses in educational foundations, adolescence, women and education, and school and society. Her publications include *Collaborative Action Research: A Developmental Process* and several articles. Her research focuses on classroom-based research with teachers, life/case history as a basis for understanding school practice, and investigations into the role of gender in teachers' and administrators' work experience.

Margaret Stephenson is Assistant Professor of Psychology at the University of Massachusetts, Amherst, where she teaches courses in adolescent development, multicultural issues in psychology, and constructivist approaches to psychotherapy. Her research focuses on the study of the acculturation process of cross-cultural groups in the United States and the development of instruments to measure that process. She is currently working on a study investigating the relations among acculturation process, environmental factors, and psychopathology.

BIBLIOGRAPHY

Adelson, J., & Douvan, E. (1975). "Adolescent friendships." In J. J. Conger, P. H. Mussen, and J. Kagan (Eds.), *Basic and Contemporary Issues in Developmental Psychology* (pp. 277–290). New York: Harper and Row.

Adelson, J., & O'Neil, R. (1975). "Growth of political ideas in adolescence: The sense of community." In J. J. Conger, P. H. Mussen, and J. Kagan *Basic and Contemporary Issues in Developmental Psychology* (pp. 53–70). New York: Harper and Row.

Adler, N. (1975). "Emotional responses of women following therapeutic abortion." *American Journal of Orthopsychiatry, 45,* 446–456.

American Psychological Association: Interdivisional Committee on Adolescent Abortion. (1987). "Adolescent abortion: Psychological and legal issues." *American Psychologist, 42*(1), 763–778.

Ames, N., & Miller, E. (1994). *Changing Middle Schools: How to Make Schools Work for Young Adolescents.* San Francisco: Jossey-Bass.

Aristotle. (1941). *Rhetorica.* New York: Random House. (Original work published ca. 334–332 B.C.)

Bakan, D. (1972). "Adolescence in America: From idea to social fact." In J. Kagan and R. Coles (Eds.), *Twelve to Sixteen: Early Adolescence* (pp. 73–89). New York: W. W. Norton.

Baptiste, D. A. (1993). "Immigrant families, adolescents and acculturation: Insight for therapists." *Marriage-and-Family Review, 19*(3–4), 341–363.

Bardige, B. (1988). "Things so finely human: Moral sensibilities at risk in adolescence." In Gilligan et al., (Eds.), *Mapping the Moral Domain* (pp. 87–110). Cambridge, MA: Harvard University Press.

Baumrind, D. (1987). "Development perspectives on adolescent risk-taking in contemporary America." In C. E. Irwin (Ed.), *Adolescent Social Behavior and Health* (pp. 93–125). San Francisco: Jossey-Bass.

———. (in press). "Rearing competent children." In W. Damon (Ed.), *New Directions for Child Development: Child Development Today and Tomorrow.* San Francisco: Jossey-Bass.

Beardslee, W. R. (1981). "Self-understanding and coping with cancer." In G. P. Koocher & J. E. O'Malley (Eds.), *The Damocles Syndrome: Psychosocial Consequences of Surviving Childhood Cancer* (pp. 144–163). New York: McGraw-Hill.

———. (1989). "The role of self understanding in resilient individuals: The development of a perspective." *American Journal of Orthopsychiatry, 59*(2), 266–278.

Bell, A. P., Weinberg, M. S., & Hammersmith, S. K. (1981). *Sexual Preference: Its Development in Men and Women.* Bloomington, IN: Indiana University Press.

Benedict, R. (1950). *Patterns of Culture.* New York: New American Library.

Berndt, T. (1981). "Relations between social cognition, non-social cognition, and social behavior: The case of friendship." In J. Flavell & L. Ross (Eds.), *Social Cognitive Development: Frontiers and Possible Futures* (pp. 176–199). Cambridge, England: Cambridge University Press.

———. (1982). "The features and effects of friendship in early adolescence." *Child Development, 55,* 151–162.

Berndt, T. J., & Ladd, G. W. (1989). *Peer Relationships in Child Development.* New York: John Wiley.

Berndt, T. J., & Perry, T. B. (1990). "Distinctive features and effects of early adolescent friendships." In R. Montemayor (Ed.), *Advances in Adolescent Research.* Greenwich, CT: JAI Press.

Berry, G. L. & Asamen, J. K. (Eds.). (1989). *Black Students: Psychosocial Issues and Academic Achievement.* Beverley Hills, CA: Sage Focus.

Berry, J. W. (1986). "Multiculturalism and psychology in plural societies." In L. H. Ekdtrand (Ed.), *Ethnic Minorities and Immigrants in a Cross-Cultural Perspective.* (pp. 37–51). The Netherlands: Swets and Zeitlinger.

Berry, J. W., Kim, U., Minde, T., & Mok, D. (1987). "Comparative studies of acculturative stress." *International Migration Review, 21*(3), 491–511.

Berry, J. W., & Sam, D. (1996). "Acculturation and adaptation." In J. W. Berry, M. H. Segall, & Kagitcibasi (Eds.), *Handbook of Cross-Cultural Psychology: Vol. 3. Social Behavior and Applications.* Boston: Allyn and Bacon.

Bibb, A., & Casimir, G. J. (1996). " Haitian families." In M. McGoldrick, J. Giordano, & J. K Pearce (Eds.), *Ethnicity and Family Theory* (2nd ed., pp. 97–111). New York: Guilford Press.

Blos, P. (1962). *On Adolescence: A Psychoanalytic Interpretation*. New York: Free Press.

———. (1972). "The child analyst looks at the young adolescent." In J. Kagan & R. Coles (Eds.), *Twelve to Sixteen: Early Adolescence*. New York: W. W. Norton.

Blyth, D., Hill, J., & Thiel, K. (1982). "Early adolescents' significant others: Grade and gender differences in perceived relationships with familial and non-familial adults and young people." *Journal of Youth and Adolescence, 11,* 425–450.

Bracken, M., Hachamovitch, M., & Grossman, A. (1974). "The decision to abort and psychological sequelae." *Journal of Nervous and Mental Disorders, 15,* 155–161.

Bracken, M., Klerman, L., & Bracken, M. (1978). "Coping with pregnancy resolution among never-married women." *American Journal of Orthopsychiatry, 48,* 320–333.

Brown, L. M. (in press). "Telling a girl's life." *Women and Therapy.*

Brown, L. M., & Gilligan, C. (1992). *Meeting at the Crossroads.* Cambridge, MA: Harvard University Press.

Buhrmester, D., & Furman, W. (1987). "The development of companionship and intimacy." *Child Development, 58,* 1101–1113.

Bukowski, W., Newcomb, A. & Hartup, W. (Eds). (1996). *The Company They Keep: Friendship in Childhood and Adolescence.* Cambridge, England: Cambridge University Press.

Burleson, B. (1982). "The development of comforting communication skills in childhood and adolescence." *Child Development, 53,* 1578–1588.

Chodorow, N. (1974). "Family structure and feminine personality." In M. Z. Rosaldo and L. Lamphere (Eds.), *Woman, Culture, and Society* (pp. 43–66). Stanford, CA: Stanford University Press.

———. (1989). *Feminism and Psychoanalysis.* New Haven, CT: Yale University Press.

Clark. R. (1983). *Family Life and School Achievement: Why Poor Black Children Succeed or Fail.* Chicago: University of Chicago Press.

Coleman, J. C. (1987). "Friendship and the peer group in adolescence." In J. Adelson (Ed.), *Handbook of Adolescent Psychology* (pp. 408–431). New York: Wiley.

Coles, R., & Stokes, G. (1985). *Sex and the American Teenager.* New York: Harper and Row.

Cooley, C. H. (1902). *Human Nature and the Social Order.* New York: Scribners.

Côté, J., & Levine, C. (1987). "A formulation of Erikson's theory of ego identity formation." *Developmental Review, 7,* 273–325.

Cottle, T. J. (1972). "The connections of adolescence." In J. Kagan & R. Coles (Eds.), *Twelve to Sixteen: Early Adolescence* (pp. 294-336). New York: W. W. Norton.

Crockett, L., Losoff, M., & Peterson, A. C. (1984). "Perceptions of the peer group and friendship in early adolescence." *Journal of Early Adolescence, 4*(2), 155–181.

Csikszentmihalyi, M., & Larson, R. (1984). *Being Adolescent.* New York: Basic Books.

Cvejic, H., Lipper, I., Kinch, R. A., & Benjamin, P. (1977). "Follow-up of 50 adolescent girls two years after abortion." *Canadian Medical Association Journal, 116,* 44–46.

Diaz, R., & Berndt, T. (1982). "Children's knowledge of a best friend: Fact or fantasy?" *Developmental Psychology, 18,* 787–794.

Dickinson, E. (1960/1924). *Complete Poems.* Boston: Little, Brown.

Elder, G. (1980). "Adolescence in historical perspective." In J. Adelson (Ed.), *Handbook of Adolescent Psychology* (pp. 3–46). New York: John Wiley.

Erikson, E. H. (1959). "Identity and the life cycle." *Psychological Issues, 1,* 1–171.

———. (1964). *Insight and Responsibility.* New York: W. W. Norton.

———. (1966). *The Challenge of Youth.* New York: Anchor Paperback.

———. (1968). *Identity: Youth and Crisis.* New York: W. W. Norton.

———. (1975). *Life History and the Historical Moment.* New York: W. W. Norton.

———. (1980). *Identity and the Life Cycle: A Reissue.* New York: W. W. Norton.

Ewing, J. A., & Rouse, B. A. (1973). "Therapeutic abortion and a prior psychiatric history." *American Journal of Psychiatry, 130,* 37–40.

Feldman, S., & Elliott, G. (1990). *At the Threshold: The Developing Adolescent.* Cambridge, MA: Harvard University Press.

Finkelhor, D. (1984). *Child Sexual Abuse: New Theory and Research.* New York: Free Press.

Ford, C., Castelnuovo-Tedesco, P., & Long, K. (1971). "Abortion: Is it a therapeutic procedure in psychiatry?" *Journal of the American Medical Association, 218,* 1173.

Fordham, S. (1988). "Racelessness as a factor in Black students' school success: Pragmatic strategy or pyrrhic victory?" *Harvard Educational Review, 58*(1), 54–84.

Fordham, S., & Ogbu, J. (1986). "Black students' school success: Coping with the burden of acting white." *The Urban Review, 18*(3), 176–206.

Fowler, J. W. (1981). "Adolescence," in *Stages of Faith: The Psychology of Human Development and the*

Quest for Meaning (pp. 69–77). San Francisco: Harper and Row.

Freud, A. (1946). *The Ego and Mechanisms of Defense* (C. Baines, Trans.). New York: International Universities Press.

———. (1958). "Adolescence," in *Psychoanalytic Study of the Child,* (Vol. 13). New York: International Universities Press.

Freud, S. (1962). "The transformations of puberty," in *Three Essays on the Theory of Sexuality* (pp. 73–74, 85–96). New York: Basic Books.

Fritz, G. K., Williams, J. R., & Amylon, M. (1988). "After treatment ends: Psychosocial sequelae on pediatric cancer survivors." *American Journal of Orthopsychiatry, 58*(4), 552–561.

Garcia-Preto, M. (1996). "Puerto Rican families." In M. McGoldrick, J. Giordano, & J. K. Pearce (Eds), *Ethnicity and Family Therapy* (2nd ed., pp. 183–199). New York: Guilford Press.

Garmezy, N. (1985). "Stress-resistant children: The search for protective factors." In J. E. Stevenson (Ed.), *Recent Research in Developmental Psychopathology* (pp. 213–233). Oxford: Pergamon Press.

———. (1987). "Stress, competence, and development: Continuities in the study of schizophrenic adults, children vulnerable to psychopathology, and the search for stress-resistant children." *American Journal of Orthopsychiatry, 57*(2), 159–174.

Garrod, A., & Larimore, C. (1997). *First Person First Peoples: Native American College Graduates Tell Their Life Stories.* Ithaca, NY: Cornell University Press.

Gibbs, J. T. (1984). "Black adolescents and youth: An endangered species." *American Journal of Orthopsychiatry, 54*(1), 6–23.

Giles, H. C. (1990). "Counseling Haitian students and their families: Issues and interventions." *Journal of Counseling and Development, 68,* 317–319.

Gilligan, C. (1977). "In a different voice: Women's conceptions of self and morality." *Harvard Educational Review, 47*(4), 481–516.

———. (1982). *In a Different Voice.* Cambridge, MA: Harvard University Press.

———. (1987). "Adolescent development reconsidered." In C. Irwin (Ed.), *Adolescent Social Behavior and Health* (pp. 63–92). San Francisco: Jossey-Bass.

———. (1989). "Teaching Shakespeare's sister." In C. Gilligan, N. Lyons, & T. Hanmer (Eds.), *Making Connections* (pp. 6–29). Cambridge, MA: Harvard University Press.

———. (1990). "Joining the resistance: Psychology, politics, girls and women." *Michigan Quarterly Review 29*(4), 501–536.

Gilligan, C., & Murphy, J. (1979). "Deveopment from adolescence to adulthood: The philosopher and the dilemma of the fact." In D. Kuhn (Ed.), *Intellectual Development Beyond Childhood* (pp. 85–99). San Francisco: Jossey-Bass.

Gilligan, C., Brown, L. M., & Rogers, A. (1990). "Psyche embedded: A place for body, relationships and culture in personality theory." In A. Rabin et al., (Eds.), *Studying Persons and Lives* (pp. 86–147). New York: Springer.

Gilligan, C., Lyons, N., & Hanmer, T. (Eds.). (1989). *Making Connections: The Relational Worlds of Adolescent Girls at Emma Willard School.* Troy, NY: Emma Willard School.

Goethals, G. W., & Klos, D. S. (1976). *Experiencing Youth: First Person Accounts.* Boston: Little, Brown.

Goldberger, N., Tarule, J., Clincy, B., & Belenky, M. (Eds.). (1996). *Knowledge, Difference and Power.* New York: Basic Books.

Gordon, S., & Gilgun, J. F. (1987). "Adolescent sexuality." In V. B. Van Hasselt & M. Hersen (Eds.), *Handbook of Adolescent Psychology* (pp. 147–167). New York: Joh Wiley.

Gottman, J. M., & Parker, J. G. (Eds.). (1987). *Conversations with Friends.* New York: Cambridge University Press.

Grotevant, H. D., & Cooper, C. R. (1986). "Individuation in family relationships." *Human Development, 29,* 82–100.

Hall, C., & Lindzey, G. (1978). *Theories of Personality.* New York: John Wiley.

Hall, G. S. (1904). *Adolescence: Its Psychology and Its Relations to Physiology, Anthropology, Sociology, Sex, Crime, Religion, and Education.* New York: Appleton-Century-Crofts.

Hatcher, S. (1976). "Understanding adolescent pregnancy and abortion." *Primary Care, 3,* 407–425.

Hauser, S. T., Houlihan, J., Powers, S. I., Jacobson, A. M., Noam, G., Weiss-Perry, B., & Follansbee, D. (1987). "Interaction sequences in families of psychiatrically hospitalized and non-patient adolescents." *Psychiatry, 50,* 308–319.

Hauser, S. T., Powers, S. I., Noam, G., Jacobson, A. M., Weiss, B., & Follansbee, D. (1984). "Familial contexts of adolescent ego development." *Child Development, 55,* 195–213.

Havighurst, R. J., Bosman, P. H., Liddle, G., Mathews, C. V., & Pierce, J. V. (1962). *Growing Up in River City.* New York: John Wiley.

Hill, J. P. (1987). "Research on adolescents and their families: Past and prospect." In C. E. Irwin

(Ed.), *Adolescent Social Behavior and Health* (pp. 13–31). San Francisco: Jossey-Bass.

Hollingshead, A. B. (1949). *Elmstown's Youth.* New York: John Wiley.

Jackson, J. S., McCullough, W. R., & Gurin, G. (1981). "Group identity development within black families." In H. McAdoo (Ed.), *Black Families* (pp. 252–263). Beverly Hills, CA: Sage.

Jordan, D. (1971). *Parental Antecedents and Personality Characteristics of Ego Identity Statuses.* Unpublished doctoral dissertation, State University of New York at Buffalo.

Josselson, R. (1987). *Finding Herself: Pathways to Identity Development in Women.* San Francisco: Jossey-Bass.

Kohlberg, L., & Gilligan, C. (1972). "The adolescent as philosopher: The discovery of the self in a postconventional world." In J. Kagan & R. Coles (Eds.), *Twelve to Sixteen: Early Adolescence.* New York: W. W. Norton.

Koocher, G., & O'Malley, J. (1981). *The Damocles Syndrome: Psychosocial Consequences of Surviving Childhood Cancer.* New York: McGraw-Hill.

LaFromboise, T., Coleman, H. L. K., & Gerton, J. (1993). "Psychological impact of biculturalism: Evidence and theory." *Psychological Bulletin, 144*(3), 395–412.

Leadbetter, B., & Way, N. (1996). *Urban Girls: Resisting Stereotypes, Creating Identities.* New York: New York University Press.

Leung, P. K., & Boehnlein, J. (1996). "Vietnamese families." In M. McGoldrick, J. Giordano, & J. K. Pearce (Eds.), *Ethnicity and Family Therapy* (2nd ed., pp. 295–306). New York: Guilford Press.

Lewin, K. (1939). "Field theory and experiment in social psychology: Concepts and methods." *The American Journal of Sociology, 44,* 868–897.

Lewis, C. C. (1987). "Minors' competence to consent to abortion." *American Psychologist, 42*(1), 84–88.

Lyons, N. (1983). "Two perspectives: On self, relationships, and morality." *Harvard Educational Review, 53*(2), 125–136.

Mague, K., & Stephenson, M. (1997). *Identity Development from Multicultural Context: Individuation and Connectedness in Haitian-American Young Adults.* Unpublished manuscript.

Manaster, G. J. (1989). *Adolescent Development: A Psychological Interpretation.* Itasca, IL: F. E. Peacock.

Marcia, J. (1966). "Development and validation of ego identity: Status." *Journal of Personality and Social Psychology, 3,* 551–558.

———. (1967). "Ego identity status: Relationship to change in self-esteem." *Journal of Personality, 35,* 118–133.

———. (1980). "Identity in adolescence." In J. Adelson, (Ed.), *Handbook of Adolescent Psychology.* New York: John Wiley.

Margolis, A. J., Davidson, L. A., Hanson, D. H., Loos, S. A., & Mikelson, C. A. (1971). "Therapeutic abortion: Follow-up study." *American Journal of Obstetrical Gynecology, 110,* 243–249.

Martin, K. (1996). *Puberty, Sexuality and the Self: Girls and Boys at Adolescence.* New York: Routledge.

Masten, A. S., & Garmezy, N. (1985). "Risk, vulnerability, and protective factors in developmental psychopathology." In B. B. Lahey & A. E. Kazdin (Eds.), *Advances in Clinical Child Psychology* (Vol. 8). New York: Plenum Press.

Matsuoka, J. K. (1990). "Differential acculturation among Vietnamese refugees." *Social Work, 35*(4), 341–345.

McAdoo, H. P., & McAdoo, J. (1985). *Black Children: Social, Educational and Parental Environments.* Beverly Hills, CA: Sage Focus.

McGoldrick, M., & Giordano, J. (1996). "Overview: Ethnicity and family therapy." In M. McGoldrick, J. Giordano, & J. K. Pearce (Eds.), *Ethnicity and family therapy* (2nd ed., pp 1–27). New York: Guilford Press.

McLaughlin, M., & Heath, S. (Eds.). (1993). *Inner City Youth: Beyond Ethnicity and Gender.* New York: Teachers College Press.

Mead, G. H. (1934). *Mind, Self and Society.* Chicago: University of Chicago Press.

Mead, M. (1930). *Growing Up in New Guinea.* New York: W. Morrow.

Mead, M. (1958). "Adolescence in primitive and modern society." In E. Maccoby, J. Newcomb, & E. Hartly (Eds.), *Readings in Social Psychology.* (pp. 341–349). New York: W. W. Norton.

Miller, A. (1983). *The Drama of the Gifted Child.* New York: Basic Books.

Miller, J. B. (1976). *Toward a New Psychology of Women.* Boston: Beacon Press.

Monsour, K., & Stewart, B. (1973). "Abortion and sexual behavior in college women." *American Journal of Orthopsychiatry, 43,* 803–814.

Montemayor, R. (1983). "Parents and adolescents in conflict: All families some of the time and some families most of the time." *Journal of Early Adolescence, 3,* 83–103.

Montemayor, R., & Hanson, E. (1985). "A naturalistic view of conflict between adolescents and their parents and siblings." *Journal of Early Adolescence, 5,* 23–30.

Mosley, D. T., Follingshead, D. R., Harley, H., & Heckel, R. V. (1981). "Psychological factors that predict reaction to abortion." *Journal of Clinical Psychology, 37,* 276–279.

Muuss, R. (1988). *Theories of Adolescence.* New York: Random House.

Noam, G. (1988). "The theory of biography and transformation: Foundation for clinical-developmental therapy." In S. Shirk (Ed.), *Cognitive Development and Child Psychotherapy* (pp. 273–317). New York: Plenum Press.

Noam, G., Powers, S., Kilkenny, R., & Beedy, J. (1990). "The interpersonal self in life-span developmental perspective: Theory, measurement and longitudinal case analysis." In P. Baltes, D. Featherman, & R. Learner (Eds.), *Life-Span Development and Behavior* (Vol. 10, pp. 59–104). Hillsdale, NJ: Erlbaum.

Oetting, E. R., & Beauvais, F. (1990–1991). "Orthogonal cultural identification theory: The cultural identification of minority adolescents." *International Journal of the Addictions, 25,* 655–685.

Olson, L. (1980). "Social and psychological correlates of pregnancy resolution among adolescent women: A review." *American Journal of Orthopsychiatry, 50,* 432–445.

Parker, J. G., & Gottman, J. M. (1989). "Social and emotional development in a relational context: Friendship interaction from early childhood to adolescence." In T. J. Berndt & G. W. Ladd (Eds.), *Peer Relations in Child Development* (pp. 95–131). New York: John Wiley.

Payne, E. C., Kravitz, A. R., Notman, M. T., & Anderson, J. V. (1976). "Outcome following therapeutic abortion." *Archives of General Psychiatry, 33,* 725–733.

Perry, W. A. (1970). *Forms of Intellectual and Ethical Development in the College Years: A Scheme.* New York: Holt, Rinehart, and Winston.

Peterson, L. (1989). "Coping by children undergoing stressful medical procedures: Some conceptual, methodological, and therapeutic issues." *Journal of Consulting and Clinical Psychology, 57*(3), 380–387.

Piaget, J. (1972). "Intellectual evolution from adolescence to adulthood." *Human Development, 15,* 1–12.

Plato. (1921). *Republic.* Oxford: Clarendon Press. (Original work published ca. 379 B.C.)

Powers, S. I. (1988). "Moral judgment in the family." *Journal of Moral Education, 17,* 209–219.

Powers, S. I., Hauser, S. T., Schwartz, J., Noam, G., & Jacobson, A. M. (1983). "Adolescent ego development and family interaction: A structural-developmental perspective." In H. D. Grotevant & C. R. Cooper (Eds.), *Adolescent Development within the Family.* San Francisco: Jossey-Bass.

Pritchett, V. S. (1971). *Midnight Oil.* London: Chatto and Windus.

Redfield, R., Linton, R., & Herskovits, M. J. (1936). "Memorandum on the study of acculturation." *American Anthroplogists, 38,* 149–152.

Remafedi, G. (1987). "Adolescent homosexuality: Psychosocial and medical implications." *Pediatrics, 79,* 331–337.

———. (1987). "Male homosexuality: The adolescent's perspective." *Pediatrics, 79,* 326–330.

Roesler, T., & Deisher, R. (1972). "Youthful male homosexuality." *Journal of the American Medical Association, 219*(8), 1018–1023.

Rogers, A. (in press). "A feminist poetics of psychotherapy." *Women and Therapy.*

Rogler, L. H., Cortes, D. E., & Malgady, R. G. (1991). "Acculturation and mental health status among Hispanics." *American Psychologist, 46,* 585–597.

Rosen, R. H. (1980). "Adolescent pregnancy decision-making: Are parents important?" *Adolescence, 15,* 43–54.

Ruddick, S. (1989). *Maternal Thinking.* Boston: Beacon Press.

Rutter, M. (1975). "Attainment and adjustment in two geographical areas. I: The prevalence of psychiatric disorder." *British Journal of Psychiatry, 126,* 493–509.

———. (1979). "Protective factors in children's responses to stress and disadvantage." In M. W. Kent & J. Rolf (Eds.), *Primary Prevention of Psychopathology: III: Social Competence in Children.* Hanover, NH: University Press of New England.

———. (1987). "Psychosocial resilience and protective mechanisms." *American Journal of Orthopsychiatry, 57*(3), 316–331.

Rutter, M., Graham, P., Chadwick, O., & Yule, W. (1976). "Adolescent turmoil: Fact or fiction?" *Journal of Child Psychology and Psychiatry, 17,* 35–56.

Rutter, M., & Quinton, D. (1984). "Long-term follow-up of women institutionalized in childhood: Factors promoting good functioning in adult life." *British Journal of Developmental Psychology, 18,* 225–234.

Santrock, J. W. (1990). *Adolescence* (4th ed.). Dubuque, IA: Wm. C. Brown.

Savin-Williams, R. C. (1990). *Gay and Lesbian Youth: Expressions of Identity.* Washington, DC: Hemisphere.

Schiller, P. M. (1987). "Biculturalism and psychosocial adjustment among Native American university students." *Dissertation Abstracts International, 48,* 1542A. (University Microfilms No. DA8720632)

Selman, R. (1979). "A structural-developmental model of social cognition: Implications for intervention research." In R. L. Mosher (Ed.), *Adolescents' Development and Education* (pp. 123–132). Berkeley, CA: McCutchan.

———. (1980). *The Growth of Interpersonal Understanding.* New York. Academic Press.

Sharabany, R., Gershoni, R., & Hofman, J. (1981). "Girl-friend, boy-friend: Age and sex differences in intimate friendship." *Developmental Psychology, 17,* 800–808.

Sisson, L., Hersen, M., & Van Hasselt, V. (1987). "Historical perspectives." In V. Van Hasselt & M. Hersen (Eds.), *Handbook of Adolescent Psychology* (pp. 3–10). New York: Pergamon Press.

Slater, E. J., Stewart, K. J., & Linn, M. W. (1983). "The effects of family disruption on adolescent males and females." *Adolescence, 17*(72), 203–214.

Slaughter, D. (1972). "Becoming an African-American woman." *School Review, 80*(2), 299–318.

Sluzki, C. E. (1979). "Migration and family conflict." *Family Process, 18*(4), 379–390.

Smith, E. M. (1973). "A follow-up study of women who request abortion." *American Journal of Orthopsychiatry, 43,* 574–585.

Spaulding, J. G., & Cavenar, J. O. (1978). "Psychoses following therapeutic abortion." *American Journal of Psychiatry, 135,* 364–365.

Sullivan, H. S. (1953). *The Interpersonal Theory of Psychiatry.* New York: W. W. Norton.

Surrey, J. (1984). "The self-in-relation." In *Work in Progress.* Wellesley, MA: Stone Center for Developmental Services and Studies.

Taylor, R. (1976). "Psychosocial development among black children and youth: A reexamination." *American Journal of Orthopsychiatry, 46*(1), 4–19.

———. (1989). "Black youth, role models and the social construction of identity." In R. Jones (Ed.), *Black Adolescents.* Berkeley, CA: Cobbs and Henry.

Unks, G. (Ed.). (1996). *The Gay Teen.* New York: Routledge.

Van der Kolk, B. A. (1987). *Psychological Trauma.* Washington, DC: American Psychiatric Press.

Ward, J. (1989). "Racial identity formation and transformation." In C. Gilligan, N. Lyons, & T. Hanmer (Eds.), *Making Connections: The Relational Worlds of Adolescent Girls at Emma Willard School* (pp. 215–232). Troy, NY: Emma Willard School.

Weiss, L., & Fine, M. (1993). *Beyond Silenced Voices: Class, Race and Gender in U.S. Schools.* Albany, NY: SUNY Press.

Werner, E. (1989). "High-risk children in young adulthood: A longitudinal study from birth to 32 years." *American Journal of Orthopsychiatry, 59*(1), 72–81.

Youniss, J., & Smollar, J. (1985). *Adolescent Relations with Mothers, Fathers, and Friends.* Chicago: University of Chicago Press.

Zeldin, R., Small, S., & Savin-Williams, R. (1982). "Prosocial interactions in two mixed-sex adolescent groups." *Child Development, 53,* 1492–1498.